EXPOSITORY THOUGHTS ON
LUKE

VOLUME 2

J. C. Ryle — when he was Vicar of Stradbroke, Suffolk.

EXPOSITORY THOUGHTS ON

LUKE

Volume 2

J. C. Ryle

THE BANNER OF TRUTH TRUST

THE BANNER OF TRUTH TRUST

Head Office
3 Murrayfield Road
Edinburgh, EH12 6EL
UK

North America Office
610 Alexander Spring Road
Carlisle, PA 17015
USA

banneroftruth.org

❧

First published 1858
First Banner of Truth Trust edition 1986
Reprinted 1998
This retypeset edition 2012,
Reprinted 2015 (clothbound), 2015 (paperback),
2020 (clothbound), 2023 (clothbound)

© The Banner of Truth Trust 2012

❧

ISBN
Print (clothbound): 978 1 84871 131 0
Print (paperback): 978 1 84871 609 4
EPUB: 978 1 84871 210 2
Seven-volume set ISBN: 978 1 84871 136 5

❧

Typeset in 10/14 Berkeley Oldstyle Medium
at The Banner of Truth Trust, Edinburgh

Printed in the USA by
Versa Press Inc.,
East Peoria, IL.

TABLE OF CONTENTS

CONTENTS

TABLE OF CONTENTS
OF NOTES

CHAPTER XII

Verse

CONTENTS OF NOTES

CHAPTER XIV

Verse

CHAPTER XV

Verse

CHAPTER XVI

CONTENTS OF NOTES

CHAPTER XVII

CHAPTER XVIII

CHAPTER XX

Verse

CHAPTER XXI

CONTENTS OF NOTES

CONTENTS OF NOTES

CONTENTS OF NOTES

CHAPTER XXIV

Verse

CONTENTS OF NOTES

LUKE 11:1-4

1 And it came to pass, that, as he was praying in a certain place, when he ceased, one of his disciples said unto him, Lord, teach us to pray, as John also taught his disciples.

2 And he said unto them, When ye pray, say, Our Father which art in heaven, Hallowed be thy name. Thy kingdom come. Thy will be done, as in heaven, so in earth.

3 Give us day by day our daily bread.

4 And forgive us our sins; for we also forgive every one that is indebted to us. And lead us not into temptation; but deliver us from evil.

THESE verses contain the prayer commonly called the Lord's Prayer. Few passages of Scripture perhaps are so well known as this. The most benighted Roman Catholic can tell us that there is a prayer called 'Pater Noster.' The most ignorant English child has heard something about 'Our Father.'

The importance of the Lord's Prayer appears in the simple fact, that our Lord Jesus Christ delivered it twice with very slight variations. He who never spake a word without good reason, has thought fit to teach us this prayer upon two distinct occasions. Twice the Lord God wrote the Ten Commandments on tables of stone (*Deut.* 9:10; 10:4). Twice the Lord Jesus delivered the Lord's Prayer.

The occasion of the Lord's Prayer being delivered a second time, in the verses before us, is full of interest. It appears that 'one of the disciples' said, 'Lord, teach us to pray.' The answer to that request was the well-known prayer which we are now considering. Who this 'disciple' was we do not know. What he did will be remembered as long as the world stands. Happy are those who partake of his feelings, and often cry, 'Lord, teach me to pray.'

The substance of the Lord's Prayer is a mine of spiritual treasure. To expound it fully in a work like this, is manifestly impossible. The prayer, on which volumes have been written, does not admit of being handled properly in a few pages. For the present it must suffice us to notice its leading divisions, and to mark the leading trains of thought which it should suggest to us for private meditation.

The first division of the Lord's Prayer *respects the God whom we worship*. We are taught to approach him as our Father in heaven,—our

1

Father no doubt as our Creator, but specially as our Father reconciled to us in Christ Jesus,—our Father whose dwelling is 'in heaven,' and whom no temple on earth can contain. We then make mention of three great things,—our Father's name, our Father's kingdom, and our Father's will.

We are taught to pray that the name of God may be sanctified: 'Hallowed be thy name.' In using these words, we do not mean that God's name admits of degrees of holiness, or that any prayers of ours can make it more holy than it is. But we declare our hearty desire that God's character, and attributes, and perfections, may be more known and honoured, and glorified by all his intelligent creatures. In fact it is the very petition which the Lord Jesus himself puts up on another occasion. 'Father, glorify thy name' (*John* 12:28).

We are next taught to pray that God's kingdom may come: 'Thy kingdom come.' In so saying, we declare our desire that the usurped power of Satan may speedily be cast down,—that all mankind may acknowledge God as their lawful King, and that the kingdoms of this world may become in fact, as they are in promise, the kingdoms of our God and of his Christ. The final setting up of this kingdom has been long predicted, even from the day of Adam's fall. The whole creation groans in expectation of it. The last prayer in the Bible points to it. The canon of Scripture almost closes with the words, 'Come, Lord Jesus' (*Rev.* 11:15; *Gen.* 3:15; *Rom.* 8:22; *Rev.* 22:20).

We are taught, thirdly, to pray that God's will may be done: 'Thy will be done on earth as it is in heaven.' In so saying, we express our longing desire that the number of God's converted and obedient people on earth may greatly increase, that his enemies who hate his laws, may be minished and brought low, and that the time may speedily arrive when all men shall do their willing service to God on earth, even as all the angels do in heaven (*Hab.* 2:14; *Heb.* 8:11).

Such is the first division of the Lord's Prayer. Its marvellous fulness and deep importance cannot be overrated. Blessed indeed are those Christians who have learned that God's name is far more honourable than that of any earthly potentate,—God's kingdom the only kingdom that shall stand for ever,—and God's law the rule to which all laws ought to be conformed! The more these things are understood and believed in a land, the happier that land will be. The days when all acknowledge these things will be the 'days of heaven upon earth.'

The second division of the Lord's Prayer *respects our own daily wants*. We are taught to make mention of two things which we need every day. These two things are, one of them temporal, and the other spiritual. One of them is 'bread.' The other is 'forgiveness of sins.'

We are taught to ask for bread: 'Give us this day our daily bread.' Under this word 'bread,' no doubt, is included everything which our bodies can require. We acknowledge our entire dependence upon God for life, and breath, and all things. We ask him to take charge of us, and provide for us in all that concerns this world. It is the prayer of Solomon under another form, 'Feed me with food convenient for me' (*Prov.* 30:8).

We are taught to ask, in the next place, for forgiveness: 'Forgive us our sins; for we also forgive every one that is indebted to us.' In so saying, we confess that we are fallen, guilty, and corrupt creatures, and in many things offend daily. We make no excuse for ourselves. We plead nothing in our own behalf. We simply ask for the free, full, gracious mercy of our Father in Christ Jesus. And we accompany the petition by the only profession which the whole Lord's Prayer contains. We profess that we 'forgive every one that is indebted to us.'

The combined simplicity and richness of the second division of the Lord's Prayer can never be sufficiently admired. How soon the words are spoken! And yet how much the words take in! Daily bread and daily mercy are by far the first and principal things that mortal man wants. He is the rich man who possesses them. He is the wise man who is not ashamed to pray for them every day. The child of God, no doubt, is fully justified before God, and all things are working for his good. But it is the life of true faith to apply daily for fresh supplies of all our wants. Though the promises are all ours, our Father likes his children to remind him of them. Though washed, we need daily to wash our feet (*John* 13:10).

3

The third division of the Lord's Prayer *respects our daily dangers*. We are taught to make mention of two things which we ought to fear every day, and which we must expect to meet with as long as we are in this world. One of these things is 'temptation.' The other is 'evil.'

We are taught to pray against temptation: 'Lead us not into temptation.' We do not mean by this expression that God is the author of evil, or that he tempts man to sin (*James* 1:13). But we entreat him who orders all things in heaven and earth, and without whom nothing can happen, so to order the course of our lives, that we may not be tempted above what we can bear. We confess our weakness and readiness to fall. We entreat our Father to preserve us from trials, or else to make a way for us to escape. We ask that our feet may be kept, and that we may not bring discredit on our profession and misery on our souls.

We are taught, lastly, to pray against evil: 'Deliver us from evil.' We include under the word evil, everything that can hurt us, either in body or soul, and especially every weapon of that great author of evil, the devil. We confess that ever since the fall the world 'lieth in the wicked one' (*1 John* 5:19). We confess that evil is in us, and about us, and near us, and on every side, and that we have no power to deliver ourselves from it. We apply to the strong for strength. We cast ourselves on him for protection. In short we ask what our Saviour himself asked for us, when he said, 'I pray not that thou shouldest take them out of the world, but that thou shouldest keep them from the evil' (*John* 17:15).

Such is the last division of the Lord's Prayer. In real importance it is not a whit inferior to the two other divisions, which we have already considered. It leaves man precisely in the position which he ought to occupy. It puts in his mouth the language of humility. The most dangerous state in which we can be, is not to know and feel our spiritual danger.

And now let us use the Lord's Prayer for the trial of our own state before God. Its words have probably passed over our lips thousands of times. But have we really felt it?—Do we really desire its petitions to be granted?—Is God really our Father?—Are we born again, and made his children by faith in Christ?—Do we care much for his name and will?—Do we really wish the kingdom of God to come?—Do we feel our need of daily temporal mercies, and of daily pardon of sin?—Do we fear falling into temptation?—Do we dread evil above all things?—These are serious questions. They deserve serious consideration.

Let us strive to make the Lord's Prayer our model and pattern in all our approaches to God. Let it suggest to us the sort of things which we should pray for and pray against. Let it teach us the relative place and proportion which we should give to each subject in our prayers. The more we ponder and examine the Lord's Prayer, the more instructive and suggestive shall we find it to be.

Notes—Luke 11:1-4

1.—[*As he was praying.*] We see in this place another instance of our Lord's diligence in private prayer. In this respect he has left a pattern which all Christians ought to copy.

[*Teach us to pray.*] Quesnel calls attention to the benefit which this man's request has obtained for the whole church of Christ:—'One single person, moved and edified by the good example of our Lord praying, conceives a love for prayer, desires to know how to pray, is sensible that of himself he is not capable of doing it, addresses himself to Christ, obtains from him this divine pattern, procures this treasure for the rest of the disciples, and for the whole church, and becomes the occasion of the infinite good which the prayer has produced, and will produce, to the end of the world.'

2.—[*When ye pray, say.*] Let it be carefully noted that the Lord's Prayer was twice delivered by our Lord, upon two distinct occasions. This accounts for the slight variations in its form, which appear on comparison.—Mede remarks, 'As Joseph said to Pharaoh, the dream is doubled unto Pharaoh, because the thing is established, so the delivery of this prayer was doubled,

that we may know the more certainly that our Saviour intended and commanded it for a set form of prayer to his church.'

[*Our Father.*] Chrysostom and Augustine both remark that to address God as 'Father,' is peculiar to the New Testament dispensation, and that the Old Testament saints never use the expression.—The remark is undoubtedly true, but requires fencing with cautions.—We must be careful not to suppose that the Old Testament saints were destitute of the Holy Ghost, as some say, and were not born again. Their light was undoubtedly far less than ours. The way into the holiest was not made manifest. The precise manner in which God would be just and yet justify the ungodly, was not clearly understood by them. They could not therefore look up to God with that boldness and freedom which the Christian believer can, as to a reconciled Father. But to say that God was in no sense the Father of Old Testament believers would be going much too far. He is the Father of all who are saved by Christ, and without Christ no man was ever saved.

The expression 'Our' in the beginning of the Lord's Prayer, should not be overlooked. It teaches believers that in all their prayers they should think of others as well as themselves. They should remember all the members of Christ's mystical body as their brethren and sisters in the Lord.

[*Thy name.*] To see the full meaning of this expression we should note the many places in which it is used in the Psalms. Such, for instance, as these, 'I will declare thy name unto my brethren.' Psalm 22:22.—'They that know thy name will put their trust in thee.' Psalm 9:10.—'I will wait on thy name.' Psalm 52:9.—'Unto thy name give glory.' Psalm 115:1.—'The righteous shall give thanks unto thy name.' Psalm 140:13.—In all these cases, and many more, the idea is evidently that of 'God's revealed character and attributes.'

[*Thy kingdom.*] The plainest and simplest sense of this word is the promised kingdom which God is one day to take to himself over all the world, foretold by Daniel and the other prophets, when Satan shall cease to be 'prince of this world,' and the millennium shall begin.

[*Thy will be done, as in heaven, so in earth.*] To see the full beauty of this prayer, we should read the description of angels, in Psalm 103:20 and 21. Heaven is the only place now where God's will is done perfectly, constantly, unhesitatingly, cheerfully, immediately, and without asking any questions.

3.—[*Give us day by day our daily bread.*] The English translation of the Greek words in this verse admits of some question. The literal sense appears to be, 'Give us for the day, or day by day, the bread which is sufficient for our subsistence.'

The Greek word which we have rendered 'daily,' is only found in this place, and in Matthew 6:11.

Some think that the words should be translated, 'our super-substantial bread,' understanding by it, the bread in the Lord's supper. This is a most unlikely and improbable sense. Even Stella, the Spanish commentator, remarks that the Eucharist is not bread for every day.

Some think that the words should be rendered, 'Give us day by day our tomorrow's bread—a future bread.' This seems a very harsh and awkward sense.

The true meaning appears to be that which has been already given, 'the bread which is convenient, or sufficient, for our daily subsistence.' This is the interpretation maintained by Chrysostom, Theophylact, and Suidas, and ably defended by Parkhurst.

4.—[*Forgive us our sins.*] Let this expression be carefully noted. It provides an answer to those who say that the believer ought never to ask for pardon of sins. One text like this is worth a hundred arguments. The Lord Jesus bids us do it, and therefore it ought to be done.

The justification of every believer no doubt is a finished and perfect work, and one admitting of no degrees, no increase, and no diminution. The moment a man believes on Christ, he is as much justified as St Paul or St John, and cannot be more justified if he lives to the age of Methuselah. But all this is no reason why he should not daily confess his sins, and daily seek fresh application of Christ's blood to his conscience. In fact, it is the life of faith to do so. The words of our Lord, in another place, are very teaching: 'He that is washed needeth not save to wash his feet' (*John* 13:10).

[*Indebted to us.*] Whitby and Hammond both remark that this expression has a sense much stronger than it appears, at first sight, to bear. Hammond says that in the Syriac language, which our Lord very probably spoke, a sinner is called 'a debtor.'

Let it not be forgotten that every unforgiving and implacable man, who uses the Lord's Prayer, is practically praying that his own sin may not be forgiven at all. He is professing a lie.

[*Lead us.*] The Greek word rendered 'lead' is only used seven times in the New Testament. Excepting in the Lord's Prayer, our translators have always rendered it 'bring into.' Luke 5:18, 19; Acts 17:20; 1 Timothy 6:7; Hebrews 13:11.

[*From evil.*] The words so translated might have been rendered, with equal correctness, 'the evil one,' that is, 'the devil.' They are so rendered in Matthew 13:19, 38; 1 John 2:13, 14; 3:12; 5:18.

I cannot leave the subject of the Lord's Prayer, without remarking that those who profess to believe in a 'unanimous consent of the Fathers' in the interpretation of Scripture, would do well to observe the exceedingly various senses which the Fathers attach to the several clauses of the Lord's Prayer. No man can investigate this point without discovering that the Fathers are no more agreed among themselves as to the meaning of Scripture, than Gill and A. Clarke, or Thomas Scott and Mant. A summary of various interpretations of the Lord's Prayer by the Fathers will be found in Cumming's *Lectures for the Times*. (Edit. 1845 p. 174.)

LUKE 11:5-13

5 And he said unto them, Which of you shall have a friend, and shall go unto him at midnight, and say unto him, Friend, lend me three loaves;

6 For a friend of mine in his journey is come to me, and I have nothing to set before him?

7 And he from within shall answer and say, Trouble me not: the door is now shut, and my children are with me in bed; I cannot rise and give thee.

8 I say unto you, Though he will not rise and give him, because he is his friend, yet because of his importunity he will rise and give him as many as he needeth.

9 And I say unto you, Ask, and it shall be given you; seek, and ye shall find; knock, and it shall be opened unto you.

10 For every one that asketh receiveth; and he that seeketh findeth; and to him that knocketh it shall be opened.

11 If a son shall ask bread of any of you that is a father, will he give him a stone? or if *he ask* a fish, will he for a fish give him a serpent?

12 Or if he shall ask an egg, will he offer him a scorpion?

13 If ye then, being evil, know how to give good gifts unto your children: how much more shall *your* heavenly Father give the Holy Spirit to them that ask him?

IN these verses our Lord Jesus Christ instructs us about prayer. The subject is one which can never be too strongly impressed on our attention. Prayer lies at the very root of our practical Christianity. It is part of the daily business of our religious life. We have reason to thank God, that upon no point has our Lord Jesus Christ spoken so fully and frequently as upon prayer.

We learn for one thing from these verses, *the importance of perseverance in prayer.* This lesson is conveyed to us in the simple parable, commonly called the 'Friend at Midnight.' We are there reminded what man can obtain from man by dint of importunity. Selfish and indolent as we naturally are, we are capable of being roused to exertion by continued asking. The man who would not give three loaves at midnight for friendship's sake, at length gave them to save himself the trouble of being further entreated. The application of the parable is clear and plain. If importunity succeeds so well between man and man, how much more may we expect it to obtain mercies when used in prayer to God.

The lesson is one which we shall do well to remember. It is far more easy to begin a habit of prayer than to keep it up. Myriads of professing Christians are regularly taught to pray when they are young, and then gradually leave off the practice as they grow up. Thousands take up a habit of praying for a little season, after some special mercy or special affliction, and then little by little become cold about it, and at last lay it aside. The secret thought comes stealing over men's minds, that 'it is no use to pray.' They see no visible benefit from it. They persuade themselves that they get on just as well without prayer. Laziness and unbelief prevail over their hearts, and at last they altogether 'restrain prayer before God' (*Job* 15:4).

Let us resist this feeling, whenever we feel it rising within us. Let us resolve by God's grace, that however poor and feeble our prayers may seem to be, we will pray on. It is not for nothing that the Bible tells us so frequently, to 'watch unto prayer,' to 'pray without ceasing,' to 'continue in prayer,' to 'pray always and not to faint,' to be 'instant in prayer.' These expressions all look one way. They are all meant to remind us of a danger and to quicken us to a duty. The time and way in which our prayers shall be answered are matters which we must leave entirely to God. But that every petition which we offer in faith shall certainly be answered, we need not doubt. Let us lay our matters before God again and again, day after day, week after week, month after month, year after year. The answer may be long in coming, as it was in the cases of Hannah and Zacharias (*1 Sam.* 1:27; *Luke* 1:13). But though it tarry, let us pray on and wait for it. At the right time it will surely come and not tarry.

We learn for another thing from these verses, *how wide and encouraging are the promises which the Lord Jesus holds out to prayer.* The striking words in which they are clothed are familiar to us if any are in the Bible: 'Ask, and ye shall receive; seek, and ye shall find; knock, and it shall be opened unto you.'—The solemn declaration which follows, appears intended to make assurance doubly sure: 'Every one that asketh receiveth; and he that seeketh findeth; and to him that knocketh it shall be opened.'—The heart-searching argument which concludes the passage, leaves faithlessness and unbelief without excuse: 'If ye then being evil, know how to give good gifts unto your children: how much more shall your heavenly Father give the Holy Spirit to them that ask him?'

There are few promises in the Bible so broad and unqualified as those contained in this wonderful passage. The last in particular deserves especial notice. The Holy Spirit is beyond doubt the greatest gift which God can bestow upon man. Having this gift, we have all things, life, light, hope, and heaven. Having this gift, we have God the Father's boundless love, God the Son's atoning blood, and full communion with all three persons of the blessed Trinity. Having this gift, we have grace and peace in the world that now is, glory and honour in the world to come. And yet this mighty gift is held out by our Lord Jesus Christ as a gift to be obtained by prayer! 'Your heavenly Father shall give the Holy Spirit to them that ask him.'

There are few passages in the Bible which so completely strip the unconverted man of his common excuses as this passage. He says he is 'weak and helpless.' But does he ask to be made strong?—He says he is 'wicked and corrupt.' But does he seek to be made better?—He says he 'can do nothing of himself.' But does he knock at the door of mercy, and pray for the grace of the Holy Spirit?—These are questions to which many, it may be feared, can make no answer. They are what they are, because they have no real desire to be changed. They have not, because they ask not. They will not come to Christ, that they may have life; and therefore they remain dead in trespasses and sins.

And now, as we leave the passage, let us ask ourselves whether we know anything of real prayer? Do we pray at all?—Do we pray in the name of Jesus, and as needy sinners?—Do we know what it is to 'ask,' and 'seek,' and 'knock,' and wrestle in prayer, like men who feel that it is a matter of life or death, and that they must have an answer?—Or are we content with saying over some old form of words, while our thoughts are wandering, and our hearts far away? Truly we have learned a great lesson when we have learned that 'saying prayers' is not praying!

If we do pray, let it be a settled rule with us, never to leave off the habit of praying, and never to shorten our prayers. A man's state before God may always be measured by his prayers. Whenever we begin to feel careless about our private prayers, we may depend upon it, there is something very wrong in the condition of our souls. There are breakers ahead. We are in imminent danger of a shipwreck.

Notes—Luke 11:5-13

5.—[*Which of you shall have a friend, etc.*] Here, as in many other cases, we should notice the lowly condition of life, and simple range of social circumstances, from which our Lord drew his illustrations of spiritual truth. This is one of the reasons why the Bible is so peculiarly suited to that class of mankind which is always most numerous,—the poor.

[*Three loaves.*] We may conclude from this expression, that a loaf of bread in the New Testament days was much smaller in size than it commonly is now. Three of our loaves would be more than sufficient for the wants of one man. This fact should be remembered as it throws light on the miracle of feeding the multitude with a few loaves.

6.—[*In his journey.*] In order to understand the arrival of a friend from a journey at midnight, we must remember that in hot countries people often travel by night, and rest during the day. All who have travelled in India will see the reasonableness of this circumstance in the parable.

7.—[*My children are with me in bed.*] The family of a poor man in Eastern climates often all sleep in one common sleeping chamber. This appears to be the simple meaning of the expression here used:—'We have all retired to our sleeping chamber. We are all in bed.'

8.—[*Importunity.*] The Greek word so translated is only used here in the New Testament. It would be rendered more literally 'shamelessness.' It signifies a continual asking and entreating, in spite of rebuffs, like the asking of an impudent beggar.

11.—[*If a son shall ask bread, etc.*] The sentence so translated would be rendered more literally, 'What father of you will his son ask bread, will he give him a stone?'

There is an evident resemblance implied between the appearances of a loaf and a stone, a fish and a serpent.

12.—[*An egg ... a scorpion.*] Bishop Pearce shows, by a quotation from Bochart, that the large kind of scorpions, when coiled and rolled up, had a white body not unlike an egg.

[*Will he offer.*] The Greek word so translated is the same which is rendered in the preceding verse 'will he give.'

13.—[*Being evil.*] Let this expression be

noted. It is one of those which show the natural wickedness of man. He is by nature only evil. 'Every imagination of the thought of his heart is only evil continually.' Genesis 6:5.

[*Your heavenly Father.*] There is a notable distinction between the Greek words so translated and those rendered 'Father which art in heaven,' in the Lord's Prayer. Here it signifies 'Father *from* heaven.' There it is 'Father *in* heaven.'—Alford remarks that 'when we address God, he is our Father in heaven,—when he answers us, he is our Father from heaven. In the former case we go up to him and his abode. In the latter case he comes down to us.'

I cannot leave the above passage without expressing my own dissent from the allegorical signification which the Fathers and other commentators have thought fit to place on many of its expressions. I cannot hold, with Augustine, that the three loaves represent the Trinity, man's food and life, or faith, hope, and charity,—nor yet that the 'fish' represents faith, or the 'egg' hope.—I cannot hold with Bede, that the guest newly arrived is the spirit of man, weary and hungry,—the host, natural man unable to satisfy his soul,—and the appeal to the friend, application to God for help.—I cannot hold with Vitringa, that the guest is the heathen world, the host who receives him, the disciples of Jesus, who must receive bread of life from God for the relief of the heathen, and solicit it with all perseverance.—I cannot hold with others, that the children in bed are the angels, or the saints who are already in glory. Several of these interpretations will be found in Trench on Parables.

I leave all such explanations of Scripture to those who can receive them. I for one cannot.—To some minds they may appear wise, clever, and beautiful. To me they appear fanciful, dangerous, destitute of sobriety, and unwarrantable additions to the mind of Christ.—Most parables are intended to convey one great lesson. Even those in which almost every part has a meaning, such as the ten virgins and the prodigal son, require to be handled with great caution. In the parable of the friend at midnight I am unable to see any warrant for searching out far-fetched allegorical meanings. We have no right to enquire what the words of Scripture can be twisted, and strained, and wrested into meaning. We have only to consider what was the original scope or intention of the Holy Ghost when the words were written, and by that to abide. The protest of Stella, the Spanish commentator, on this subject in his commentary on this very place, is well worthy of remark.

It is fair to observe, that the broad promise at the end of the passage, 'Your heavenly Father shall give the Holy Spirit to them that ask him,' is differently explained by different theologians.—Some would interpret it as a general promise, graciously held out to all mankind, as an inducement and encouragement to pray.—Others would confine it to God's children and true believers, and interpret it only as an argument for converted people asking much that they may have much.

The reader of my exposition will perceive that I am unable to place the more confined and narrow view upon the promise. I feel obliged, in fairness and honesty, to regard the words as one of those great, broad sentences, in which God holds out his hands to the unconverted, and sets before them an open door.—That no man can pray acceptably without the Holy Spirit, I am well aware.—In what way a man can ask for the Holy Spirit unless he has first received the Holy Spirit, I do not pretend to explain. I only know that I find the words of this promise plainly laid before us, and that fair interpretation seems to require them to be *generally* applied. I desire to receive the promise as a little child, and to press it on unconverted people. I dare not be more systematic in my theology than Scripture itself.

LUKE 11:14-20

14 And he was casting out a devil, and it was dumb. And it came to pass, when the devil was gone out, the dumb spake; and the people wondered.

15 But some of them said, He casteth out devils through Beelzebub the chief of the devils.

16 And others, tempting *him*, sought of him a sign from heaven.

17 But he, knowing their thoughts, said unto them, Every kingdom divided against itself is brought to desolation; and a house *divided* against a house falleth.

18 If Satan also be divided against himself, how shall his kingdom stand? because ye say that I cast out devils through Beelzebub.

19 And if I by Beelzebub cast out devils, by whom do your sons cast *them* out? therefore shall they be your judges.

20 But if I with the finger of God cast out devils, no doubt the kingdom of God is come upon you.

THE connection between these verses and those which immediately precede them, is striking and instructive. In the preceding verses, our Lord Jesus Christ had been showing the power and importance of prayer. In the verses before us, he delivers a man from a dumb devil. The miracle is evidently intended to throw fresh light on the lesson. The same Saviour who encourages us to pray, is the Saviour who destroys Satan's power over our members, and restores our tongues to their proper use.

Let us notice, firstly, in these verses, *the variety of ways in which Satan exhibits his desire to injure man.* We read of a dumb devil. Sometimes in the Gospels we are told of an 'unclean' devil. Sometimes we are told of a raging and violent devil. Here we are told of one under whose influence the unhappy person possessed by him became 'dumb.' Many are the devices of Satan. It is foolish to suppose that he always works in the same manner. One thing only is the common mark of all his operations,—he delights to inflict injury and do harm.

There is something very instructive in the case before us. Do we suppose, because bodily possession by Satan is not so glaringly manifest as it once was, that the great enemy is less active in doing mischief than he used to be?—If we think so we have much to learn.—Do we suppose that there is no such thing as the influence of a 'dumb' devil in the present day? If we do, we had better think again.—What shall we say of those who never speak to God, who never use their tongues in prayer and praise, who never employ that organ which is a man's 'glory,' in the service of him who made it? What shall we say, in a word, of those who can speak to everyone but God?—What can we say but that Satan has despoiled them of the truest use of a tongue? What ought we to say but that they are possessed with a 'dumb devil?' The prayerless man is dead while he lives. His members are rebels against the God who made them. The 'dumb devil' is not yet extinct.

Let us watch and pray that we may never be given over to the influence of a dumb spirit. Thanks be to God, that same Jesus still lives, who can make the deaf to hear and the dumb to speak! To him let us flee for help. In him let us abide. It is not enough to avoid open profligacy, and to keep clear of glaring sins. It is not enough to be moral, and proper, and respectable in our lives. All this is negative goodness, and nothing more. Is there anything positive about our religion? Do we yield our members as instruments of righteousness to God? (*Rom.* 6:13). Having eyes, do we see God's kingdom? Having ears, do we hear Christ's voice? Having a tongue, do we use it for God's praise? These are very serious inquiries. The number of persons who are deaf and dumb before God is far greater than many suppose.

Let us notice, secondly, in these verses, *the amazing power of prejudice over the hearts of unconverted men.* We read, that when our Lord cast out the dumb spirit, there were some who said, 'He casteth out devils through Beelzebub the chief of the devils.' They could not deny the miracle. They then refused to allow that it was wrought by divine power. The work before their eyes was plain and indisputable. They then attempted to discredit the character of him who did it, and to blacken his reputation by saying that he was in league with the devil.

The state of mind here described, is a most formidable disease, and one unhappily not uncommon. There are never wanting men who are determined to see no good in the servants of Christ, and to believe all manner of evil about them. Such men appear to throw aside their common sense. They refuse to listen to evidence, or to attend to plain arguments. They seem resolved to believe that whatever a Christian does must be wrong, and whatever he says must be false!—If he does right at any time, it must be from corrupt motives! If he speaks truth, it must be with sinister views! If he does good works, it is from interested reasons! If he casts out devils, it is through Beelzebub!—Such prejudiced men are to be found in many a congregation. They are the sorest trials of the ministers of Christ. No wonder that St Paul said, 'Pray that we may be delivered from unreasonable as well as wicked men' (2 Thess. 3:1–2).

Let us strive to be of a fair, and honest, and candid spirit in our judgment of men and things in religion. Let us be ready to give up old and cherished opinions the moment that anyone can show us a 'more excellent way.' The honest and good heart is a great treasure (Luke 8:15). A prejudiced spirit is the very jaundice of the soul. It affects a man's mental eyesight, and makes him see everything in an unnatural colour. From such a spirit may we pray to be delivered!

Let us notice, lastly, in these verses, the great evil of religious divisions. This is a truth which our Lord impresses on us in the answer he gives to his prejudiced enemies. He shows the folly of their charge that he cast out devils by Beelzebub. He quotes the proverbial saying that 'a house divided against itself falleth.' He infers the absurdity of the idea that Satan would cast out Satan, or the devil cast out his own agents. And in so doing, he teaches Christians a lesson which they have been mournfully slow to learn in every age of the church. That lesson is the sin and folly of needless divisions.

Religious divisions of some kind there must always be, so long as false doctrine prevails, and men will cleave to it. What communion can there be between light and darkness? How can two walk together except they be agreed? What unity can there be where there is not the unity of the Spirit? Division and separation from those who adhere to false and unscriptural doctrine is a duty, and not a sin.

But there are divisions of a very different kind, which are deeply to be deplored. Such, for example, are divisions between men who agree on main points,—divisions about matters not needful to salvation,—divisions about forms and ceremonies, and ecclesiastical arrangements upon which Scripture is silent. Divisions of this kind are to be avoided and discouraged by all faithful Christians. The existence of them is a melancholy proof of the fallen state of man, and the corruption of his understanding as well as his will. They bring scandal on religion, and weakness on the church. 'Every kingdom divided against itself is brought to desolation.'

What are the best remedies against needless divisions? A humble spirit, a readiness to make concessions, and an enlightened acquaintance with Holy Scripture. We must learn to distinguish between things in religion which are essential, and things which are not essential,—things which are needful to salvation, and things which are not needful,—things which are of first-rate importance, and things which are of second-rate importance. On the one class of things we must be stiff and unbending as the oak tree: 'If any man preach any other gospel than that which we have preached, let him be accursed' (*Gal.* 1:8).—On the other we may be yielding and compliant as the willow: 'I am made all things to all men, that I might by all means save some' (*1 Cor.* 9:22). To draw such nice distinctions requires no small practical wisdom. But such wisdom is to be had for the asking. 'If any man lack wisdom, let him ask of God' (*James* 1:5). When Christians keep up needless divisions they show themselves more foolish than Satan himself.

Notes—Luke 11:14-20

14.—[*It was dumb.*] The expression here used should be noted and compared with the one which follows in the same verse, 'the dumb spake.'—It was the *devil* which was dumb. It was the *man* who spake.—The words would have been more clearly rendered, 'The dumb man spake.' The action of the evil spirit making the possessed man dumb, and the action of the man released from his power, should be carefully distinguished.

15.—[*Beelzebub.*] The meaning of this name is said to be the 'Lord of flies.' Beelzebub is mentioned as 'the god of Ekron,' in 2 Kings 1:3. For what reason so peculiar a name was given to the chief of the devils is a question which has never been fully settled. How great the plague of flies is in a hot country those who have travelled there have always mentioned.

16.—[*Sought of him a sign.*] Let it be noted that it is always one mark of a thoroughly unbelieving heart, to pretend to want more evidence of the truth of religion.

17.—[*Every kingdom divided ... desolation.*] It may be doubted whether our Lord's words in this place are not meant to refer to the many intestine divisions and dissensions which prevailed among the Jews, even to the very day when Titus took Jerusalem. In this light the verse contained a solemn prophecy. It is notorious that the divisions of the Jews were one cause of the success of the Roman army.

19.—[*Your sons cast them out.*] It is not agreed among commentators to whom our Lord refers in this expression. Bishop Jewel thinks that he refers to his own disciples, John, James, Peter, Andrew, and the rest, and calls them 'sons of the Jews.' Others, however, think that he refers to certain persons among the Jews who had power to cast out devils, though they were not disciples of Christ. That there were such persons seems likely from Acts 19:13.

[*Shall they be your judges.*] The meaning of this expression is, 'They shall condemn your supposition that I cast out devils by Beelzebub, as unreasonable and absurd. They shall be witnesses that devils are not cast out by devils, but by the power of God.'

20.—[*The kingdom of God is come upon you.*] The argument here appears to be this,—'If these miracles which I work are really worked by the finger of God, and I am clearly proved by them to be one sent from God, then, whether you will allow it or not, the times of Messiah have evidently arrived. The kingdom of God has come down upon you unawares, and these miracles are signs that it is so.'—This argument reduced the enemies of our Lord to a dilemma. Either they must deny that our Lord cast out devils,—this they could not do;—or else they must admit that their own sons cast out devils by the power of Beelzebub;—this they would not do.—The nature of the argument appears to show that when our Lord spake of 'your sons casting out devils,' he could not have meant his own disciples.

LUKE 11:21-26

21 When a strong man armed keepeth his palace, his goods are in peace:

22 But when a stronger than he shall come upon him, and overcome him, he taketh from him all his armour wherein he trusted, and divideth his spoils.

23 He that is not with me is against me: and he that gathereth not with me scattereth.

24 When the unclean spirit is gone out of a man, he walketh through dry places, seeking rest; and finding none, he saith, I will return unto my house whence I came out.

25 And when he cometh, he findeth *it* swept and garnished.

26 Then goeth he, and taketh *to him* seven other spirits more wicked than himself; and they enter in, and dwell there: and the last *state* of that man is worse than the first.

THE subject of these words of Christ is mysterious, but deeply important. They were spoken concerning Satan and his agency. They throw light on the power of Satan, and the nature of his operations. They deserve the close attention of all who would war the Christian warfare with success. Next to his friends and allies, a soldier ought to be well acquainted with his enemies. We ought not to be ignorant of Satan's devices.

Let us observe in these verses *what a fearful picture our Lord draws of Satan's power.* There are four points in his description, which are peculiarly instructive.

Christ speaks of Satan as a 'strong man.' The strength of Satan has been only too well proved by his victories over the souls of men. He who tempted Adam and Eve to rebel against God, and brought sin into the world,—he who has led captive the vast majority of mankind, and robbed them of heaven;—that evil one is indeed a mighty foe. He who is called the 'prince of this world,' is not an enemy to be despised. The devil is very strong.

Christ speaks of Satan as a 'strong man, armed.' Satan is well supplied with defensive armour. He is not to be overcome by slight assaults, and feeble exertions. He that would overcome him must put forth all his strength. 'This kind goeth not out but by prayer and fasting.'—And Satan is also well supplied with offensive weapons. He is never at a loss for means to injure the soul of man. He has snares of every kind, and engines of every description. He knows exactly how every rank, and class, and age, and nation, and people can be assailed with most advantage. The devil is well armed.

Christ speaks of man's heart as being Satan's 'palace.' The natural heart is the favourite abode of the evil one, and all its faculties and powers are his servants and do his will. He sits upon the throne which God ought to occupy, and governs the inward man. The devil is the 'spirit that worketh in the children of disobedience' (*Eph.* 2:2).

Christ speaks of Satan's 'goods being at peace.' So long as a man is dead in trespasses and sin, so long his heart is at ease about spiritual things. He has no fear about the future. He has no anxiety about his soul. He has no dread of falling into hell. All this is a false peace no doubt. It is a sleep which cannot last, and from which there must be one day an awful waking. But there is such a peace beyond question. Thoughtless, stolid, reckless insensibility about eternal things is one of the worst symptoms of the devil reigning over a man's soul.

Let us never think lightly of the devil. That common practice of

17

idle jesting about Satan which we may often mark in the world, is a great evil. A prisoner must be a very hardened man who jests about the executioner and the gallows. The heart must be in a very bad state, when a man can talk with levity about hell and the devil.

Let us thank God that there is One who is stronger even than Satan. That One is the Friend of sinners, Jesus the Son of God. Mighty as the devil is, he was overcome by Jesus on the cross, when he triumphed over him openly. Strong as the devil is, Christ can pluck his captives out of his hands, and break the chains which bind them. May we never rest till we know that deliverance by experience, and have been set free by the Son of God!

Let us observe, for another thing in these verses, *how strongly our Lord teaches the impossibility of neutrality.* He says, 'he that is not with me is against me: and he that gathereth not with me, scattereth.'

The principle laid down in these words should be constantly remembered by all who make any profession of decided religion. We all naturally love an easy Christianity. We dislike collisions and separation. We like, if possible, to keep in with both sides. We fear extremes. We dread being righteous overmuch. We are anxious not to go too far.—Such thoughts as these are full of peril to the soul. Once allowed to get the upper hand, they may do us immense harm. Nothing is so offensive to Christ as lukewarmness in religion. To be utterly dead and ignorant, is to be an object of pity as well as blame. But to know the truth and yet 'halt between two opinions,' is one of the chiefest of sins.

Let it be the settled determination of our minds, that we will serve Christ with all our hearts, if we serve him at all. Let there be no reserve, no compromise, no half-heartedness, no attempt to reconcile God and mammon in our Christianity. Let us resolve, by God's help, to be 'with Christ,' and 'gather' by Christ's side, and allow the world to say and do what it will.—It may cost us something at first. It will certainly repay us in the long run. Without decision there is no happiness in religion. He that follows Jesus most fully, will always follow him most comfortably.—Without decision in religion, there is no usefulness to others. The half-hearted Christian attracts none by the beauty of his life, and wins no respect from the world.

Let us observe finally, in these verses, *how dangerous it is to be content with any change in religion short of thorough conversion to God.* This is a truth which our Lord teaches by an awful picture of one from whom a devil has been cast forth, but into whose heart the Holy Spirit has not entered. He describes the evil spirit, after his expulsion, as seeking rest and finding none.—He describes him planning a return to the heart which he once inhabited, and carrying his plan into execution.—He describes him finding that heart empty of any good, and like a house 'swept and garnished' for his reception.—He describes him as entering in once more, with seven spirits worse than himself, and once more making it his abode. And he winds up all by the solemn saying, 'the last state of that man is worse than the first.'

We must feel in reading these fearful words, that Jesus is speaking of things which we faintly comprehend. He is lifting a corner of the veil which hangs over the unseen world. His words, no doubt, illustrate the state of things which existed in the Jewish nation during the time of his own ministry. But the main lesson of his words, which concerns us, is the danger of our own individual souls. They are a solemn warning to us, never to be satisfied with religious reformation without heart conversion.

There is no safety excepting in thorough Christianity. To lay aside open sin is nothing, unless grace reigns in our hearts. To cease to do evil is a small matter, if we do not also learn to do well.—The house must not only be swept and whitewashed. A new tenant must be introduced, or else the leprosy may yet appear again in the walls.—The outward life must not only be garnished with the formal trappings of religion. The power of vital religion must be experienced in the inward man.—The devil must not only be cast out. The Holy Ghost must take his place. Christ must dwell in our hearts by faith. We must not only be moralized, but spiritualized. We must not only be reformed, but born again.

Let us lay these things to heart. Many professing Christians, it may be feared, are deceiving themselves. They are not what they once were, and so they flatter themselves, they are what they ought to be. They are no longer sabbath-breaking, daring sinners, and so they dream that they are Christians. They see not that they have only changed one kind of devil for another. They are governed by a decent, Pharisaic devil, instead of an audacious, riotous, unclean devil.—But the tenant within is the devil still. And their last end will be worse than their first. From such an end may we pray to be delivered! Whatever we are in religion, let us be thorough. Let us not be houses swept and garnished, but uninhabited by the Spirit. Let us not be potsherds covered with silver, fair without, but worthless within. Let our daily prayer be, 'Search me, O God;—and see whether there be any wicked way in me, and lead me in the way everlasting' (*Psa.* 139:23, 24).

Notes—Luke 11:21-26

21.—[*A strong man.*] The Greek expression so translated, would be more literally rendered 'the strong one.' The word 'man' is not in the Greek. The same remark applies to Matthew 12:29, and Mark 3:27. The literal translation brings out the character of the devil, and the applicability of the whole passage to him with much force.

[*His goods.*] The literal meaning of the Greek expression so translated is, 'the things that are his,—that belong to him.'

22.—[*A stronger than he.*] This expression again would be more literally rendered, 'the One stronger than he.' It evidently refers to our Lord, the great conqueror of Satan. There is a probable reference to Isaiah 53:12. John the Baptist calls our Lord 'the mightier one,' in Mark 1:7, and Luke 3:16. In both these places the Greek is the same as it is here.

[*Divideth his spoils.*] It admits of a question whether our Lord did not mean us to put a literal sense on these words, and to interpret them of that new application of man's faculties and powers which he makes when he converts a soul. He takes

possession of the affections and intellectual capacities, over which the devil once exercised dominion, and uses them for his own glory. Ford quotes a saying of Bishop Reynolds; 'God maketh use of that art, wealth, power, learning, wisdom, intellect, which Satan used against Christ's kingdom, as instruments and ornaments unto the gospel; as, when a magazine in war is taken, the General makes use of those arms, which were provided against him, for his own service.'

23.—[*He that is not with me is against me.*] The application of this expression is differently interpreted by different commentators. Some think that it should be confined strictly to the subject of which our Lord is speaking,—that is, the utter division which exists between his kingdom and that of the devil. They think our Lord is enforcing the absurdity of the idea that he cast out devils by Beelzebub, and that his argument is 'There can be no alliance between me and Satan. He is not with me, and so he is against me. He is not gathering with me, and so he scatters.'—Others think that the expression is of much wider application, and that it is a general truth concerning all waverers, and doubters, and half-hearted, and excuse-making people, of whom no doubt there were many among our Lord's hearers. They argue that our Lord is exposing the awful danger of many of his Jewish hearers, who had been a little roused by John the Baptist, and seemed likely to receive Christ when he appeared. And yet, when he did appear, they hung back and affected to be troubled with doubts, and so continued neutral and undecided.—This last opinion appears to me by far the most probable, and is confirmed by the passage which immediately follows. The sentence is directed against undecided Jews, who were like the man from whom the unclean spirit had gone forth. Their hesitating neutrality was a most dangerous position. Their last end was likely to be worse than their first.

At first sight, it seems difficult to reconcile our Lord's words in this verse with his words in another place. We find him saying of one who cast out devils in his name, but did not follow his disciples, 'Forbid him not: for he that is not against us is for us' (Luke 9:50). Here, however, we find him saying, 'He that is not with us, is against us.'

The reconciliation of the two sentences in reality is not difficult. They were spoken of two entirely different classes of persons. In the former case, our Lord was speaking of one who was really working for Christ, and against the devil, and was doing good, though perhaps not in the wisest way. Of him he says, 'He that is not against us, is for us.' He works against the same enemy that we work against, and therefore he is on our side.—In the case before us, our Lord is speaking of men who refused to join him and become his disciples, who held aloof from him, and were afraid or ashamed of his service. Of them he says, 'He that is not with us is against us.' He does not avow himself our friend, and so he becomes practically one of our foes.

24.—[He walketh through dry places.] The expression translated 'walketh,' is more frequently rendered, 'passeth, or goeth through.' Let it be noted, that it is

the 'spirit,' and not the man, of whom this is said.—The expression, 'dry places,' is a difficult one. The literal signification of the Greek words would be,—'places without water.' According to some, it means 'uninhabited or wilderness-places,' where the devil finds no rest, finding no one to injure.—According to others it signifies the *Gentiles*, over whom Satan exercised special power before the gospel was preached to them, and the *heathen*, over whom Satan specially reigns now.—Our inability to make out clearly the meaning of the expression, arises, in a great measure, from our ignorance of what is going on in the unseen world of spirits, both evil and good. To an immaterial creature, like a devil, the expression would probably be quite plain.

[*Seeking rest.*] This is an awful expression! It shows the restless unwearied craving to do mischief, and inflict injury on God's creatures, which seems at present a special attribute of the devil, during the period that he is permitted to do evil.

[*He saith, I will return unto my house.*] This is another most awful expression. How many men and women are being daily watched by the devil, and mischief planned against them, while they, in their folly, never dream of what Satan is doing!

25.—[*And when he cometh, he findeth.*] Let it be carefully noted both here and in the following verse, that it is the evil spirit, and not the man, of whom these things are said. Literally translated, the Greek words should be, 'When it cometh, it findeth, etc.'

[*Swept and garnished.*] These expressions must of course be regarded as figurative. They are borrowed from the condition of a house, and applied to the state of a reformed, but unconverted, people or heart.

Let it be remembered that there may be much moral cleanliness, and even much 'garnishing,' about one who is unsanctified. There may be much that is fair to the eye, and yet no grace.

26.—[*Seven other spirits.*] The number seven is often used in Scripture proverbially, to denote great increase in number, or size, or quantity, or intensity. Thus, Psalm 119:164; Proverbs 24:16; Matthew 18:21; Daniel 3:19.

[*More wicked than himself.*] This expression seems to denote that even among devils there are degrees of wickedness and malice. Just so there are degrees of glory in heaven, grace on earth, and punishment in hell.

[*Last state … worse than the first.*] The Greek expressions so rendered mean literally 'the last things,' and the 'first things.'

The tendency of a backslider, or a man who has at one time professed religion, but afterwards turned back to the world, to become worse than he ever was before, is a painful fact, but a notorious one.—The possession of clear knowledge of the gospel combined with deliberate choice of sin and the world, seems the parent of the most hardened state of soul to which mortal man can attain. Ford quotes a striking sentence from Cowper's Letters on this subject: 'I have observed that when a man who once seemed a Christian has put off that character, and resumed his old one, he loses, together with the grace which he seemed to possess, the most amiable parts of the character that he resumes. The best features of his natural face seem to be struck out, that after having worn religion only as a mask, he may make a more disgusting appearance than he did before he assumed it '

The story of the unclean spirit in this passage admits of a three-fold application. 1.—It describes the history of the Jewish nation before Christ came upon earth. For a time after the giving of the law they seemed better than the Gentiles, and like a house swept and garnished. But when they became proud, self-righteous, and unholy, the evil spirit returned to them. They were cast off by God, and given over to be oppressed and scattered by the Babylonians, Syrians, and the Romans. And forty years after our Lord was upon earth, their last state was worse than their first. 2.—It describes the history of the Gentile churches since the time when Christ was on earth. For many centuries they seemed like a house swept and garnished. The evil spirit seemed cast out. But in the vast majority of cases they have departed from their first things. The Spirit of God has left them. The evil spirit has returned. Their end seems likely to be worse than their beginning. 3.—Above all, the passage describes the state of individuals who are content with reformation without conversion. This is a sense which ought never to be lost sight of. Historical and prophetical interpretations are useful, but they must not be allowed to overlay and bury the lessons that concern each one of ourselves.

LUKE 11:27-32

27 And it came to pass, as he spake these things, a certain woman of the company lifted up her voice, and said unto him, Blessed is the womb that bare thee, and the paps which thou hast sucked.

28 But he said, Yea rather, blessed *are* they that hear the word of God, and keep it.

29 And when the people were gathered thick together, he began to say, This is an evil generation: they seek a sign; and there shall no sign be given it, but the sign of Jonas the prophet.

30 For as Jonas was a sign unto the Ninevites, so shall also the Son of man be to this generation.

31 The queen of the south shall rise up in the judgment with the men of this generation, and condemn them: for she came from the utmost parts of the earth to hear the wisdom of Solomon; and, behold, a greater than Solomon *is* here.

32 The men of Nineve shall rise up in the judgment with this generation, and shall condemn it: for they repented at the preaching of Jonas; and, behold, a greater than Jonas *is* here.

A WOMAN is brought before us in this passage of Scripture of whose name and history we know nothing. We read that, as our Lord spake, 'A certain woman of the company lifted up her voice, and said unto him, Blessed is the womb that bare thee.' At once our Lord founds on her remark a great lesson. His perfect wisdom turned every incident within his reach to profit.

We should observe in these verses *how great are the privileges of those who hear and keep God's Word.* They are regarded by Christ with as much honour as if they were his nearest relatives. It is more blessed to be a believer in the Lord Jesus than it would have been to have been one of the family in which he was born after the flesh. It was a greater honour to the Virgin Mary herself to have Christ dwelling in her heart by faith, than to have been the mother of Christ, and to have nursed him on her bosom.

Truths like these we are generally very slow to receive. We are apt to fancy that to have seen Christ, and heard Christ, and lived near Christ, and been a relative of Christ according to the flesh, would have had some mighty effect upon our souls. We are all naturally inclined to attach great importance to a religion of sight, and sense, and touch, and eye, and ear. We love a sensuous, tangible, material Christianity, far better than one of faith. And we need reminding that seeing is not always believing. Thousands saw Christ continually, while he was on earth, and yet clung to their sins. Even his brethren at one time 'did not believe in him' (*John* 7:5). A mere fleshly knowledge of Christ saves no one. The words of St Paul are very instructive:—'Though we have known Christ after the flesh, yet now henceforth know we him no more' (*2 Cor.* 5:16).

Let us learn from our Lord's words before us that the highest privileges our souls can desire are close at hand, and within our reach, if we only believe. We need not idly wish that we had lived near Capernaum, or hard by Joseph's house at Nazareth. We need not dream of a deeper love and a more thorough devotion if we had really pressed Christ's hand, or heard Christ's voice, or been numbered among Christ's relatives. All this could have done nothing more for us than simple faith can do now. Do we hear Christ's voice and follow him? Do we take him for our only Saviour and our only Friend, and forsaking all other hopes, cleave only unto him? If this be so, all things are ours. We need no higher privilege. We can have no higher, until Christ comes again. No man can be nearer and dearer to Jesus than the man who simply believes.

We should observe, secondly, in these verses, *the desperate unbelief of the Jews in our Lord's time.* We are told that though they 'gathered thick together' to hear Christ preach, they still professed to be waiting for a sign. They pretended to want more evidence before they believed. Our Lord declares that the Queen of Sheba and the men of Nineveh would put the Jews to shame at the last day. The Queen of Sheba had such faith that she travelled a vast distance in order to hear the wisdom of Solomon. Yet Solomon, with all his wisdom, was an erring and imperfect king. The Ninevites had such faith that they believed the message which Jonah brought from God, and repented. Yet even Jonah was a weak and unstable prophet. The Jews of our Lord's time had far higher light and infinitely clearer teachings than either Solomon or Jonah could supply. They had among them the King of kings, the Prophet greater than Moses. Yet the Jews neither repented nor believed!

Let it never surprise us to see unbelief abounding, both in the church and in the world. So far from wondering that there have been men like Hobbes, and Payne, and Rousseau, and Voltaire, we ought rather to wonder that such men have been so few. So far from marvelling that the vast majority of professing Christians remain unaffected and unmoved by the preaching of the gospel, we ought to marvel that any around us believe at all. Why should we wonder to see that old disease which began with Adam and Eve infecting all their children? Why should we expect to see more faith among men and women now than was seen in our Lord's time? The enormous amount of unbelief and hardness on every side may well grieve and pain us. But it ought not to cause surprise.

Let us thank God if we have received the gift of faith. It is a great thing to believe all the Bible. We do not sufficiently realize the corruption of human nature. We do not see the full virulence of the disease by which all Adam's children are infected, and the small number of those who are saved.—Have we faith, however weak and small? Let us praise God for the privilege. Who are we that God should have made us to differ? Let us watch against unbelief. The root of it often lies within us even after the tree is cut down. Let us guard our faith with a godly jealousy. It is the shield of the soul. It is the grace above all others which Satan labours to overthrow. Let us hold it fast. Blessed are they that believe!

We should observe, lastly, in these verses, *how our Lord Jesus Christ testifies to the truth of a resurrection, and a life to come.* He speaks of the queen of the south, whose name and dwelling place are now alike unknown to us. He says 'she shall rise up in the judgment.' He speaks of the men of Nineveh, a people who have passed away from the face of the earth. He says of them also, 'they shall rise up.'

There is something very solemn and instructive in the language which our Lord here uses. It reminds us that this world is not all, and that the life which man lives in the body on earth is not the only life of which we ought to think. The kings and queens of olden time are all to live again one day, and to stand before the bar of God. The vast multitudes who once swarmed round the palaces of Nineveh are all to come forth from their graves, and to give an account of their works. To our eyes they seem to have passed away for ever. We read with wonder of their empty halls, and talk of them as a people who have completely perished. Their dwelling places are a desolation. Their very bones are dust. But to the eye of God they all live still. The queen of the south and the men of Nineveh will all rise again. We shall yet see them face to face.

Let the truth of the resurrection be often before our minds. Let the life to come be frequently before our thoughts. All is not over when the grave receives its tenant, and man goes to his long home. Other people may dwell in our houses, and spend our money. Our

25

very names may soon be forgotten. But still all is not over! Yet a little time and we all shall live again. 'The earth shall cast out the dead' (*Isa.* 26:19). Many, like Felix, may well tremble when they think of such things. But men who live by faith in the Son of God, like St Paul, should lift up their heads and rejoice.

Notes—Luke 11:27-32

27.—[*A certain woman.*] We are not told who this woman was. Her exclamation seems to have been the expression of mingled pleasure and wonder, such as the impressible heart of a Jewish woman would utter. It would be too much to conclude that she was a disciple and a believer.

[*Of the company.*] This expression would be more literally rendered, 'out of the crowd or multitude.'

28.—[*Yea rather.*] The Greek word so translated is only found in three other places, and in each is variously rendered. 'Nay but' (*Rom.* 9:20). 'Yes, verily' (*Rom.* 10:18). 'Yea, doubtless' (*Phil.* 3:8).

We cannot doubt that the words of this verse were spoken with a prophetic foresight of that unscriptural worship of the Virgin Mary, which was one day to arise and prevail so extensively in the church of Christ. By no ingenuity, or torturing process, can the words be made to bear any but one plain meaning. They declare, that to hear the Word of God and keep it, is to be more blessed than to be connected with Christ by the ties of flesh, and that to be the mother of Christ according to the flesh does not confer on anyone greater honour and privileges than to believe and obey the gospel.

29.—[*Gathered thick together.*] The Greek word so rendered is only found here. Parkhurst says that it means 'crowding upon.'

[*They seek a sign.*] The extraordinary perverseness of the Jews in ever wanting some sign to produce in them faith, is noteworthy. Heart unbelief always professes to want evidence. It is not evidence, but a right will which is needful, if a man's soul is to be saved.

30.—[*Jonas was a sign.*] The likeness between Jonas and our Lord has been variously explained. The three days and nights during which Jonah was in the whale's belly, and his coming forth alive at the end of them, are undoubtedly the principal point. They were a type of our Lord being in the grave, and rising again the third day.—The forty days after which Nineveh was to be destroyed are probably another point. They were a type of the forty years which elapsed between our Lord's ministry and the destruction of Jerusalem.—The mighty fact of the resurrection is unquestionably the main point in the type. It was the hinge on which the whole gospel turned, and the truth which the apostles constantly pressed on the Jews.

31.—[*The queen of the south.*] It need hardly be remarked that the person so described is the Queen of Sheba of the Old Testament (*1 Kings* 10:1). Her name is not known at all. Her dominions are not known with certainty. Some think that they were in Arabia. Some think they were in Ethiopia. 'The utmost parts of the earth' must be interpreted with qualification, as a very distant land.

[*A greater than Solomon.*] Let it be noted, that both here and in the end of the following verses, the Greek word translated 'a greater,' is literally 'a greater thing.' It is not improbable that the 'thing' referred to is 'the sign.'—There is one here who is a sign of far greater moment than either Jonah or Solomon.

Let it be observed, that the point in which the queen of the south surpassed the Jews of our Lord's time and put them to shame, was 'faith.' She had faith enough to come a long journey to hear a wise man.

The Jews, on the other hand, had 'the wisdom of God' actually in the midst of them, preaching and teaching for three years, and yet they would not believe.

Let it be observed, that the point in which the Ninevites surpassed the Jews and put them to shame, was repentance. They had among them for a short time a prophet, and a very weak and erring prophet too. Yet they repented and turned to God. The Jews had among them the mightiest and most faithful preacher that ever warned a people, and yet they would not repent.

In this, as well as in other passages, we should not fail to remark that our Lord speaks of the story of Jonah as an undoubtedly true story, and of Jonah himself and the queen of Sheba as real persons. The modern theory which says that the histories of the Old Testament are nothing better than amusing fables, finds no countenance in the New Testament.

Here again, as well as elsewhere, we see the general judgment and the resurrection spoken of as events which will undoubtedly take place, and events in which the saints of the Old Testament are as much and really interested as those who lived after Christ's ministry began.

LUKE 11:33-36

33 No man, when he hath lighted a candle, putteth it in a secret place, neither under a bushel, but on a candlestick, that they which come in may see the light.

34 The light of the body is the eye: therefore when thine eye is single, thy whole body also is full of light; but when *thine eye* is evil, thy body also *is* full of darkness.

35 Take heed therefore that the light which is in thee be not darkness.

36 If thy whole body therefore *be* full of light, having no part dark, the whole shall be full of light, as when the bright shining of a candle doth give thee light.

WE learn from these words of the Lord Jesus, *the importance of making a good use of religious light and privileges.* We are reminded of what men do when they light a candle. They do not 'put it in a secret place,' under a bushel measure. They place it on a candlestick, that it may be serviceable and useful by giving light.

When the gospel of Christ is placed before a man's soul, it is as if God offered to him a lighted candle. It is not sufficient to hear it, and assent to it, and admire it, and acknowledge its truth. It must be received into the heart, and obeyed in the life. Until this takes place the gospel does him no more good than if he were an African heathen, who has never heard the gospel at all. A lighted candle is before him, but he is not turning it to account. The guilt of such conduct is very great. God's light neglected will be a heavy charge against many at the last day.

But even when a man professes to value the light of the gospel he must take care that he is not selfish in the use of it. He must endeavour to reflect the light on all around him. He must strive to make others acquainted with the truths which he finds good for himself. He must let his light so shine before men, that they may see whose he is and whom he serves, and may be induced to follow his example, and join the Lord's side. He must regard the light which he enjoys as a loan, for the use of which he is accountable. He must strive to hold his candle in such a way, that many may see it, and as they see it, admire and believe.

Let us take heed to ourselves that we do not neglect our light. The sin of many in this matter is far greater than they suppose. Thousands flatter themselves that their souls are not in a very bad state, because they abstain from gross and glaring acts of wickedness, and are decent and respectable in their outward lives. But are they neglecting the gospel when it is offered to them? Are they coolly sitting still year after year, and taking no decided steps in the service of Christ? If this be so, let them know that their guilt is very great in the sight of God. To have the light and yet not walk in the light, is of itself a great sin. It is to treat with contempt and indifference the King of kings.

Let us beware of selfishness in our religion, even after we have learned to value the light. We should labour to make all men see that we have found 'the pearl of great price,' and that we want them to find it as well as ourselves. A man's religion may well be suspected when he is content to go to heaven alone. The true Christian will have a large heart. If a parent, he will long for the salvation of his children. If a master, he will desire to see his servants converted. If a landlord, he will want his tenants to come with him into God's kingdom. This is healthy religion! The Christian who is satisfied to burn his candle alone, is in a very weak and sickly state of soul.

We learn, secondly, from these verses, *the value of a single and undivided heart in religion*. This is a lesson which our Lord illustrates from the office of the eye in the human body. He reminds us that when the eye is 'single,' or thoroughly healthy, the action of the whole body is influenced by it. But when, on the contrary, the eye is evil or diseased, it affects the physical comfort and activity of the whole man. In an Eastern country, where eye diseases are painfully common, the illustration is one which would be particularly striking.

But when can it be truly said that a man's heart is single in religion? What are the marks of a single heart? The question is one of deep importance. Well would it be for the church and the world if single hearts were more common!

The single heart is a heart which is not only changed, converted, and renewed; but thoroughly, powerfully, and habitually under the influence of the Holy Ghost. It is a heart which abhors all compromises, all lukewarmness, all halting between two opinions in religion. It sees one mighty object,—the love of Christ dying for sinners. It has one mighty aim,—to glorify God and do his will. It has one mighty desire,—to please God and be commended by him. Compared with such objects, aims, and desires, the single heart knows nothing worthy to be named. The praise and favour of man are nothing. The blame and disapprobation of man are trifles light as air. 'One thing I desire,—one thing I do,—one thing I live for:' this is the language of the single heart (*Psa.* 27:4; *Luke* 10:42; *Phil.* 3:13). Such were the hearts of Abraham, and Moses, and David, and Paul, and Luther, and Latimer. They all had their weaknesses and infirmities. They erred no doubt in some things. But they all had this grand peculiarity. They were men of one thing. They had single hearts. They were unmistakably 'men of God.'

The blessings of a single heart in religion are almost incalculable. He who has it, does good by wholesale. He is like a lighthouse in the midst of a dark world. He reflects light on hundreds whom he knows nothing of. 'His whole body is full of light.' His Master is seen through every window of his conversation and conduct. His grace shines forth in every department of his behaviour. His family, his servants, his relations, his neighbours, his friends, his enemies, all see the bias of his character, and all are obliged to confess, whether they like it or not, that his religion is a real and influential thing. And not least, the man of a single heart finds a rich reward in the inward experience of his own soul. He has meat to eat the world knows not of. He has a joy and peace in believing to which many indolent Christians never attain. His face is towards the sun, and so his heart is seldom cold.

Let us pray and labour that we may have a single eye and a whole heart in our Christianity. If we have a religion, let us have a thorough one. If we are Christians, let us be decided. Inward peace and outward usefulness are at stake in this matter. Our eye must be single, if our whole body is to be full of light.

Notes—Luke 11:33-36

33.—[*No man ... lighted a candle, etc.*] The saying of this verse is evidently intended to be a rebuke to the unbelieving Jews, who had the light, but would not use it,—and a warning to our Lord's disciples, who believed in the light, that they ought not to conceal the light, but display it to the world. A candle is intended to be placed on a candlestick and give light. So also God's truth is intended to be imparted to others, and exhibited to all around us.

It is hard to conceive a more striking example of putting the light 'under a bushel' than the treatment of the Bible by the Church of Rome. The Church of Rome possesses that Word which is given to be the light of man's soul, and yet discourages its reading and opposes its circulation.

34.—[*When thine eye is single, etc.*] The eye is to the body, what the heart is to the man. If the eye is dimmed—does not see objects clearly, the whole action of the body is more or less affected. If the heart is double-minded and compromising, the whole character of the man will be influenced by it. His course will be wavering and unstable. His life will be trimming and inconsistent.

Parkhurst says, that the Greek word rendered 'single,' when applied to the eye, means clear. Doddridge says, 'it is opposed to an eye overgrown with film, which would obstruct the sight.' Campbell says that it means 'sound and healthy' and that both Chrysostom and Theophylact interpret it in that sense.

35.—[*Take heed, therefore, etc.*] The meaning of this verse appears to be 'Take heed lest that faculty in thee, which ought to be the eye of the soul, become so dimmed and obscured by sin, sloth, or unbelief, that it be as useless as if it were in utter darkness. Take heed, lest by hardening thy heart against the light of my gospel, thou become utterly callous, and be given over to a reprobate mind.'

It must be remembered that the expression is parabolic and figurative. It must not be so strained and wrested as to convey the idea that man has naturally an 'inward light' which can save his soul. Such an interpretation would contradict other plain texts of Scripture, and tend to Pelagianism.

36.—[*If thy whole body, etc.*] The meaning of this verse is at first sight nothing more than the assertion of a simple truism. It seems nothing more than saying, 'If thy body shall be light, it shall be light.' This, however, is plainly not the full meaning of our Lord's words.

The meaning of the words appears to be as follows. 'If the eye of thy soul is thoroughly healthy, and thy heart thoroughly right in the sight of God, so that thy whole character is enlightened and influenced by it, then shall thy whole character shine after the manner of a candle which enlightens thee by its shining. Thou shalt not only have light for thyself, but reflect light on others.' The second expression, 'full of light,' should be read in close connection with the likeness of the candle which immediately follows.—If thou art really full of light, thou shalt be like a lighted candle on a candlestick. Thou shalt be a light to the world.

The marginal reading gives a more literal translation of the conclusion of the verse than the authorized version. The literal rendering of the Greek is, 'as when a candle, by its bright, flashing shining, enlightens thee.'

LUKE 11:37-44

37 And as he spake, a certain Pharisee besought him to dine with him: and he went in, and sat down to meat.

38 And when the Pharisee saw *it*, he marvelled that he had not first washed before dinner.

39 And the Lord said unto him, Now do ye Pharisees make clean the outside of the cup and platter; but your inward part is full of ravening and wickedness.

40 *Ye* fools, did not he that made that which is without make that which is within also?

41 But rather give alms of such things as ye have; and, behold, all things are clean unto you.

42 But woe unto you, Pharisees! for ye tithe mint and rue and all manner of herbs, and pass over judgment and the love of God: these ought ye to have done, and not to leave the other undone.

43 Woe unto you, Pharisees! for ye love the uppermost seats in the synagogues, and greetings in the markets.

44 Woe unto you, scribes and Pharisees, hypocrites! for ye are as graves which appear not, and the men that walk over *them* are not aware *of them.*

L ET us notice in this passage, *our Lord Jesus Christ's readiness, when needful, to go into the company of the unconverted.* We read that 'a certain Pharisee besought him to dine with him.' The man was evidently not one of our Lord's disciples. Yet we are told that 'Jesus went in and sat down to meat.'

The conduct of our Lord on this occasion, as on others, is meant to be an example to all Christians. Christ is our pattern as well as our propitiation. There are evidently times and occasions when the servant of Christ must mix with the ungodly and the children of this world. There may be seasons when it may be a duty to hold social intercourse with them, to accept their invitations, and sit down at their tables. Nothing of course, must induce the Christian to be a partaker in the sins or frivolous amusements of the world. But he must not be uncourteous. He must not entirely withdraw himself from the society of the unconverted, and become a hermit or an ascetic. He must remember, that good may be done in the private room as well as in the pulpit.

One qualification however should never be forgotten, when we act upon our Lord's example in this matter. Let us take heed that we go down into the company of the unconverted in the same spirit in which Christ went. Let us remember his boldness in speaking of the things of God. He was always 'about his Father's business.'—Let us remember his faithfulness in rebuking sin. He spared not even the sins of those that entertained him, when his attention was publicly called to them. Let us go into company in the same frame of mind, and our souls will take no harm. If we feel that we dare not imitate Christ in the company which we are invited to join, we may be sure that we had better stay at home.

Let us notice, secondly, in this passage, *the foolishness which accompanies hypocrisy in religion.* We are told that the Pharisee with whom our Lord dined marvelled that our Lord 'had not first washed before dinner.' He thought, like most of his order, that there was something unholy in not doing it, and that the neglect of it was a sign of moral impurity. Our Lord points out the absurdity of attaching such importance to the mere cleansing of the body, while the cleansing of the heart is overlooked. He reminds his host that God looks at the inward part of us, the hidden man of the heart, far more than at our skins. And he asks the searching question, 'Did not he that made that which is without, make that which is within also?' The same God who formed our poor dying bodies, is the God who gave us a heart and soul.

For ever let us bear in mind that the state of our hearts is the principal thing that demands our attention, if we would know what we are in religion. Bodily washings, and fastings, and gestures and postures, and self-imposed mortification of the flesh, are all utterly useless if the heart is wrong. External devoutness of conduct, a grave face, and a bowed head, and a solemn countenance, and a loud amen, are all abominable in God's sight, so long as our hearts are not washed from their wickedness, and renewed by the Holy Ghost. Let this caution never be forgotten. The idea that men can be devout before they are converted, is a grand delusion of the devil, and one against which we all need to be on our guard. There are two Scriptures which are very weighty on this subject. In one it is written, 'Out of the heart are the issues of life' (*Prov.* 4:23). In the other it is written, 'Man looketh on the outward appearance, but the Lord looketh on the heart' (*1 Sam.* 16:7). There is a question which we should always ask ourselves in drawing near to God, whether in public or private. We should say to ourselves, 'Where is my heart?'

Let us notice, thirdly, in this passage, *the gross inconsistency which is often exhibited by hypocrites in their religion.* We read that our Lord says to the Pharisees, 'Ye tithe mint and rue and all manner of herbs, and pass over judgment and the love of God.' They carried to an extreme their zeal to pay tithes for the service of the temple;—and yet they neglected the plainest duties towards God and their neighbours. They were scrupulous to an extreme about small matters in the ceremonial law;—and yet they were utterly regardless of the simplest first principles of justice to man and love toward God. In the one direction they were rigidly careful to do even more than was needful. In the other direction they would do nothing at all. In the secondary things of their religion they were downright zealots and enthusiasts. But in the great primary things they were no better than the heathen.

The conduct of the Pharisees in this matter, unhappily, does not stand alone. There have never been wanting religious professors who have exalted the second things of Christianity far above the first, and in their zeal for the second things have finally neglected the first things entirely. There are thousands at the present day who make a great ado about daily services, and keeping Lent, and frequent communion, and turning to the East in churches, and a gorgeous ceremonial, and intoning public prayers,—but never get any further. They know little or nothing of the great practical duties of humility, charity, meekness, spiritual-mindedness, Bible reading, private devotion, and separation from the world. The plunge into every gaiety with greediness. They are to be seen at every worldly assembly and revel, at the race, the opera, the theatre, and the ball. They exhibit nothing of the mind of Christ in their daily life. What is all this but walking in the steps of the Pharisees? Well says the wise man, 'There is no new thing under the sun' (*Eccles.* 1:9). The generation which tithed mint, but passed over 'judgment and the love of God,' is not yet extinct.

Let us watch and pray that we may observe a scriptural proportion in our religion. Let us beware of putting the second things out of their place, and so by degrees losing sight of the first entirely. Whatever importance we attach to the ceremonial part of Christianity, let us never forget its great practical duties. The religious teaching which inclines us to pass them over, has something about it which is radically defective.

Let us notice, lastly, *the falseness and hollowness which character-ize the hypocrite in religion.* We read that our Lord compared the Pharisees to 'graves which appear not, and the men that walk over them are not aware of them.' Even so these boasting teachers of the Jews were inwardly full of corruption and uncleanness, to an extent of which their deluded hearers had no conception.

The picture here drawn is painful and disgusting. Yet the accuracy and truthfulness of it have often been proved by the conduct of hypocrites in every age of the church. What shall we say of the lives of monks and nuns, which were exposed at the time of the Reformation? Thousands of so-called 'holy' men and women were found to be sunk in every kind of wickedness. What shall we say of the lives of some of the leaders of sects and heresies who have professed a peculiarly pure standard of doctrine? Not infrequently the very men who have promised to others liberty have turned out to be themselves 'servants of corruption.' The morbid anatomy of human nature is a loathsome study. Hypocrisy and unclean living have often been found side by side.

Let us leave the whole passage with a settled determination to watch and pray against hypocrisy in religion. Whatever we are as Christians, let us be real, thorough, genuine, and sincere. Let us abhor all canting, and affectation, and part-acting in the things of God, as that which is utterly loathsome in Christ's eyes. We may be weak, and erring, and frail, and come far short of our aims and desires. But at any rate, if we profess to believe in Christ, let us be true.

Notes—Luke 11:37-44

37.—[*A certain Pharisee.*] We do not know who this Pharisee was. It seems clear that he was not a disciple of Christ. Yet our Lord accepted his invitation, and dined with him. From this circumstance the conclusion is often drawn by weak believers that it is lawful and desirable to keep up social intercourse with unconverted people. As to the lawfulness there can be no doubt. As to the desirableness and expediency, everyone must judge for himself, and consider what he can do, and what he cannot. Those Christians who plead our Lord's example as an argument for dining with unconverted people, would do well to mark our Lord's conduct and conversation at the tables of those with whom he dined. Let them copy him in his conversation as well as in the acceptance of invitations. Unhappily, there are many who will accept the invitation as our Lord accepted, but will not talk at table as our Lord talked.

38.—[*That he had not first washed.*] Let this expression be carefully noted. The Greek word literally translated would be rendered, 'that he had not first been baptized' before dinner. It is clear that the washing spoken of cannot be a washing of the whole body, but a partial washing, as of the hands and feet, or a sprinkling of water on the hands, after the manner of Eastern nations (2 *Kings* 3:11). The opinion held by some Baptists that the Greek word to 'baptize' is never used except in the sense of a total immersion of the body, is one that cannot be reconciled with the expression used in this text.

39.—[*Your inward part.*] This of course means your inward man—your heart. It is what St Peter calls 'the hidden man of the heart' (*1 Pet.* 3:4).

40.—[*Ye fools.*] The literal meaning of the Greek word so translated is, 'persons without mind or understanding.' It is the same word that St Paul uses (*1 Cor.* 15:36). It is not the word that our Lord forbids to be used in the Sermon on the Mount (*Matt.* 5:22).

[*Did not he that made that which is without, etc.*] Our Lord's meaning in this verse appears to be that it is absurd and unreasonable to suppose that God can be pleased with mere external and ceremonial purity, while inward purity and the cleansing of the heart are neglected. He who made all things, made the inner man as well as the outward, and requires the heart to be washed from its wickedness, as well as the hands from uncleanness.

41.—[*But rather give alms, etc.*] This is a very difficult verse. The variety of interpretations of it shows plainly that it has perplexed the commentators.

Some think that the whole verse is ironical, and that our Lord means, 'Go on in your practice of giving alms of such things as ye have, and then indeed ye are very holy people! All things are clean unto you!—Give alms and keep up the ceremonial law, and then no doubt, ye are the people! None so holy as ye!' This is the opinion of Lightfoot, who thinks that our Lord is quoting the tenets of the Pharisees 'in mere scoff and displeasure.' However it does not seem a satisfactory mode of explaining the verse, and is unlike our Lord's usual mode of speaking. This interpretation may therefore be dismissed at once.

The real difficulty of the verse no doubt lies in the words which we translate 'such things as ye have.' Some think that this expression is elliptical, and that it means, 'Give alms everyone according to his ability.' This is the view of Euthymius, Maldonatus, Cocceius, Hammond, Whitby, Schoettgen, and Doddridge.—Others think that the expression means, 'Give as alms to the poor those things that ye have,' that is, the things that ye have obtained by avarice and plunder, as Zacchæus did.—Others think that the expression means, 'All that ye have—all your property.'—Others think that it means, 'That which is over and above,—your superfluities,—give them as alms.'—Others think that it means, 'Give alms with all your might.'—Others think that it means, 'Give alms, which is the only remedy left to you.'

All these interpretations appear very unsatisfactory. None of them meets the grave objection, that, taken in connection with the concluding sentence of the verse, they teach false doctrine. Alms do not make our souls clean, and all our actions pure, no matter how, or in what way, or to what extent we give them.

I take leave to suggest another explanation, which seems to me to deserve consideration. The literal meaning of the Greek words is as follows,—'But rather give *the things that are in*, as alms.'—The simplest sense of this sentence appears to be, 'Give first the offering of the inward man. Give your heart, your affections, and your will to God, as the first great alms which you bestow, and then all your other actions, proceeding from a right heart, are an acceptable sacrifice, and a clean offering in the sight of God.—Give the inner man first, and then the gifts and service of the external man will be acceptable.—Give yourselves first to the Lord, and then he will be pleased with your gifts. See that your persons are first accepted, and then your works will be acceptable. To the pure all things are pure.' Let the expression in this sense be compared with Romans 12:1; Psalm 51:17; 2 Corinthians 8:5.

42.—[*Woe unto you.*] Here, as in other places, the stern and severe language of our Lord deserves notice. Gracious and loving as he was, he could rebuke when there was need. Nothing seems so odious in his eyes as hypocrisy.

[*Ye tithe mint, etc.*] This expression means that the Pharisees pretended to such excessive scrupulosity about giving a tenth of all their possessions to the service of the temple and to the maintenance of the ceremonial law, that they were not content with tithing their corn. They even tithed their garden herbs. Yet all this time they entirely neglected the plain duties of justice to man, and real love to God.

The neglect of distinction between that which is great and that which is small, that which is first and that which is second, that which is essential and that which is non-essential, has been the source of enormous evil in every age of the church. It is a distinction which the never-dying school of the Pharisees is unable to draw.

43.—[*Ye love the uppermost seats, etc.*] Let it be noted, that ambition and the love of precedence are common marks of the formalist and the self-righteous. To exalt themselves under pretence of honouring the *church*, and to obtain power under cover of obtaining respect for their own *order*, has been the practice of Pharisees all over the world and in every age of the church of Christ.

Our Lord, in this verse, exposes the hollowness of the motives by which his enemies were actuated. Self, and self-aggrandizement, were the true spring of all their conduct.

44.—[*Ye are as graves which appear not.*] There is a remarkable difference between the comparison which our Lord draws here and that which he draws in St Matthew 23:27, where he likens the Pharisees to whitened sepulchres.

In the comparison before us he rebukes the cunning with which they concealed their own inward corruption, so that men were not aware of it.—In the one in St Matthew he exposes the false profession which they made outwardly to the eye, in having a beautiful semblance of religion, while there was nothing corresponding in the state of their hearts.—In the case before us he exposes what men did not see in the Pharisees. In the case in St Matthew he rather exposes what men did see.—In the one case it was a grave full of corruption, but a grave concealed from the eye. In the other it was a grave equally full of corruption, but outwardly beautiful and white, so as to deceive a beholder as to the nature of its contents.—In the one case there was corruption, but made outwardly beautiful and harmless. In the other there was corruption hidden, concealed, and entirely kept back from the eye.—In both cases the heart was the same. The whitened sepulchre and the sepulchre concealed were both sepulchres full of corruption.

LUKE 11:45-54

45 Then answered one of the lawyers, and said unto him, Master, thus saying thou reproachest us also.

46 And he said, Woe unto you also, ye lawyers! for ye lade men with burdens grievous to be borne, and ye yourselves touch not the burdens with one of your fingers.

47 Woe unto you! for ye build the sepulchres of the prophets, and your fathers killed them.

48 Truly ye bear witness that ye allow the deeds of your fathers: for they indeed killed them, and ye build their sepulchres.

49 Therefore also said the wisdom of God, I will send them prophets and apostles, and *some* of them they shall slay and persecute:

50 That the blood of all the prophets, which was shed from the foundation of the world, may be required of this generation;

51 From the blood of Abel unto the blood of Zacharias, which perished between the altar and the temple: verily I say unto you, It shall be required of this generation.

52 Woe unto you, lawyers! for ye have taken away the key of knowledge: ye entered not in yourselves, and them that were entering in ye hindered.

53 And as he said these things unto them, the scribes and the Pharisees began to urge *him* vehemently, and to provoke him to speak of many things:

54 Laying wait for him, and seeking to catch something out of his mouth, that they might accuse him.

T HE passage before us is an example of our Lord Jesus Christ's faithful dealing with the souls of men. We see him without fear or favour rebuking the sins of the Jewish expounders of God's law. That false charity which calls it 'unkind' to say that anyone is in error, finds no encouragement in the language used by our Lord. He called things by their right names. He knew that acute diseases need severe remedies. He would have us know that the truest friend to our souls, is not the man who is always 'speaking smooth things,' and agreeing with everything we say, but the man who tells us the most truth.

We learn, firstly, from our Lord's words, *how great is the sin of professing to teach others what we do not practise ourselves.* He says to the lawyers, 'Ye lade men with burdens grievous to be borne, and ye yourselves touch not the burdens with one of your fingers.' They required others to observe wearisome ceremonies in religion which they themselves neglected. They had the impudence to lay yokes upon the consciences of other men, and yet to grant exemptions from these yokes for themselves. In a word, they had one set of measures and weights for their hearers, and another set for their own souls.

The stern reproof which our Lord here administers, should come home with special power to certain classes in the church. It is a word in season to all teachers of young people. It is a word to all masters of families and heads of households. It is a word to all fathers and mothers. Above all, it is a word to all clergymen and ministers of religion. Let all such mark well our Lord's language in this passage. Let them beware of telling others to aim at a standard which they do not aim at themselves. Such conduct, to say the least, is gross inconsistency.

Perfection, no doubt, is unattainable in this world. If nobody is to lay down rules, or teach, or preach, until he is faultless himself, the whole fabric of society would be thrown into confusion. But we have a right to expect some agreement between a man's words and a man's works,—between his teaching and his doing,—between his preaching and his practice. One thing at all events is very certain. No lessons produce such effects on men as those which the teacher illustrates by his own daily life. Happy is he who can say with Paul, 'Those things which ye have heard and seen in me, do' (*Phil.* 4:9).

We learn, secondly, from our Lord's words, *how much more easy it is to admire dead saints than living ones.* He says to the lawyers, 'Ye build the sepulchres of the prophets, and your fathers killed them.' They professed to honour the memory of the prophets, while they lived in the very same ways which the prophets had condemned! They openly neglected their advice and teaching, and yet they pretended to respect their graves!

The practice which is here exposed has never been without followers in spirit, if not in the letter. Thousands of wicked men in every age of the church have tried to deceive themselves and others by loud professions of admiration for the saints of God after their decease. By so doing they have endeavoured to ease their own consciences, and blind the eyes of the world. They have sought to raise in the minds of others the thought, 'If these men love the memories of the good so dearly, they must surely be of one heart with them.' They have forgotten that even a child can see that 'dead men tell no tales,' and that to admire men when they can neither reprove us by their lips, nor put us to shame by their lives, is a very cheap admiration indeed.

Would we know what a man's religious character really is? Let us inquire what he thinks of true Christians while they are yet alive.—Does he love them, and cleave to them, and delight in them, as the excellent of the earth?—Or does he avoid them, and dislike them, and regard them as fanatics, and enthusiasts, and extreme, and righteous over-much?—The answers to these questions are a pretty safe test of a man's true character. When a man can see no beauty in living saints, but much in dead ones, his soul is in a very rotten state. The Lord Jesus has pronounced his condemnation. He is a hypocrite in the sight of God.

We learn, thirdly, from our Lord's words, *how surely a reckoning day for persecution will come upon the persecutors.* He says that the 'blood of all the prophets shall be required.'

There is something peculiarly solemn in this statement. The number of those who have been put to death for the faith of Christ in every age of the world, is exceedingly great. Thousands of men and women have laid down their lives rather than deny their Saviour, and have shed their blood for the truth. At the time they died they seemed to have no helper. Like Zacharias, and James, and Stephen, and John the Baptist, and Ignatius, and Huss, and Hooper, and Latimer, they died without resistance. They were soon buried and forgotten on earth, and their enemies seemed to triumph utterly. But their deaths were not forgotten in heaven. Their blood was had in remembrance before God. The persecutions of Herod, and Nero, and Diocletian, and bloody Mary, and Charles IX, are not forgotten. There shall be a great assize one day, and then all the world shall see that 'precious in the sight of the Lord is the death of his saints' (*Psa.* 116:15).

Let us often look forward to the judgment day. There are many things going on in the world which are trying to our faith. The frequent triumphing of the wicked is perplexing. The frequent depression of the godly is a problem that appears hard to solve. But it shall all be made clear one day. The great white throne and the books of God shall put all things in their right places. The tangled maze of God's providences shall be unravelled. All shall be proved to a wondering world to have been 'well done.' Every tear that the wicked have caused the godly to shed shall be reckoned for. Every drop of righteous blood that has been spilled shall at length be required.

We learn, lastly, from our Lord's words, *how great is the wickedness of keeping back others from religious knowledge.* He says to the lawyers, 'Ye have taken away the key of knowledge: ye entered not in yourselves, and them that were entering in ye hindered.'

The sin here denounced is awfully common. The guilt of it lies at far more doors than at first sight many are aware. It is the sin of the Romish priest who forbids the poor man to read his Bible.—It is the sin of the unconverted Protestant minister who warns his people against 'extreme views,' and sneers at the idea of conversion.—It is the sin of the ungodly, thoughtless husband who dislikes his wife becoming 'serious.'—It is the sin of the worldly-minded mother who cannot bear the idea of her daughter thinking of spiritual things, and giving up theatres and balls. All these, wittingly or unwittingly, are bringing down on themselves our Lord's emphatic 'woe.' They are hindering others from entering heaven!

Let us pray that this awful sin may never be ours. Whatever we are ourselves in religion, let us dread discouraging others, if they have the least serious concern about their souls. Let us never check any of those around us in their religion, and specially in the matter of reading the Bible, hearing the gospel, and private prayer. Let us rather cheer them, encourage them, help them, and thank God if they are better than ourselves. 'Deliver me from blood-guiltiness,' was a prayer of David's (*Psa.* 51:14). It may be feared that the blood of relatives will be heavy on the heads of some at the last day. They saw them about to 'enter' the kingdom of God, and they 'hindered' them.

Notes—Luke 11:45-54

45.—[*One of the lawyers.*] The lawyers, be it remembered, were a class of men among the Jews who devoted themselves to the study of the law of God. We generally find them in league with the scribes and Pharisees in the gospel history.

46.—[*Woe unto you also, ye lawyers.*] These words are a striking instance of our Lord's boldness in rebuking sinners. He is appealed to in an angry tone, and he tells those who appeal to him their sins and wickedness to their face.

[*Ye lade men with burdens.*] These burdens mean the many vexatious and trifling rules laid down by the Jewish expounders of the law, as requiring men's attention, if they would be saved. Chemnitius remarks the close resemblance between these Jewish teachers and the Roman Catholic priests, who hedged up the way to heaven with a long list of things to be observed,—penances, pilgrimages, fastings, flagellations, contritions, attritions, confessions, and the like.

47.—[*Ye build the sepulchres of the prophets.*] Let it be remembered that in every age of the church, true Christians have been more admired and praised when they were dead than when they were alive. Chemnitius observes that the conduct of these lawyers related in this verse is that of the Roman Catholic Church. No people can be more zealous than the Romish priests in honouring the tombs and relics of saints and martyrs, and building costly churches in honour of them. And yet the doctrines of these saints are not believed, and their lives are not imitated!

48.—[*Ye bear witness that ye allow the deeds of your fathers.*] The meaning of these words can only be that the lives of the Jewish teachers were clear evidence that they agreed with those who murdered the prophets more than with the prophets. A man's life is the best proof of a man's opinions. It is absurd and hypocritical to pretend admiration of dead saints, if we do not at the same time endeavour to walk

41

in their steps. Poole remarks, 'It is gross hypocrisy for men to magnify the servants of God in former ages, and in the meantime to malign and persecute the servants of the same God in a present age, owning the same truth, and living by the same rule.'

49.—[*Said the wisdom of God.*] It is a disputed question what these words mean. Alford thinks that they simply refer to the description of the death of Zechariah, in the book of Chronicles (2 *Chron.* 24:18-22) and that our Lord gives a paraphrase and summary of the lessons contained in that passage. The more common opinion is that our Lord speaks of himself under the name of 'Wisdom,' and that comparing the passage with Matthew 23:34, it means, 'I, the eternal wisdom of God, have said.'

50.—[*Of this generation.*] Both here and in the following verse, it seems probable that the word generation means nation or people, as in Matthew 24:34. It is a certain fact that the greater part of the men who were alive when our Lord said these things, must have been dead forty years after, when the great inquisition for blood took place, at the destruction of Jerusalem.

51.—[*Zacharias.*] There can be little doubt that this Zacharias was the son of Jehoiada, who was murdered in the days of Joash (2 *Chron.* 24:20). Lightfoot gives some remarkable quotations from rabbinical writers, proving how very great a crime this murder was regarded by the Jews themselves.

[*The temple.*] Let it be noted, that the Greek word so translated, is commonly rendered, 'The house.'

[*It shall be required.*] This is one of those fearful passages of Scripture which teach us that sins are not forgotten by God because not punished at the time of commission. There are evidently many sins recorded in the book of God's remembrance which will all be brought to light and reckoned for one day.

52.—[*Ye have taken away the key of knowledge.*] It is a doubtful question whether these words should not have been rendered 'Ye have borne, or taken up, and carried the key of knowledge.' Let the expression be compared with John 1:29, and the marginal reading in that place; and with such phrases as that translated, 'Take up his cross,' in Luke 9:23. The meaning would then be, 'Ye have been by profession the instructors of the Jews in spiritual knowledge. Ye have, so to speak, carried the keys. Yet ye made no use of them yourselves, and allowed nobody else to use them.' According to Watson, the Jewish teachers of the law had a key formally given to them, when they were ordained or set apart for the office of teaching.

Baxter remarks on this verse, 'This is just the description of a wicked clergy.'—It certainly describes the Church of Rome.

53.—[*To provoke him to speak of many things.*] The Greek verb in this expression is remarkable, and is only found here in the New Testament. Parkhurst says that it means 'To draw or force words from the mouth of another, to question magisterially, as a master does his scholars.' Hammond says on this text, 'They did ask questions to hear what Christ would say, as an angry schoolmaster that seeks occasion against a scholar.' Hesychius says it is 'to require another to recite from memory.' The meaning is obvious. Our Lord's enemies knew that 'In the multitude of words there wanteth not sin,' and they hoped to find occasion against him.

54.—[*To catch.*] The original idea of the Greek word so translated is 'to hunt,' or to lay hold of and catch in hunting.

We should remember the words of St James. 'If any man offend not in word, the same is a perfect man.' The perfect meekness of our Lord is strikingly shown in his never losing his temper under abounding provocations, and his perfect wisdom in never saying a word on which his deadliest enemies could justly lay hold.

LUKE 12:1-7

1 In the mean time, when there were gathered together an innumerable multitude of people, insomuch that they trode one upon another, he began to say unto his disciples first of all, Beware ye of the leaven of the Pharisees, which is hypocrisy.

2 For there is nothing covered, that shall not be revealed; neither hid, that shall not be known.

3 Therefore whatsoever ye have spoken in darkness shall be heard in the light; and that which ye have spoken in the ear in closets shall be proclaimed upon the housetops.

4 And I say unto you my friends, Be not afraid of them that kill the body, and after that have no more that they can do.

5 But I will forewarn you whom ye shall fear: Fear him, which after he hath killed hath power to cast into hell; yea, I say unto you, Fear him.

6 Are not five sparrows sold for two farthings, and not one of them is forgotten before God?

7 But even the very hairs of your head are all numbered. Fear not therefore: ye are of more value than many sparrows.

THE words which begin this chapter are very striking when we consider its contents. We are told that 'an innumerable multitude of people were gathered together, insomuch that they trode one upon another.' And what does our Lord do? In the hearing of this multitude he delivers warnings against false teachers, and denounces the sins of the times in which he lived unsparingly, unflinchingly, and without partiality. This was true charity. This was doing the work of a physician. This was the pattern which all his ministers were intended to follow. Well would it have been for the church and the world if the ministers of Christ had always spoken out as plainly and faithfully as their Master used to do! Their own lives might have been made more uncomfortable by such a course of action. But they would have saved far more souls.

The first thing that demands our attention in these verses is *Christ's warning against hypocrisy*. He says to his disciples, 'Beware ye of the leaven of the Pharisees, which is hypocrisy.'

This is a warning of which the importance can never be overrated. It was delivered by our Lord more than once, during his earthly ministry. It was intended to be a standing caution to his whole church in every age, and in every part of the world. It was meant to remind us that the principles of the Pharisees are deeply engrained in human nature, and that Christians should be always on their guard against them. Pharisaism is a subtle leaven which the natural heart is always ready to receive. It is a leaven which once received into the heart infects the whole character of a man's Christianity. Of this leaven says our Lord, in words that should often ring in our ears,—of this leaven, beware!

Let us ever nail this caution in our memories, and bind it on our hearts. The plague is about us on every side. The danger is at all times. What is the essence of Romanism, and semi-Romanism, and formalism, and sacrament-worship and church-adorning, and ceremonialism? What is it all but the leaven of the Pharisees under one shape or another? The Pharisees are not extinct. Pharisaism lives still.

If we would not become Pharisees, let us cultivate a heart religion. Let us realize daily that the God with whom we have to do, looks far below the outward surface of our profession, and that he measures us by the state of our hearts. Let us be real and true in our Christianity. Let us abhor all part-acting, and affectation, and semblance of devotion, put on for public occasions, but not really felt within. It may deceive man, and get us the reputation of being very religious, but it cannot deceive God. 'There is nothing covered that shall not be revealed.' Whatever we are in religion, let us never wear a cloak or a mask.

The second thing that demands our attention in these verses is *Christ's warning against the fear of man.* 'Be not afraid,' he says, 'of them which kill the body, and after that have no more that they can do.' But this is not all. He not only tells us whom we ought not to fear, but of whom we ought to be afraid. 'Fear him,' he says, 'which after he hath killed, hath power to cast into hell; yea, I say unto you, Fear him.' The manner in which the lesson is conveyed is very striking and impressive. Twice over the exhortation is enforced. 'Fear him,' says our Lord,—'yea, I say unto you, Fear him.'

The fear of man is one of the greatest obstacles which stand between the soul and heaven.—'What will men say of me? What will they think of me? What will they do to me?'—How often these little questions have turned the balance against the soul, and kept men bound, hand and foot by sin and the devil! Thousands would never hesitate a moment to storm a breach or face a lion, who dare not face the laughter of relatives, neighbours, and friends. Now if the fear of man has such influence in these times, how much greater must its influence have been in the days when our Lord was upon earth! If it be hard to follow Christ through ridicule and ill-natured words, how much harder must it have been to follow him through prisons, beatings, scourgings, and violent deaths! All these things our Lord Jesus knew well. No wonder that he cries, 'Be not afraid.'

But what is the best remedy against the fear of man? How are we to overcome this powerful feeling, and break the chains which it throws around us? There is no remedy like that which our Lord recommends. We must supplant the fear of man by a higher and more powerful principle,—the fear of God. We must look away from those who can only hurt the body to him who has all dominion over the soul. We must turn our eyes from those who can only injure us in the life that now is, to him who can condemn us to eternal misery in the life to come. Armed with this mighty principle, we shall not play the coward. Seeing him that is invisible, we shall find the lesser fear melting away before the greater, and the weaker before the stronger. 'I fear God,' said Colonel Gardiner, 'and therefore there is no one else that I need fear.'—It was a noble saying of martyred Bishop Hooper, when a Roman Catholic urged him to save his life by recanting at the stake,—'Life is sweet and death is bitter. But eternal life is more sweet, and eternal death is more bitter.'

The last thing that demands our attention in these verses, is *Christ's encouragement to persecuted believers.* He reminds them of God's providential care over the least of his creatures:—'Not one sparrow is forgotten before God.' He goes on to assure them that the same Fatherly care is engaged on behalf of each one of themselves:—'The very hairs of your head are all numbered.' Nothing whatever, whether great or small, can happen to a believer, without God's ordering and permission.

The providential government of God over everything in this world is a truth of which the Greek and Roman philosophers had no conception. It is a truth which is specially revealed to us in the Word of God. Just as the telescope and microscope show us that there is order and design in all the works of God's hand, from the greatest planet down to the least insect, so does the Bible teach us that there is wisdom, order, and design in all the events of our daily life. There is no such thing as 'chance,' 'luck,' or 'accident' in the Christian's journey through this world. All is arranged and appointed by God. And all things are 'working together' for the believer's good (*Rom.* 8:28).

Let us seek to have an abiding sense of God's hand in all that befalls us, if we profess to be believers in Jesus Christ. Let us strive to realize that a Father's hand is measuring out our daily portion, and that our steps are ordered by him. A daily practical faith of this kind, is one grand secret of happiness, and a mighty antidote against murmuring and discontent. We should try to feel in the day of trial and disappointment, that all is right and all is well done. We should try to feel on the bed of sickness, that there must be a 'needs be.' We should say to ourselves, 'God could keep away from me these things if he thought fit. But he does not do so, and therefore they must be for my advantage. I will lie still, and bear them patiently. I have "an everlasting covenant, ordered in all things, and sure" (*2 Sam.* 23:5). What pleases God shall please me.'

Notes—Luke 12:1-7

1.—[*An innumerable multitude.*] The Greek word so translated means literally, 'The myriads,' or tens of thousands of the people. Lightfoot thinks that these words are an evidence of the success of the seventy disciples.

[*He began to say.*] Let it be observed, that the discourse which follows these words is remarkable for the great number of sayings which it contains which were also said by our Lord upon other occasions. It is clear that our Lord repeated the same words in different places, and taught the same lessons on different occasions. All teachers and instructors repeat their lessons over and over again, in order to impress them on the minds of those they teach. It is absurd and unreasonable to suppose that our Lord Jesus Christ did not do so. To maintain, as some do, that St Luke, in this chapter, is only stringing together for convenience' sake, sayings which our Lord used on many different occasions, appears to me a very irreverent mode of dealing with an inspired writing, and a very needless explanation of the repetitions which the chapter contains. The things repeated are things which it is especially important for Christians to know, and therefore our Lord repeats them, and Luke was inspired to write them.

46

Burgon remarks, 'Of the fifty-nine verses which compose the present chapter, no less than thirty-five prove to have been delivered on quite distinct occasions; not in single verses only, but by seven, eight, and even ten verses at a time.'

An excessive desire to harmonize the various Gospel histories has led to many strange dealings with Scripture. 'Harmonies,' however well meant, have done little good to the church of Christ.

[*Beware ye of the leaven of the Pharisees.*] This is a warning which is given in another place, on a totally distinct occasion. It is a great standing caution to the church against formality and hypocrisy. Few warnings have been so much needed and so much overlooked. 'Leaven' is the word used to express false doctrine, because it works secretly and silently,—because its quantity is small compared to the whole mass of dough,—and because, once mingled, it alters the whole character of the bread. This is precisely the case with false doctrine. It seems 'a little one.' It works stealthily and noiselessly. Insensibly it poisons the whole gospel. If men will add to or take away from the great prescription for the cure of souls, the divine medicine is spoiled.

2.—[*Nothing covered ... revealed.*] This verse seems to admit of two interpretations. It is a general statement of the uselessness of hypocrisy. Everything shall appear in its true colours at last. It is an injunction to the disciples to reserve and keep back nothing in their teaching. They are to 'declare all the counsel of God.' The distinction between interior and exterior doctrines, inward truths for the learned and outward truths for the unlearned, however approved by some philosophers, finds no countenance in the gospel.

3.—[*Darkness ... light ... closets ... housetops.*] These expressions all seem to be proverbial. They all teach the duty of keeping nothing back in teaching the gospel. To understand the 'housetops,' we should remember that Eastern houses generally had flat roofs, which were much used by the inhabitants.

4.—[*Them that kill the body, etc.*] The distinction between body and soul, and the separate existence of the soul after the body is dead, are clearly brought out in this passage. The use which martyrs have often made of this verse at the moment of death, is a striking and remarkable fact in church history.

5.—[*Fear him ... hath power ... hell.*] Some commentators think with Stier, that this means the devil. This however seems very unlikely. The power of life and death is not in the hands of the devil. Most think that it means God, who alone kills and makes alive, casts down and raises up. This view is fully and clearly set forth by Chemnitius.

The reality and fearfulness of hell stand out awfully on the face of this verse. There is a hell after death. The state of the wicked man after this life is not annihilation. There is a hell which ought to be feared. There is a just God who will finally cast into hell the obstinately impenitent and unbelieving.

Let us not fail to notice that 'fear' is an argument that ought sometimes to be pressed on professing Christians. Christ himself used it. Burkitt says, 'It is good to raise a friend's fear, when that fear is for his good.' To say, as some ignorantly do, that love, and not fear, is the only argument which should be addressed to believers, is a modern and unscriptural notion.

6.—[*Not one of them is forgotten.*] The providential care of God over all his creatures is strikingly taught in this and the following verse. Nothing was too little for God to create. Nothing is too little for God to preserve. Nothing that concerns God's people is too little for him to manage, or for them to bring before him in prayer. Our least matters are in God's hands. Major remarks, that this providence of God over the least things was a truth of which the heathen philosophers had no conception. The Epicureans, the Academics, the followers of Aristotle and others, maintained that the gods regarded the universe in general, but not particular persons and things.

LUKE 12:8-12

8 Also I say unto you, Whosoever shall confess me before men, him shall the Son of man also confess before the angels of God:

9 But he that denieth me before men shall be denied before the angels of God.

10 And whosoever shall speak a word against the Son of man, it shall be forgiven him: but unto him that blasphemeth against the Holy Ghost it shall not be forgiven.

11 And when they bring you unto the synagogues, and *unto* magistrates, and powers, take ye no thought how or what thing ye shall answer, or what ye shall say:

12 For the Holy Ghost shall teach you in the same hour what ye ought to say.

WE are taught, firstly, in these verses, that *we must confess Christ upon earth, if we expect him to own us as his saved people at the last day.* We must not be ashamed to let all men see that we believe in Christ, and serve Christ, and love Christ, and care more for the praise of Christ than for the praise of man.

The duty of confessing Christ is incumbent on all Christians in every age of the church. Let us never forget that. It is not for martyrs only, but for all believers, in every rank of life. It is not for great occasions only, but for our daily walk through an evil world. The rich man among the rich, the labourer among labourers, the young among the young, the servant among servants,—each and all must be prepared, if they are true Christians, to confess their Master. It needs no blowing a trumpet. It requires no noisy boasting. It needs nothing more than using the daily opportunity. But one thing is certain;—if a man loves Jesus, he ought not to be ashamed to let people know it.

The difficulty of confessing Christ is undoubtedly very great. It never was easy at any period. It never will be easy as long as the world stands. It is sure to entail on us laughter, ridicule, contempt, mockery, enmity, and persecution. The wicked dislike to see anyone better than themselves. The world which hated Christ will always hate true Christians. But whether we like it or not, whether it be hard or easy, our course is perfectly clear. In one way or another Christ must be confessed.

The grand motive to stir us up to bold confession is forcibly brought before us in the words which we are now considering. Our

Lord declares, that if we do not confess him before men, he will 'not confess us before the angels of God' at the last day. He will refuse to acknowledge us as his people. He will disown us as cowards, faithless, and deserters. He will not plead for us. He will not be our Advocate. He will not deliver us from the wrath to come. He will leave us to reap the consequences of our cowardice, and to stand before the bar of God helpless, defenceless, and unforgiven. What an awful prospect is this! How much turns on this one hinge of 'confessing Christ before men!' Surely we ought not to hesitate for a moment. To doubt between two such alternatives is the height of folly. For us to deny Christ or be ashamed of his gospel, may get us a little of man's good opinion for a few years, though it will bring us no real peace. But for Christ to deny us at the last day will be ruin in hell to all eternity! Let us cast away our cowardly fears. Come what will, let us confess Christ.

We are taught, secondly, in these verses, that *there is such a thing as an unpardonable sin.* Our Lord Jesus Christ declares, that 'unto him that blasphemeth against the Holy Ghost, it shall not be forgiven.'

These awful words must doubtless be interpreted with scriptural qualification. We must never so expound one part of Scripture as to make it contradict another. Nothing is impossible with God. The blood of Christ can cleanse away all sin. The very chief of sinners have been pardoned in many instances. These things must never be forgotten. Yet notwithstanding all this, there remains behind a great truth which must not be evaded. There is such a thing as a sin 'which shall not be forgiven.'

The sin to which our Lord refers in this passage, appears to be the sin of deliberately rejecting God's truth with the heart, while the truth is clearly known with the head. It is a combination of light in the understanding and determined wickedness in the will. It is the very sin into which many of the scribes and Pharisees appear to have fallen, when they rejected the ministration of the Spirit after the day of Pentecost, and refused to believe the preaching of the apostles. It is a sin into which, it may be feared, many constant hearers of the gospel nowadays fall, by determined clinging to the world. And worst of all, it is a sin which is commonly accompanied by utter deadness, hardness, and insensibility of heart. The man whose sins will not be forgiven, is precisely the man who will never seek to have them forgiven. This is exactly the root of his awful disease. He might be pardoned, but he will not seek to be pardoned. He is gospel-hardened and 'twice dead.' His conscience is 'seared with a hot iron' (*1 Tim.* 4:2).

Let us pray that we may be delivered from a cold, speculative, unsanctified head-knowledge of Christianity. It is a rock on which thousands make shipwreck to all eternity. No heart becomes so hard as that on which the light shines, but finds no admission. The same fire which melts the wax hardens the clay. Whatever light we have, let us use it. Whatever knowledge we possess, let us live fully up to it. To be an ignorant heathen, and bow down to idols and stones, is bad enough. But to be called a Christian, and know the theory of the gospel and yet cleave to sin and the world with the heart, is to be a candidate for the worst and lowest place in hell.—It is to be as like as possible to the devil.

We are taught, lastly, in this passage, that *Christians need not be over-anxious as to what they shall say, when suddenly required to speak for Christ's cause.*

The promise which our Lord gives on this subject, has a primary reference no doubt, to public trials like those of Paul before Felix and Festus. It is a promise which hundreds in similar circumstances have found fulfilled to their singular comfort. The lives of many of the Reformers, and others of God's witnesses, are full of striking proofs, that the Holy Ghost can teach Christians what to say in time of need.

But there is a secondary sense, in which the promise belongs to all believers, which ought not be overlooked. Occasions are constantly arising in the lives of Christians, when they are suddenly and unexpectedly called upon to speak on behalf of their Master, and to render a reason of their hope. The home circle, the family fireside, the society of friends, the intercourse with relatives, the very business of the world, will often furnish such sudden occasions. On such occasions the believer should fall back on the promise now before us. It may be disagreeable, and especially to a young Christian, to be suddenly required to speak before others of religion, and above all if religion is attacked. But let us not be alarmed, and flurried, or cast down, or excited. If we remember the promise of Christ, we have no cause to be afraid.

Let us pray for a good memory about Bible promises. We shall find it an inestimable comfort. There are far more, and far wider promises laid down in Scripture for the comfort of Christ's people, than most of Christ's people are aware of. There are promises for almost every position in which we can be placed, and every event that can befall us. Among other promises, let us not forget the one which is now before us. We are sometimes called upon to go into company which is not congenial to us, and we go with a troubled and anxious heart. We fear saying what we ought not to say, and not saying what we ought. At such seasons, let us remember this blessed promise, and put our Master in remembrance of it also. So doing he will not fail us or forsake us. A mouth shall be given to us and wisdom to speak rightly. 'The Holy Ghost shall teach us' what to say.

Notes—Luke 12:8-12

8.—[*Before the angels of God.*] The time referred to in these words as well as in those in the next verse, must doubtless be the day of judgment. The angels shall be specially employed in that day in gathering together God's elect, and separating the wicked from among them.

The time referred to in the expression, 'before men,' must necessarily be, this present life, while we are among men.

The 'confessing Christ' in this verse must not be confined merely to confessing him when placed on our trial, or at the stake. We confess him whenever we boldly avow ourselves to be his servants and disciples in the midst of an evil world.

9.—[*He that denieth.*] Let it be noted, that the Greek words translated 'he that denieth,' would be rendered more literally, 'he that has denied.'

We must be careful not to confine 'denying Christ' to such open acts as Peter's denial of him. We deny Christ when from unbelief, or indolence, or love of the world, or fear of man, we shrink from confessing him as our Saviour and our King.

10.—[*Whosoever shall speak a word, etc.*] The language of this verse is deep and mysterious. There are sins which are unpardonable.—The distinction drawn between 'speaking against the Son of man,' and 'blaspheming against the Holy

Ghost,' ought not to be overlooked. The explanation is probably something of this kind.—The sin against the Son of man was committed by those who did not know Christ to be the Messiah in the days of his humiliation, and did not receive him, believe him, or obey him, but ignorantly rejected him, and crucified him. Many of those who so sinned were pardoned, we cannot doubt; as, for example, on the day of Pentecost, after Peter's preaching.—The sin against the Holy Ghost was committed by those, who, after the day of Pentecost, and the outpouring of the Spirit, and the full publication of the gospel, persisted in unbelief and obstinate impenitence, and were given over to a reprobate mind. These especially grieved the Spirit, and resisted the ministration of the Holy Ghost. That this was the state of many of the Jews appears from several places in the Acts, and especially Acts 28:25-28. See also 1 Thessalonians 2:15, 16.

The blasphemy against the Holy Ghost of which those were guilty, who said that our Lord cast out devils by Beelzebub, appears to be another form of sin. It is not clear to me that our Lord refers to it in this place.

The great question of the unpardonable sin, and the possibility of falling into it in modern days, is a distinct branch of the subject, and is not the chief point in the passage before us. That there is such a sin is clear. That it consists of the union of the clearest head-knowledge of the gospel with deliberate rejection of it, and deliberate choice of sin and the world, seems highly probable. That those who are troubled with fear that they have committed it, are just the persons who have not committed it, is the judgment of all the soundest divines. Utter hardness, callousness, and insensibility of conscience, are probably leading characteristics of the man who has sinned the unpardonable sin. He is 'let alone,' and given over to a reprobate mind.

Let it be noted, that the word we translate 'him that blasphemeth,' would be more literally rendered, 'him that has blasphemed.'

11.—[*When they bring you.*] Let it be noted, that the word 'they,' in this expression, refers to no persons especially, and must be taken indefinitely. It means, 'When ye are brought.' Let the expression be compared with Luke 16:9.

[*Unto magistrates and powers.*] We have examples of the disciples being brought before such 'powers,' in the case of Peter and John before the council, and Paul before Felix, Festus, and Agrippa.

[*Take ye no thought.*] The Greek word so rendered means literally, 'Be not anxious,— be not solicitous,—be not careful.' It is the same word that is used in the expressions, 'Take no thought for the morrow' (*Matt.* 6:34). 'Careth for the things of the world' (*1 Cor.* 7:34). 'Be careful for nothing' (*Phil.* 4:6).

We must not suppose that our Lord meant his disciples to neglect study and reading, upon all proper occasions. We might as well forbid all teaching in schools, because of the promise 'They shall not teach every man his neighbour' (*Heb.* 8:11). St Paul, at the very end of his ministry, took thought for his 'books and parchments' (*2 Tim.* 4:13).

To apply such promises as this to ministers in modern times, and to justify men in making no preparation for their Sunday sermons, is irreverent and unwarrantable trifling with Scripture.

12.—[*The Holy Ghost shall teach you.*] The fulfilment of this promise is remarkably seen in Paul's defence of himself before the Jews at Jerusalem, on the steps of the castle, and before Felix, Festus, and Agrippa. It has also been seen in modern times, in the histories of Wickliffe, Huss, Luther, Latimer, Ridley, Cranmer, and others, and especially in the case of some female martyrs, such as Alice Driver, at the English Reformation.

LUKE 12:13-21

13 And one of the company said unto him, Master, speak to my brother, that he divide the inheritance with me.

14 And he said unto him, Man, who made me a judge or a divider over you?

15 And he said unto them, Take heed, and beware of covetousness: for a man's life consisteth not in the abundance of the things which he possesseth.

16 And he spake a parable unto them, saying, The ground of a certain rich man brought forth plentifully:

17 And he thought within himself, saying, What shall I do, because I have no room where to bestow my fruits?

18 And he said, This will I do: I will pull down my barns, and build greater; and there will I bestow all my fruits and my goods.

19 And I will say to my soul, Soul, thou hast much goods laid up for many years; take thine ease, eat, drink, *and* be merry.

20 But God said unto him, *Thou* fool, this night thy soul shall be required of thee: then whose shall those things be, which thou hast provided?

21 So *is* he that layeth up treasure for himself, and is not rich toward God.

T HE passage we have now read affords a singular instance of man's readiness to bring the things of this world into the midst of his religion. We are told that a certain hearer of our Lord asked him to assist him about his temporal affairs. 'Master,' he said, 'speak to my brother, that he divide the inheritance with me.' He probably had some vague idea that Jesus was going to set up a kingdom in this world, and to reign upon earth. He resolves to make an early application about his own pecuniary matters. He entreats our Lord's interference about his earthly inheritance. Other hearers of Christ might be thinking of a portion in the world to come. This man, was one whose chief thoughts evidently ran upon this present life.

How many hearers of the gospel are just like this man! How many are incessantly planning and scheming about the things of time, even under the very sound of the things of eternity! The natural heart of man is always the same. Even the preaching of Christ did not arrest the attention of all his hearers. The minister of Christ in the present day must never be surprised to see worldliness and inattention in the midst of his congregation. The servant must not expect his sermons to be more valued than his Master's.

Let us mark, in these verses, *what a solemn warning our Lord pronounces against covetousness.* 'He said unto them, Take heed, and beware of covetousness.'

It would be vain to decide positively which is the most common sin in the world. It would be safe to say that there is none, at any rate, to which the heart is more prone, than covetousness. It was this sin which helped to cast down the angels who fell. They were not content with their first estate. They coveted something better. It was this sin which helped to drive Adam and Eve out of paradise, and bring death into the world. Our first parents were not satisfied with the things which God gave them in Eden. They coveted, and so they fell.—It is a sin which, ever since the fall, has been the fertile cause of misery and unhappiness upon earth. Wars, quarrels, strifes, divisions, envyings, disputes, jealousies, hatreds of all sorts, both public and private, may nearly all be traced up to this fountain-head.

Let the warning which our Lord pronounces, sink down into our hearts, and bear fruit in our lives. Let us strive to learn the lesson which St Paul had mastered, when he says, 'I have learned, in whatever state I am, therewith to be content' (*Phil.* 4:11). Let us pray for a thorough confidence in God's superintending providence over all our worldly affairs, and God's perfect wisdom in all his arrangements concerning us. If we have little, let us be sure that it would be not good for us to have much. If the things that we have are taken away, let us be satisfied that there is a needs be. Happy is he who is persuaded that whatever is, is best, and has ceased from vain wishing, and has become 'content with such things as he has' (*Heb.* 13:5).

Let us mark, secondly, in these verses, *what a withering exposure our Lord makes of the folly of worldly-mindedness.* He draws the picture of a rich man of the world, whose mind is wholly set on earthly things. He paints him scheming and planning about his property, as if he was master of his own life, and had but to say, 'I will do a thing,' and it would be done. And then he turns the picture, and shows us God requiring the worldling's soul, and asking the heart-searching question, 'Whose shall those things be, which thou hast provided?' 'Folly,' he bids us learn, nothing less than 'folly,' is the right word by which to describe the conduct of the man who thinks of nothing but his money. The man who 'lays up treasure for himself, and is not rich towards God,' is the man whom God declares to be a 'fool.'

It is an awful thought that the character which Jesus brings before us in this parable, is far from being uncommon. Thousands in every age of the world have lived continually doing the very things which are here condemned. Thousands are doing them at this very day. They are laying up treasure upon earth, and thinking of nothing but how to increase it. They are continually adding to their hoards, as if they were to enjoy them for ever, and as if there was no death, no judgment, and no world to come. And yet these are the men who are called clever, and prudent, and wise! These are the men who are commended, and flattered, and held up to admiration! Truly the Lord seeth not as man seeth! The Lord declares that rich men who live only for this world are 'fools.'

Let us pray for rich men. Their souls are in great danger. 'Heaven,' said a great man on his death-bed, 'is a place to which few kings and rich men come.' Even when converted, the rich carry a great weight, and run the race to heaven under great disadvantages. The possession of money has a most hardening effect upon the conscience. We never know what we may do when we become rich. 'The love of money is the root of all evil: Which while some have coveted after, they have erred from the faith, and pierced themselves through with many sorrows' (1 Tim. 6:10). Poverty has many disadvantages. But riches destroy far more souls than poverty.

Let us mark, lastly, in these verses, *how important it is to be rich towards God.* This is true wisdom. This is true providing for time to come. This is genuine prudence. The wise man is he who does not think only of earthly treasure, but of treasure in heaven.

When can it be said of a man, that he is rich towards God? Never till he is rich in grace, and rich in faith, and rich in good works! Never till he has applied to Jesus Christ, and bought of him gold tried in the fire! (Rev. 3:18). Never till he has a house not made with

55

hands, eternal in the heavens! Never till he has a name inscribed in the book of life, and is an heir of God and a joint heir with Christ! Such a man is truly rich. His treasure is incorruptible. His bank never breaks. His inheritance fadeth not away. Man cannot deprive him of it. Death cannot snatch it out of his hands. All things are his already,—life, death, things present, and things to come (*1 Cor.* 3:22). And best of all, what he has now is nothing to what he will have hereafter.

Riches like these are within reach of every sinner who will come to Christ and receive them. May we never rest till they are ours! To obtain them may cost us something in this world. It may bring on us persecution, ridicule, and scorn. But let the thought console us, that the Judge of all says, 'Thou art rich' (*Rev.* 2:9). The true Christian is the only man who is really wealthy and wise.

Notes—Luke 12:13-21

13.—[*One of the company said.*] We know nothing of this man. His question gave occasion for a striking lesson on covetousness. The number of instances in which our Lord turns a bystander's remark to a spiritual use, in the Gospel of St Luke, is well worthy of notice. It is probable that this man was filled with the common notion that Messiah was going to be a temporal ruler, and to set all things right in the world.

14.—[*Who made me a judge?*] The question here is equivalent to a strong negation.—'I am not come to be a judge of temporal matters.' The wisdom of our Lord's line of conduct on this occasion deserves notice. The slightest interference with the office of the civil government would have given occasion to his enemies, and placed them in their power.

Ministers of Christ would do well in modern times to mark our Lord's conduct in this case, and, as far as possible, to walk in his steps. The less ministers have to do with secular things, and especially with the administration of law, the better. The magistrates' bench, as a general rule, is not a fitting position for a minister of the gospel to occupy. When the preacher of the gospel undertakes any work except that of his calling, his proper work and business are usually neglected, or worse done than they would have been if he had confined himself exclusively to them, and been a man of one thing. 'Give thyself wholly to these things,' is a sentence which should never be forgotten.

15.—[*Take heed and beware of covetousness.*] Those who possess Latimer's works should read his sermon on this text. He begins by repeating the words three times, and then says, 'And what if I should say nothing else?'

[*A man's life.*] The meaning of this must be, 'A man's true interest,'—the real end and object of man's being,—the purpose for which God made him, and gave him breath. He was not made only to amass wealth, but to glorify God on earth, and enjoy him hereafter in heaven.

17.—[*He thought within himself.*] The anxious thoughts, and scheming and planning, which increase of wealth always brings with it, are strikingly described in this verse. The more acres a man has, the more cares. The more his money increases, the more of his time is generally consumed and eaten up in thinking about it.

18.—[*My barns.*] It is doubtful whether the word translated 'barns' exactly means what we understand by a barn in our language. It means literally a 'repository.' It is not improbable, as is often the case in some countries, that the rich man's barns were holes in the ground, or caves, prepared for the keeping of corn.

Let it be observed, that the rich man talks of 'my' barns, 'my' fruits, 'my' goods, with all the self-sufficiency and petty importance of one who knows no will but his own, and no master but his own selfishness. It should remind us of Nabal's language in 1 Samuel 25:11. Of him too it is written, 'Fool is his name, and folly is with him' (*1 Sam.* 25:25).

19.—[*I will say to my soul.*] This is the language of genuine worldliness. And yet he talks of 'soul!' He speaks of 'goods laid up for many years,' and yet ignores the eternity which must come at last, and the necessity of a hope laid up in heaven!

The secret thoughts and schemes of rich worldlings are strikingly exposed in this verse. The Lord Jesus knows exactly what such men are thinking of.

Basil remarks, 'If this man had only had the sense of a hog, what other thing could he have said?'

20.—[*But God said unto him.*] Our Lord does not inform us in what way God spoke to the rich man; whether directly or by a messenger, as he spake by Nathan to David. What he has not thought fit to explain, it is useless for us to conjecture.

[*Thou fool.*] The Greek word so translated means literally, without mind, or sense, or understanding. It is the same word as in Luke 11:40. Let us mark, that just when the rich man was scheming cunningly, and thinking himself very wise, God says to him, 'Thou fool.'

[*Thy soul shall be required.*] The Greek words so translated would be literally rendered, 'They shall require thy soul.' It is an example of the indefinite use of 'they,' as already observed on verse 11.

Let it be noted, that this expression is one of those which show the separate existence of the soul when the body is dead.

[*Whose shall those things be?*] The argument here appears to be much the same as that in Ecclesiastes 5:15, and Psalm 39:6. A man cannot possess his property a moment after he is dead. Grace is the only lasting possession.

21.—[*Layeth up treasure for himself.*] This describes all who labour only for themselves, and the life that now is.

[*Is not rich toward God.*] This is the character of him who gives nothing to God's glory,—neither money, affection, thought, time, nor interest. There are thousands of this character. They are rich toward everything but God. They have plenty to give to the world, but nothing to give to God. Ask them to help a worldly scheme, and they can find money, time, and attention. Ask them to do something for God, and they have no money, or no time! Those are the truly rich who have property which will be recognized at the day of judgment. Many owners of millions of pounds are paupers before God. They are not rich either in grace, or faith, or good works.

LUKE 12:22-31

22 And he said unto his disciples, Therefore I say unto you, Take no thought for your life, what ye shall eat; neither for the body, what ye shall put on.

23 The life is more than meat, and the body *is more* than raiment.

24 Consider the ravens: for they neither sow nor reap; which neither have storehouse nor barn; and God feedeth them: how much more are ye better than the fowls?

25 And which of you with taking thought can add to his stature one cubit?

26 If ye then be not able to do that thing which is least, why take ye thought for the rest?

27 Consider the lilies how they grow: they toil not, they spin not; and yet I say unto you, that Solomon in all his glory was not arrayed like one of these.

28 If then God so clothe the grass, which is to day in the field, and to morrow is cast into the oven; how much more *will he clothe* you, O ye of little faith?

29 And seek not ye what ye shall eat, or what ye shall drink, neither be ye of doubtful mind.

30 For all these things do the nations of the world seek after: and your Father knoweth that ye have need of these things.

31 But rather seek ye the kingdom of God; and all these things shall be added unto you.

WE have in these verses *a collection of striking arguments against over-anxiety about the things of this world.* At first sight they may seem to some minds simple and commonplace. But the more they are pondered, the more weighty will they appear. An abiding recollection of them would save many Christians an immense amount of trouble.

Christ bids us consider the ravens. 'They neither sow nor reap. They have neither storehouse nor barn. But God feedeth them.' Now if the Maker of all things provides for the wants of birds, and orders things so that they have a daily supply of food, we ought surely not to fear that he will let his spiritual children starve.

Christ bids us look at the lilies. 'They toil not, they spin not. Yet Solomon in all his glory was not arrayed like one of these.' Now if God every year provides these flowers with a fresh supply of living leaves and blossoms, we surely ought not to doubt his power and willingness to furnish his believing servants with all needful clothing.

Christ bids us remember that a Christian man should be ashamed of being as anxious as a heathen. The 'nations of the world' may well be careful about food, and raiment, and the like. They are sunk in deep ignorance, and know nothing of the real nature of God. But the man who can say of God, 'he is my Father,' and of Christ, 'he is my Saviour,' ought surely to be above such anxieties and cares. A clear faith should produce a light heart.

Finally, Christ bids us think of the perfect knowledge of God. 'Our Father knows that we have need' of food and raiment. That thought alone ought to make us content. All our wants are perfectly known to the Lord of heaven and earth. He can relieve those wants, whenever he sees fit. He will relieve them, whenever it is good for our souls.

Let the four arguments now adduced sink deep into our hearts, and bear fruit in our lives. Nothing is more common than a careful and troubled spirit, and nothing so mars a believer's usefulness, and minishes his inward peace. Nothing, on the contrary, glorifies God so much as a cheerful spirit in the midst of temporal troubles. It carries a reality with it which even the worldly can understand. It commends our Christianity, and makes it beautiful in the eyes of men. Faith, and faith only, will produce this cheerful spirit. The man who can say boldly, 'The Lord is my shepherd,' is the man who will be able to add, 'I shall not want' (*Psa.* 23:1).

We have, secondly, in these verses, *a high standard of living commended to all Christians.* It is contained in a short and simple injunction, 'Seek ye the kingdom of God.' We are not to give our principal thoughts to the things of this world. We are not so to live as if we had nothing but a body. We are to live like beings who have immortal souls to be lost or saved,—a death to die,—a God to meet,—a judgment to expect,—and an eternity in heaven or in hell awaiting us.

When can we be said to 'seek the kingdom of God?' We do so when we make it the chief business of our lives to secure a place in the number of saved people,—to have our sins pardoned, our hearts renewed, and ourselves made meet for the inheritance of the saints in light. We do so when we give a primary place in our minds to the interests of God's kingdom,—when we labour to increase the number of God's subjects,—when we strive to maintain God's cause, and advance God's glory in the world.

The kingdom of God is the only kingdom worth labouring for. All other kingdoms shall, sooner or later, decay and pass away. The statesmen who rear them are like men who build houses of cards, or children, who make palaces of sand on the sea shore. The wealth which constitutes their greatness is as liable to melt away as the snow in spring. The kingdom of God is the only kingdom which shall endure for ever. Happy are they who belong to it, love it, live for it, pray for it, and labour for its increase and prosperity. Their labour shall not be in vain. May we give all diligence to make our calling into this kingdom sure! May it be our constant advice to children, relatives, friends, servants, neighbours, 'Seek the kingdom!' Whatever else you seek, 'Seek first the kingdom of God!'

We have, lastly, in these verses, *a marvellous promise held out to those who seek the kingdom of God.* Our Lord Jesus declares, 'All these things shall be added unto you.'

We must take heed that we do not misunderstand the meaning of this passage. We have no right to expect that the Christian tradesman, who neglects his business under pretence of zeal for God's kingdom, will find his trade prosper, and his affairs do well. To place such a sense upon the promise would be nothing less than fanaticism and enthusiasm. It would encourage slothfulness in business, and give occasion to the enemies of God to blaspheme.

The man to whom the promise before us belongs, is the Christian who gives to the things of God their right order and their right place. He does not neglect the worldly duties of his station, but he regards them as of infinitely less importance than the requirements of God. He does not omit due attention to his temporal affairs, but he looks on them as of far less moment than the affairs of his soul. In short, he aims in all his daily life to put God first and the world second,— to give the second place to the things of his body, and the first place to the things of his soul. This is the man to whom Jesus says, 'All these things shall be added unto thee.'

But how is the promise fulfilled? The answer is short and simple. The man who seeks first God's kingdom shall never lack anything that is for his good. He may not have so much health as some. He may not have so much wealth as others. He may not have a richly spread table, or royal dainties. But he shall always have *enough*. 'Bread shall be given him; his water shall be sure' (*Isa.* 33:16). 'All things shall work together for good to them that love God' (*Rom.* 8:28). 'No good thing will the Lord withhold from them that walk uprightly' (*Psa.* 84:11). 'I have been young,' said David, 'and now am old; yet have I not seen the righteous forsaken, nor his seed begging bread' (*Psa.* 37:25).

Notes—Luke 12:22-31

22.—[*He said unto his disciples.*] Let it be noted that our Lord in this passage addresses himself especially to his disciples. He turns to them from the man for whom he had refused to be a judge and a divider, and from the mixed multitude to whom he had spoken the parable of the rich fool. He knew the readiness of a believer's heart to be anxious about the things of this world, and supplied his followers with comforting arguments against care.

[*Take no thought.*] The same remark which has been already made on this expression may be repeated here. The meaning of the Greek word is, 'Take no anxious thought,—be not anxiously careful.'

[*Life ... body.*] The maintenance of animal life and the clothing of the body, are the two primary objects of thought and care. St Paul refers to this when he says, 'Having food and raiment let us be therewith content' (*1 Tim.* 6:8).

23.—[*More.*] This expression means 'more excellent,—more valuable.' It is translated 'greater' in Luke 11:31, 32; and 'more excellent' in Hebrews 11:4.

24.—[*Ravens.*] Let it be noted that the ravens are specially mentioned in Psalm 147:9 and Job 38:41, as objects of God's care. In the history of Elijah, the Holy Ghost shows us the ravens providing for others, as well as providing for themselves (*1 Kings* 17:6).

25.—[*To his stature, one cubit.*] It admits of grave doubt whether the Greek word which we translate 'stature,' ought not to have been translated 'life,' or 'age.'—It is so translated in John 9:21 and 23, and Hebrews 11:11. The idea of a person being anxious to increase his stature is undoubtedly somewhat strange, and the addition of a cubit to it would hardly be called in the following verse 'that thing which is least.'—Anxiety about a longer term of life is much more common and intelligible. The application of the word 'cubit' to an increase of life, is quite justified by the expression in the Psalms 'Thou hast made my days as an handbreadth' (*Psa.* 39:5). The figure is also used in classical writers.

27.—[*The lilies.*] It is not clear that the flowers which are translated 'lilies,' are the lilies of our climate. Major quotes Sir J. E. Smith's saying, 'There is reason to suppose that the lily mentioned by our Saviour, is the Amaryllis Lutea or Autumnal Narcissus. The flower is described by travellers, as appearing in profusion in the fields of countries in the Levant, and covering them in autumn with a vivid golden brilliancy, so as to admit of a peculiarly apt comparison with Solomon in all his glory.'

[*Solomon in all his glory.*] Let it be observed that the kingdom and glory of Solomon are spoken of here as real and true things, and not as mere myths and fables.

28.—[*The grass.*] The word so translated signifies herbage in general, including flowers.

29.—[*Neither be ye of doubtful mind.*] The Greek word so translated is only found here in the New Testament. Its meaning has been variously explained, and our own translators seem to have felt its difficulty by their marginal reading 'live not in careful suspense.'

According to Hammond, the idea is borrowed from clouds or birds, high in the air, and tossed to and fro by the wind.

The vulgate translation appears to regard the expression as a warning against high and ambitious thoughts, 'be not lifted up on high.'

The true idea is probably that which is given by Suicer. The expression is one borrowed from ships out at sea, which, especially when seen from the shore, appear lifted up, tossed to and fro, and restless. Thucydides has a similar expression, when describing the condition of men's minds in Greece, just at the beginning of the Peloponnesian war (*Thuc.* 2:7). It implies a state of suspense, doubt, and anxiety about the future.

30.—[*The nations.*] Doddridge paraphrases this sentence thus, 'The Gentile nations of the world, who know little of Providence or of a future state, seek after all these lower things with great solicitude; and they are more excusable in doing it.'

LUKE 12:32-40

32 Fear not, little flock; for it is your Father's good pleasure to give you the kingdom.

33 Sell that ye have, and give alms; provide yourselves bags which wax not old, a treasure in the heavens that faileth not, where no thief approacheth, neither moth corrupteth.

34 For where your treasure is, there will your heart be also.

35 Let your loins be girded about, and *your* lights burning;

36 And ye yourselves like unto men that wait for their lord, when he will return from the wedding; that when he cometh and knocketh, they may open unto him immediately.

37 Blessed are those servants, whom the lord when he cometh shall find watching: verily I say unto you, that he shall gird himself, and make them to sit down to meat, and will come forth and serve them.

38 And if he shall come in the second watch, or come in the third watch, and find *them* so, blessed are those servants.

39 And this know, that if the goodman of the house had known what hour the thief would come, he would have watched, and not have suffered his house to be broken through.

40 Be ye therefore ready also: for the Son of man cometh at an hour when ye think not.

LET us mark *what a gracious word of consolation this verse contains for all true believers.* The Lord Jesus knew well the hearts of his disciples. He knew how ready they were to be filled with fears of every description,—fears because of the fewness of their number,—fears because of the multitude of their enemies,—fears because of the many difficulties in their way,—fears because of their sense of weakness and unworthiness. He answers these many fears with a single golden sentence,—'Fear not, little flock; for it is your Father's good pleasure to give you the kingdom.'

Believers are a 'little flock.' They always have been, ever since the world began. Professing servants of God have sometimes been very many. Baptized people at the present day are a great company. But true Christians are very few. It is foolish to be surprised at this. It is vain to expect it will be otherwise until the Lord comes again. 'Strait is the gate, and narrow is the way, that leadeth unto life, and few there be that find it' (*Matt.* 7:14).

Believers have a glorious 'kingdom' awaiting them. Here upon earth they are often mocked, and ridiculed, and persecuted, and, like their Master, despised and rejected of men. But 'the sufferings of this present time are not worthy to be compared with the glory which shall be revealed.' 'When Christ, who is our life, shall appear, then shall ye also appear with him in glory' (*Rom.* 8:18; *Col.* 3:4).

Believers are tenderly loved by God the Father. It is 'the Father's good pleasure' to give them a kingdom. He does not receive them grudgingly, unwillingly, and coldly. He rejoices over them as members of his beloved Son in whom he is well pleased. He regards them as his dear children in Christ. He sees no spot in them. Even now, when he looks down on them from heaven, in the midst of their infirmities, he is well pleased, and hereafter, when presented before his glory, he will welcome them with exceeding joy (*Jude* 24).

Are we members of Christ's little flock? Then surely we ought not to be afraid. There are given to us exceeding great and precious promises (2 *Pet.* 1:4). God is ours, and Christ is ours. Greater are those that are for us than all that are against us. The world, the flesh, and the devil, are mighty enemies. But with Christ on our side we have no cause to fear.

Let us mark, secondly, *what a striking exhortation these verses contain to seek treasure in heaven.* 'Sell that ye have,' said our Lord, 'and give alms.' 'Provide yourselves bags which wax not old, a treasure in the heavens which faileth not.' But this is not all. A mighty, heart-searching principle is laid down to enforce the exhortation. 'Where your treasure is, there will your heart be also.'

The language of this charge is doubtless somewhat figurative. Yet the meaning of it is clear and unmistakable. We are to *sell*,—to give up anything, and deny ourselves anything which stands in the way of our soul's salvation. We are to *give*,—to show charity and kindness to everyone, and to be more ready to spend our money in relieving others, than to hoard it for our own selfish purposes. We are to *provide* ourselves treasures in heaven,—to make sure that our names are in the book of life,—to lay hold of eternal life,—to lay up for ourselves evidences which will bear the inspection of the day of judgment. This is true wisdom. This is real prudence. The man who does well for himself is the man who gives up everything for Christ's sake. He makes the best of bargains. He carries the cross for a few years in this world, and in the world to come has everlasting life. He obtains the best of possessions. He carries his riches with him beyond the grave. He is rich in grace here, and he is rich in glory hereafter. And, best of all, what he obtains by faith in Christ he never loses. It is 'that good part which is never taken away.'

Would we know what we are ourselves? Let us see whether we have treasure in heaven, or whether all our good things are here upon earth.—Would we know what our treasure is? Let us ask ourselves what we love most? This is the true test of character. This is the pulse of our religion. It matters little what we say, or what we profess, or what preaching we admire, or what place of worship we attend. What do we love? On what are our affections set? This is the great question. 'Where our treasure is there will our hearts be also.'

Let us mark, lastly, what an *instructive picture these verses contain of the frame of mind which the true Christian should endeavour to keep up.* Our Lord tells us that we ought to be 'like unto men that wait for their Lord.' We ought to live like servants who expect their Master's return, fulfilling our duties in our several stations, and doing nothing which we would not like to be found doing when Christ comes again.

The standard of life which our Lord has set up here is an exceedingly high one,—so high, indeed, that many Christians are apt to flinch from it, and feel cast down. And yet there is nothing here which ought to make a believer afraid. Readiness for the return of Christ to this world implies nothing which is impossible and unattainable. It requires no angelical perfection. It requires no man to forsake his family, and retire into solitude. It requires nothing more than the life of repentance, faith, and holiness. The man who is living the life of faith in the Son of God is the man whose 'loins are girded,' and whose 'light is burning.' Such a man may have the care of kingdoms on him, like Daniel,—or be a servant in a Nero's household, like some in Paul's time. All this matters nothing. If he lives looking unto Jesus, he is a servant who can 'open to him immediately.' Surely it is not too much to ask Christians to be men of this kind. Surely it was not for nothing that our Lord said, 'The Son of man cometh at an hour when ye think not.'

Are we ourselves living as if we were ready for the second coming of Christ? Well would it be if this question were put to our consciences more frequently. It might keep us back from many a false step in our daily life. It might prevent many a backsliding. The true Christian should not only believe in Christ, and love Christ. He should also look and long for Christ's appearing. If he cannot say from his heart, 'Come, Lord Jesus,' there must be something wrong about his soul.

Notes—Luke 12:32-40

32.—[*Little flock.*] The Greek word which we render 'flock,' is a diminutive, meaning literally 'little flock.' The addition of the adjective which we translate 'little,' increases the tenderness of the whole expression.

[*It is your Father's good pleasure.*] This would be rendered literally, 'Your Father is well pleased.' It is the same expression which is used in the well-known places, Matthew 3:17; 17:5; Mark 1:11; Luke 3:22. Let it be noted that our Lord lays special stress in this passage on the Fatherly relation of God to all believers, as an antidote to over-carefulness and anxiety.

33.—[*Sell that ye have, etc.*] This

expression, if not confined to the apostles, but applied generally to all believers, must evidently be interpreted with some scriptural limitation. There is nothing in the Acts or the Epistles, which shows that believers, in the primitive church, were expected to sell all their property, as soon as they were converted. On the contrary, St Peter's words to Ananias, seem to show that it was quite optional with converts to sell their property or keep it (*Acts* 5:4). St Paul goes even further, and says that 'if a man provides not for his own, he has denied the faith, and is worse than an infidel' (*1 Tim.* 5:8).

The whole verse is a strong figurative exhortation to self-denial, liberality, and careful provision for the soul. An excessively literal interpretation lands us in insuperable difficulties. It will surely not be said that Christians ought literally to provide themselves 'bags.' Once concede that a figure is used, and a figurative explanation of the whole verse must be reasonably conceded.

The 'thief' in the verse represents sudden and violent loss, the 'moth' gradual and silent waste or exhaustion.

35.—[*Loins be girded.*] This is a figure drawn from the habits of dressing which prevailed in our Lord's time, and which are general at the present day throughout the East. Long flowing garments were the ordinary attire that men wore. When anything was to be done requiring bodily exertion, the first thing needful was to gird up the loins, or tie the garments tightly round the waist.

[*Your lights burning.*] To see the full force of this expression, we should read the parable of the ten virgins (*Matt.* 25:1–13). Marriages often took place in the evening. It was the duty of the servants to meet the wedding party with lighted torches. The verse before us is an exhortation to be in an attitude of constant preparation to meet the bridegroom Jesus Christ at his second advent.

37.—[*He shall gird himself, etc.*] This is perhaps one of the most wonderful promises which is made to believers anywhere in the New Testament. It must probably be interpreted figuratively. The meaning evidently is, that there is no degree of honour and glory which the Lord Jesus will not gladly bestow on those who are found ready to meet him, in the day of his second advent. Some think that there will be, in some way, a literal fulfilment of this promise, and that our Lord refers to this, when he says at the last supper, 'I will not drink of the fruit of the vine, until the kingdom of God shall come' (*Luke* 22:18). A reference to the same literal fulfilment is also supposed to exist in Isaiah 25:6.

Pearce says 'We may gather from this verse that it was the custom in those days, as it was not long since among us, for the bridegroom at a wedding supper to wait upon the company as a servant.'

38.—[*Second watch ... third watch.*] These expressions are figurative. The night was divided into four watches. The second watch was from nine to twelve, and the third from twelve to three. The uncertainty of the time of the Lord's advent, and the duty of being always ready for it, are the lessons of the verse.

39.—[*What hour the thief would come.*] This is a parabolic sentence, intended to teach us that the 'day of the Lord so cometh as a thief in the night' (*1 Thess.* 5:2); and that there is no safety for Christians, excepting in constant readiness for it.

40.—[*The Son of man cometh.*] Let it be noted that the coming here spoken of, is the second personal advent of our Lord Jesus Christ, at the end of this dispensation. To apply the expression, as some do, to death, is an entire perversion of Scripture. The coming of the Lord is one thing, and death is another.

LUKE 12:41-48

41 Then Peter said unto him, Lord, speakest thou this parable unto us, or even to all?

42 And the Lord said, Who then is that faithful and wise steward, whom *his* lord shall make ruler over his household, to give *them their* portion of meat in due season?

43 Blessed *is* that servant, whom his lord when he cometh shall find so doing.

44 Of a truth I say unto you, that he will make him ruler over all that he hath.

45 But and if that servant say in his heart, My lord delayeth his coming; and shall begin to beat the menservants and maidens, and to eat and drink, and to be drunken;

46 The lord of that servant will come in a day when he looketh not for *him*, and at an hour when he is not aware, and will cut him in sunder, and will appoint him his portion with the unbelievers.

47 And that servant, which knew his lord's will, and prepared not *himself*, neither did according to his will, shall be beaten with many *stripes*.

48 But he that knew not, and did commit things worthy of stripes, shall be beaten with few *stripes*. For unto whomsoever much is given, of him shall be much required: and to whom men have committed much, of him they will ask the more.

WE learn from these verses, *the importance of doing, in our Christianity.* Our Lord is speaking of his own second coming. He is comparing his disciples to servants waiting for their master's return, who have each their own work to do during his absence. 'Blessed,' he says, 'is that servant, whom his lord, when he cometh, shall find so *doing.*'

The warning has doubtless a primary reference to ministers of the gospel. They are the stewards of God's mysteries, who are specially bound to be found 'doing,' when Christ comes again. But the words contain a further lesson, which all Christians would do well to consider. That lesson is, the immense importance of a working, practical, diligent, useful religion.

The lesson is one which is greatly needed in the churches of Christ. We hear a great deal about people's intentions, and hopes, and wishes, and feelings, and professions. It would be well if we could hear more about people's practice. It is not the servant who is found wishing and professing, but the servant who is found 'doing' whom Jesus calls 'blessed.'

The lesson is one which many, unhappily, shrink from giving, and many more shrink from receiving. We are gravely told that to talk of 'working,' and 'doing,' is legal, and brings Christians into bondage!

Remarks of this kind should never move us. They savour of ignorance or perverseness. The lesson before us is not about justification, but about sanctification,—not about faith, but about holiness. The point is not *what a man should do to be saved*,—but *what ought a saved man to do?* The teaching of Scripture is clear and express upon this subject. A saved man ought to be 'careful to maintain good works' (*Titus* 3:8). The desire of a true Christian ought to be, to be found 'doing.'

If we love life, let us resolve by God's help, to be 'doing' Christians. This is to be like Christ,—he 'went about doing good' (*Acts* 10:38). This is to be like the apostles,—they were men of deeds even more than of words. This is to glorify God,—'Herein is my Father glorified, that ye bear much fruit' (*John* 15:8). This is to be useful to the world,—'Let your light so shine before men, that they may see your good works, and glorify your Father in heaven' (*Matt.* 5:16).

We learn, secondly, from these verses, *the awful danger of those who neglect the duties of their calling.* Of such our Lord declares, that they shall be 'cut in sunder, and their portion appointed with the unbelievers.' These words no doubt apply especially to the ministers and teachers of the gospel. Yet we must not flatter ourselves that they are confined to them. They are probably meant to convey a lesson to all who fill offices of high responsibility. It is a striking fact that when Peter says at the beginning of the passage, 'Speakest thou this parable to us, or even to all?' our Lord gives him no answer. Whosoever occupies a position of trust, and neglects his duties, would do well to ponder this passage, and learn wisdom.

The language which our Lord Jesus uses about slothful and unfaithful servants, is peculiarly severe. Few places in the Gospels contain such strong expressions as this. It is a vain delusion to suppose that the gospel speaks nothing but 'smooth things.' The same loving Saviour who holds out mercy to the uttermost to the penitent and believing, never shrinks from holding up the judgments of God against those who despise his counsel. Let no man deceive us on this subject. There is a hell for such a one as goeth on still in his wickedness, no less than a heaven for the believer in Jesus. There is such a thing as 'the wrath of the Lamb' (*Rev.* 6:16).

Let us strive so to live, that whenever the heavenly Master comes, we may be found ready to receive him. Let us watch our hearts with a godly jealousy, and beware of the least symptom of unreadiness for the Lord's appearing. Specially let us beware of any rising disposition to lower our standard of Christian holiness,—to dislike persons who are more spiritually-minded than ourselves, and to conform to the world. The moment we detect such a disposition in our hearts, we may be sure that our souls are in great peril. The Christian professor who begins to persecute God's people, and to take pleasure in worldly society, is on the high road to ruin.

We learn, lastly, from these verses, that *the greater a man's religious light is, the greater is his guilt if he is not converted.* The servant which 'knew his lord's will, but did it not, shall be beaten with many stripes.' 'Unto whomsoever much is given, of him shall be much required.'

The lesson of these words is one of wide application. It demands the attention of many classes. It should come home to the conscience of every British Christian. His judgment shall be far more strict than that of the heathen who never saw the Bible.—It should come home to every Protestant who has the liberty to read the Scriptures. His responsibility is far greater than that of the priest-ridden Romanist, who is debarred from the use of God's Word.—It should come home to every hearer of the gospel. If he remains unconverted he is far more guilty than the inhabitant of some dark parish, who never hears any teaching but a sort of semi-heathen morality.—It should come home to every child and servant in religious families. All such are far more blameworthy, in God's sight, than those who live in houses where there is no honour paid to the Word of God and prayer. Let these things never be forgotten. Our judgment at the last day will be according to our light and opportunities.

What are we doing ourselves with our religious knowledge? Are we using it wisely, and turning it to good account? Or are we content with the barren saying, 'We know it,—we know it,' and secretly flat-tering ourselves that the knowledge of our Lord's will makes us better than others, while that will is not done? Let us beware of mistakes. The day will come, when knowledge unimproved will be found the most perilous of possessions. Thousands will awake to find that they are in a lower place than the most ignorant and idolatrous heathen. Their knowledge not used, and their light not followed, will only add to their condemnation.

Notes—Luke 12:41-48

42.—[*And the Lord said.*] Let it be noted that our Lord Jesus Christ did not give any direct reply to the question which Peter asked. Major remarks, 'The meaning of our Saviour's reply appears to be this: The precepts that I have given apply to every individual, but with greater force to you who are in the situation of stewards, to whom much has been entrusted, and from whom consequently much will be required.'

The whole passage, down to the forty-eighth verse, appears to be parabolic and figurative; and we must be careful not to strain any particular expression in it, further than is warranted by the general scope of the context.

[*Steward.*] This word, it should be noted, is specially used by St Paul as descriptive of the ministerial office (*1 Cor.* 4:1). It would seem to show that ministers are primarily pointed at in our Lord's teaching in this parable.

44.—[*Make him ruler over all that he hath.*] This expression should be compared with similar expressions in the parables of the talents and of the pounds.

45.—[*Beat the menservants, etc.*] Stella, though a Roman Catholic commentator, remarks how closely this verse describes the conduct of cardinals and bishops at Rome in the beginning of the seventeenth century.

46.—[*Will cut him in sunder.*] It admits of some doubt whether the Greek word so translated will bear so strong a sense as

our translators have put upon it. It is only found in this passage, and a similar passage in Matthew 24:51.

Parkhurst thinks that it means, 'shall scourge with the utmost severity.' Others think that it means, 'shall separate, or remove, from his office;—shall dismiss.' It certainly is worthy of note, that after using this expression, our Lord speaks of the unfaithful servant as yet alive: 'He shall appoint him his portion with the unbelievers.'

[*With the unbelievers.*] Some think that this expression means simply 'with the unfaithful servants,' in contradistinc-tion to the 'faithful servants,' described in the forty-second verse. Comparison with Matthew 25:21, favours this idea.

48.—[*Knew not ... commit things worthy of stripes.*] Watson thinks that the ignorance here must be 'taken comparatively, and not absolutely.' Few expressions in the Bible are more unfavourable to the heathen who die in ignorance of the gospel than this. It is vain to conceal from ourselves the solemn truth, that no degree of ignorance makes a man entirely guiltless and excusable in the sight of God. Our very ignorance is part of our sin.

[*Unto whomsoever much is given, etc.*] In this sentence our Lord lays down a great principle in his kingdom, as an appropriate conclusion to the parable he has just been speaking.

Baxter remarks on this verse, 'Great gifts are to be used with great diligence; and great trusts, and powers, and charges, are rather to be feared than sought. Little do the conquerors of the world, or those that strive for church preferments, believe and consider what duty, or what deep damnation, they labour for.'

LUKE 12:49-53

49 I am come to send fire on the earth; and what will I, if it be already kindled?

50 But I have a baptism to be baptized with; and how am I straitened till it be accomplished!

51 Suppose ye that I am come to give peace on earth? I tell you, Nay; but rather division:

52 For from henceforth there shall be five in one house divided, three against two, and two against three.

53 The father shall be divided against the son, and the son against the father; the mother against the daughter, and the daughter against the mother; the mother in law against her daughter in law, and the daughter in law against her mother in law.

THE sayings of the Lord Jesus in these five verses are peculiarly weighty and suggestive. They unfold truths which every true Christian would do well to mark and digest. They explain things in the church, and in the world, which at first sight are hard to be understood.

We learn, for one thing, from these verses, *how thoroughly the heart of Christ was set on finishing the work which he came into the world to do.* He says, 'I have a baptism to be baptized with,'—a baptism of suffering, of wounds, of agony, of blood, and of death. Yet none of these things moved him. He adds, 'How am I straitened till this baptism is accomplished!' The prospect of coming trouble did not deter him for a moment. He was ready and willing to endure all things in order to provide eternal redemption for his people. Zeal for the cause he had taken in hand was like a burning fire within him. To advance his Father's glory, to open the door of life to a lost world, to provide a fountain for all sin and uncleanness by the sacrifice of himself, were continually the uppermost thoughts of his mind. He was pressed in spirit till this mighty work was finished.

For ever let us bear in mind that all Christ's sufferings on our behalf were endured willingly, voluntarily, and of his own free choice. They were not submitted to patiently merely because he could not avoid them. They were not borne without a murmur merely because he could not escape them. He lived a humble life for thirty-three years because he loved to do so. He died a death of agony with a willing and a ready mind. Both in life and death he was carrying out the eternal counsel whereby God was to be glorified and sinners were to be saved. He carried it out with all his heart, mighty as the struggle was which it entailed on his flesh and blood. He delighted to do God's will. He was straitened till it was accomplished.

Let us not doubt that the heart of Christ in heaven is the same that it was when he was upon earth. He feels as deep an interest now about the salvation of sinners as he did formerly about dying in their stead. Jesus never changes. He is the same yesterday, and today, and for ever. There is in him an infinite willingness to receive, pardon, justify, and deliver the souls of men from hell. Let us strive to realize that willingness, and learn to believe it without doubting, and repose on it without fear. It is a certain fact, if men would only believe it, that Christ is far more willing to save us than we are to be saved.

Let the zeal of our Lord and Master be an example to all his people. Let the recollection of his burning readiness to die for us be like a glowing coal in our memories, and constrain us to live to him, and not to ourselves. Surely the thought of it should waken our sleeping hearts, and warm our cold affections, and make us anxious to redeem the time, and do something for his praise. A zealous Saviour ought to have zealous disciples.

We learn, for another thing, from these verses, *how useless it is to expect universal peace and harmony from the preaching of the gospel.* The disciples, like most Jews of their day, were probably expecting Messiah's kingdom immediately to appear. They thought the time was at hand when the wolf would lie down with the lamb, and men would not hurt or destroy any more (*Isa.* 11:9). Our Lord saw what was in their hearts, and checked their untimely expectations with a striking saying,—'Suppose ye that I am come to send peace on earth? I tell you, Nay; but rather division.'

There is something at first sight very startling in this saying. It seems hard to reconcile it with the song of angels, which spoke of 'peace on earth' as the companion of Christ's gospel (*Luke* 2:14). Yet startling as the saying sounds, it is one which facts have proved to be literally true. Peace is undoubtedly the result of the gospel wherever it is believed and received. But wherever there are hearers of the gospel who are hardened, impenitent, and determined to have their sins, the very message of peace becomes the cause of division. They that are after the flesh will hate those that are after the Spirit. They that are resolved to live for the world will always be evil affected towards those that are resolved to serve Christ. We may lament this state of things, but we cannot prevent it. Grace and nature can no more amalgamate than oil and water. So long as men are disagreed upon first principles in religion, there can be no real cordiality between them. So long as some men are converted and some are unconverted, there can be no true peace.

Let us beware of unscriptural expectations. If we expect to see people of one heart and one mind, before they are converted, we shall continually be disappointed. Thousands of well-meaning persons nowadays are continually crying out for more 'unity' among Christians. To attain this they are ready to sacrifice almost anything, and to throw overboard even sound doctrine, if, by so doing, they can secure peace. Such people would do well to remember that even gold may be bought too dear, and that peace is useless if purchased at the expense of truth. Surely they have forgotten the words of Christ, 'I came not to send peace, but division.'

Let us never be moved by those who charge the gospel with being the cause of strife and divisions upon earth. Such men only show their ignorance when they talk in this way. It is not the gospel which is to blame, but the corrupt heart of man. It is not God's glorious remedy which is in fault, but the diseased nature of Adam's race, which, like a self-willed child, refuses the medicine provided for its cure. So long as some men and women will not repent and believe, and some will, there must needs be division. To be surprised at it is the height of folly. The very existence of division is one proof of Christ's foresight, and of the truth of Christianity.

Let us thank God that a time is coming when there shall be no more divisions on earth, but all shall be of one mind. That time shall be when Jesus, the Prince of Peace, comes again in person, and puts down every enemy under his feet. When Satan is bound, when the wicked are separated from the righteous, and cast down to their own place, then, and not till then, will be perfect peace. For that blessed time let us wait, and watch, and pray. The night is far spent. The day is at hand. Our divisions are but for a little season. Our peace shall endure to eternity.

Notes—Luke 12:49-53

49.—[*I am come to send fire.*] Commentators differ widely about the meaning of the word 'fire' in this verse.

1. Some think that it means the Holy Spirit, and refers to the gift of the Holy Ghost which was bestowed on the day of Pentecost. This, in the main, is the opinion of Chrysostom, Origen, Jerome, Athanasius, Ambrose, Gregory, Bede, Bernard, Cocceius, Cornelius à Lapide, Alford, and Stier.

2. Some think that it means the 'preaching of the gospel.' This is the opinion of Theophylact, Cyril, Bucer, and Chemnitius.

3. Some think that it means the 'Word of God.' This is the opinion of Bullinger, Gualter, and Watson.

4. Some think that it means 'love.' This is the opinion of Jansenius, Stella, Bengel, and, in part, of Euthymius.

5. Some think that it means the persecutions, afflictions, dissensions, and strifes which were to accompany the introduction of the gospel into the world. This is the opinion of Tertullian, Brentius, Beza, Poole, Calovius, Trapp, Maldonatus, Hammond, Lightfoot, Whitby, Burkitt, Henry, Pearce, Scott, Barnes, and Burgon.

I decidedly adhere to this last opinion. The other four interpretations appear to me far-fetched and inconsistent with the context. Fire is an expression not infrequently used in Scripture as an emblem of trouble and affliction. See Psalm 66:12 and Isaiah 43:2. Moreover, it is worthy of remark, that 'to send fire' is a common figure of speech in the Old Testament, to express sending trouble and affliction. Let the following passages be examined: Lamentations 1:13; Ezekiel 39:6; Hosea 8:14; Amos 2:2, 5.

[*What will I, if it be already kindled?*] The Greek words so translated, are so remarkable, that some have thought they ought to be rendered, 'What will I? Oh! that it were already kindled.' This is the opinion of Cocceius and Hammond. But I see no reason for disputing the correctness of our received translation.

Trapp's paraphrase is a fair exposition of the meaning of the sentence: 'Let the fire kindle as soon as it will, I am contented. I know much good will come of it.'

Barnes paraphrases the sentence thus: 'What would I, but that it were kindled. Since it is necessary for the advancement of religion that such divisions should take place,—since the gospel cannot be established without conflicts, strifes, and hatreds, I am even desirous that they should come.'

Lightfoot says,—'"What will I," seems to be used after the manner of the schools, where "what do I say" is the same with "I do say this;" and "what do I decree," the same with, "I do decree this." So, "what will I" is the same with "this I will." The meaning is, "This I will, that it be already kindled."'

50.—[*A baptism.*] This baptism is plainly not that of water, nor that of the Holy Ghost, but the baptism of suffering. It is the same baptism of which our Lord said to James and John, 'Ye shall be baptized with the baptism that I am baptized with.'

The expression is one of those which shows the wisdom of our translators of the Bible in adhering to the word 'baptism,' and not rendering it either 'immersion,' or 'sprinkling.'

The effect of either of these words in the present verse, instead of 'baptism,' needs only to be tried. Few would like to substitute for our present translation, 'I have an immersion to be immersed with;' or, 'I have a sprinkling to be sprinkled with.'

[*How am I straitened.*] The Greek word so translated is the same that is rendered in Acts 18:5, 'pressed;' and in 2 Corinthians 5:14, 'constrains.' It is supposed by some that the feeling our Lord meant to express, was that of pain and distress in the prospect of his coming sufferings and crucifixion. This is the opinion of Stier. It seems, however, highly improbable.—It is supposed by others that the expression is like John 12:27 and Luke 22:42, and is meant to imply the conflict between our Lord's human will which naturally shrank from suffering, and his divine will which was set on accomplishing the work he came to do. This opinion is supported by many. Yet it does not seem quite to harmonize with the context, and is not altogether satisfactory.—The most probable view appears to be that which I have ventured to maintain in the exposition. The expression, 'I am straitened,' was intended to show us the burning desire by which our Lord was constrained to accomplish the work of our redemption. It is like the saying, 'With desire I have desired to eat the passover with you.' Theophylact and Euthymius both support this view.

51.—[*Nay; but rather division, etc.*] The words of Burkitt on this passage are worth reading, 'Our Saviour declares what will be the accidental event and effect, but not the natural tendency of his religion. We must distinguish between the intentional aim of Christ's coming and the accidental event of it. Christ's intentional aim was to plant, propagate, and promote peace in the world. But through the lust and corruption of man's nature, the issue and event of his coming is war and division; not that these are the genuine and natural fruits of the gospel, but occasional and accidental only.'

52.—[*Five in one house divided, etc.*] The expressions in this and the following verse must not be pressed too literally. In some houses there are not five persons. In others there are many more than five.—In some families, where the work of conversion begins, the father and son are entirely of one mind, and so also are the mother and daughter.—The expressions are manifestly proverbial. The plain lesson they are meant to convey is this, that the gospel will often produce divisions in families, and that even two persons who are most nearly related, may become estranged from one another, in consequence of one being converted and the other not. That this is constantly the case, is well known to all who know anything of true religion. Few believers can look round the circle of their relatives and acquaintances, and not see striking illustrations of the truth of our Lord's prophecy in this passage. Melancholy as it seems, it is a fact that nothing annoys some persons so much as the conversion of their relatives.

LUKE 12:54-59

54 And he said also to the people, When ye see a cloud rise out of the west, straightway ye say, There cometh a shower; and so it is.

55 And when *ye see* the south wind blow, ye say, There will be heat; and it cometh to pass.

56 *Ye* hypocrites, ye can discern the face of the sky and of the earth; but how is it that ye do not discern this time?

57 Yea, and why even of yourselves judge ye not what is right?

58 When thou goest with thine adversary to the magistrate, *as thou art* in the way, give diligence that thou mayest be delivered from him; lest he hale thee to the judge, and the judge deliver thee to the officer, and the officer cast thee into prison.

59 I tell thee, thou shalt not depart thence, till thou hast paid the very last mite.

THE first thing which this passage teaches us is *the duty of noticing the signs of the times.* The Jews in our Lord's days neglected this duty. They shut their eyes against events occurring in their own day of the most significant character. They refused to see that prophecies were being fulfilled around them which were bound up with the coming of Messiah, and that Messiah himself must be in the midst of them. The sceptre had departed from Judah, and the lawgiver from between his feet. The seventy weeks of Daniel were fulfilled (*Gen.* 49:10; *Dan.* 9:24). The ministry of John the Baptist had excited attention from one end of the land to the other. The miracles of Christ were great, undeniable, and notorious. But still the eyes of the Jews were blinded. They still obstinately refused to believe that Jesus was the Christ. And hence they drew from our Lord the question,—'How is that ye do not discern this time?'

It becomes the servants of God, in every age, to observe the public events of their own day, and to compare them with the predictions of unfulfilled prophecy. There is nothing commendable in an ignorant indifference to contemporary history. The true Christian should rather watch the career of governments and nations with a jealous watchfulness, and hail with gladness the slightest indication of the day of the Lord being at hand. The Christian who cannot see the hand of God in history, and does not believe in the gradual movement of all kingdoms towards the final subjection of all things to Christ, is as blind as the Jew.

Have we no signs of the times to observe? The question is soon answered. The history of the last seventy years is full of events which demand the prayerful attention of every servant of Christ. The things that have happened within these seventy years ought to send us to our watch towers, and raise in us great searchings of heart. The rise and progress of a missionary spirit among all Protestant churches,— the widespread interest felt about the Jews,—the evident decay of the Mahometan power,—the shaking of all the kingdoms of Europe by the French revolution,—the extraordinary spread of knowledge and education,—the marvellous revival of Romanism,—the steady growth of the most subtle forms of infidelity,—all these are facts which cannot be denied, and facts which ought to speak loudly to every well-informed Christian. Surely they deserve to be called signs of our times.

Let us remember the words of our Lord in the passage before us, and not err after the manner of the Jews. Let us not be blind, and deaf, and insensible to all that God is doing, both in the church and in the world. The things of which we have just been reminded are surely not without meaning. They have not come on the earth by chance or by accident, but by the appointment of God. We ought not to doubt that they are a call to watchfulness, and to preparation for the day of God. May we all have an ear to hear, and a heart to understand! May we not sleep as do many, but watch and discern our time! It is a solemn saying in the book of Revelation: 'If therefore thou shalt not watch, I will come on thee as a thief, and thou shalt not know what hour I will come upon thee' (*Rev.* 3:3).

The second thing which this passage teaches us, is *the immense importance of seeking reconciliation with God before it be too late.* This is a lesson which our Lord illustrates by a parable or comparison. He compares us to a man on his way to a magistrate with an adversary, in consequence of a difference or dispute, and describes the course which such a man ought to take.—Like him, we are upon our way to the presence of a Judge. We shall all stand at the bar of God.—Like him, we have an adversary. The holy law of God is against us, and contrary to us, and its demands must be satisfied.—Like him, we ought to give diligence to get our case settled, before it comes before the Judge. We ought to seek pardon and forgiveness before we die.— Like him, if we let our opportunity slip, the judgment will go against us, and we shall be cast into the prison of hell. Such appears to be the meaning of the parable in the passage before us. It is a vivid picture of the care which men ought to take in the great matter of reconciliation with God.

Peace with God is by far the first thing in religion. We are born in sin, and children of wrath. We have no natural love towards God. The carnal mind is enmity against God. It is impossible that God can take pleasure in us. 'The wicked his soul hateth' (*Psa.* 11:5). The chief and foremost desire of everyone who professes to have any religion, should be to obtain reconciliation. Till this is done, nothing is done. We have got nothing worth having in Christianity, until we have peace with God. The law brings us in guilty. The judgment is sure to go against us. Without reconciliation, the end of our life's journey will be hell.

Peace with God is the principal thing which the gospel of Christ offers to the soul. Peace and pardon stand in the forefront of its list of privileges, and are tendered freely to everyone that believes on Jesus. There is One who can deliver us from the adversary. Christ is the end of the law for righteousness to everyone that believeth. Christ hath redeemed us from the curse of the law, being made a curse for us. Christ has blotted out the handwriting that was against us, and has taken it out of the way, nailing it to his cross. Being justified by faith, we have peace with God, through our Lord Jesus Christ. There is no condemnation to them that are in Christ Jesus. The claims of our adversary are all satisfied by Christ's blood. God can now be just, and yet the justifier of everyone that believeth on Jesus. A full atonement has been made. The debt has been completely paid. The Judge can say, 'Deliver them, I have found a ransom' (*Job* 33:24).

Let us never rest till we know and feel that we are reconciled to God. Let it not content us to go to church, use means of grace, and be reckoned Christians, without knowing whether our sins are pardoned, and our souls justified. Let us seek to know that we are one with Christ, and Christ in us,—that our iniquities are forgiven, and our sins covered. Then, and then only, may we lie down in peace, and look forward to judgment without fear. The time is short. We are travelling on to a day when our lot for eternity must be decided. Let us give diligence that we may be found safe in that day. The souls that are found without Christ shall be cast into a hopeless prison.

Notes—Luke 12:54-59

54.—[*He said to the people.*] Let it be noted, that the concluding portion of the Lord's discourse in this chapter is specially addressed to 'the people,' and not to the disciples as the preceding verses were. It consists of a general rebuke of the blindness of the Jewish nation in not seeing the signs of the times, and the fulfilment of prophecy, and a general exhortation to seek reconciliation with God, before it be too late.

[*A cloud rise out of the west ... a shower.*] It should be remembered that the Mediterranean sea lies on the West of the whole Jewish territory. It was from this quarter that rain generally came. The 'little cloud' rising out of the sea, which Elijah's servant saw from Mount Carmel, and which brought rain, is an illustration of our Lord's words (1 Kings 18:44).

55.—[*The south wind blow ... heat.*] It should be remembered, that the great wilderness of Sinai and the hot deserts of Arabia, lie to the south of the Jewish territory. This accounts for winds from this quarter bringing heat (Jer. 4:11, 12).

56.—[*Ye hypocrites, ye can discern the face of the sky.*] Our Lord's argument appears to be that the signs of his advent as the true Messiah, were so clear and intelligible, that it required no more discernment to see them, than it did to foretell heat or rain from observation of the heavens and the winds. If the Jews would honestly and impartially consider the signs of their times, they could not avoid the conclusion

that Christ was the Messiah. The truth was that they were not honest in their inquiries, but prejudiced and unbelieving. He therefore calls them 'hypocrites.'

57.—[*Why even of yourselves judge ye not ... right?*] We must be careful not to interpret this verse so as to make it contradict other Scriptures. Our Lord does not mean to say that the Jews could understand spiritual things, and see the kingdom of God by their own unassisted judgment, and without the teaching of the Holy Ghost. His meaning is, 'why do ye not of yourselves, by simply observing what is going on around you, form a right judgment about my claim to be received as the Messiah, and a just decision upon the matters in dispute between me and your teachers, the scribes and Pharisees?'

The Greek word translated 'right,' is more commonly rendered 'just' or 'righteous.'

58.—[*When thou goest with thine adversary, etc.*] It is worthy of remark that the contents of this verse and the following, are found in the Sermon on the Mount, in an entirely different connection. It is evident that our Lord made use of the same illustration on two different occasions and with two entirely different applications. In the Sermon on the Mount, the words are used to enforce the great duty of forgiveness of injuries. In the passage before us, our Lord's object appears to be to enforce the solemn duty of seeking timely reconciliation with God. Life is the way. The law of God is the adversary. The magistrate represents the last judgment. The prison represents hell. This certainly appears to me the only satisfactory exposition of the passage. The other view, that it is only a repetition of the lesson in Matthew 5:25, is liable to this grave objection, that it makes our Lord conclude a solemn discourse by a most abrupt introduction of a subject which has no connection with the context. On the other hand, to enforce on the multitude around him, the great duty of seeking reconciliation with God before it was too late, appears a natural termination of the whole address.

Stier remarks, 'The mere reference to placability towards a brother with whom I may have matter of litigation, would not be a distinctive conclusion of this discourse (although it was occasioned by the contention of brothers about an inheritance), and would be an inexplicable subsidence of the strain into a matter quite foreign to verses 55-57.'

59.—[*Not depart thence, till thou hast paid.*] The meaning of this expression is, 'Thou shalt never depart at all.' Poole remarks, 'It is a sign the Papists are at a woeful loss for arguments to prove purgatory, when they make use of this text, as if it spake of a prison for souls, from which there is an outlet.' Such an argument would prove many absurdities, if applied to other texts where the expression 'until' is used. See Psalm 72:7 and 110:1; and Matthew 1:25.

Theophylact remarks, 'If we shall remain in prison until we pay the uttermost farthing, and are never able to pay it, it is manifest that future punishment is eternal.'

Euthymius says, 'This means, Thou shalt never come out from prison at all.'

Stella, the Spanish commentator, says, 'The wicked shall be placed in hell until they pay their debt to the uttermost farthing; and as they never will pay it, it is certain that they will be there to all eternity.'

LUKE 13:1-5

1 There were present at that season some that told him of the Galilæans, whose blood Pilate had mingled with their sacrifices.

2 And Jesus answering said unto them, Suppose ye that these Galilæans were sinners above all the Galilæans, because they suffered such things?

3 I tell you, Nay: but, except ye repent, ye shall all likewise perish.

4 Or those eighteen, upon whom the tower in Siloam fell, and slew them, think ye that they were sinners above all men that dwelt in Jerusalem?

5 I tell you, Nay: but except ye repent, ye shall all likewise perish.

T HE murder of the Galileans, mentioned in the first verse of this passage, is an event of which we know nothing certain. The motives of those who told our Lord of the event, we are left to conjecture. At any rate, they gave him an opportunity of speaking to them about their own souls, which he did not fail to employ. He seized the event, as his manner was, and made a practical use of it. He bade his informants look within, and think of their own state before God. He seems to say, 'What though these Galileans did die a sudden death? What is that to you? Consider your own ways. Except ye repent ye shall all likewise perish.'

Let us observe, for one thing, in these verses, *how much more ready people are to talk of the deaths of others than their own.* The death of the Galileans, mentioned here, was probably a common subject of conversation in Jerusalem and all Judæa. We can well believe that all the circumstances and particulars belonging to it were continually discussed by thousands who never thought of their own latter end. It is just the same in the present day. A murder,—a sudden death,—a shipwreck, or a railway accident, will completely occupy the minds of a neighbourhood, and be in the mouth of everyone you meet. And yet these very persons dislike talking of their own deaths, and their own prospects in the world beyond the grave. Such is human nature in every age. In religion, men are ready to talk of anybody's business rather than their own.

The state of our own souls should always be our first concern. It is eminently true that real Christianity will always begin at home. The converted man will always think first of his own heart, his own life, his own deserts, and his own sins. Does he hear of a sudden death? He will say to himself, 'Should I have been found ready, if this had happened to me?'—Does he hear of some awful crime, or deed of wickedness? He will say to himself, 'Are *my* sins forgiven? and have I really repented of my own transgressions?'—Does he hear of worldly men running into every excess of sin? He will say to himself, 'Who has made *me* to differ? What has kept me from walking in the same road, except the free grace of God?' May we ever seek to be men of this frame of mind! Let us take a kind interest in all around us. Let us feel tender pity and compassion for all who suffer violence, or are removed by sudden death. But let us never forget to look at home, and to learn wisdom for ourselves from all that happens to others.

Let us observe, for another thing, in these verses, *how strongly our Lord lays down the universal necessity of repentance.* Twice he declares emphatically, 'Except ye repent, ye shall all likewise perish.'

The truth here asserted, is one of the foundations of Christianity. 'All have sinned and come short of the glory of God.' All of us are born in sin. We are fond of sin, and are naturally unfit for friendship with God. Two things are absolutely necessary to the salvation of every one of us. We must repent, and we must believe the gospel. Without repentance towards God, and faith towards our Lord Jesus Christ, no man can be saved.

The nature of true repentance is clearly and unmistakably laid down in Holy Scripture. It begins with knowledge of sin. It goes on to work sorrow for sin. It leads to confession of sin before God. It shows itself before man by a thorough breaking off from sin. It results in producing a habit of deep hatred for all sin. Above all, it is inseparably connected with lively faith in the Lord Jesus Christ. Repentance like this is the characteristic of all true Christians.

The necessity of repentance to salvation will be evident to all who search the Scriptures, and consider the nature of the subject.— Without it there is no forgiveness of sins. There never was a pardoned man who was not also a penitent. There never was one washed in the blood of Christ who did not feel, and mourn, and confess, and hate his own sins.—Without it there can be no meetness for heaven. We could not be happy if we reached the kingdom of glory with a heart loving sin. The company of saints and angels would give us no pleasure. Our minds would not be in tune for an eternity of holiness. Let these things sink down into our hearts. We must repent as well as believe, if we hope to be saved.

Let us leave the subject with the solemn inquiry,—Have we ourselves repented? We live in a Christian land. We belong to a Christian church. We have Christian ordinances and means of grace. We have heard of repentance with the hearing of the ear, and that hundreds of times. But have we ever repented? Do we really know our own sinfulness? Do our sins cause us any sorrow? Have we cried to God about our sins, and sought forgiveness at the throne of grace? Have we ceased to do evil, and broken off from our bad habits? Do we cordially and heartily hate everything that is evil? These are serious questions. They deserve serious consideration. The subject before us is no light matter. Nothing less than life—eternal life—is at stake! If we die impenitent, and without a new heart, we had better never have been born.

If we never yet repented, let us begin without delay. For this we are accountable. 'Repent ye, and be converted,' were the words of Peter to the Jews who had crucified our Lord (*Acts* 3:19). 'Repent and pray,' was the charge addressed to Simon Magus when he was in the 'gall of bitterness and bond of iniquity' (*Acts* 8:22). There is everything to encourage us to begin. Christ invites us. Promises of Scripture are held out to us. Glorious declarations of God's willingness to receive us abound throughout the Word. 'There is joy in heaven over one sinner that repenteth.' Then let us arise and call upon God. Let us repent without delay.

If we have already repented in time past, let us go on repenting to the end of our lives. There will always be sins to confess and infirmities to deplore, so long as we are in the body. Let us repent more deeply, and humble ourselves more thoroughly, every year. Let every returning birthday find us hating sin more, and loving Christ more. He was a wise old saint who said, 'I hope to carry my repentance to the very gate of heaven.'

Notes—Luke 13:1-5

1.—[*The Galilæans, whose blood, etc.*] We know nothing about the event here mentioned. Josephus speaks of the slaughter of certain Samaritans by Pilate upon Mount Gerizim. But they seem to have been rebels and fanatics, and to have died in battle. It is far more probable that the case reported to our Lord was that of certain Galileans who had come up to Jerusalem to worship, and were slain by Pilate's soldiers in some popular tumult.

2.—[*Suppose ye ... sinners above all etc.*] It is evident that our Lord's informants were filled with the vulgar opinion that sudden deaths were special judgments, and that if a man died suddenly, he must have committed some special sin. Our Lord bids them understand that this opinion was a mere baseless delusion. We have no right whatever to conclude that God is angry with a man because he removes him suddenly from the world.

Ford gives a quotation from Perkins which deserves reading, 'The common opinion is, that if a man die quietly, and go away like a lamb (which in some diseases, as consumption, any man may do), then he goes straight to heaven. But if the violence of the disease stirs up impatience, and causes frantic behaviour, then men use to say, "There is a judgment of God, serving either to discover a hypocrite or to plague a wicked man." But the truth is otherwise.—A man may die like a lamb, and yet go to hell; and one dying in exceeding torment and strange behaviour of body, may go to heaven.'—(Perkins' *Salve for a Sick Man.*)

3.—[*Ye shall all likewise perish.*] It is highly probable that these words were spoken with a prophetic meaning, and that our Lord had in view the tremendous slaughter of the Jews by the Roman army under Titus, which was to take place in a few years at the siege of Jerusalem.

4.—[*Those eighteen … tower in Siloam.*] We know nothing about the circumstance which our Lord here mentions. It is probable it was something which had lately happened, and was the common subject of conversation among dwellers in Jerusalem, just as any great accident is among ourselves at the present day.

The word translated 'sinners' in this verse, means literally, 'debtors.'

5.—[*Except ye repent, etc.*] The repetition of this sentence shows the general importance of repentance, and the great need in which the Jews in particular stood of it. Ford quotes a saying of Philip Henry's, which is worth reading: 'Some people do not like to hear much of repentance. But I think it so necessary, that if I should die in the pulpit, I should desire to die preaching repentance, and if I should die out of the pulpit, I should desire to die practising it.'

LUKE 13:6-9

6 He spake also this parable; A certain *man* had a fig-tree planted in his vineyard; and he came and sought fruit thereon, and found none.

7 Then said he unto the dresser of his vineyard, Behold, these three years I come seeking fruit on this fig-tree, and find none: cut it down; why cumbereth it the ground?

8 And he answering said unto him, Lord, let it alone this year also, till I shall dig about it, and dung *it*:

9 And if it bear fruit, *well*: and if not, *then* after that thou shalt cut it down.

THE parable we have now read is peculiarly humbling and heart-searching. The Christian who can hear it, and not feel sorrow and shame as he looks at the state of Christendom, must be in a very unhealthy state of soul.

We learn, first, from this passage, that *where God gives spiritual privileges he expects proportionate returns.*

Our Lord teaches this lesson by comparing the Jewish church of his day to a 'fig-tree planted in a vineyard.' This was exactly the position of Israel in the world. They were separated from other nations by the Mosaic laws and ordinances, no less than by the situation of their land. They were favoured with revelations of God, which were granted to no other people. Things were done for them which were never done for Egypt, or Nineveh, or Babylon, or Greece, or Rome. It was only just and right that they should bear fruit to God's praise. It might reasonably be expected that there would be more faith, and penitence, and holiness, and godliness in Israel than among the heathen. This is what God looked for. The owner of the fig-tree 'came seeking fruit.'

But we must look beyond the Jewish church if we mean to get the full benefit of the parable before us.—We must look to the Christian churches. They have light, and truth, and doctrines, and precepts, of which the heathen never hear. How great is their responsibility! Is it not just and right that God should expect from them 'fruit?'— We must look to our own hearts. We live in a land of Bibles, and liberty, and gospel preaching. How vast are the advantages we enjoy compared to the Chinese and Hindoo! Never let us forget that God expects from us 'fruit.'

These are solemn truths. Few things are so much forgotten by men as the close connection between privilege and responsibility. We are all ready enough to eat the fat and drink the sweet, and bask in the sunshine of our position both as Christians and Englishmen,—and even to spare a few pitying thoughts for the half-naked savage who bows down to stocks and stones. But we are very slow to remember that we are accountable to God for all we enjoy; and that to whomsoever much is given, of them much will be required. Let us awake to a sense of these things. We are the most favoured nation upon earth. We are in the truest sense 'a fig-tree planted in a vineyard.' Let us not forget that the great Master looks for 'fruit.'

We learn, secondly, from this passage, that *it is a most dangerous thing to be unfruitful under great religious privileges.*

The manner in which our Lord conveys this lesson to us is deeply impressive. He shows us the owner of the barren fig-tree complaining that it bore no fruit: 'These three years I come seeking fruit and find none.'—He describes him as even ordering the destruction of the tree as a useless cumberer of the ground: 'Cut it down; why cumbereth it the ground?' He brings in the dresser of the vineyard pleading for the fig-tree, that it may be spared a little longer: 'Lord, let it alone this year also.' And he concludes the parable by putting these awful words into the vinedresser's mouth: 'If it bear fruit, well: and if not, then after that thou shalt cut it down.'

There is a plain warning here to all professing churches of Christ. If their ministers do not teach sound doctrine, and their members do not live holy lives, they are in imminent peril of destruction. God is every year observing them, and taking account of all their ways. They may abound in ceremonial religion. They may be covered with the leaves of forms, and services, and ordinances. But if they are destitute of the fruits of the Spirit, they are reckoned useless cumberers of the ground. Except they repent, they will be cut down. It was so with the Jewish church forty years after our Lord's ascension. It has been so since with the African churches. It will be so yet with many others, it may be feared, before the end comes. The axe is lying near the root of many an unfruitful church. The sentence will yet go forth, 'Cut it down.'

There is a plainer warning still in the passage for all unconverted Christians. There are many in every congregation who hear the gospel, who are literally hanging over the brink of the pit. They have lived for years in the best part of God's vineyard, and yet borne no fruit. They have heard the gospel preached faithfully for hundreds of Sundays, and yet have never embraced it, and taken up the cross, and followed Christ. They do not perhaps run into open sin. But they do nothing for God's glory. There is nothing positive about their religion. Of each of these the Lord of the vineyard might say with truth, 'I come these many years seeking fruit on this tree and find none. Cut it down. It cumbereth the ground.' There are myriads of respectable professing Christians in this plight. They have not the least idea how near they are to destruction. Never let us forget that to be content with sitting in the congregation and hearing sermons, while we bear no fruit in our lives, is conduct which is most offensive to God. It provokes him to cut us off suddenly, and that without remedy.

We learn, lastly, from this parable, *what an infinite debt we all owe to God's mercy and Christ's intercession.* It seems impossible to draw any other lesson from the earnest pleading of the dresser of the vineyard: 'Lord, let it alone this year also.' Surely we see here, as in a glass, the lovingkindness of God, and the mediation of Christ.

Mercy has been truly called the darling attribute of God. Power, justice, purity, holiness, wisdom, unchangeableness, are all parts of God's character, and have all been manifested to the world in a thousand ways, both in his works and in his Word. But if there is one part of his perfections which he is pleased to exhibit to man more clearly than another, beyond doubt that part is mercy. He is a God that 'delighteth in mercy' (*Mic.* 7:18).

Mercy founded on the mediation of a coming Saviour, was the cause why Adam and Eve were not cast down to hell, in the day that they fell. Mercy has been the cause why God has borne so long with this sin-laden world, and not come down to judgment. Mercy is even now the cause why unconverted sinners are so long spared, and not cut off in their sins. We have probably not the least conception how much we all owe to God's long-suffering. The last day will prove that all mankind were debtors to God's mercy, and Christ's mediation. Even those who are finally lost will discover to their shame, that it was 'of the Lord's mercies they were not consumed' long before they died. As for those who are saved, covenant-mercy will be all their plea.

And now are we fruitful or unfruitful? This, after all, is the question that concerns us most. What does God see in us year after year? Let us take heed so to live that he may see in us fruit.

Notes—Luke 13:6-9

6.—[*A certain man had a fig-tree, etc.*] There can be no doubt that our Lord's primary object in this parable was to show the danger of the Jewish church and nation, at the time when he spoke. It is worthy of remark, that 'the barren fig-tree' to which our Lord said, 'No man eat fruit of thee hereafter for ever' (*Mark* 11:14), was meant to be an emblem of the Jewish church. But the primary application of this parable must not shut out the secondary one. It was meant for individuals, as well as for the Jewish church.

7.—[*These three years.*] The meaning of these 'three years,' has called forth much ingenious conjecture from commentators. Gregory thinks that the three years signify the times of Israel before the law, in the law, and after the law. Ambrose thinks that they signify the times of natural law, of written law, and of evangelical law.—Theophylact applies them to the times of children, of youth, and of old age.—Stella explains them to mean the times before the Babylonian captivity, the times after the return from Babylon, and the times of our Lord's own first advent. Others apply them to the three years of our Lord's earthly ministry.—If any of these senses is true, the last appears most likely. It may, however, be seriously questioned, whether our Lord had any of these meanings in his mind, when he spoke this parable, and whether we ought not to regard the 'three years' as simply an accessory circumstance of the story, the interpretation of which must not be carried too far.

[*Cumbereth.*] The Greek word so translated is only rendered thus in this passage. It is generally translated, 'make void,'—'make of none effect,'—'destroy,'—'bring to nothing,'—'abolish.'

The expression is probably intended to teach the deep lesson, that unfruitful members of God's church are not merely injuring themselves and perilling their own souls. They are an injury to the church generally, and do public harm. The common idea that an unconverted person 'does no harm,'—is 'no man's enemy but his own,'—and the like, is a miserable man-made delusion, based on no warrant of Scripture. To be unfruitful is to be a cumberer of the ground. We are always doing either good or harm.

8.—[*Lord, let it alone, etc.*] Who is meant by the dresser of the vineyard, who thus intercedes, is a question on which wide and strange differences of opinion prevail. Augustine says that it signifies 'every saint,' because all intercede.—Ambrose and Stella say that it signifies the 'apostles.' Jerome says that it signifies 'Michael and Gabriel,' the archangels, who had the special charge of the Jewish synagogue.—Alford thinks that it signifies the Holy Spirit.—All these interpretations appear to me incorrect. The most probable view is that of Euthymius and Theophylact, who consider the interceding vineyard dresser to be an emblem of Christ himself. Matthew Henry says truly, 'that had it not been for Christ's intercession, the whole world had been cut down.'

[*Dig about it and dung it.*] This part of the parable signifies the extraordinary means which were used with the Jewish church at the latter period of its existence, in order to awaken it to repentance.

9.—[*After that thou shalt cut it down.*] It is very probable that all unconverted members of Christ's church will be found at the last day to have had their special 'time of visitation,' and to have been 'digged about' by special providences, at some period of their lives. Hence their final condemnation will be proved most just.

The final cutting down of the tree of the Jewish church, was, undoubtedly, most justly brought on the Jews by their obstinate neglect of all the messages which God sent them in the fifty years immediately preceding the destruction of Jerusalem by the ministry of John the Baptist, of our Lord Jesus Christ, and of the apostles. If ever there was a fig-tree which was long spared, and patiently digged about, and had every means used to make it fruitful, that tree was the Jewish church.

LUKE 13:10-17

10 And he was teaching in one of the synagogues on the sabbath.

11 And, behold, there was a woman which had a spirit of infirmity eighteen years, and was bowed together, and could in no wise lift up *herself*.

12 And when Jesus saw her, he called *her to him*, and said unto her, Woman, thou art loosed from thine infirmity.

13 And he laid *his* hands on her: and immediately she was made straight, and glorified God.

14 And the ruler of the synagogue answered with indignation, because that Jesus had healed on the sabbath day, and said unto the people, There are six days in which men ought to work: in them therefore come and be healed, and not on the sabbath day.

15 The Lord then answered him, and said, *Thou* hypocrite, doth not each one of you on the sabbath loose his ox or *his* ass from the stall, and lead *him* away to watering?

16 And ought not this woman, being a daughter of Abraham, whom Satan hath bound, lo, these eighteen years, be loosed from this bond on the sabbath day?

17 And when he had said these things, all his adversaries were ashamed: and all the people rejoiced for all the glorious things that were done by him.

WE see in these verses *a striking example of diligence in the use of means of grace*. We are told of a 'woman which had a spirit of infirmity eighteen years, and was bowed together, and could in no wise lift up herself.' We know not who this woman was. Our Lord's saying that she was 'a daughter of Abraham,' would lead us to infer that she was a true believer. But her name and history are hidden from us. This only we know, that when Jesus was 'teaching in one of the synagogues on the sabbath,' this woman was there. Sickness was no excuse with her for tarrying from God's house. In spite of suffering and infirmity, she found her way to the place where the day and the Word of God were honoured, and where the people of God met together. And truly she was blessed in her deed! She found a rich reward for all her pains. She came sorrowing, and went home rejoicing.

The conduct of this suffering Jewess may well put to shame many a strong and healthy professing Christian. How many in the full enjoyment of bodily vigour, allow the most frivolous excuses to keep them away from the house of God! How many are constantly spending the whole Sunday in idleness, pleasure-seeking, or business, and scoffing and sneering at those who 'keep the sabbath holy!' How many think it a great matter if they attend the public worship of God once on Sunday, and regard a second attendance as a needless excess of zeal akin to fanaticism! How many find religious services a weariness while they attend them, and feel relieved when they are over! How few know anything of David's spirit, when he said, 'I was glad when they said unto me, Let us go into the house of the Lord.'—'How amiable are thy tabernacles, O Lord of hosts!' (*Psa.* 122:1; *Psa.* 84:1).

Now what is the explanation of all this? What is the reason why so few are like the woman of whom we read this day? The answer to these questions is short and simple. The most have no heart for God's service. They have no delight in God's presence or God's day. 'The carnal mind is enmity against God.' The moment a man's heart is converted, these pretended difficulties about attending public worship vanish away. The new heart finds no trouble in keeping the sabbath holy. Where there is a will there is always a way.

Let us never forget that our feelings about Sundays are sure tests of the state of our souls. The man who can find no pleasure in giving God one day in the week, is manifestly unfit for heaven. Heaven itself is nothing but an eternal sabbath. If we cannot enjoy a few hours in God's service once a week in this world, it is plain that we could not enjoy an eternity in his service in the world to come. Happy are they who walk in the steps of her of whom we read today! They shall find Christ and a blessing while they live, and Christ and glory when they die.

We see, secondly, in these verses, *the almighty power of our Lord Jesus Christ.* We are told that when he saw the suffering woman of whom we are reading, 'he called her to him, and said unto her, Woman, thou are loosed from thine infirmity. And he laid his hands on her.' That touch was accompanied by miraculous healing virtue. At once a disease of eighteen years' standing gave way before the Lord of Life. 'Immediately she was made straight, and glorified God.'

We need not doubt that this mighty miracle was intended to supply hope and comfort to sin-diseased souls. With Christ nothing is impossible. He can soften hearts which seem hard as the nether millstone. He can bend stubborn wills which 'for eighteen years' have been set on self-pleasing, on sin, and the world. He can enable sinners who have been long poring over earthly things, to look upward to heaven, and see the kingdom of God. Nothing is too hard for the Lord. He can create, and transform, and renew, and break down, and build, and quicken, with irresistible power. He lives who formed the world out of nothing, and he never changes.

Let us hold fast this blessed truth, and never let it go. Let us never despair about our own salvation. Our sins may be countless. Our lives may have been long spent in worldliness and folly. Our youth may have been wasted in soul-defiling excesses, of which we are sorely ashamed. But are we willing to come to Christ, and commit our souls to him? If so, there is hope. He can heal us thoroughly, and say 'thou art loosed from thine infirmity.'—Let us never despair about the salvation of others so long as they are alive. Let us name them before the Lord night and day, and cry to him on their behalf. We may perhaps have relatives whose case seems desperate because of their wickedness. But it is not really so. There are no incurable cases with Christ. If he were to lay his healing hand on them, they would be 'made straight, and glorify God.' Let us pray on, and faint not. That saying of Job is worthy of all acceptation: 'I know that thou canst do everything' (*Job* 42:2). Jesus is 'able to save to the uttermost.'

We see, lastly, in these verses, *the right observance of the sabbath day asserted and defended by our Lord Jesus Christ.* The ruler of the synagogue in which the infirm woman was healed, found fault with her as a breaker of the sabbath. He drew down upon himself a stern but just rebuke: 'Thou hypocrite, doth not each one of you on the sabbath loose his ox or his ass from the stall, and lead him away to watering?' If it was allowable to attend to the wants of beasts on the sabbath, how much more to human creatures! If it was no breach of the fourth commandment to show kindness to oxen and asses, much less to show kindness to a daughter of Abraham.

The principle here laid down by our Lord is the same that we find elsewhere in the Gospels. He teaches us that the command to 'do no work' on the sabbath, was not intended to prohibit works of necessity and mercy. The sabbath was made for man's benefit, and not for his hurt. It was appointed to promote man's best and highest interests, and not to debar him of anything that is really for his good. It requires nothing but what is reasonable and wise. It forbids nothing that is really necessary to man's comfort.

Let us pray for a right understanding of the law of the sabbath. Of all the commandments that God has given, none is more essential to the happiness of man, and none is so frequently misrepresented, abused, and trampled under foot. Let us lay down for ourselves two special rules for the observance of the sabbath. For one thing let us do no work which is not absolutely needful. For another let us keep the day 'holy,' and give it to God. From these two rules let us never swerve. Experience shows that there is the closest connection between sabbath sanctification and healthy Christianity.

Notes—Luke 13:10-17

11.—[*Which had a spirit of infirmity.*] The nature of this woman's disease we are left to conjecture. It seems to have been some ailment mysteriously connected with possession by an unclean spirit, and caused by it. There is no other case precisely like it in the New Testament.

12.—[*He called her to him.*] Let it be noted, that this miracle was one of those which our Lord worked unsolicited and unasked. The widow at Nain is another instance. In both cases the person to whom kindness was shown, was a woman.

There are some beautiful remarks in Stella's commentary on this passage. He observes that it is a striking instance of our Lord's love and compassion towards sinners. If he does so much for a person, when unsolicited, how much more will he do for those who call upon him in prayer.

14.—[*There are six days, etc.*] The bitterness and sarcasm of this unhappy speech, are very remarkable. The very sight of a miracle, which ought to have convinced the ruler of the synagogue that Jesus was the Messiah, seems to have called forth all the corruption of his heart. The same thing may often be remarked in some unconverted men. The nearer the kingdom of God comes to them, the more bitter and angry they are.

[*Men ought to work.*] Let it be noted, that the Greek expression so translated, would be more literally rendered, 'it is fit, or becoming to work.' The word 'men' is not in the Greek.

Stella observes that there was a striking similarity between the character of this ruler of the synagogue, and that of many of the prelates and judges of his own day. They often pretended great zeal for the cause of religion, and persecuted anyone who gave them offence. Yet this zeal in reality was only in behalf of their own dignity and office, and not for the glory of God.

16.—[*A daughter of Abraham.*] This expression certainly appears to me to make it highly probable, that this woman whom our Lord healed, was a true believer. When Zacchæus was converted our Lord said, 'He also is a son of Abraham' (*Luke* 19:9). To regard the expression as only meaning a 'daughter of Abraham according to natural descent, a Jewess,' seems to me a tame and unsatisfactory interpretation.

[*Whom Satan hath bound.*] This expression is remarkable. It would seem to imply that Satan has a permissive power to inflict bodily disease and infirmity. It should be compared with the two first chapters of Job, and with St Paul's expression, 'to deliver such an one unto Satan for the destruction of the flesh' (*1 Cor.* 5:5).

LUKE 13:18-21

18 Then said he, Unto what is the kingdom of God like? and whereunto shall I resemble it?

19 It is like a grain of mustard seed, which a man took, and cast into his garden; and it grew, and waxed a great tree; and the fowls of the air lodged in the branches of it.

20 And again he said, Whereunto shall I liken the kingdom of God?

21 It is like leaven, which a woman took and hid in three measures of meal, till the whole was leavened.

THERE is a peculiar interest belonging to the two parables contained in these verses. We find them twice delivered by our Lord, and at two distinct periods in his ministry. This fact alone should make us give the more earnest heed to the lessons which the parables convey. They will be found rich both in prophetical and experimental truths.

The parable of the mustard seed is intended to show *the progress of the gospel in the world.*

The beginnings of the gospel were exceedingly small. It was like 'the grain of seed cast into the garden.' It was a religion which seemed at first so feeble, and helpless, and powerless, that it could not live. Its first founder was One who was poor in this world, and ended his life by dying the death of a malefactor on the cross.—Its first adherents were a little company, whose number probably did not exceed a thousand when the Lord Jesus left the world.—Its first preachers were a few fishermen and publicans, who were, most of them, unlearned and ignorant men.—Its first starting point was a despised corner of the earth, called Judæa, a petty tributary province of the vast empire of Rome.—Its first doctrine was eminently calculated to call forth the enmity of the natural heart. Christ crucified was to the Jews a stumbling-block, and to the Greeks foolishness.—Its first movements brought down on its friends persecution from all quarters. Pharisees and Sadducees, Jews and Gentiles, ignorant idolaters and self-conceited philosophers, all agreed in hating and opposing Christianity. It was a sect everywhere spoken against.—These are no empty assertions. They are simple historical facts, which no one can deny. If ever there was religion which was a little grain of seed at its beginning, that religion was the gospel.

But the progress of the gospel, after the seed was once cast into the earth, was great, steady, and continuous. The grain of mustard seed 'grew, and waxed a great tree.' In spite of persecution, opposition, and violence, Christianity gradually spread and increased. Year after year its adherents became more numerous. Year after year idolatry withered away before it. City after city, and country after country, received the new faith. Church after church was formed in almost every quarter of the earth then known. Preacher after preacher rose up, and missionary after missionary came forward to fill the place of those who died. Roman emperors and heathen philosophers, sometimes by force and sometimes by argument, tried in vain to check the progress of Christianity. They might as well have tried to stop the tide from flowing, or the sun from rising. In a few hundred years, the religion of the despised Nazarene,—the religion which began in the upper chamber at Jerusalem,—had overrun the civilized world. It was professed by nearly all Europe, by a great part of Asia, and by the whole northern part of Africa. The prophetic words of the parable before us were literally fulfilled. The grain of mustard seed 'waxed a great tree; and the fowls of the air lodged in the branches of it.' The Lord Jesus said it would be so. And so it came to pass.

Let us learn from this parable never to despair of any work for Christ, because its first beginnings are feeble and small. A single minister in some large neglected town-district,—a single missionary amidst myriads of savage heathen,—a single reformer in the midst of a fallen and corrupt church,—each and all of these may seem at first sight utterly unlikely to do any good. To the eye of man, the work may appear too great, and the instrument employed quite unequal to it. Let us never give way to such thoughts. Let us remember the parable before us, and take courage. When the line of duty is plain, we should not begin to count numbers, and confer with flesh and blood. We should believe that one man with the living seed of God's truth on his side, like Luther or Knox, may turn a nation upside down. If God is with him, none shall stand against him. In spite of men and devils, the seed that he sows shall wax a great tree.

The parable of the leaven is intended to show *the progress of the gospel in the heart of a believer.*

The first beginnings of the work of grace in a sinner are generally exceedingly small. It is like the mixture of leaven with a lump of dough. A single sentence of a sermon, or a single verse of Holy Scripture,—a word of rebuke from a friend, or a casual religious remark overheard,—a tract given by a stranger, or a trifling act of kindness received from a Christian,—some one of these things is often the starting point in the life of a soul.—The first actings of the spiritual life are often small in the extreme,—so small, that for a long time they are not known except by him who is the subject of them, and even by him not fully understood. A few serious thoughts and prickings of conscience,—a desire to pray really and not formally,— a determination to begin reading the Bible in private,—a gradual drawing towards means of grace,—an increasing interest in the subject of religion,—a growing distaste for evil habits and bad companions,—these, or some of them, are often the first symptoms of grace beginning to move the heart of man. They are symptoms which worldly men may not perceive, and ignorant believers may despise, and even old Christians may mistake. Yet they are often the first steps in the mighty business of conversion. They are often the 'leaven' of grace working in a heart.

The work of grace once begun in the soul will never stand still. It will gradually 'leaven the whole lump.' Like leaven once introduced, it can never be separated from that with which it is mingled. Little by little it will influence the conscience, the affections, the mind, and the will, until the whole man is affected by its power, and a thorough conversion to God takes place. In some cases no doubt the progress is far quicker than in others. In some cases the result is far more clearly marked and decided than in others. But wherever a real work of the Holy Ghost begins in the heart, the whole character is sooner or later leavened and changed. The tastes of the man are altered. The whole bias of his mind becomes different. 'Old things pass away, and all things become new' (2 Cor. 5:17). The Lord Jesus said that it would be so, and all experience shows that so it is.

Let us learn from this parable never to 'despise the day of small things' in religion (Zech. 4:10). The soul must creep before it can walk, and walk before it can run. If we see any symptom of grace beginning in a brother, however feeble, let us thank God, and be hopeful. The leaven of grace once planted in his heart, shall yet leaven the whole lump. 'He that begins the work will perform it unto the day of Jesus Christ' (Phil. 1:6).

Let us ask ourselves whether there is any work of grace in our own hearts. Are we resting satisfied with a few vague wishes and convictions? Or do we know anything of a gradual, growing, spreading, increasing, leavening process going on in our inward man? Let nothing short of this content us. The true work of the Holy Ghost will never stand still. It will leaven the whole lump.

Notes—Luke 13:18-21

19.—[*Like a grain of mustard seed.*] Some think that the grain of seed here means Christ himself, who died, and was buried in a garden, and allege in favour of this view, the text, 'Except a corn of wheat fall into the ground and die, it abideth alone: but if it die, it bringeth forth much fruit' (*John* 12:24).

I am unable to see this sense in the parable. The words are distinct and plain. It is the 'kingdom of God,' which is like the seed.

[*Waxed a great tree.*] The growth of the grain of mustard seed into a tree of comparatively great size, ought not to be wondered at, when we remember the rapidity of vegetation in a hot climate. Parkhurst's Lexicon, on the Greek word translated 'mustard-seed,' mentions several facts which prove the correctness of our Lord's language.

[*Fowls of the air lodged, etc.*] It is thought by many that this expression was meant to denote the corruption which crept into the church of Christ, when it grew into a large body, and was favoured by the powers of this world. The idea may possibly be true, though it seems to me more likely that the circumstance is only mentioned in order to show the size of the tree.

It may be well to remark that there is nothing in this parable to justify the idea that the visible church shall gradually increase, till the whole world is converted. It is not said that the mustard tree would bear good fruit, and be never cut down. The lesson taught, is simply this, that, from a small beginning, the visible church of Christ shall become very large.

21.—[*It is like leaven.*] It is thought by many, that 'leaven,' in this parable, was intended by our Lord to mean, an evil and corrupt principle, and that the object of the parable was to describe the silent entrance and rapid growth of corruption and false doctrine in the church of Christ. In defence of this view it is alleged, that the word 'leaven' is always used as an emblem of something evil. The doctrine of the Pharisees and Sadducees, for example, is called 'leaven.'

I am quite unable to see the correctness of this view.

For one thing, it seems to me very improbable that our Lord would speak two parables in a breath, both beginning with the expression, 'the kingdom of God,' and compare this kingdom, in one case, with that which is healthy and prosperous, and in the other case, with that which is poisonous and corrupting. To my eyes his object in both parables seems one and the same. Had he meant 'evil' when he spoke of leaven, he would surely have said, 'whereunto shall I liken the kingdom of the evil one.'

For another thing, I can see no force in the objection that 'leaven' is generally used as an emblem of that which is evil, and therefore must be so used here. I do not see why the word is to be rigorously tied down to be only an emblem of evil; and why it may not be in this case an emblem of good.

The goat in the twenty-fifth of Matthew is an emblem of the wicked: yet the goat in the Old Testament is a clean animal, and appointed to be used in some sacrifices, as well as the sheep. The serpent is generally regarded as an emblem of evil. Our Lord calls the Pharisees 'serpents.' And yet in another place, he says to the disciples, 'Be wise as serpents.' In short I believe that the same word may be used in one place as a figure of that which is good, and in another as a figure of that which is evil. In some places leaven certainly means 'false doctrine.' In the passage before us, I believe it means 'grace.'

Stella supports the view which I have maintained by quotations from Augustine and Gregory.

[*A woman ... three measures of meal.*] There are some who see allegorical meanings in the 'woman,' the number 'three,' and the 'meal.' I will only record my own conviction, that these meanings were not in our Lord's mind when the parable was spoken. One great truth was intended to be conveyed. That truth was the small beginning of grace in a heart, and the influence which it gradually acquires over the whole character. To this view let us adhere.

LUKE 13:22-30

22 And he went through the cities and villages, teaching, and journeying toward Jerusalem.

23 Then said one unto him, Lord, are there few that be saved? And he said unto them,

24 Strive to enter in at the strait gate: for many, I say unto you, will seek to enter in, and shall not be able.

25 When once the master of the house is risen up, and hath shut to the door, and ye begin to stand without, and to knock at the door, saying, Lord, Lord, open unto us; and he shall answer and say unto you, I know you not whence ye are:

26 Then shall ye begin to say, We have eaten and drunk in thy presence, and thou hast taught in our streets.

27 But he shall say, I tell you, I know you not whence ye are; depart from me, all *ye* workers of iniquity.

28 There shall be weeping and gnashing of teeth, when ye shall see Abraham, and Isaac, and Jacob, and all the prophets, in the kingdom of God, and you *yourselves* thrust out.

29 And they shall come from the east, and *from* the west, and from the north, and *from* the south, and shall sit down in the kingdom of God.

30 And, behold, there are last which shall be first, and there are first which shall be last.

WE see in these verses *a remarkable question asked*. We are told that a certain man said to our Lord, 'Are there few that be saved?'

We do not know who this inquirer was. He may have been a self-righteous Jew, trained to believe that there was no hope for the uncircumcised, and no salvation for any but the children of Abraham. He may have been an idle trifler with religion, who was ever wasting his time on curious and speculative questions. In any case, we must all feel that he asked a question of deep and momentous importance.

He that desires to know the number of the saved, in the present dispensation, need only turn to the Bible, and his curiosity will be satisfied. He will read in the Sermon on the Mount these solemn words, 'Strait is the gate, and narrow is the way, that leadeth unto life, and few there be that find it' (*Matt.* 7:14).—He has only to look around him, and compare the ways of the many with the Word of God, and he will soon come to the conclusion, if he is an honest man, that the saved are few. It is an awful conclusion. Our souls naturally turn away from it. But Scripture and facts alike combine to shut us up to it. Salvation to the uttermost is offered to men. All things are ready on God's part. Christ is willing to receive sinners. But sinners are not willing to come to Christ. And hence few are saved.

We see, secondly, in these verses, *a striking exhortation given.* We are told that when our Lord Jesus Christ was asked whether few would be saved, he said, 'Strive to enter in at the strait gate.' He addressed these words to the whole company of his hearers. He thought it not good to gratify the curiosity of his questioner by a direct reply. He chose rather to press home on him, and all around him, their own immediate duty. In minding their own souls, they would soon find the question answered. In striving to enter in at the strait gate they would soon see whether the saved were many or few.

Whatever others may do in religion the Lord Jesus would have us know that our duty is clear. The gate is strait. The work is great. The enemies of our souls are many. We must be up, and doing. We are to wait for nobody. We are not to inquire what other people are doing, and whether many of our neighbours, and relatives, and friends, are serving Christ. The unbelief and indecision of others will be no excuse at the last day. We must never follow a multitude to do evil. If we go to heaven alone we must resolve that by God's grace we will go. Whether we have many with us or a few, the command before us is plain,—'Strive to enter in.'

Whatever others may think in religion the Lord Jesus would have us know that we are responsible for exertion. We are not to sit still in sin and worldliness, waiting for the grace of God. We are not to go on still in our wickedness, sheltering ourselves under the vain plea that we can do nothing till God draws us. We are to draw near to him in the use of means of grace. How we can do it is a question with which we have nothing to do. It is in obedience that the knot will be untied. The command is express and unmistakable,—'Strive to enter in.'

We see, thirdly, in these verses, *a day of awful solemnity described.* We are told of a time when 'the master of the house shall rise and shut the door,' when some shall 'sit down in the kingdom of God,' and others be 'shut out' for evermore. About the meaning of these words there can be no doubt. They describe the second coming of Christ and the day of judgment.

A day is coming on the earth when the long-suffering of God towards sinners shall have an end. The door of mercy, which has been so long open, shall at last be shut. The fountain opened for all sin and uncleanness shall at length be closed. The throne of grace shall be removed, and the throne of judgment shall be set up in its place. The great assize of the world shall begin. All that are found impenitent and unbelieving shall be thrust out for ever from God's presence. Men shall find that there is such a thing as 'the wrath of the Lamb' (*Rev.* 6:16).

A day is coming when believers in Christ shall receive a full reward. The Master of the great house in heaven shall call his servants together, and give to each a crown of glory, that fadeth not away. They shall sit down with Abraham, and Isaac, and Jacob, and rest for ever from warfare and work. They shall be shut in with Christ, and saints, and angels, in the kingdom of heaven, and sin, and death, and sorrow, and the world, and the devil, shall be eternally shut out. Men shall see at last that 'To him that soweth righteousness shall be a sure reward' (*Prov.* 11:18).

We see, lastly, in these verses, *a heart-searching prophecy delivered.* Our Lord tells us that in the day of his second coming, 'Many will seek to enter in at the strait gate, and shall not be able.'—They will 'knock at the door, saying, Lord, Lord, open to us,' but will find no admission.—They will even plead earnestly, that 'they have eaten and drunk in Christ's presence, and that he has taught in their streets.'—But their plea will be unavailing. They will receive the solemn answer, 'I know you not whence ye are; depart from me, all ye workers of iniquity.' Religious profession, and formal knowledge of Christ will save none who have served sin and the world.

There is something peculiarly striking in our Lord's language in this prophecy. It reveals to us the awful fact, that men may see what is right when it is too late for them to be saved. There is a time coming when many will repent too late, and believe too late,—sorrow for sin too late, and begin to pray too late,—be anxious about salvation too late, and long for heaven too late. Myriads shall wake up in another world, and be convinced of truths which on earth they refused to believe. Earth is the only place in God's creation where there is any infidelity. Hell itself is nothing but truth known too late.

The recollection of this passage should help us to set a right estimate on things around us. Money, and pleasure, and rank, and greatness, occupy the first place now in the world. Praying, and believing, and holy living, and acquaintance with Christ, are despised, and ridiculed, and held very cheap. But there is a change coming one day! The last shall be first, and the first last. For that change let us be prepared.

And now let us ask ourselves whether we are among the many or among the few. Do we know anything of striving and warring against sin, the world, and the devil? Are we ready for the Master's coming to shut the door? The man who can answer these questions satisfactorily is a true Christian.

Notes—Luke 13:23-30

23.—[*Are there few that be saved?*] Whitby remarks, 'This question seems to have been propounded agreeably to that sentiment of the Jews, that all Israelites should have their portion in the world to come.'—Perhaps the question would be translated more literally, 'Are the saved few?'

It may be well to remark here, that we have no warrant for supposing that the aggregate number of those who are lost will prove finally to be greater than the number of the saved. When all the infants who die without knowing good from evil, and all the 'nations of the saved,' who shall be converted after the calling in of the Jews, are added to the ranks of God's elect under the present dispensation, they shall be a multitude that no man can number. They will probably far exceed in number those who are lost.

[*He said unto them.*] Let it be noted, that our Lord's answer was not directed only to the man who asked the question, but to all the people round him. He probably knew that the question arose from a common opinion prevalent among all Jews, and that his questioner was only the mouthpiece of many. He therefore addresses his reply to all his hearers.

24, 25, etc.—[*Strive, etc.*] Major says, 'In these verses allusion is made to nuptial feasts. These were celebrated by night. The house was filled with lights. Thus they who were admitted have the benefit of light; but they who were excluded were in darkness outside the house,—"outer darkness,"—which necessarily appeared more gloomy compared with the light within.' The guests entered by a narrow wicket gate, at which the porter stood to prevent the unbidden from rushing in. When all that had been invited were arrived, the door was shut, and not opened to those who stood without, however much they knocked.

[*Strive to enter in.*] The Greek word rendered 'strive,' is that from which we take our English word 'agonize.' It implies great exertion and conflict. It is elsewhere translated, 'labour fervently,' and 'fight' (*Col.* 4:12; *1 Tim.* 6:12).

[*At the strait gate.*] The Greek preposition which we here render 'at,' is almost always translated 'through,' when found in sentences so constructed as the one before us.

[*Many ... will seek ... not be able.*] Stier labours to make out a distinction here between 'seeking' to enter, and 'striving' to enter. He appears to think that our Lord is speaking of things which happen while men are alive, and that the reason why many are not able to enter in, is to be found in the defective manner of their attempts. They indolently 'seek,' but do not earnestly 'strive.'

This distinction appears to me over-refined and quite unnecessary. The time when men shall 'seek to enter,' and 'not be able,' seems to me, most plainly, to be at the last day, when the door of mercy is shut for ever. The whole context shows this, and the language used is parallel to that in the parable of the wise and foolish virgins (*Matt.* 25:1–13).

Moreover the Greek word which we translate 'seek' happens to be the very same which is used in the famous promise, 'Seek, and ye shall find: knock, and it shall be opened unto you' (*Matt.* 7:7). To argue therefore from this passage, that men may seek to enter in at the gate of life and not be able, while they are alive, appears to me a harsh and needless straining of Scripture. That there is a state of mind to which some may come in which they shall seek God after a manner, and yet not find him, I do not deny. It is taught in Proverbs 1:28. All I maintain is that it is not taught here. The lesson taught here is simply this, that there will be a time when men shall find the gate of life closed, and shall desire entrance in vain when it is too late.

It appears to me very doubtful whether there ought to be a 'full stop' at the end of the twenty-fourth verse, and whether the sense does not indicate that a comma only is sufficient.

25.—[*When once the master.*] The language used in this verse is clearly that of parable.

[*I know you not.*] Let this expression be noted. It is again emphatically used in the twenty-seventh verse. It is not safe to lay too much stress on expressions used in parables in the establishment of doctrine. Nevertheless this repeated sentence, 'I know you not,' appears hard to be reconciled with the opinion that saints may fall away and be lost. The lost in the passage before us are clearly people whom the Lord does not know, and never did know.

26.—[*We have eaten and drunk in thy presence.*] It does not appear that these words have any necessary reference to the sacrament of the Lord's supper. The expression, 'eat and drink' is frequently used in the New Testament to describe familiar intercourse. (See *Luke* 5:30 and 22:30.)

27.—[*Depart from me ... iniquity.*] The similarity between this expression and Matthew 25:41, appears to show clearly that the time described is the second coming of Christ, and the judgment day.

28.—[*Ye shall see.*] This expression seems to prove that the lost shall see afar off the glory and blessedness of the saved, and that the sight shall add to their misery.

[*Abraham, and Isaac, and Jacob ... in the kingdom of God.*] Let this expression be noted. It shows that Old Testament saints will share the glory of the kingdom of God with Gentile believers. There seems no room here for the opinion, which some hold, that Old Testament saints and believers who have lived since the day of Pentecost shall not be together in glory;—and that Abraham, Isaac, and Jacob are not members of that church which is the bride and the Lamb's wife. Both the present verse, and the one following and the kindred passage in Matthew (*Matt.* 8:11), appear distinctly to contradict this notion.

29.—[*They shall come.*] This verse

describes the calling of the Gentiles of all nations, and people, and tongues into the church. They are to sit down in the same kingdom with the patriarchs and prophets.

[*East ... west ... north ... south.*] Bengel suggests the idea that these points of the compass are intentionally arranged thus, to show the order in which the Gentiles would be called in all over the world. It certainly is a fact that the gospel first took root in Syria and Asia Minor, then spread on to the west of Europe and along the shores of the Mediterranean, then turned northward to the Scandinavian nations and Britain, and since that time has spread, wherever it has spread, toward the south, in Africa, Asia,

South America, and the South Pacific Ocean.

30.—[*There are last ... first ... are first ... last.*] This is a proverbial expression which was literally fulfilled when the gospel was first preached, and has often been fulfilled since, both in churches and individuals. The Jews who were first became last, and the Gentiles who were last became first. The churches of Asia Minor and Africa were called first, and were famous when Britain was only a field for missionaries. But now those churches have become last, and the British churches fill the foremost position in Christendom. And they too, 'if they continue not in God's goodness, will be cut off' (*Rom.* 11:22).

LUKE 13:31-35

31 The same day there came certain of the Pharisees, saying unto him, Get thee out, and depart hence: for Herod will kill thee.

32 And he said unto them, Go ye, and tell that fox, Behold, I cast out devils, and I do cures to day and to morrow, and the third *day* I shall be perfected.

33 Nevertheless I must walk to day, and to morrow, and the *day* following: for it cannot be that a prophet perish out of Jerusalem.

34 O Jerusalem, Jerusalem, which killest the prophets, and stonest them that are sent unto thee; how often would I have gathered thy children together, as a hen *doth gather* her brood under *her* wings, and ye would not!

35 Behold, your house is left unto you desolate: and verily I say unto you, Ye shall not see me, until *the time* come when ye shall say, Blessed *is* he that cometh in the name of the Lord.

L ET us learn from these verses, *how entirely our times are in God's hands.* Our Lord Jesus Christ teaches us this lesson by his reply to those who bade him depart, because Herod would kill him. He said, 'I cast out devils, and I do cures today and tomorrow.' His time was not yet come for leaving the world. His work was not yet finished. Until that time came it was not in the power of Herod to hurt him. Until that work was finished no weapon forged against him could prosper.

There is something in our Lord's words which demands the

attention of all true Christians. There is a frame of mind exhibited to us which we should do well to copy. Our Lord, no doubt, spoke with a prophetic foresight of coming things. He knew the time of his own death, and he knew that this time was not yet come. Foreknowledge like this, of course, is not granted to believers in the present day. But still there is a lesson here which we ought not to overlook. We ought, in a certain measure, to aim at having the mind that was in Christ Jesus. We ought to seek to possess a spirit of calm, unshaken confidence about things to come. We should study to have a heart 'not afraid of evil tidings,' but quiet, steady, and trusting in the Lord (*Psa.* 112:7).

The subject is a delicate one, but one which concerns our happiness so much that it deserves consideration. We are not intended to be idle fatalists, like the Mahometans, or cold, unfeeling statues, like the Stoics. We are not to neglect the use of means, or to omit all prudent provision for the unseen future. To neglect means is fanaticism, and not faith.—But still, when we have done all, we should remember, that though duties are ours, events are God's. We should therefore endeavour to leave things to come in God's hands, and not to be over-anxious about health, or family, or money, or plans. To cultivate this frame of mind would add immensely to our peace. How many of our cares and fears are about things which never come to pass! Happy is that man who can walk in our Lord's steps, and say, 'I shall have what is good for me. I shall live on earth till my work is done, and not a moment longer. I shall be taken when I am ripe for heaven, and not a minute before. All the powers of the world cannot take away my life, till God permits. All the physicians on earth cannot preserve it, when God calls me away.'

Is there anything beyond the reach of man in this spirit? Surely not. Believers have a covenant ordered in all things and sure. The very hairs of their heads are numbered. Their steps are ordered by the Lord. All things are working together for their good. When they are afflicted, it is for their profit. When they are sick, it is for some wise purpose. All things are said to be theirs,—life, death, things present, and things to come (*2 Sam.* 23:5; *Matt.* 10:30; *Psa.* 37:23; *Rom.* 8:28; *Heb.* 12:10; *John* 11:4; *1 Cor.* 3:22). There is no such thing as chance, luck, or accident, in the life of a believer. There is but one thing needful, in order to make a believer calm, quiet, unruffled, undisturbed in every position, and under every circumstance. That one thing is faith in active exercise. For such faith let us daily pray. Few indeed know anything of it. The faith of most believers is very fitful and spasmodic. It is for want of steady, constant faith, that so few can say with Christ, 'I shall walk today, and tomorrow, and not die till my work is done.'

Let us learn, for another thing, from these verses, *how great is the compassion of our Lord Jesus Christ towards sinners.* We see this brought out in a most forcible manner by our Lord's language about Jerusalem. He knew well the wickedness of that city. He knew what crimes had been committed there in times past. He knew what was coming on himself, at the time of his crucifixion. Yet even to Jerusalem he says, 'How often would I have gathered thy children together as a hen doth gather her brood under her wings, and ye would not.'

It grieves the Lord Jesus Christ to see sinners going on still in their wickedness. 'As I live,' are his words, 'I have no pleasure in the death of the wicked' (*Ezek.* 33:11). Let all unconverted people remember this. It is not enough that they grieve parents, and ministers, and neighbours, and friends. There is one higher than all these, whom they deeply grieve by their conduct. They are daily grieving Christ.

The Lord Jesus is willing to save sinners. 'He is not willing that any should perish, but that all should come to repentance.' 'He would have all men saved and come to the knowledge of the truth' (*2 Pet.* 3:9; *1 Tim.* 2:4). This is a mighty principle of the gospel, and one which sorely perplexes narrow-minded and shallow theologians. But what says the Scripture? The words before us, no less than the texts just quoted, are distinct and express. 'I would have gathered thy children,' says Christ, 'and ye would not.' The will of poor hardened unbelieving man, and not the will of Christ, is the cause why sinners are lost for evermore. Christ 'would' save them, but they will 'not be' saved.

Let the truth before us sink down into our hearts, and bear fruit in our lives. Let us thoroughly understand that if we die in our sins and go to hell, our blood will be upon our own heads. We cannot lay the blame on God the Father, nor on Jesus Christ the Redeemer, nor on the Holy Ghost the Comforter. The promises of the gospel are wide, broad, and general. The readiness of Christ to save sinners is unmistakably declared. If we are lost, we shall have none to find fault with but ourselves. The words of Christ will be our condemnation: 'Ye will not come to me, that ye might have life' (*John* 5:40).

Let us take heed, with such a passage as this before us, that we are not more systematic than Scripture. It is a serious thing to be 'wise above that which is written.' Our salvation is wholly of God. Let that never be forgotten. None but the elect shall be finally saved. 'No man can come unto Christ except the Father draw him' (*John* 6:44). But our ruin, if we are lost, will be wholly of ourselves. We shall reap the fruit of our own choice. We shall find that we have lost our own souls. Linked between these two principles lies truth which we must maintain firmly, and never let go. There is doubtless deep mystery about it. Our minds are too feeble to understand it now. But we shall understand it all hereafter. God's sovereignty and man's responsibility shall appear perfectly harmonious one day. In the meantime, whatever we doubt, let us never doubt Christ's infinite willingness to save.

Notes—Luke 13:31-35

31.—[*There came certain ... Herod will kill thee.*] It is thought by some that this message was an invention of the Pharisees, intended to alarm our Lord, and stop his preaching, and that Herod never really intended to kill our Lord. Yet it seems impossible to reconcile this theory with the message that our Lord in reply sends to Herod in the next verse. It is more probable that Herod wished to make away with One whose ministry reminded him of John the Baptist, and who publicly testified that John the Baptist, whom Herod had murdered, was a prophet. He had probably expressed this wish publicly to his courtiers, and the Pharisees came to repeat it to our Lord, hoping that the report would silence him.

[*Depart hence: or Herod will kill thee.*] This expression shows that our Lord was in Galilee at this time. We are expressly told (*Luke* 23:7) that Galilee belonged to Herod's jurisdiction.

Let it be noted that the literal translation of the Greek here would be, 'Herod is willing,—has a will,—wishes,—means,—to kill thee.' It is not a future tense merely. It is like 'Ye *will* not come to me' (*John* 5:40).

32.—[*That fox.*] This remarkable expression is variously interpreted. Some think that our Lord did not apply it to Herod at all but to the Pharisee who brought the message. This, however, seems a very unnatural and forced application of the word. The most common opinion is, that our Lord applied it to Herod himself, in virtue of his office as a prophet. Whitby remarks, 'To impose this ignominious name on Herod is not contrary to the command "not to speak ill of the ruler of thy people." It is the office of prophets not to spare kings when they expose their offences (*Jer.* 1:10). Christ, therefore, uses his prophetical power in giving this tyrant a name suitable to his actions' (compare *Zeph.* 3:3; *Ezek.* 22:27).

Maldonatus thinks that our Lord purposely called Herod 'that fox,' in order to show the Pharisees how little he feared him.

One word of caution is needful. The use of this expression by our Lord is no warrant to Christians to employ violent and contemptuous epithets in speaking of the wicked, and especially of the wicked in high places. He that would use such language about his ruler as Christ here used about Herod, must first prove his prophetical commission, and satisfy us that he has a special mission from God.

[*Today, and tomorrow, and the third day.*] This is a difficult expression, and one which has received three different interpretations. The expression in the next verse is only another way of saying the same thing.

Some think that our Lord meant three literal days. Bishop Pearce says, 'This, and what follows to the end of the chapter, seem to have been spoken about two or three days before Jesus was crucified.' This seems a very improbable and unsatisfactory interpretation.

Some think that by days our Lord meant years, according to the theory which makes prophetic days always mean years. This again seems an unsatisfactory view. According to it our Lord spoke these words in the first year of his three years' ministry. Yet it appears more likely that he spoke them in the last.

Some think that this expression is indefinite, and a proverbial form of speech, signifying merely a short space of time:—'I am yet a little time with you, and during that time I shall continue my work, notwithstanding Herod's threats; and at the end of that time, and not before, I shall be perfected, or finish my course by death.' Similar modes of speaking occur in Hosea 6:2; and in the marginal readings of Genesis 30:33; 31:2; Exodus 4:10; 13:14; Deuteronomy 6:20; 19:6; Joshua 3:5; 4:6; 22:24; 1 Samuel 19:7.

I am disposed to adhere to this last opinion, as on the whole most probable one. Major gives quotations from Euripides and Arrian which justify the interpretation of the three days in a proverbial sense by the usage of profane writers.

[*I shall be perfected.*] This is a remarkable expression. In the Greek it is in the present tense. The meaning seems to be 'I shall be perfected by my death,—I shall finish the work which I came to do.' The same word is applied to our Lord in Hebrews 2:10 and 5:9.

33.—[*I must walk.*] The meaning of this expression seems to be, 'I must continue in the course I have begun,—I must go on (to use a common English phrase) as I have hitherto.' It is the same word which is used in Luke 1:6; 1 Peter 4:3; 2 Peter 2:10; 3:3; Jude 16. In each place it is rendered 'walk,' and in each means 'maintaining an habitual course of life.'

[*It cannot be that a prophet ... Jerusalem.*] This is a peculiar expression. The Greek word rendered, 'it cannot be,' is only found here in the New Testament, and means literally 'it is impossible.' Yet it is clear that this cannot be our Lord's literal meaning. John the Baptist, to say nothing of other prophets, did not die at Jerusalem. The sense must be, as Euthymius and Heinsius maintain, 'it would be an unusual thing,—an exception to a rule,—for a prophet to die in any place but Jerusalem.

When I do die, it will be at Jerusalem. But I am not there yet, but in Galilee.'

Barradius thinks that our Lord meant, 'it is not possible that I, the great prophet, fore-told by Moses, can perish out of Jerusalem.' This however seems very improbable.

Drusius and A. Clarke say, that a man professing to be a prophet could be tried on that ground only by the great Sanhedrim, which always resided at Jerusalem.

34.—[*O Jerusalem, etc.*] This remark-able passage is found in St Matthew's Gospel (*Matt.* 23:37), at the very end of our Lord's ministry, in almost the same words. I cannot see any satisfactory explanation of this circumstance excepting that our Lord must have twice used the same expression about Jerusalem in the course of his minis-try on earth.

To suppose that our Lord was at the end of his ministry in this part of St Luke's Gospel is, on the face of the narrative, utterly improbable. To suppose that St Luke thrust in this remarkable saying about Jerusalem at this particular point of his Gospel, out of its place and order, and without any connection with the context, is equally improbable.

I see on the other hand no improbability whatever in the supposition that our Lord made use of this remarkable saying about Jerusalem on two distinct occasions during his ministry. I can quite understand that his mighty and feeling heart was deeply touched with sorrow for the sin and hard-ness of that wicked but privileged city. And it seems to me both likely and natural that language like that before us would fall from his lips on more than one occasion.

[*How often.*] I cannot think, as some do, that this expression refers to many visits which our Lord had made to Jerusalem dur-ing his ministry. I rather refer it to all the messages and invitations which for many centuries he had sent to Jerusalem by his servants, the prophets.

[*Would I ... ye would not!*] The Greek word in both these phrases is stronger than appears from our English translation. It is literally, 'I willed, and ye willed not.'

Few passages in the Bible throw the responsibility of the loss of the soul so distinctly on those who are lost.—'I would,'

'ye would not.'—Two wills are expressly mentioned, the will of Christ to do good, and the will of man to refuse good when offered.

Let it be noted that our Lord does not say, 'thou wouldest not,' but 'ye would not.'—By this mode of speaking, he makes it plain that he charges the guilt of Jerusalem on its inhabitants, the men and women who dwelt there, and specially on the priests, and scribes, and Pharisees who governed the city. They were neither willing to be gathered themselves, nor to let others round them be gathered. They neither entered in themselves into the kingdom, nor allowed others to enter. Christ was willing, but they were unwilling.

We must be careful, however, not to confine 'ye would not,' to the scribes, Pharisees, and rulers. The verse which fol-lows shows clearly that our Lord includes all the inhabitants of Jerusalem.

35.—[*Your house is left ... desolate.*] These words mean, 'Your temple, in which you glory, your holy and beautiful house, is now deprived of its glory. God has departed from it, and has no longer any pleasure in it.'

[*Ye shall not see me until, etc.*] The meaning of these words, and the manner of their fulfilment, are points on which com-mentators are not agreed.

Some think that our Lord refers to his own triumphal entry into Jerusalem, when he rode in upon an ass, just before his crucifixion, and all the city met him, crying 'Hosanna!'

Some think that our Lord refers to the approaching destruction of Jerusalem, when the fulfilment of all his predictions would oblige the Jews to confess that he was the Messiah. Bishop Pearce says, 'They will then remember what they did to me when I was among them, and will acknow-ledge that I am the Christ, the person who came in the name of the Lord. Accordingly, Eusebius tells us, that upon seeing that destruction, vast multitudes came over to the faith of Christ.'

Some think that our Lord's words are not yet fulfilled, and that they refer to the last times, when the Jews after their last tribulation shall 'look on him, whom they pierced,' and believe, at the time of his second advent in glory.

I decidedly adhere to this last opinion. The triumphant entry into Jerusalem was a faint type, no doubt, of the honour which Christ will one day see in Jerusalem. But the Jewish nation, as a nation, never saw our Lord and honoured him as the Messiah, during the whole period of his first advent. But 'when he cometh with clouds every eye shall see him, and they also which pierced him' (*Rev.* 1:7).

LUKE 14:1-6

1 And it came to pass, as he went into the house of one of the chief Pharisees to eat bread on the sabbath day, that they watched him.

2 And, behold, there was a certain man before him which had the dropsy.

3 And Jesus answering spake unto the lawyers and Pharisees, saying, Is it lawful to heal on the sabbath day?

4 And they held their peace. And he took *him*, and healed him, and let him go;

5 And answered them, saying, Which of you shall have an ass or an ox fallen into a pit, and will not straightway pull him out on the sabbath day?

6 And they could not answer him again to these things.

L ET us mark in this passage, *how our Lord Jesus Christ accepted the hospitality of those who were not his disciples.* We read that 'he went into the house of one of the chief Pharisees to eat bread.' We cannot reasonably suppose that this Pharisee was a friend of Christ. It is more probable that he only did what was customary for a man in his position. He saw a stranger teaching religion, whom some regarded as a prophet, and he invited him to eat at his table. The point that most concerns us, is this, that when the invitation was given it was accepted.

If we want to know how our Lord carried himself at a Pharisee's table, we have only to read attentively the first twenty-four verses of this chapter. We shall find him the same there that he was elsewhere, always about his Father's business. We shall see him first defending the true observance of the sabbath day,—then expounding to those who were bidden together with him the nature of true humility,—then urging on his host the character of true hospitality,—and finally delivering that most apposite and striking parable, the parable of the great supper. And all this is done in the most wise, and calm, and dignified manner. The words are all words in season. The speech is 'always with grace, seasoned with salt' (*Col.* 4:6). The perfection of our Lord's conduct appears on this, as on all other occasions. He always said the right thing, at the right time, and in the right way. He never forgot for a moment, who he was and where he was.

The example of Christ in this passage deserves the close attention of all Christians, and specially of ministers of the gospel. It throws strong light on some most difficult points,—our intercourse with unconverted people,—the extent to which we should carry it,—the manner in which we should behave when we are with them. Our Lord has left us a pattern for our conduct in this chapter. It will be our wisdom to endeavour to walk in his steps.

We ought not to withdraw entirely from all intercourse with unconverted people. It would be cowardice and indolence to do so, even if it were possible. It would shut us out from many opportunities of doing good. But we ought to go into their society moderately, watchfully, and prayerfully, and with a firm resolution to carry our Master and our Master's business with us. The house from which Christ is deliberately excluded, is not the house at which Christians ought to receive hospitalities, and keep up intimacy.—The extent to which we should carry our intercourse with the unconverted, is a point which each believer must settle for himself. Some can go much further than others in this direction, with advantage to their company, and without injury to themselves. 'Every man hath his proper gift' (*1 Cor.* 7:7). There are two questions which we should often put to ourselves, in reference to this subject. 'Do I, in company, spend all my time in light and worldly conversation?—Or do I endeavour to follow, however feebly, the example of Christ?' The society in which we cannot answer these questions satisfactorily, is society from which we had better withdraw.—So long as we go into company as Christ went to the Pharisee's house, we shall take no harm.

Let us mark, secondly, in this passage, *how our Lord was watched by his enemies.* We read that when he went to eat bread on the sabbath day, in the house of a Pharisee, 'they watched him.'

The circumstance here recorded, is only a type of what our Lord was constantly subjected to, all through his earthly ministry. The eyes of his enemies were continually observing him. They watched for his halting, and waited eagerly for some word or deed on which they could lay hold, and build an accusation. Yet they found none. Our blessed Lord was ever holy, harmless, undefiled, and separate from evil. Perfect indeed must that life have been, in which the bitterest enemy could find no flaw, or blemish, or spot, or wrinkle, or any such thing!

He that desires to serve Christ must make up his mind to be 'watched' and observed, no less than his Master. He must never forget that the eyes of the world are upon him, and that the wicked are looking narrowly at all his ways. Specially ought he to remember this when he goes into the society of the unconverted. If he makes a slip there, in word or deed, and acts inconsistently, he may rest assured it will not be forgotten.

Let us endeavour to live daily as in the sight of a holy God. So living, it will matter little how much we are 'watched' by an ill-natured and malicious world. Let us exercise ourselves to have a conscience void of offence toward God and man, and to do nothing which can give occasion to the Lord's enemies to blaspheme. The thing is possible. By the grace of God it can be done. The haters of Daniel were obliged to confess, 'we shall not find any occasion against this Daniel, except we find it against him concerning the law of his God' (*Dan.* 6:5).

Let us mark, lastly, in this passage, *how our Lord asserts the lawfulness of doing works of mercy on the sabbath day.* We read that he healed a man who had the dropsy on the sabbath day, and then said to the lawyers and Pharisees, 'Which of you shall have an ass or an ox fallen into a pit, and will not straightway pull him out on the sabbath day?' This was a home-thrust, which could not be parried. It is written, 'They could not answer him again.'

The qualification which our Lord here puts on the requirements of the fourth commandment is evidently founded on Scripture, reason, and common sense. The sabbath was made for man,—for his benefit, not for his injury,—for his advantage, not for his hurt. The interpretation of God's law respecting the sabbath was never intended to be strained so far as to interfere with charity, kindness, and the real wants of human nature. All such interpretations only defeat their own end. They require that which fallen man cannot perform, and thus bring the whole commandment into disrepute. Our Lord saw this clearly, and laboured throughout his ministry to restore this precious part of God's law to its just position.

The principle which our Lord lays down about sabbath observance needs carefully fencing with cautions. The right to do works of *necessity* and *mercy* is fearfully abused in these latter days. Thousands of Christians appear to have thrown down the hedge, and burst the bounds entirely with respect to this holy day. They seem to forget that though our Lord repeatedly explains the requirements of the fourth commandment, he never struck it out of the law of God, or said that it was not binding on Christians at all.

Can anyone say that Sunday travelling, except on very rare emergencies, is a work of *mercy*?—Will anyone tell us that Sunday trading, Sunday dinner parties, Sunday excursion-trains on railways, Sunday deliveries of letters and newspapers, are works of *mercy*?—Have servants, and shopmen, and engine-drivers, and coachmen, and clerks, and porters, no souls? Do they not need rest for their bodies and time for their souls, like other men?—These are serious questions, and ought to make many people think.

Whatever others do, let us resolve to 'keep the sabbath holy.' God has a controversy with the churches about sabbath desecration. It is a sin of which the cry goes up to heaven, and will be reckoned for one day. Let us wash our hands of this sin, and have nothing to do with it. If others are determined to rob God, and take possession of the Lord's day for their own selfish ends, let us not be partakers in their sins.

Notes—Luke 14:1-6

1.—[*He went into ... house ... Pharisees.*] Inns and places of reception for travellers were doubtless far more uncommon in our Lord's time than they are now. The duty of entertaining strangers, in consequence, often devolved on the chief man in each village or town.

Stella thinks that one object that our Lord had in view in going to the Pharisee's house, was to benefit the servants of the family, who had few opportunities of hearing truth. He remarks that in his own time, in Spain, servants had hardly any opportunity of hearing sermons, from the demands which their masters made upon their time on Sundays.

[*To eat bread on the sabbath day.*] Lightfoot says that 'the Jews' tables were generally better spread on the sabbath, than on any other days; and that, as they themselves reckoned, on account of religion and piety.' He proves this by quotations from rabbinical writers.

2.—[*Before him.*] Some think that the dropsical man placed himself 'before Christ' in faith, hoping that he would see and heal him. Others think that he was purposely placed there by our Lord's enemies, in order to lay a trap in our Lord's way, and procure an occasion of accusing him as a sabbath-breaker.

3.—[*Answering spake.*] Let it be noted here that we are told of nothing that was said, or spoken by the lawyers and Pharisees, and yet we read both here, and at verse 5, that our Lord 'answered.' It is plain that he answered their thoughts.

Whitby observes, 'In this and all similar cases, there is an answer to some inward conception or reasoning; or to some action expressive of their sentiments concerning him.' The same remark applies to Matthew 22:1; Luke 5:22; 7:39, 40; Mark 14:48; Matthew 11:25.

[*To heal on the sabbath day.*] Let it be noted that our Lord seems frequently to have chosen the sabbath day on purpose, as the day on which he would work miracles of mercy. See Mark 1:21; Luke 6:6; Luke 13:10; John 9:14.

5.—[*An ass or an ox.*] Stella makes some severe remarks, in his commentary on this verse, upon the prelates of his day. He charges them with caring more about the horses and mules which drew their equipages, than about the sick, the poor, and the needy in their diocese. He observes that they were not like Job, who did not rend his garments when he lost his oxen and camels, but when his sons and his daughters died.

[*Straightway.*] This word is more commonly rendered 'immediately.' It signifies that there was no delay about saving the life of the ox and the ass, and so there ought to be no delay about healing a sick man, or doing a work of mercy on the sabbath day.

LUKE 14:7-14

7 And he put forth a parable to those which were bidden, when he marked how they chose out the chief rooms; saying unto them,

8 When thou art bidden of any *man* to a wedding, sit not down in the highest room; lest a more honourable man than thou be bidden of him;

9 And he that bade thee and him come and say to thee, Give this man place; and thou begin with shame to take the lowest room.

10 But when thou art bidden, go and sit down in the lowest room; that when he that bade thee cometh, he may say unto thee, Friend, go up higher: then shalt thou have worship in the presence of them that sit at meat with thee.

11 For whosoever exalteth himself shall be abased; and he that humbleth himself shall be exalted.

12 Then said he also to him that bade him, When thou makest a dinner or a supper, call not thy friends, nor thy brethren, neither thy kinsmen, nor *thy* rich neighbours; lest they also bid thee again, and a recompense be made thee.

13 But when thou makest a feast, call the poor, the maimed, the lame, the blind:

14 And thou shalt be blessed; for they cannot recompense thee: for thou shalt be recompensed at the resurrection of the just.

LET us learn from these verses *the value of humility*. This is a lesson which our Lord teaches in two ways. Firstly, he advises those who are bidden to a wedding to 'sit down in the lowest room.' Secondly, he backs up his advice by declaring a great principle, which frequently fell from his lips:—'Whosoever exalteth himself shall be abased; and he that humbleth himself shall be exalted.'

Humility may well be called the queen of the Christian graces. To know our own sinfulness and weakness, and to feel our need of Christ, is the very beginning of saving religion.—It is a grace which has always been a distinguishing feature in the character of the holiest saints in every age. Abraham, and Moses, and Job, and David, and Daniel, and Paul, were all eminently humble men.—Above all, it is a grace within the reach of every true Christian. All have not money to give away. All have not time and opportunities for working directly for Christ. All have not gifts of speech, and tact, and knowledge, in order to do good in the world. But all converted men should labour to adorn the doctrine they profess by humility. If they can do nothing else, they can strive to be humble.

Would we know the root and spring of humility? One word describes it. The root of humility is right *knowledge*. The man who really knows himself and his own heart,—who knows God and his infinite majesty and holiness,—who knows Christ, and the price at which he was redeemed,—that man will never be a proud man. He will count himself, like Jacob, unworthy of the least of all God's mercies. He will say of himself, like Job, 'I am vile.' He will cry, like Paul, 'I am chief of sinners' (*Gen.* 32:10; *Job* 40:4; *1 Tim.* 1:15). He will think anything good enough for him. In lowliness of mind he will esteem everyone else to be better than himself (*Phil.* 2:3). Ignorance—nothing but sheer ignorance—ignorance of self, of God, and of Christ, is the real secret of pride. From that miserable self-ignorance may we daily pray to be delivered! He is the wise man who knows himself;—and he who knows himself, will find nothing within to make him proud.

Let us learn, secondly, from these verses, *the duty of caring for the poor.* Our Lord teaches this lesson in a peculiar manner. He tells the Pharisee who invited him to his feast, that, when he made 'a dinner or a supper,' he ought not to 'call his friends,' or kinsmen, or rich neighbours. On the contrary, he says, 'When thou makest a feast, call the poor, the maimed, the lame, the blind.'

The precept contained in these words must evidently be interpreted with considerable limitation. It is certain that our Lord did not intend to forbid men showing any hospitality to their relatives and friends. It is certain that he did not mean to encourage a useless and profuse expenditure of money in giving to the poor. To interpret the passage in this manner would make it contradict other plain Scriptures. Such interpretations cannot possibly be correct.

But when we have said this, we must not forget that the passage contains a deep and important lesson. We must be careful that we do not limit and qualify that lesson till we have pared it down and refined it into nothing at all. The lesson of the passage is plain and distinct. The Lord Jesus would have us care for our poorer brethren, and help them according to our power. He would have us know that it is a solemn duty never to neglect the poor, but to aid them and relieve them in their time of need.

Let the lesson of this passage sink down deeply into our hearts.

'The poor shall never cease out of the land' (*Deut.* 15:11). A little help conferred upon the poor judiciously and in season, will often add immensely to their happiness, and take away immensely from their cares, and promote good feeling, between class and class in society. This help it is the will of Christ that all his people who have the means should be willing and ready to bestow. That stingy, calculating spirit, which leads some people to talk of 'the workhouse,' and condemn all charity to the poor, is exceedingly opposed to the mind of Christ. It is not for nothing that our Lord declares that he will say to the wicked in the day of judgment, 'I was an hungred, and ye gave me no meat:—I was thirsty and ye gave me no drink.'—It is not for nothing that St Paul writes to the Galatians, 'They would that I should remember the poor; the same which I also was forward to do' (*Matt.* 25:42; *Gal.* 2:10).

Let us learn, lastly, from these verses, *the great importance of looking forward to the resurrection of the dead.* This lesson stands out in a striking manner in the language used by our Lord on the subject of showing charity to the poor. He says to the Pharisee who entertained him, 'The poor cannot recompense thee:—thou shalt be recompensed at the resurrection of the just.'

There is a resurrection after death. Let this never be forgotten. The life that we live here in the flesh is not all. The visible world around us is not the only world with which we have to do. All is not over when the last breath is drawn, and men and women are carried to their long home in the grave. The trumpet shall one day sound, and the dead shall be raised incorruptible. All that are in the graves shall hear Christ's voice and come forth: they that have done good to the resurrection of life, and they that have done evil to the resurrection of damnation. This is one of the great foundation truths of the Christian religion. Let us cling to it firmly, and never let it go.

Let us strive to live like men who believe in a resurrection and a life to come, and desire to be always ready for another world. So living, we shall look forward to death with calmness. We shall feel that there remains some better portion for us beyond the grave.—So living, we shall take patiently all that we have to bear in this world. Trials, losses, disappointments, ingratitude, will affect us little. We shall not look for our reward here. We shall feel that all will be rectified one day, and that the Judge of all the earth will do right (*Gen.* 18:25).

But how can we bear the thought of a resurrection? What shall enable us to look forward to a world to come without alarm? Nothing can do it, but faith in Christ. Believing on him, we have nothing to fear. Our sins will not appear against us. The demands of God's law will be found completely satisfied. We shall stand firm in the great day, and none shall lay anything to our charge (*Rom.* 8:33). Worldly men, like Felix, may well tremble when they think of a resurrection. But believers, like Paul, may rejoice.

Notes—Luke 14:7-14

7.—[*He marked.*] The Greek word so rendered is only used five times in the New Testament. It means literally 'gave attention,' or 'observed.' It is elsewhere translated 'gave heed' (*Acts* 3:5).

[*The chief rooms.*] The Greek word so rendered does not literally mean 'rooms,' or 'chambers,' as if our Lord meant that the guests chose the best apartments in the house. It signifies the 'best seats,' or reclining places at table. Major gives a quotation, showing that 'the most honourable station at an entertainment among the Romans, was the middle part of the middle couch, each couch holding three.'

9.—[*Give this man place ... lowest room.*] It should be observed in this verse, that it is the same Greek word which is translated 'place' and 'room.' The sentence should either have been translated, 'give this man place,' and 'take the lowest place,'—or 'give this man room,' and 'take the lowest room.'

[*Begin.*] This shows the tardiness, and reluctance, and unwillingness with which the move would be made.

10.—[*Go and sit down in the lowest room.*] The following quotation from Paley is worth reading. 'Some of the passages in the Gospels about humility, especially the Lord's advice to the guests at an entertainment, seem to extend his rules to what we call *manners*, which was both regular in point of consistency, and not so much beneath the dignity of our Lord's mission, as may at first sight be supposed; for bad manners are bad morals.' (Paley's *Evidences.* Part 2 chapter 2.1.)

[*Worship.*] The Greek word so translated means literally 'glory,' or 'honour.' Our translation is unfortunate. It must however be remembered that the meaning of words changes with time. The word 'worship' did not mean exclusively religious worship, when the last revision of the Bible took place in England. The sense in which the word is here used, still lingers among us in the epithet 'worshipful,' applied to 'mayors,' and 'worship' to magistrates. In the marriage service of the Church of England, the word also occurs in the sense of 'honour.'

11.—[*Whosoever exalteth himself, etc.*] Let it be noted that hardly any saying of our Lord's is so frequently repeated as this sentence about humility.

12.—[*Call not thy friends, etc.*] This is a remarkable direction. There are few sayings of our Lord's in which we are so plainly required by the equity of interpretation, to put a qualified sense on his command. Just as it is impossible to put a literal construction on his saying, 'if any man come after me and *hate* not his father, etc., he cannot be my disciple,' so it is impossible to put a literal sense on his words here.

Poole remarks, 'Many things are delivered in Scripture, in the form of a universal and absolute prohibition, which must not be so understood, among which this is one instance. None must think that our Saviour doth here absolutely or universally forbid an invitation of brethren, kinsmen, rich neighbours, friends, to dine with us. There was nothing more ordinarily practised among the Jews, and Christ himself was at divers meals. But Christ teacheth us here,

'1. That inviting friends is no act of charity. It was a lawful act of humanity and civility, and of a good tendency to procure unity and friendship among neighbours and friends, but no such act of charity as they could expect a heavenly reward for.

'2. That such feastings ought not to be upheld in prejudice to our duty in relieving the poor, that is, they ought not to be maintained in such excesses and immoderate degrees, as by them to disable us from that relief of the poor, which God requireth of us as our duty.'

The evil consequences of an excessively literal interpretation of this passage, may be seen in the well-meant but grossly abused charities to the poor, which were so prevalent in this country before the Reformation, and which are still to be seen in Roman Catholic countries on the Continent at the present day. It is notorious that profuse charity to the poor, given indiscriminately, and without inquiry, does no real good, fosters idleness, rears up a class of professional mendicants, promotes dissolute and profligate habits among beggars, and enormously increases the very evil which it is meant to relieve.

Such instances of literal obedience to our Lord's command in this passage, as Cornelius à Lapide quotes in his commentary, are melancholy instances of useless and mischievous kindness. He tells us how St Louis of France used daily to feed a hundred and twenty poor people, and how St Hedwig, Duchess of Poland, used daily to feed nine hundred poor people! The slightest knowledge of human nature will tell us that such liberality would certainly be grossly abused, and could never have been meant by our Lord. The words of St Paul are distinct and unmistakable, 'If any man will not work, neither shall he eat' (2 *Thess.* 3:10).

We must beware however in England that we do not go into the other extreme. There is a disposition in some quarters to discourage all charity and almsgiving whatsoever. There are many who say that to give relief checks exertion, and makes the poor do nothing for themselves. Such arguments no doubt have a grain of truth in them, and certainly save men's pockets. But we must be careful that we do not carry them too far. In a densely peopled country like England, there always will be many cases of real poverty and distress, which rich people ought to consider and relieve. Relief should of course be given judiciously, and after due enquiry. But to say that nothing should ever be given to a poor person, under any circumstances, excepting what the law allows, is evidently contrary to the mind of Christ, and flatly contradictory to the spirit of the passage before us.

14.—[*Thou shalt be recompensed.*] This expression is worthy of notice. It confirms the doctrine of a reward according to works, though not on account of works, in the judgment day.

The similarity between the Lord's language in this place, and that used in the description of the judgment day, in the 25th chapter of St Matthew, ought to be observed. It seems to contradict the opinion which some hold, that in St Matthew our Lord is speaking only of the judgment of the heathen who never heard the gospel. Some arguments by which this view is maintained, would apply to the passage before us. Yet here it is plain, that our Lord is speaking of his own hearers and disciples. It appears more probable that both here and in St Matthew our Lord speaks of the general judgment, and that the importance of works as an evidence of faith, is the truth which he desires to impress on our minds.

[*The resurrection of the just.*] This expression is remarkable. I cannot think that our Lord used it in deference to an opinion common among the Jews, that resurrection was the special privilege of the righteous. It seems to me far more probable that our Lord refers to the first resurrection, spoken of in the twentieth chapter of Revelation. It is hard to put any other sense on the expression than this, that there is a resurrection of which none but the just shall be partakers,—a resurrection which shall be the peculiar privilege of the righteous, and shall precede that of the wicked.

LUKE 14:15-24

15 And when one of them that sat at meat with him heard these things, he said unto him, Blessed *is* he that shall eat bread in the kingdom of God.

16 Then said he unto him, A certain man made a great supper, and bade many:

17 And sent his servant at supper time to say to them that were bidden, Come; for all things are now ready.

18 And they all with one *consent* began to make excuse. The first said unto him, I have bought a piece of ground, and I must needs go and see it: I pray thee have me excused.

19 And another said, I have bought five yoke of oxen, and I go to prove them: I pray thee have me excused.

20 And another said, I have married a wife, and therefore I cannot come.

21 So that servant came, and shewed his lord these things. Then the master of the house being angry, said to his servant, Go out quickly into the streets and lanes of the city, and bring in hither the poor, and the maimed, and the halt, and the blind.

22 And the servant said, Lord, it is done as thou hast commanded, and yet there is room.

23 And the lord said unto the servant, Go out into the highways and hedges, and compel *them* to come in, that my house may be filled.

24 For I say unto you, That none of those men which were bidden shall taste of my supper.

THE verses before us contain one of our Lord's most instructive parables. It was spoken in consequence of a remark made by one who was sitting at meat with him in a Pharisee's house. 'Blessed,' said this man, 'is he that shall eat bread in the kingdom of God.'—The object of this remark we are left to conjecture. It is far from unlikely that he who made it was one of that class of people who wish to go to heaven, and like to hear good things talked of, but never get any further. Our Lord takes occasion to remind him and all the company, by means of the parable of the great supper, that men may have the kingdom of God offered to them, and yet may wilfully neglect it, and be lost for ever.

We are taught, firstly, in this parable, that *God has made a great provision for the salvation of men's souls.* This is the meaning of the words, 'a certain man made a great supper, and bade many.' This is the gospel.

The gospel contains a full supply of everything that sinners need in order to be saved. We are all naturally starving, empty, helpless, and ready to perish. Forgiveness of all sin, and peace with God;—justification of the person and sanctification of the heart;—grace by the way, and glory in the end,—are the gracious provision which God has prepared for the wants of our souls. There is nothing that sin-laden hearts can wish, or weary consciences require, which is not spread before men in rich abundance in Christ. Christ, in one word, is the sum and substance of the 'great supper.' 'I am the bread of life,' he declares,—'he that cometh unto me shall never hunger, and he that believeth on me shall never thirst.'—'My flesh is meat indeed, and my blood is drink indeed.'—'He that eateth my flesh and drinketh my blood, hath eternal life' (*John* 6:35, 55-56).

We are taught, secondly, in this parable, that *the offers and invitations of the gospel are most broad and liberal.* We read that he who made the supper 'sent his servant at supper time to say to them that were bidden, Come; for all things are now ready.'

There is nothing wanting on God's part for the salvation of man. If man is not saved, the fault is not on God's side. The Father is ready to receive all who come to him by Christ. The Son is ready to cleanse all from their sins who apply to him by faith. The Spirit is ready to come to all who ask for him. There is an infinite willingness in God to save man, if man is only willing to be saved.

There is the fullest warrant for sinners to draw near to God by Christ. The word 'Come,' is addressed to all without exception.—Are men labouring and heavy-laden? 'Come unto me,' says Jesus, 'and I will give you rest' (*Matt.* 11:28).—Are men thirsting? 'If any man thirst,' says Jesus, 'let him come unto me, and drink' (*John* 7:37).— Are men poor and hungry? 'Come,' says Jesus, 'buy wine and milk without money and without price' (*Isa.* 55:1). No man shall ever be able to say that he had no encouragement to seek salvation. That word of the Lord shall silence every objector,—'Him that cometh to me, I will in no wise cast out' (*John* 6:37).

We are taught, thirdly, in this parable, that *many who receive gospel invitations refuse to accept them*. We read that when the servant announced that all things were ready, those who were invited 'all with one consent began to make excuse.' One had one trivial excuse, and another had another. In one point only all were agreed. They would not come.

We have in this part of the parable a vivid picture of the reception which the gospel is continually meeting with wherever it is proclaimed. Thousands are continually doing what the parable describes. They are invited to come to Christ, and they will not come.—It is not ignorance of religion that ruins most men's souls. It is want of will to use knowledge, or love of this present world.—It is not open profligacy that fills hell. It is excessive attention to things which in themselves are lawful.—It is not avowed dislike to the gospel which is so much to be feared. It is that procrastinating, excuse-making spirit, which is always ready with a reason why Christ cannot be served *today*.—Let the words of our Lord on this subject sink down into our hearts. Infidelity and immorality, no doubt, slay their thousands. But decent, plausible, smooth-spoken *excuses* slay their tens of thousands. No excuse can justify a man in refusing God's invitation, and not coming to Christ.

We are taught, lastly, in this parable, that *God earnestly desires the salvation of souls, and would have all means used to procure acceptance for his gospel*. We read that when those who were first invited to the supper refused the invitation, 'the master of the house said to his servant, Go out quickly into the streets and lanes of the city, and bring in hither the poor, and the maimed, and the halt, and the blind.' We read that when this was done, and there was yet room, 'the lord said unto his servant, Go out into the highways and hedges, and compel them to come in, that my house may be filled.'

The meaning of these words can admit of little dispute. They surely justify us in asserting the exceeding love and compassion of God towards sinners. His longsuffering is inexhaustible. If some will not receive the truth, he will have others invited in their stead. His pity for the lost is no feigned and imaginary thing. He is infinitely willing to save souls.—Above all, the words justify every preacher and teacher of the gospel in employing all possible means to awaken sinners, and to turn them from their sins. If they will not come to us in public, we must visit them in private. If they will not attend our preaching in the congregation, we must be ready to preach from house to house. We must even not be ashamed to use a gentle violence. We must be instant in season, out of season (2 *Tim.* 4:2). We must deal with many an unconverted man, as one half-asleep, half out of his mind, and not fully conscious of the state he is in. We must press the gospel on his notice again and again. We must cry aloud and spare not. We must deal with him as we would with a man about to commit suicide. We must try to snatch him as a brand from the burning. We must say, 'I cannot,—I will not,—I dare not let you go on ruining your own soul.' The men of the world may not understand such earnest dealing. They may sneer at all zeal and fervour in religion as fanaticism. But the 'man of God,' who desires to do the work of an evangelist, will heed little what the world says. He will remember the words of our parable. He will 'compel men to come in.'

Let us leave this parable with serious self-inquiry. It ought to speak to us in the present day. To us this invitation of the gospel is addressed as well as to the Jews. To us the Lord is saying constantly, 'Come unto the supper,—Come unto me.'—Have we accepted his invitation? Or are we practically saying, 'I cannot come'? If we die without having come to Christ, we had better never have been born.

Notes—Luke 14:15-24

15.—[*Blessed is he that shall eat bread, etc.*] The motive of this remark, and the real character of him who made it, we are left to conjecture.

Gill thinks it likely that the man was a Jew, who was imbued with the gross notions which were commonly held about feasting and banqueting in the kingdom of Messiah. He shows, from rabbinical writers, that 'the Jews suppose, that God will then make a splendid feast, in which, beside bread, which they call the bread of the kingdom, there will be great variety of flesh, fish, and fowl, plenty of generous wine, and all sorts of delicious fruit. Particularly they speak of a great ox, which they suppose to be the Behemoth in Job, which will then be prepared;—and of Leviathan, and his mate, which will there be dressed;—and of a large fowl, called Ziz, of mountain bigness;—and of old wine, kept from the creation of the world;—and fruits of the garden of Eden, which will then be served up.' I have given this quotation at length, as an instructive instance of the rubbish contained in rabbinical writers.

I am myself unable to see, what some think, that this man was a believer, or even a pious-minded person. To me his remark appears nothing better than the indolent, vague wish of a man who thinks it proper to say something religious, when religion is spoken of in his company. This is well worked out by Stier. The whole tone of the parable which the remark called forth, appears to me irreconcilable with the idea that the remark was to be praised.

16.—[*A certain man made a great supper.*] There is a great similarity between this parable and the one reported by St Matthew (*Matt.* 22:2). Yet it is clear that the two parables are distinct, and were spoken on different occasions.

The primary object of the parable, no doubt, is to show the wickedness and unbelief of the Jews, and the calling of the Gentiles in their stead. The Jews had the first offer of Christ. When they rejected it, they were cut off, and the offer was made to the Gentiles. Yet the parable is evidently meant to apply to the history of the gospel offer, and the reception it meets with, in every age of the church.

17.—[*All things are now ready .... supper time.*] These expressions denote the completion of the whole work of redemption, which was announced to the Jews and Gentiles, after Christ rose again. Then and not till then, could it be said literally 'all things are ready.'

18.—[*Began to make excuse, etc.*] The various excuses which those who were invited made, are types of the various worldly reasons with which men excuse themselves from closing with the offer of Christ's gospel. Let it be noted, that all the things mentioned were in themselves innocent and lawful.

[*Bought ... and I must needs go and see.*] Stella sees in this expression an intentional illustration of the folly of worldly men. They are spending their time, and thoughts, and strength, on things of which they do not know the real worth. If the man had been wise, he says, 'he would first have seen the land, and afterwards bought it.'

20.—[*I have married a wife, etc.*] The Roman Catholic writers do not fail to draw from this expression arguments in favour of the unmarried estate. Yet they can make nothing of it. By parity of reasoning, we might prove that buying oxen, or land, is more sinful than hoarding up money and not spending it. They overlook the beautiful point of this part of the parable, which is this. It is not so much the open breach of God's law, as an excessive attention to lawful and innocent things which ruins many men's souls. Few truths are so completely overlooked.

21.—[*Shewed his lord.*] This seems to teach the duty of a minister. He must report to his Master in heaven, what success he meets with.

[*Being angry.*] It is evident that this expression must not be strained into a proof that God is liable to the passion of anger, as the giver of a feast, whose feast is despised. Yet the words are meant to teach us that unbelief and rejection of the gospel are very provoking to God. And there is a sense, we must never forget, in which 'God is angry with the wicked every day.'

[*The poor ... maimed ... halt ... blind.*] These words describe primarily the Gentiles, who were just in this miserable condition as compared to the Jews. Secondly, they describe all sinners to whom the gospel is offered, who feel their sins, and acknowledge their own spiritual need and poverty.

22.—[*Yet there is room.*] This expression seems to show that there is more willingness on God's part to save sinners, than there is on the part of sinners to be saved, and more grace to be given, than there are hearts willing to receive it.

Bengel remarks, 'neither nature nor grace can endure a vacuum, or empty space.'

23.—[*Compel them to come in.*] This expression must be carefully interpreted. It does not sanction any literal compulsion, or force, in pressing the gospel on men's acceptance. Least of all does it sanction the least approach to intolerance or persecution of men because of their religious opinions.

Bishop Pearce says, 'Compel them by arguments, not by force. The nature of the parable shows this plainly. It was a feast to which they were invited.'

The word translated 'compel,' is only used nine times in the New Testament. In four of the places it is rendered 'constrain.'

Matthew 14:22; Mark 6:45; Acts 28:19; Galatians 6:12. It is evident from these passages, that the word does not necessarily imply any employment of force and violence.

Alford's idea that in the words 'compel them to come in,' there is possibly 'an allusion to infant-baptism,' appears to me exceedingly improbable.

24.—[*None ... bidden shall taste, etc.*] This expression primarily applies to the Jews. Rejecting Christ's gospel they were cut off for a season, until it shall please God to graft them in again (*Rom.* 11:23). Secondarily it illustrates a mournful truth about those who reject the gospel among ourselves. They are sometimes let alone, and given over to a reprobate mind. To refuse truth brings down on man God's heaviest displeasure. Our Lord's words about Chorazin and Bethsaida should often be studied.

LUKE 14:25-35

25 And there went great multitudes with him: and he turned, and said unto them,

26 If any *man* come to me, and hate not his father, and mother, and wife, and children, and brethren, and sisters, yea, and his own life also, he cannot be my disciple.

27 And whosoever doth not bear his cross, and come after me, he cannot be my disciple.

28 For which of you, intending to build a tower, sitteth not down first, and counteth the cost, whether he have *sufficient* to finish *it*?

29 Lest haply, after he hath laid the foundation, and is not able to finish *it*, all that behold *it* begin to mock him,

30 Saying, This man began to build, and was not able to finish.

31 Or what king, going to make war against another king, sitteth not down first, and consulteth whether he be able with ten thousand to meet him that cometh against him with twenty thousand?

32 Or else, while the other is yet a great way off, he sendeth an ambassage, and desireth conditions of peace.

33 So likewise, whosoever he be of you that forsaketh not all that he hath, he cannot be my disciple.

34 Salt *is* good: but if the salt have lost his savour, wherewith shall it be seasoned?

35 It is neither fit for the land, nor yet for the dunghill; *but* men cast it out. He that hath ears to hear, let him hear.

WE learn, firstly, from this passage, that *true Christians must be ready, if need be, to give up everything for Christ's sake.* This is a lesson which is taught in very remarkable language. Our Lord says, 'If any man come to me, and hate not his father and mother, and wife, and children, and brethren, and sisters, yea, and his own life also, he cannot be my disciple.'

This expression must doubtless be interpreted with some qualification. We must never explain any text of Scripture in such a manner as to make it contradict another. Our Lord did not mean us to understand that it is the duty of Christians to hate their relatives. This would have been to contradict the fifth commandment. He only meant that those who follow him must love him with a deeper love even that their nearest and dearest connections, or their own lives.— He did not mean that it is an essential part of Christianity to quarrel with our relatives and friends. But he did mean that if the claims of our relatives and the claims of Christ come into collision, the claims of relatives must give way. We must choose rather to displease those we love most upon earth, than to displease him who died for us on the cross.

The demand which our Lord makes upon us here is peculiarly stringent and heart-searching. Yet it is a wise and a necessary one. Experience shows, both in the church at home, and in the mission-field abroad, that the greatest foes to a man's soul are sometimes those of his own house. It sometimes happens that the greatest hindrance in the way of an awakened conscience, is the opposition of relatives and friends. Ungodly fathers cannot bear to see their sons 'taking up new views' of religion. Worldly mothers are vexed to see their daughters unwilling to enter into the gaieties of the world. A collision of opinion takes place frequently, as soon as grace enters into a family. And then comes the time when the true Christian must remember the spirit of our Lord's words in this passage. He must be willing to offend his family, rather than offend Christ.

The line of duty in such cases is doubtless very painful. It is a heavy cross to disagree with those we love, and specially about spiritual things. But if this cross be laid upon us, we must remember that firmness and decision are true kindness. It can never be true love to relatives to do wrong, in order to please them. And, best of all, firmness accompanied by gentleness and consistency, in the long run of life, often brings its own reward. Thousands of Christians will bless God at the last day, that they had relatives and friends who chose to displease them rather than Christ. That very decision was the first thing that made them think seriously, and led finally to the conversion of their souls.

We learn, secondly, from this passage, that *those who are thinking of following Christ should be warned to 'count the cost.'* This is a lesson which was intended for the multitudes who followed our Lord without thought and consideration, and was enforced by examples drawn from building and from war. It is a lesson which will be found useful in every age of the church.

It costs something to be a true Christian. Let that never be forgotten. To be a mere nominal Christian, and go to church, is cheap and easy work. But to hear Christ's voice, and follow Christ, and believe in Christ, and confess Christ, requires much self-denial. It will cost us our sins, and our self-righteousness, and our ease, and our worldliness. All—all must be given up. We must fight an enemy, who comes against us with twenty thousand followers. We must build a tower in troublous times. Our Lord Jesus Christ would have us thoroughly understand this. He bids us 'count the cost.'

Now, why did our Lord use this language? Did he wish to discourage men from becoming his disciples? Did he mean to make the gate of life appear more narrow than it is? It is not difficult to find an answer to these questions. Our Lord spoke as he did to prevent men following him lightly and inconsiderately, from mere animal feeling or temporary excitement, who in time of temptation would fall away. He knew that nothing does so much harm to the cause of true religion as backsliding, and that nothing causes so much backsliding as enlisting disciples without letting them know what they take in hand. He had no desire to swell the number of his followers by admitting soldiers who would fail in the hour of need. For this reason he raises a warning voice. He bids all who think of taking service with him count the cost before they begin.

Well would it be for the church and the world if the ministers of Christ would always remember their Master's conduct in this passage. Often,—far too often,—people are built up in self-deception, and encouraged to think they are converted when in reality they are not converted at all. Feelings are supposed to be faith. Convictions are supposed to be grace. These things ought not so to be. By all means let us encourage the first beginnings of religion in a soul. But never let us urge people forward without telling them what true Christianity entails. Never let us hide from them the battle and the toil. Let us say to them 'come with us,'—but let us also say 'count the cost.'

We learn, lastly, from this passage, *how miserable is the condition of backsliders and apostates.* This is a lesson which is intimately connected with the preceding one. The necessity of 'counting the cost' is enforced by a picture of the consequences of neglecting to do so. The man who has once made a profession of religion, but has afterwards gone back from it, is like salt which has 'lost its savour.' Such salt is comparatively useless. 'It is neither fit for the land, nor yet for the dunghill: but men cast it out.' Yet the state of that salt is a lively emblem of the state of a backslider. No wonder that our Lord said, 'He that hath ears to hear let him hear.'

The truth which our Lord brings out in this place is very painful, but very useful and needful to be known. No man, be it remembered, is in so dangerous a state as he who has once known the truth and professed to love it, and has afterwards fallen away from his profession, and gone back to the world. You can tell such a man nothing that he does not know. You can show him no doctrine that he has not heard. He has not sinned in ignorance like many. He has gone away from Christ with his eyes open. He has sinned against a known, and not an unknown God. His case is well-nigh desperate. All things are possible with God. Yet it is written, 'It is impossible for those who were once enlightened,—if they shall fall away, to renew them again unto repentance' (*Heb.* 6:4-6).

Let us ponder these things well. The subject is one which is not sufficiently considered. Let us never be afraid of beginning to serve Christ. But let us begin seriously, thoughtfully, and with a due consideration of the step we take. And having once begun, let us pray for grace that we may persevere, and never fall way.

Notes—Luke 14:25-35

25.—[*Great multitudes ... he turned and said, etc.*] The conduct of our Lord on this occasion stands out in strong contrast to that of many ministers of the gospel, in the present day.

The temptation to admit people to full communion, and endorse and approve them as true Christians, before they have given evidence of decided grace, is very strong. The inclination to set before young inquirers the joys and comforts of the gospel, without any proportionate exhibition of the cross and the fight, requires constant watching against.

The close imitation of our Lord's conduct in this passage would probably greatly lessen the number of our communicants. But it may be doubted whether we should not gain in quality what we lost in quantity, and whether we should not be freed from many of those disgraceful backslidings, and gross inconsistencies, which so often nowadays bring discredit on religion.

It may be laid down as a general rule that communicants cheaply admitted are worth little, and that to call people Christians upon lower terms than those which our Lord sets forth, in the long run does more harm than good.

26.—[*Come to me, and hate not.*] The expression 'hate,' in this verse, must evidently be taken comparatively. The following quotation from Pearce deserves reading.

'Besides the proof from Matthew 10:37, that the word "hate" here means "love less," it may be added, that in Matthew 6:24, the word "hate" is used after the same manner. So also when we read in Romans 9:13, "Jacob have I loved, but Esau have I hated," the meaning is, that I have loved Jacob more than Esau. That this is no arbitrary interpretation of the word "hate," but one agreeable to the Hebrew idiom, appears from what is said in Genesis 29:30, 31, where Leah being "hated," is explained by Rachel being loved more than Leah. See also Deuteronomy 21:15-17.'

28.—[*To build a tower.*] The following note from Doddridge deserves reading.

'The phrase, "build a tower," naturally suggests to us the idea of a more magnificent edifice, than our Lord's hearers might probably think of on this occasion. It is plain that towers were frequently run up, probably of slight materials, to lodge those who had the care of keeping vineyards or flocks; and they were built pretty high in proportion to their base, that they might command the larger prospect.'

There is reason in this comment, when we mark our Lord's words, 'which of you.'

31.—[*What king, etc.*] Some regard this 'king' as an emblem of a believer, and the king coming 'with twenty thousand,' as Satan. I am quite unable to see this. Both here and in the preceding three verses, I believe our Lord is only borrowing an illustration from familiar subjects, and that we are not meant to look further.

33.—[*Forsaketh.*] The Greek word so rendered is more commonly translated, 'bid farewell,' or 'take leave.' The meaning evidently is that a man cannot be Christ's disciple unless he is deliberately prepared to give up everything for his sake, if need be, and to encounter any enemy, and make any sacrifice.

34.—[*Salt have lost his savour.*] The following quotation from Maundrell deserves reading. He is describing the valley of salt in his travels, and he says, 'Along, on one side, there is a small precipice, occasioned by the continual taking away of the salt. I broke a piece of it, of which the part exposed to the rain, sun, and air, though it had the sparks and particles of salt, had completely lost its savour. The inner part which was connected with the rock, retained its savour.'

Schoettgen speaks of a species of salt in Judæa, brought from the Dead Sea, and called bituminous salt, which was easily rendered vapid, and of no other use but to 'spread in a part of the temple, on the pavement, to prevent slipping in wet weather.'

This striking and solemn saying about the 'salt which has lost its savour,' is found on no less than three distinct occasions in the Gospels (see *Matt.* 5:13, and *Mark* 9:50). The spiritual lesson of the passage is fearfully overlooked. The sinfulness of sins against light and knowledge, and the possibility of being given over to a reprobate mind, are points not sufficiently dwelt upon by preachers, or considered by hearers. Men seem to forget that there is such a thing as an unpardonable sin,—and that if salt has once lost its savour it cannot be seasoned again.

I should not like to be mistaken in saying this. I cannot find in Scripture any clear proof that there is any decreed reprobation. I hold that the destruction of those who are lost is the consequence of their own sins, and not of God's predestination. I believe that we have no right to say of any sinner, that he is too bad to be saved.

But the general teaching of the New Testament appears to be that nothing is so displeasing to God as the misuse of knowledge, and the wilful turning away from truth once seen and acknowledged, to the service of sin and the world. The Bible teaches, in fact, that no sinner is so unlikely to be saved as the man who after making a high spiritual profession, falls away and returns to the world, and no heart so unlikely to be changed as the heart which once professed to love the gospel, but afterwards became cold and indifferent to it.

I can certainly testify, after sixteen years' ministry, that by far the most hopeless and painful death-beds I have attended have been those of backsliders. I have seen some such persons go out of the world without hope, whose conscience really appeared dead, buried, and gone, and on whom every truth, and doctrine, and argument appeared alike thrown away. They seemed to have lost the power of feeling, and could only lie still and despair. I fear the true account of such persons' state of soul was the sentence of our Lord, on which I have now been dwelling.

LUKE 15:1-10

1 Then drew near unto him all the publicans and sinners for to hear him.

2 And the Pharisees and scribes murmured, saying, This man receiveth sinners, and eateth with them.

3 And he spake this parable unto them, saying,

4 What man of you, having an hundred sheep, if he lose one of them, doth not leave the ninety and nine in the wilderness, and go after that which is lost, until he find it?

5 And when he hath found *it*, he layeth *it* on his shoulders, rejoicing.

6 And when he cometh home, he calleth together *his* friends and neighbours, saying unto them, Rejoice with me; for I have found my sheep which was lost.

7 I say unto you, that likewise joy shall be in heaven over one sinner that repenteth, more than over ninety and nine just persons, which need no repentance.

8 Either what woman having ten pieces of silver, if she lose one piece, doth not light a candle, and sweep the house, and seek diligently till she find *it*?

9 And when she hath found *it*, she calleth *her* friends and *her* neighbours together, saying, Rejoice with me; for I have found the piece which I had lost.

10 Likewise, I say unto you, there is joy in the presence of the angels of God over one sinner that repenteth.

THE chapter which begins with these verses is well known to Bible readers if any is in the Scriptures. Few chapters perhaps have done more good to the souls of men. Let us take heed that it does good to us.

We should first observe in these verses, *the striking testimony which was borne to our Lord by his enemies.* We read that when 'all the publicans and sinners drew near to hear him, the scribes and Pharisees murmured, saying, This man receiveth sinners, and eateth with them.'

These words were evidently spoken with surprise and scorn, and not with pleasure and admiration. These ignorant guides of the Jews could not understand a preacher of religion having anything to do with wicked people! Yet their words worked for good. The very saying which was meant for a reproach was adopted by the Lord Jesus as a true description of his office. It led to his speaking three of the most instructive parables which ever fell from his lips.

The testimony of the scribes and Pharisees was strictly and literally true. The Lord Jesus is indeed one that 'receiveth sinners.' He receives them to pardon them, to sanctify them, and to make them meet for heaven. It is his special office to do so. For this end he came into the world. He came not to call the righteous, but sinners to repentance.

He came into the world to save sinners. What he was upon earth he is now at the right hand of God, and will be to all eternity. He is emphatically the sinner's Friend.

Have we any sense of sin? Do we feel bad, and wicked, and guilty, and deserving of God's anger? Is the remembrance of our past lives bitter to us? Does the recollection of our past conduct make us ashamed? Then we are the very people who ought to apply to Christ, just as we are, pleading nothing of our own, making no useless delay. Christ will receive us graciously, pardon us freely, and give us eternal life. He is One that 'receiveth sinners.' Let us not be lost for want of applying to him that we may be saved.

We should observe, secondly, in these verses, *the remarkable figures under which our Lord describes his own love towards sinners.* We read that in reply to the taunting remark of his enemies he spoke three parables,—the parables of the lost sheep, the lost piece of silver, and the prodigal son. The two first of these parables are now before us. All three are meant to illustrate one and the same truth. They all throw strong light on Christ's willingness to save sinners.

Christ's love is an active, working love. Just as the shepherd did not sit still bewailing his lost sheep, and the woman did not sit still bewailing her lost money, so our blessed Lord did not sit still in heaven pitying sinners. He left the glory which he had with the Father, and humbled himself to be made in the likeness of man. He came down into the world to seek and save that which was lost. He never rested till he had made atonement for our transgressions, brought in everlasting righteousness, provided eternal redemption, and opened a door of life to all who are willing to be saved.

Christ's love is a self-denying love. The shepherd brought his lost sheep home on his own shoulders rather than leave it in the wilderness. The woman lighted a candle, and swept the house, and searched diligently, and spared no pains, till she found her lost money. And just so did Christ not spare himself, when he undertook to save sinners. 'He endured the cross, despising the shame.' He 'laid down his life for his friends.' Greater love than this cannot be shown (*John* 15:13; *Heb.* 12:2).

Christ's love is a deep and mighty love. Just as the shepherd rejoiced to find his sheep, and the woman to find her money, so does the Lord Jesus rejoice to save sinners. It is a real pleasure to him to pluck them as brands from the burning. It was his 'meat and drink,' when upon earth, to finish the work which he came to do. He felt straitened in spirit till it was accomplished. It is still his delight to show mercy. He is far more willing to save sinners than sinners are to be saved.

Let us strive to know something of this love of Christ. It is a love that truly passeth knowledge. It is unspeakable and unsearchable. It is that on which we must wholly rest our souls, if we would have peace in time and glory in eternity. If we take comfort in our own love to Christ, we are building on a sandy foundation. But if we lean on Christ's love to us, we are on a rock.

We should observe, lastly, in these verses, *the wide encouragement which our Lord holds out to repentance*. We read these striking words, 'Joy shall be in heaven over one sinner that repenteth.' We read the same thought again after a few verses; 'There is joy in the presence of the angels of God over one sinner that repenteth.' The thing is doubled, to make doubt impossible. The idea is repeated, in order to meet man's unbelief.

There are deep things in these sayings, beyond doubt. Our poor weak minds are little able to understand how the perfect joy of heaven can admit of increase. But one thing, at any rate, stands out clearly on the face of these expressions. There is an infinite willingness on God's part to receive sinners. However wicked a man may have been, in the day that he really turns from his wickedness and comes to God by Christ, God is well-pleased. God has no pleasure in the death of him that dieth, and God has pleasure in true repentance.

Let the man who is afraid to repent, consider well the verses we are now looking at, and be afraid no more. There is nothing on God's part to justify his fears. An open door is set before him. A free pardon awaits him. 'If we confess our sins, God is faithful and just to forgive our sins, and to cleanse us from all unrighteousness' (*1 John* 1:9).

Let the man who is ashamed to repent, consider these verses, and cast shame aside. What though the world mocks and jests at his repentance? While man is mocking, angels are rejoicing. The very change which sinners call foolishness, is a change which fills heaven with joy.

Have we repented ourselves? This, after all, is the principal question which concerns us. What shall it profit us to know Christ's love, if we do not use it? 'If ye know these things, happy are ye if ye do them' (*John* 13:17).

Notes—Luke 15:1-10

1.—[*Then drew near.*] The Greek words so translated do not literally mean a particular act at a particular time. They would be more closely rendered, 'And there were drawing near.' Alford renders them, 'were busied in drawing near,'—'were continually about him.' The beginning of this chapter, be it observed, is an unbroken continuation of the last.

Let us mark the accessibleness and affability of our Lord's demeanour in this expression. He was one of whom people were not afraid. Such a demeanour is a great gift.

[*All the publicans and sinners.*] By the expression 'all' we are evidently meant to understand 'all' in that particular neighbourhood where our Lord at present was.

Let it be noted that no Gospel writer gives so many instances of our Lord's mercy to sinners as St Luke. It is supposed, with much reason, that this was intended for the encouragement of Gentile converts, for whom his Gospel was specially written. Observe, beside this chapter, Luke 18:10; 23:34, 43. These passages are all peculiar to St Luke.

2.—[*Murmured.*] The Greek word here is only used in one other place,—Luke 19:7. It means literally 'murmured greatly,' or 'were constantly murmuring' throughout the journey.

[*This man receiveth sinners.*] These words should be carefully noted. They are the key note to the whole chapter.

A constant recollection of them throws light on the interpretation of all the three parables which follow. The Pharisees found fault with our Lord for 'inviting sinners.' Our Lord replies, in effect, that the thing which they found fault with was the very thing he came on earth to do, and a thing of which he was not ashamed. He came to do for sinners what the shepherd did for his lost sheep, the woman did for her lost money, and the father did for the prodigal son. As for his murmuring enemies, they were like the elder brother of the prodigal son.

I am persuaded that remembrance of this expression is of great importance in the chapter, and that many strange explanations of things in the chapter have been given by commentators, for want of observing the expression.—The great object of all the three parables is one and the same. They all three exhibit the love and mercy of Christ towards sinners, but under three different aspects. I hold with Bengel, that the lost sheep represents the stupid, foolish sinner,—the lost piece of money the sinner altogether ignorant of himself,—and the younger son the daring and wilful sinner. But I also hold that the love which goes after the sheep, seeks the money, and runs to meet the prodigal, is all through intended to represent the *love of Christ.*—I cannot assent to the view that the three parables were meant to point to the work of the three persons of the Trinity. I cannot hold the view of Bengel, Alford, and Stier, that 'the woman' represents the Holy Ghost,—and the view of Ambrose and Wordsworth, that she represents the church. All these ideas I believe to be foreign to our Lord's intention when he spoke the three parables. I consider that the right way to view the three parables before us is to suppose that our Lord's meaning was as follows:—'You blame me for receiving sinners. I am not ashamed of it. I do receive them. I came on earth for that very purpose. If you would know my feeling towards sinners, mark the conduct of a shepherd seeking a lost sheep, a woman seeking a lost piece of money, and a kind father receiving a prodigal son. In the love exhibited in each of these three cases you have an emblem of my love to sinners.'

4.—[*What man of you, etc.*] Both in this and the two following verses, I must decline assigning the allegorical meanings to every part of the parable, which many commentators have discovered. The two numbers, hundred, and ninety-nine,—the wilderness,—the shepherd's laying the lost sheep on his shoulders,—the home,—the friends and neighbours,—all appear to me to be subordinate circumstances of the parable, which were simply intended to illustrate one great leading truth, the deep self-sacrificing love of Christ towards sinners, and the pleasure with which he saves them.

The beautiful fitness of the images chosen in the parable, is very striking. Our Lord speaks of himself in the tenth chapter of St John, as the good Shepherd.—Isaiah says, in the fifty-third chapter of his prophecy, 'All we, like sheep, have gone astray.'

7.—[*I say unto you.*] In this verse the Lord drops the language of parables and declares to us a great truth.

[*Likewise.*] The Greek word thus rendered here, and at the tenth verse, is more commonly translated 'so,' or 'even so.'

[*Joy shall be in heaven.*] The use of the future tense in this expression, has led some to think that our Lord is speaking of the day of judgment, when the saved souls shall be presented before the Father with exceeding joy. I cannot see this. I believe that our Lord simply means that when any

sinner shall repent, at any time in the history of the church, his repentance will be regarded with gladness in heaven, whatever murmuring there may be among Pharisees on earth.

[*One sinner.*] The exceeding value of one soul, in God's sight, appears in this expression. It also appears to overthrow the idea entertained by some, that the lost sheep represents the whole church of the elect, or the redeemed world.

Those who are cast down and dispirited in preaching and teaching, by apparently small success, should often think of this expression, and the parallel one in the 10th verse. The value of one soul is not enough considered.

[*Ninety and nine just ... no repentance.*] This expression is remarkable, and has caused much difference of opinion among commentators. Five different explanations are given.

1. Some think that it means the angels who have never sinned.

2. Some think that it means the glorified saints who can sin no more.

3. Some think that it means living saints who have not lost baptismal purity.

4. Some think that it means the inhabitants of other worlds, who have not fallen like man.

5. Some think that it means people who think themselves righteous and just, like the Pharisees, and fancy they need no repentance.

I believe the last to be the true view, and the others to be untenable. It is confirmed by Luke 5:32; 16:15; 18:9; Matthew 9:13; Mark 2:17.

8.—[*Either what woman.*] Let us note both here and in the last parable, how simple and familiar our Lord's illustrations of truth were. A shepherd, and a woman, are his chosen vehicles to convey to our minds some idea of his care for sinners.

Both in this verse, and the following verse, I adhere to the view expressed in the comments on the preceding parable. I decline to assign allegorical meanings to the expressions used. The woman,—the number ten,—the candle lighting,—the house,—the sweeping,—the friends and neighbours, all appear to me nothing more than subordinate circumstances in a story which is intended to teach one great truth, Christ's care for sinners, and pleasure in saving them.

Many commentators see much meaning in a 'piece of silver' being the type of the sinner. They dwell upon the image stamped on the coin, as significant of the image of God, in which man was originally created. Those who wish to see how far this idea may be worked out, will find it fully given in Ness's *History and Mystery of the New Testament*.

10.—[*Joy ... angels of God.*] This expression seems to show that the salvation of sinners is a matter of deep interest to the angels, and the recovery of each one carefully observed. This, be it remembered, is a very different thing from saying that angels can help our souls.

LUKE 15:11-24

11 And he said, A certain man had two sons:

12 And the younger of them said to *his* father, Father, give me the portion of goods that falleth *to me.* And he divided unto them *his living.*

13 And not many days after the younger son gathered all together, and took his journey into a far country, and there wasted his substance with riotous living.

14 And when he had spent all, there arose a mighty famine in that land; and he began to be in want.

15 And he went and joined himself to a citizen of that country; and he sent him into his fields to feed swine.

16 And he would fain have filled his belly with the husks that the swine did eat: and no man gave unto him.

17 And when he came to himself, he said, How many hired servants of my father's have bread enough and to spare, and I perish with hunger!

18 I will arise and go to my father, and will say unto him, Father, I have sinned against heaven and before thee,

19 And am no more worthy to be called thy son: make me as one of thy hired servants.

20 And he arose, and came to his father. But when he was yet a great way off, his father saw him, and had compassion, and ran, and fell on his neck, and kissed him.

21 And the son said unto him, Father, I have sinned against heaven, and in thy sight, and am no more worthy to be called thy son.

22 But the father said to his servants, Bring forth the best robe, and put *it* on him; and put a ring on his hand, and shoes on *his* feet:

23 And bring hither the fatted calf, and kill *it*; and let us eat, and be merry:

24 For this my son was dead, and is alive again; he was lost, and is found. And they began to be merry.

THE parable before us is commonly known as the parable of 'the prodigal son.' It may be truly called a mighty spiritual picture. Unlike some of our Lord's parables, it does not convey to us one great lesson only, but many. Every part of it is peculiarly rich in instruction.

We see, firstly, in this parable, *man following the natural bent of his own heart*. Our Lord shows us a 'younger son' making haste to set up for himself, going far away from a kind father's house, and 'wasting his substance with riotous living.'

We have in these words a faithful portrait of the mind with which we are all born. This is our likeness. We are all naturally proud and self-willed. We have no pleasure in fellowship with God. We depart from him, and go afar off. We spend our time, and strength, and faculties, and affections, on things that cannot profit. The covetous man does it in one fashion, the slave of lusts and passions in another, the lover of pleasure in another. In one point only all are agreed. Like sheep, we all naturally 'go astray, and turn every one to his own way' (*Isa.* 53:6). In the younger son's first conduct we see the natural heart.

He that knows nothing of these things has yet much to learn. He is spiritually blind. The eyes of his understanding need to be opened. The worst ignorance in the world is not to know ourselves. Happy is he who has been delivered from the kingdom of darkness, and been made acquainted with himself! Of too many it may be said, 'They know not, neither will they understand; they walk on in darkness' (*Psa.* 82:5).

We see, secondly, in this parable, *man finding out that the ways of sin are hard, by bitter experience*. Our Lord shows us the younger son spending all his property and reduced to want,—obliged to take service and 'feed swine,'—so hungry that he is ready to eat swine's food, and cared for by none.

These words describe a common case. Sin is a hard master, and the servants of sin always find it out, sooner or later, to their cost. Unconverted people are never really happy. Under a profession of high spirits and cheerfulness, they are often ill at ease within. Thousands of them are sick at heart, dissatisfied with themselves, weary of their own ways, and thoroughly uncomfortable. 'There be many that say, Who will show us any good?' 'There is no peace, saith my God, to the wicked' (*Psa.* 4:6; *Isa.* 57:21).

Let this truth sink down into our hearts. It is a truth, however loudly unconverted people may deny it. 'The way of transgressors is hard' (*Prov.* 13:15). The secret wretchedness of natural men is exceedingly great. There is a famine within, however much they may try to conceal it. They are 'in want.' He that 'soweth to his flesh shall of the flesh reap corruption.' No wonder that St Paul said, 'What fruit had ye then in those things whereof ye are now ashamed?' (*Gal.* 6:8; *Rom.* 6:21).

We see, thirdly, in this parable, *man awaking to a sense of his natural state, and resolving to repent.* Our Lord tells us that the younger son 'came to himself and said, how many hired servants of my father's have bread enough and to spare, and I perish with hunger! I will arise and go to my father, and say unto him, Father, I have sinned.'

The thoughts of thousands are vividly painted in these words. Thousands have reasoned in this way, and are saying such things to themselves every day. And we must be thankful when we see such thoughts arise. Thinking is not change of heart, but it may be the beginning of it. Conviction is not conversion, but it is one step, at any rate, in a right direction. The ruin of many people's souls is simply this, that they never think at all.

One caution, however, must always be given. Men must beware that they do not stop short in 'thinking.' Good thoughts are all very well, but they are not saving Christianity. If the younger son had never got beyond thinking, he might have kept from home to the day of his death.

We see, fourthly, in this parable, *man turning to God with true repentance and faith.* Our Lord shows us the younger son quitting the far country where he was, and going back to his father's house, carrying into practice the good intentions he had formed, and unreservedly confessing his sin. 'He arose and went.'

These words are a lifelike outline of true repentance and conversion. The man in whose heart a true work of the Holy Ghost has begun, will never be content with thinking and resolving. He will break off from sin. He will come out from its fellowship. He will cease to do evil. He will learn to do well. He will turn to God in humble prayer. He will confess his iniquities. He will not attempt to excuse his sins. He will say with David, 'I acknowledge my transgression.' He will say with the publican, 'God be merciful to me a sinner' (*Psa.* 51:3; *Luke* 18:13).

Let us beware of any repentance, falsely so called, which is not of this character. Action is the very life of 'repentance unto salvation.' Feelings, and tears, and remorse, and wishes, and resolutions, are all useless, until they are accompanied by action and a change of life. In fact they are worse than useless. Insensibly they sear the conscience and harden the heart.

We see, fifthly, in this parable, *the penitent man received readily, pardoned freely, and completely accepted with God.* Our Lord shows us this, in this part of the younger son's history, in the most touching manner. We read that 'When he was yet a great way off, his father saw him, and had compassion, and ran, and fell on his neck, and kissed him. And the son said unto him, Father, I have sinned against heaven and in thy sight, and am no more worthy to be called thy son. But the father said to his servants, Bring forth the best robe and put it on him; and put a ring on his hand, and shoes on his feet: And bring hither the fatted calf, and kill it; and let us eat, and be merry: for this my son was dead, and is alive again; he was lost, and is found. And they began to be merry.'

More deeply affecting words than these, perhaps, were never written. To comment on them seems almost needless. It is like gilding refined gold, and painting the lily. They show us in great broad letters the infinite love of the Lord Jesus Christ towards sinners. They teach how infinitely willing he is to receive all who come to him, and how complete, and full, and immediate is the pardon which he is ready to bestow. 'By him all that believe are justified from all things.'—'He is plenteous in mercy' (*Acts* 13:39; *Psa.* 86:5).

Let this boundless mercy of our Lord Jesus Christ be graven deeply in our memories, and sink into our minds. Let us never forget that he is One 'that receiveth sinners.' With him and his mercy sinners ought to begin, when they first begin to desire salvation. On him and his mercy saints must live, when they have been taught to repent and believe. 'The life which I now live in the flesh,' says St Paul, 'I live by the faith of the Son of God, who loved me, and gave himself for me' (*Gal.* 2:20).

Notes—Luke 15:11-24

11.—[*A certain man had two sons.*] Of all the parables in the New Testament this is perhaps the most full and instructive. Of the three in this chapter it is far the most striking. The first parable concerns one sheep out of a hundred. The second concerns one piece of money out of ten. The one before us concerns one son out of two. We must not attach too much importance to these numbers. But it is interesting to observe them.

It is common to regard the 'father' in this parable as the type of God the Father; and the sons, as types of Jews and Gentiles. I cannot assent to this view respecting the father. As to the sons, I only remark, that it was not the primary idea in our Lord's mind.

I believe that the younger son was meant to be a type of all unconverted sinners, and that his return to his father's house was an emblem of true repentance.—I believe that the father's kind reception of his son was meant to represent the Lord Jesus Christ's kindness and love toward sinners who come to him, and the free and full pardon which he bestows on them.—I believe that the elder son was meant to be a type of all narrow-minded self-righteous people in every age of the church, and specially of the scribes and Pharisees, who 'murmured' at our Lord for receiving sinners. These are what I believe to be the general lessons of the parable. So far I can go in interpreting it, but no further.

I may as well say here, once for all, that I am unable to see that the elder son represents the angels,—or that the 'citizen,' with whom the younger son took service, is the devil,—or the best robe, Christ's righteousness,—or the ring, assurance of pardon,—or the shoes, grace to walk with God,—or the servants, Christ's ministers,—

or the fatted calf, the Lord's supper. All such interpretations are doubtless very ingenious, and are held by many. Maldonatus says wisely 'they are uncertain.'

I content myself with remarking that I do not believe they represent the mind of Christ. The parable contains a story which strikingly illustrates Christ's love towards sinners. That story is told in the most striking manner, and is conveyed in imagery of the most graphic kind. But I am quite unable to see that every part of the imagery employed was intended by our Lord to bear a spiritual meaning.

12.—[*The younger of them said.*] Let it be noted that the 'younger son' was the one who exhibited self-will, and love of independence. This makes his conduct more reprehensible.

[*That falleth to me.*] Parkhurst remarks, that 'there is reference here to the laws both of Jews and Romans. In this they agreed that they did not allow the father of a family the voluntary distribution of his whole estate, but allotted a certain portion to the younger son (*Deut.* 21:16). The young man, therefore, only desired the immediate possession of that fortune which according to the common course of things, must in a few years devolve to him.'

13.—[*With riotous living.*] The word would be more literally rendered, 'living riotously.' The Greek word for 'riotously,' is only used here. It means strictly 'in such a way as to save nothing,—wastefully.'

15.—[*A citizen of that country.*] Gill says that this means, 'A Pharisaical legal preacher.' I cannot for a moment see this.

[*To feed swine.*] Let it be remembered, that our Lord was speaking to an audience of Jews. They regarded swine, by the law of Moses, as unclean animals. This circumstance of the story therefore, would probably convey to Jewish minds a most vivid idea of the degraded condition to which the younger son was reduced.

16.—[*He would fain have filled.*] Major says that this expression does not mean that he desired and was unable to gratify his desire. It rather signifies 'He was glad—he was only too happy.' See the same expression in Luke 16:21.

[*The husks.*] There seems little doubt that these husks mean the fruit of a tree called the carob tree, common in the Levant, and still used for feeding swine, but very unsuitable for the food of man. It probably answers to the beech mast, which swine eat among ourselves.

[*No man gave unto him.*] This does not mean that 'no man gave him husks,' as some have supposed. It only means, that 'No man gave him anything at all;—he was entirely neglected by everyone.'

17.—[*Came to himself.*] This expression has often called forth the remark that a man must come to himself, before he comes to God.

18.—[*Against heaven and before thee, etc.*] This is a confession of sin against God and man. It is one of the places in Scripture where 'heaven,' the place where God dwells, is used for God himself. See Daniel 4:26 and Matthew 21:25.

20.—[*He arose and came.*] The remark is sometimes made that the prodigal son's boldness in returning to his father's house, arose from the fact that, fallen as he was, he was yet 'a son.' An argument has been extracted from this circumstance in defence of baptismal regeneration. Alford remarks, 'he nowhere gives up his sonship,' and then gives the following quotation from Trench, 'What is it that gives the sinner now a sure ground of confidence, that, returning to God, he shall not be repelled, nor cast out?—The adoption of sonship which he renewed in Christ Jesus at his baptism, and his faith that the gifts and calling of God are without recall.'

I believe the above argument to be erroneous. I cannot admit that the parable before us gives any aid to the doctrine of baptismal regeneration. Parabolic expressions must never be strained into proof of doctrines. Those who see baptismal regeneration in the prodigal son's expression, 'Father, I have sinned,' and tell us to remark that, bad as he was, the young man did not forget his sonship, would do well to remember a twice-repeated expression in the parable. Twice over we are told that before the younger son came back he was 'dead.' Now to be dead is to be without life, and to be without life is to need being 'born again.' This is precisely what the younger son went through,—he was dead, but he 'lived again.' If those who hold baptismal regeneration will only concede that all unconverted sinners, whether baptized or unbaptized, are 'dead,' we ask no more. But will they do this?

The plain truth is, that parables are not those portions of Scripture to which we must turn for accurately-defined statements of doctrine. To find baptismal regeneration in this parable, is to turn entirely away from our Lord's intention in speaking it.

[*A great way off ... ran ... kissed.*] These three expressions are deeply touching. They bring out in strong relief the difficulty with which a sinner turns to Christ, and the readiness and willingness of Christ to receive him.

21.—[*To be called thy son.*] Let it be noted that the prodigal does not finish the sentence which he had intended to address to his father. The meaning of the omission probably is, that our Lord desired to impress on us the father's readiness to receive him. He did not allow him to finish his words, but interrupted him by expressions of kindness.

22.—[*The father said.*] Let it be noted that the father does not say a single word to his son about his profligacy and wickedness. There is neither rebuke nor reproof for the past, nor galling admonitions for the present, nor irritating advice for the future. The one idea that is represented as filling his mind, is joy that his son has come home. This is a striking fact.

[*The best robe.*] Some try to prove that this means that first old robe which the younger son used to wear, before he left his father's house. This is the view of Theophylact and Calovius. The idea is untenable. Our translators have given the true sense.

[*A ring.*] This was a mark of honour, and confidence, and distinction. See Genesis 41:42; Esther 3:10; James 2:2.

[*Shoes on his feet.*] This probably indicated that he was to be regarded not as a servant, as he had thought once he might be, but as a free man and a son. Prisoners and slaves were evidently barefooted (*Isa.* 20:4).

23.—[*The fatted calf.*] This expression means literally, 'the calf—that fatted one,'—one kept for a special occasion, a sacrifice, or a feast.

Stella, the Spanish commentator, seems to have been much annoyed by allegorical commentators, in his day. He says on this expression, with much quaint bluntness, 'If you ask me what the fatted calf means, I reply that it means a calf, and nothing but a calf.'

24.—[*Was dead and is alive again.*] Let this expression be carefully noted. Though part of a parable, it is worthy of remark as our Lord's language in describing the life of the prodigal son before his repentance, and the change when he repented. The one state was death. The other was life.

[*They began to be merry.*] The strong contrast between this expression and the one at the end of the 14th verse ought not to be overlooked. Unconverted, man begins to be 'in want.' Converted, he begins to be 'happy.'

In leaving this part of the parable, I feel it right to say, that I fully admit that it may be taken in a national sense, and that in that sense it makes excellent divinity. The Gentile nations who departed from God after the flood, and reaped darkness, misery, and hard bondage under Satan, by their departure, may undoubtedly be typified by the younger son.

Their repentance and return to God, through the preaching of the gospel after our Lord's ascension, may be typified by the prodigal son's return to his father's house. The envy with which the believing Gentiles were regarded by the Jews, may be typified by the conduct of the elder son. The parable would then, as is often the case, be a prophecy.

The words of our Lord are often so deep that they will admit of a double meaning. So it may be here. The parable may be interpreted both of nations and of individuals. All I maintain is, that the individual personal interpretation of it is decidedly the primary one which it ought to receive.

LUKE 15:25-32

25 Now his elder son was in the field: and as he came and drew nigh to the house, he heard musick and dancing.

26 And he called one of the servants, and asked what these things meant.

27 And he said unto him, Thy brother is come; and thy father hath killed the fatted calf, because he hath received him safe and sound.

28 And he was angry, and would not go in: therefore came his father out, and intreated him.

29 And he answering said to *his* father, Lo, these many years do I serve thee, neither transgressed I at any time thy commandment: and yet thou never gavest me a kid, that I might make merry with my friends:

30 But as soon as this thy son was come, which hath devoured thy living with harlots, thou hast killed for him the fatted calf.

31 And he said unto him, Son, thou art ever with me, and all that I have is thine.

32 It was meet that we should make merry, and be glad: for this thy brother was dead, and is alive again; and was lost, and is found.

THESE verses form the conclusion of the parable of the prodigal son. They are far less well known than the verses which go before them. But they were spoken by the same lips which described the younger son's return to his father's house. Like everything which those lips spoke, they will be found deeply profitable.

We are taught, firstly, in this passage, *how unkind and ill-natured are the feelings of self-righteous men towards sinners.*

This is a lesson which our Lord conveys to us by describing the conduct of the 'elder brother' of the prodigal son. He shows him to us 'angry' and finding fault because of the rejoicings over his brother's return. He shows him complaining that his father treated the returning prodigal too well, and that he himself had not been treated so well as his merits deserved. He shows him utterly unable to share in the joy which prevailed when his younger brother came home, and giving way to ill-natured and envious thoughts. It is a painful picture, but a very instructive one.

For one thing, this elder brother is an exact picture of the Jews of our Lord's times. They could not bear the idea of their Gentile younger brother being made partaker of their privileges. They would fain have excluded him from God's favour. They steadily refused to see that the Gentiles were to be fellow-heirs and partakers of Christ with themselves. In all this they were precisely acting the part of the 'elder brother.'

For another thing, the elder brother is an exact type of the scribes and Pharisees of our Lord's times. They objected that our Lord received sinners and ate with them. They murmured because he opened the door of salvation to publicans and harlots. They would have been better pleased if our Lord had confined his ministry to them and their party, and had left the ignorant and sinful entirely alone. Our Lord saw this state of things clearly; and never did he paint it with such graphic power as in the picture of the 'elder brother.'

Last, but not least, the elder brother is an exact type of a large class in the church of Christ in the present day. There are thousands on every side who dislike a free, full, unfettered gospel to be preached. They are always complaining that ministers throw the door too wide open, and that the doctrine of grace tends to promote licentiousness. Whenever we come across such persons, let us remember the passage we are now considering. Their voice is the voice of the 'elder brother.'

Let us beware of this spirit infecting our own hearts. It arises partly from ignorance. Men begin by not seeing their own sinfulness and unworthiness, and then they fancy that they are much better than others, and that nobody is worthy to be put by their side.—It arises partly from want of charity. Men are wanting in kind feeling towards others, and then they are unable to take pleasure when others are saved.—Above all, it arises from a thorough misunderstanding of the true nature of gospel forgiveness. The man who really feels that we all stand by grace and are all debtors, and that the best of us has nothing to boast of, and has nothing which he has not received,—such a man will not be found talking like the 'elder brother.'

We are taught, secondly, in this passage, that *the conversion of any soul ought to be an occasion of joy to all who see it.* Our Lord shows us this by putting the following words into the mouth of the prodigal's father:—'It was meet that we should make merry, and be glad: for this thy brother was dead, and is alive again; and was lost, and is found.'

The lesson of these words was primarily meant for the scribes and Pharisees. If their hearts had been in a right state, they would never have murmured at our Lord for receiving sinners. They would have remembered that the worst of publicans and sinners were their own brethren, and that if they themselves were different, it was grace alone that had made the difference. They would have been glad to see such helpless wanderers returning to the fold. They would have been thankful to see them plucked as brands from the burning, and not cast away for ever. Of all these feelings, unhappily, they knew nothing. Wrapped in their own self-righteousness they murmured and found fault, when in reality they ought to have thanked God and rejoiced.

The lesson is one which we shall all do well to lay to heart. Nothing ought to give us such true pleasure as the conversion of souls. It makes angels rejoice in heaven. It ought to make Christians rejoice on earth. What if those who are converted were lately the vilest of the vile? What if they have served sin and Satan for many long years, and wasted their substance in riotous living? It matters nothing.— 'Has grace come into their hearts? Are they truly penitent? Have they come back to their father's house? Are they new creatures in Christ Jesus? Are the dead made alive and the lost found?'—These are the only questions we have any right to ask. If they can be answered satisfactorily we ought to rejoice and be glad. Let the worldly, if they please, mock and sneer at such conversions. Let the self-righteous, if they will, murmur and find fault, and deny the reality of all great and sudden changes. But let the Christian who reads the words of Christ in this chapter, remember them and act upon them. Let him thank God and be merry. Let him praise God that one more soul is saved. Let him say, 'this my brother was dead, and is alive again; and was lost, and is found.'

What are our own feelings on the subject? This after all is the question that concerns us most. The man who can take deep interest in politics, or field-sports, or money-making, or farming, but none in the conversion of souls, is no true Christian. He is himself 'dead' and must be made 'alive again.' He is himself 'lost' and must be 'found.'

Notes—Luke 15:25-32

25.—[*His elder son.*] The part of the parable which begins here was evidently intended to apply to the scribes and Pharisees who 'murmured' at our Lord because he 'received sinners.' The unkindness, moroseness, and self-sufficiency of the elder son, are an exact type of the spirit manifested by those who found fault with our Lord for showing kindness to publicans and sinners.

It is important to keep this point clearly in view. It furnishes a clue to a right understanding of the whole passage. The elder son represents the Pharisee.

[*Musick and dancing.*] Some commentators have carefully dwelt on this expression, and have hinted, not obscurely, that it sanctions recreations and amusements from which many Christians think it better to abstain. Stier exclaims, 'A Note for the Pietists!' Alford says more gravely, 'Would these festal employments have been mentioned by our Lord on so solemn and blessed an occasion, if they really come among those works of the devil which he came into the world to destroy?'

I can see no force in arguments of this kind. There is not the slightest proof that the dancing referred to in this place was at all like the dancing of modern times. There is no proof that it was at night, or that it was a dance of men and women mingled together. Until these things can be proved, such comments on the verse before us are much to be regretted. I am not aware of any Christian objecting to music. Dancing, as it is conducted in modern times, many excellent Christians object to, and, I frankly say, I think with good reason.

28.—[*He was angry.*] Let those who think the elder son was a good man notice this expression, as well as those in the following verse. It is just the counterpart of the 'murmuring' of the scribes and Pharisees at the beginning of the chapter.

[*Entreated.*] The kindness of the father's character appears once more in this expression. He might have rebuked his ill-natured son. He only entreats him.

29.—[*Neither transgressed ... at any time.*]—Let this expression be carefully noted. It is precisely the spirit of the Pharisee, 'I am not as other men,—or even as this publican.' It shows clearly that the elder son cannot fairly be regarded as a weak believer. He is a type of the self-righteous, ignorant moralist, who cannot bear the doctrine of salvation by grace, or endure the idea of great sinners being completely pardoned and put on a level with himself.

[*Thou never gavest me a kid, etc.*] The spirit of this expression should be noted. It is the thanklessness of a proud, conceited person, who thinks that nothing is too good for him, and that he is never treated so well as he really deserves.

30.—[*This thy son.*] Mark the ill-natured tone of these words. He is speaking of his own brother. He calls him 'this thy son.' It is an expression of scorn and contempt, like 'this publican' in Luke 18:11.

[*With harlots.*] Let this expression be noted. The fact asserted is an addition to the younger son's unhappy profligacy, which we hear of for the first time. It may possibly have been true, but it is evidently brought forward here with an uncharitable intention, and in a contemptuous manner.

[*Thou hast killed the fatted calf.*] This expression should be compared with the beginning of the chapter. The Pharisee said, 'This man receiveth sinners and eateth with them.' The elder son's words here are an exact counterpart to this charge. 'Thou hast not only received thy sinful son, but hast even made a feast for him, and eaten with him.'

31.—[*Son, thou art ever with me, and all ... thine.*] These words have made some persons suppose that the elder son is the type of an erring believer, who is stumbled by seeing great sinners pardoned, but who has never departed from grace himself. This idea is untenable. We are not reading a conversation between a child of God and his heavenly Father. We are simply reading an incident in a story which is intended to show Christ's love towards sinners, and the ignorance of those who are stumbled by it. The words show us no doubt that the elder son had always lived a steady life compared to his brother's and that his father had never denied him anything. But they entirely fail to show that he was humble, charitable, or acquainted with his own heart, notwithstanding all the privileges he enjoyed. The words in short show that the elder son had no right to complain of his father, but they do not show that the father had no right to complain of him.

32.—[*It was meet, etc.*] This verse concludes the argument of the other chapter, and sums up the case between our Lord and his self-righteous enemies, the scribes and Pharisees. Whatever the elder son might say, he could not deny these two great facts. His brother, who a short time ago had been as one dead, was alive again. He was lost: he was now found. Before these facts all envious and murmuring feelings ought to go down. It was meet to make merry and be glad.

The application of the words to the case of our Lord's hearers is clear and plain. However much the Pharisees might murmur at him for receiving sinners, they must confess it was better for sinners to be saved than lost. If publicans and sinners were made alive unto God through his ministry, the Pharisees, if they had had a right spirit, would have been glad. Instead of finding fault they would have been thankful. Instead of murmuring they would have rejoiced.

Let us observe the difference between the way in which the elder brother and the father speak of the prodigal son. The elder brother says, 'this thy son,' as if he was not his own brother. The father says, 'this thy brother,' to remind him of his relationship.

If we take the secondary, or national view, of the parable, the application of it is not difficult. It rebukes the Jews for their unwillingness to see the Gentiles brought into the church of Christ, and made partakers of the gospel. The elder brother is a picture of the Jews of St Paul's time, disliking the conversion of the Gentiles, and 'forbidding him to speak to them' (*1 Thess.* 2:16). In this point of view, unhappily, the parable is again a prophecy. Our Jewish elder brother still stands without and refuses to come in.

LUKE 16:1-12

1 And he said also unto his disciples, There was a certain rich man, which had a steward; and the same was accused unto him that he had wasted his goods.

2 And he called him, and said unto him, How is it that I hear this of thee? give an account of thy stewardship; for thou mayest be no longer steward.

3 Then the steward said within himself, What shall I do? for my lord taketh away from me the stewardship: I cannot dig; to beg I am ashamed.

4 I am resolved what to do, that, when I am put out of the stewardship, they may receive me into their houses.

5 So he called every one of his lord's debtors *unto him*, and said unto the first, How much owest thou unto my lord?

6 And he said, An hundred measures of oil. And he said unto him, Take thy bill, and sit down quickly, and write fifty.

7 Then said he to another, And how much owest thou? And he said, An hundred measures of wheat. And he said unto him, Take thy bill, and write fourscore.

8 And the lord commended the unjust steward, because he had done wisely: for the children of this world are in their generation wiser than the children of light.

9 And I say unto you, Make to yourselves friends of the mammon of unrighteousness; that, when ye fail, they may receive you into everlasting habitations.

10 He that is faithful in that which is least is faithful also in much: and he that is unjust in the least is unjust also in much.

11 If therefore ye have not been faithful in the unrighteous mammon, who will commit to your trust the true *riches*?

12 And if ye have not been faithful in that which is another man's, who shall give you that which is your own?

THE passage we have now read is a difficult one. There are knots in it which perhaps will never be untied, until the Lord comes again. We might reasonably expect that a book written by inspiration, as the Bible is, would contain things hard to be understood. The fault lies not in the book, but in our own feeble understandings. If we learn nothing else from the passage before us, let us learn humility.

Let us beware, in the first place, that *we do not draw from these verses lessons which they were never meant to teach.*

The steward, whom our Lord describes, is not set before us as a pattern of morality. He is distinctly called the 'unjust steward.' The Lord Jesus never meant to sanction dishonesty, and unfair dealing between man and man. This steward cheated his master, and broke the eighth commandment.—His master was struck with his cunning and forethought, when he heard of it, and 'commended' him, as a shrewd and far-seeing man. But there is no proof that his master was *pleased* with his conduct. Above all, there is not a word to show that the man was praised by Christ. In short, in his treatment of his master, the steward is a beacon to be avoided, and not a pattern to be followed.

The caution, now laid down, is very necessary. Commercial dishonesty is unhappily very common in these latter days. Fair dealing between man and man is increasingly rare. Men do things in the way of business, which will not stand the test of the Bible. In 'making haste to be rich,' thousands are continually committing actions which are not strictly innocent (*Prov.* 28:20). Sharpness and smartness, in bargaining, and buying, and selling, and pushing trade, are often covering over things that ought not to be. The generation of 'the unjust steward' is still a very large one. Let us not forget this. Whenever we do to others what we would not like others to do to us, we may be sure, whatever the world may say, that we are wrong in the sight of Christ.

Let us observe, in the second place, that one principal lesson of the parable before us, is *the wisdom of providing against coming evil.*

The conduct of the unjust steward, when he received notice to quit his place, was undeniably dexterous and politic. Dishonest as he was in striking off from the bills of debtors anything that was due to his master, he certainly by so doing made for himself friends. Wicked as he was, he had an eye to the future. Disgraceful as his measures were, he provided well for himself. He did not sit still in idleness, and see himself reduced to poverty without a struggle. He schemed, and planned, and contrived, and boldly carried his plans into execution. And the result was that when he lost one home he secured another.

What a striking contrast between the steward's conduct about his earthly prospects, and the conduct of most men about their souls! In this general point of view, and in this only, the steward sets us all an example which we should do well to follow. Like him, we should look far forward to things to come. Like him, we should provide against the day when we shall have to leave our present habitation. Like him, we should secure 'a house in heaven,' which may be our home, when we put off our earthly tabernacle of the body (2 *Cor.* 5:1). Like him, we should use all means to provide for ourselves everlasting habitations.

The parable, in this point of view, is deeply instructive. It may well raise within us great searchings of heart. The diligence of worldly men about the things of time, should put to shame the coldness of professing Christians about the things of eternity. The zeal and per-tinacity of men of business in compassing sea and land to get earthly treasures, may well reprove the slackness and indolence of believers about treasures in heaven. The words of our Lord are indeed weighty and solemn, 'The children of this world are in their generation wiser than the children of light.' May these words sink into our hearts and bear fruit in our lives!

Let us notice lastly, in this passage, *the remarkable expressions which our Lord uses about little things,* in close connection with the parable of the unjust steward. We read that he said, 'He that is faithful in that which is least is faithful also in much: and he that is unjust in the least is unjust also in much.'

Our Lord here teaches us the great importance of strict faithful-ness about 'little things.' He guards us against supposing that such conduct about money as that of the unjust steward, ought ever to be considered a light and trifling thing among Christians. He would have us know that 'little things' are the best test of character;—and that unfaithfulness about 'little things' is the symptom of a bad state of heart.—He did not mean, of course, that honesty about money can justify our souls, or put away sin. But he did mean that dishonesty about money is a sure sign of a heart not being 'right in the sight of God.' The man who is not dealing honestly with the gold and silver of this world, can never be one who has true riches in heaven. 'If ye have not been faithful in that which is another man's, who shall give you that which is your own?'

The doctrine laid down by our Lord in this place, deserves most serious consideration in the present day. An idea appears to prevail in some men's minds, that true religion may be separated from common honesty, and that soundness about matters of doctrine may cover over swindling and cheating in matters of practice! Against this wretched idea our Lord's words were a plain protest. Against this idea let us watch and be on our guard. Let us contend earnestly for the glorious doctrines of salvation by grace, and justification by faith. But let us never allow ourselves to suppose that true religion sanctions any trifling with the second table of the law. Let us never forget for a moment, that true faith will always be known by its fruits. We may be very sure that where there is no honesty, there is no grace.

Notes—Luke 16:1-12

1.—[*And he said ... unto his disciples.*] The parable of the unjust steward is notoriously full of difficulties. The curious diversity of the explanations of it which have been given is sufficient to prove this. Those who wish to examine some of these explanations fully, will find them in Trench on Parables. I can only briefly refer to them.

Pearce thinks that the 'rich man' means God, and that every man is his steward.

Schleiermacher thinks that the rich man represents the Romans, the steward the publicans, and the debtor the Jewish nation,—and that our Lord's object was to vindicate the publicans, and prove their kindness to their countrymen.

Anselm and others, think that the rich man means God, and the steward all true penitents,—and that the steward's lowering the bills represents the first actions of repentance and charity.

Vitringa thinks that the rich man means God, and the steward the Pharisees,—that the accusation against the steward means, the charges of the prophets and of Christ,—and that the lowering of the bills means the effort made by the Pharisees to retain their position by lowering the standard of righteousness.

Jerome records an opinion ascribed to Theophilus, that the unjust steward is the Apostle Paul, who was thrust out of Judaism,—and then made himself friends by preaching the gospel.

Gaudentius, Bishop of Brescia, and Olshausen think that the unjust steward is the devil, and the creditors, whom he makes his friends, mankind.

Some have thought that the unjust steward represents Pontius Pilate or Judas Iscariot.

Many think that the parable is nothing more than an earnest exhortation to liberal almsgiving. This is the view of Irenæus, Augustine, Athanasius, Theophylact, Erasmus, Calvin, and Luther. Luther says 'It is a sermon on good works, and especially against avarice, that men abuse not wealth, but therewith help poor and needy people.'

I shall not discuss these opinions. I will only say that I cannot assent to any of them. Some seem to be very fanciful. All seem to me more or less untenable or defective. My own opinion shall be summed up in a few general remarks.

A. In interpreting this parable, we should carefully observe to whom it was addressed. It was not spoken to 'the scribes and Pharisees,' like the three last parables, but 'to the disciples.' They had heard a lesson to the proud and self-righteous. Now let them hear a lesson for themselves.

B. The connection between the parable of the unjust steward, and that of the prodigal son, which it immediately follows, is probably something of this kind. The disciples had heard of one who sinned by wasting money. They should now hear of one who sinned by dishonesty.—They had heard of one who by carelessness squandered all his property and lost all his friends. Let them now hear of one who, by cunning management of money, made friends, and secured himself a home.—They had heard of the wickedness of riotous living. Let them now hear of another kind of wickedness no less abominable in God's sight, dishonesty, cheating, and fraud.—They had heard the sins of Pharisees denounced and exposed. Let them now hear an exposure of the sins of impenitent and extortionate publicans.—They had heard what Pharisees ought to do,—to rejoice at the conversion of sinners. Let them now hear what publicans ought to do,—to be faithful in money matters, and to make themselves friends by a right use of their wealth.

These, or some of them, appear to me the connecting links between the parable before us, and the preceding chapter. It looks to me like a caution to our Lord's 'disciples.' They were not to suppose that all publicans were right in the Lord's eyes, or that the sins of publicans were not noticed by him as well as the sins of Pharisees.

C. The rich man and the steward and the debtors do not appear to me to be allegorical persons. I regard them as actors in the story, which our Lord is telling; but I cannot think that they were intended to represent any particular persons.

D. The great lessons which the parable is intended to convey, appear to me to be three.—The *first* is the wisdom of providing against the future. This is taught by the story of a rich man's steward, who by a wicked contrivance secured himself a home when he lost his office. If a wicked man can do this for an earthly home, and in a wicked way, how much more ought a righteous man to provide for himself a heavenly home, in a lawful way?—The *second* lesson is the importance of using money rightly. By prudent management of money, however dishonest, the unjust steward made himself friends. Let the disciples follow his example, but in an honest and righteous manner.—The *third* lesson is the importance of faithfulness in the least affairs of business, as a test of character. The dishonesty of the steward showed plainly the state of his heart. Let the disciples remember that unfaithfulness in money transactions, is a sure evidence of a rotten state of soul. The cheating publican who persevered in dishonesty, and the self-righteous Pharisee who trusted in his own goodness, were both alike in one respect. They were both unfit for the kingdom of God.

[*A steward.*] The steward in this parable seems to have been an agent, who received his master's rents, which were paid in kind and not in money, and through whose hands all his master's receipts passed.

[**Was accused.**] The word so translated is only found in this place in the New Testament. It is the root of the word 'devil.' The word devil means 'accuser.' It does not however mean in this place that the steward was falsely accused. On the contrary, his own language seems clearly to show that he felt the accusation to be just, and incapable of refutation.

2.—[*Thou mayest be.*] The expression so rendered means literally, 'Thou wilt not be able to be steward any longer.'—It is impossible that thou canst be. I cannot allow thee.

4.—[*I am resolved.*] The Greek word so translated means literally, 'I have known.'— I know what I will do.

[*They may receive me.*] Let it be noted that the expression 'they' is here used generally and indefinitely. We are not told to whom it is applied. Precisely the same expression will be found in the ninth verse.

6.—[*An hundred ... fifty.*] The dishonesty of the steward, we should observe, consisted in this:—he struck off part of what was due to his master. He remitted debts which were lawfully due to his lord. Instead of attending to his employer's interest, he robbed him, and made a present to his debtors. His master apparently had no means of checking this dishonesty. If his steward told him that a debtor only owed him one half, or one fifth, of his real debt, he could apparently only take it for granted that the statement was correct.

[*Of oil*] We should remember that olive oil was largely used in Eastern countries, and formed a large portion of the annual produce of the land.

8.—[*The lord commended.*] Let it be always noted in reading this parable, that the expression 'lord' here, does not mean the Lord Jesus Christ. It is the 'master or lord' of the unjust steward. He saw the result of the steward's schemes, in his reception at his creditors' houses. It is not, however, quite clear that he saw that he himself had been cheated.

Compare with this expression the words of David, 'Men will praise thee, when thou doest well to thyself' (*Psa.* 49:18).

Perhaps it is well to mention here, that some think the dealings of the steward with his lord's debtors were not really so dishonest and fraudulent as they appear to us in the present day. They say that this steward had a plenary power to remit or abate part of the debts due to his master, and that he simply exercised this power at a time when it very much promoted his own interests. If this explanation were true, it would certainly account for the absence of angry expressions on the part of the master. But it is an explanation which is slenderly supported.

[*The unjust steward.*] The Greek words here are remarkable. They mean literally the 'steward of unrighteousness.' The expression translated the 'unjust judge,' in Luke 18:6, is precisely similar.

[*Done wisely.*] The word translated 'wisely,' might have been better rendered 'prudently.' The wisdom commended in the steward, is wisdom in attending to his own interests. It is not wisdom unto salvation. The Greek adjective of the adverb 'wisely,' is the very word that is used in the Septuagint about the serpent in Genesis 3:1: 'He was more "*subtle*" than all the beasts.'

[*Children of this world.*] This expression means worldly people; and the opposite expression, 'children of light,' means godly people, people who follow the light, and walk in the light. See John 12:36: Ephesians 5:8. Compare also Luke 7:35.

[*In their generation wiser.*] The meaning of this expression is 'The children of this world are wiser towards their generation— that is, in what relates to this world—than the children of light are towards their generation—that is, in what relates to the kingdom of God.' It might even be rendered more closely, 'The children of this world are wiser towards their own generation, that is, in their intercourse with worldly people like themselves,—than the children of light are in their intercourse with their own brethren.'

9.—[*Make to yourselves friends, etc.*] The meaning of this saying of our Lord's is often much misunderstood. The true sense of it I believe to be as follows, 'Make to yourselves friends with your money,—by a right use of it,—in order that when ye die, ye may be received into everlasting habitations.'

[*Friends.*] This question is often raised who these friends are, whom we are to 'make' in life, and to be 'received by' in death. Some have thought the three persons of the Trinity are intended,—some the angels,—and some the people to whom our money has done good.

I cannot assent to any of these three views. The expression appears to me to be general and indefinite, and to be borrowed from the conduct of the unjust steward, in order to make the lesson more pointed. The meaning seems to me to be no more than this, 'Use your money with an eye to the future, as the steward did his. Spend your money in such a way that your expenditure shall be a friend to you, and not a witness against you in another world.'

[*The mammon of unrighteousness.*] This is a very remarkable expression. It means 'riches.' But why 'riches' are so called in this chapter and nowhere else in the Bible, we do not know.

The word 'mammon' is Syriac; or, according to Augustine, Punic. It means, all are agreed, riches or gain. Some think that it was a name given to the god of riches. But this is questionable.

The expression, 'riches of unrighteousness,' is very peculiar. Some think that our Lord meant 'riches acquired unrighteously,' like 'treasures of wickedness' (*Prov.* 10:2).—Some think that he meant 'riches which in the nature of things can never be got without some unrighteousness or sin.'—Some think that he meant 'uncertain, unstable riches.'—This last, compared with the expression, 'true riches,' in the 11th verse, appears most likely to be the true meaning. Pearce quotes in support of this view, John 7:18, and 2 Thessalonians 2:12. Compare 1 Timothy 6:17.

[*When ye fail.*] This expression evidently means 'when ye die.' It is very peculiar, and the Greek word is only found in this sense here. It is the root of our English word 'eclipse.'

[*They may receive you.*] I cannot believe that this expression refers either to the Trinity, the angels, or the persons whom we have helped with our money. I regard it as indefinite, and signifying only 'ye may be received.' The same sort of expression is found in Matthew 1:23; 5:15; Luke 12:20; Acts 7:6; 1 Thessalonians 5:3; Revelation 6:4.

[*Everlasting habitations.*] This expression must evidently mean heaven. The word translated 'habitations,' is translated 'tabernacles' in every other place where it is found in the New Testament.

In leaving this verse, I will mention two cautions which should always be remembered in interpreting it.—On the one hand, let us beware of supposing that by any use of money we can purchase to ourselves God's favour and the pardon of our sins. Heaven is not to be bought. Any such interpretation of the verse is most unscriptural.—On the other hand, let us beware of shutting our eyes against the doctrine which the verse unmistakably contains. That doctrine plainly is, that a right use of our money in this world, from right motives, will be for our benefit in the world to come. It will not justify us. It will not bear the severity of God's judgment, any more than other good works. But it shall be an evidence of our grace, which shall befriend our souls. There is such a thing as 'laying up treasure in heaven,' and 'laying up a good foundation against the time to come' (*Matt.* 6:20; *1 Tim.* 6:19).

10.—[*Faithful ... least ... much.*] This verse seems to be used in a proverbial way. It is an acknowledged truth that a man's conduct in little things is a sure test of what he is likely to do in great things, and that when a man is unfaithful in small matters, we do not expect him to be faithful in important ones. The application of this principle is made in the following verses.

11.—[*If therefore ... not been faithful.*] The argument in this and the following verse is one and the same, though the expressions are different. The 'unrighteous mammon' here means 'money.' The 'true riches' mean treasure in heaven. The doctrine is, that he who is dishonest and unfaithful in the discharge of his duties on earth, must not expect to have heavenly treasure, or to be saved.

12.—[*That which is another man's.*] The argument in this verse is like that of the preceding one.—Money is called 'that which is another man's,' because it passes from one to another, and is never our own for long.—Eternal life is called 'that which is your own,' because it is the only property which endures for ever. Everything else that we have is only a loan from God, and may be withdrawn any day. Grace and peace once given are an everlasting possession. Once ours they are ours to all eternity.

LUKE 16:13-18

13 No servant can serve two masters: for either he will hate the one, and love the other; or else he will hold to the one, and despise the other. Ye cannot serve God and mammon.

14 And the Pharisees also, who were covetous, heard all these things: and they derided him.

15 And he said unto them, Ye are they which justify yourselves before men; but God knoweth your hearts: for that which is. highly esteemed among men is abomination in the sight of God

16 The law and the prophets *were* until John: since that time the kingdom of God is preached, and every man presseth into it.

17 And it is easier for heaven and earth to pass, than one tittle of the law to fail.

18 Whosoever putteth away his wife, and marrieth another, committeth adultery: and whosoever marrieth her that is put away from *her* husband committeth adultery.

T HESE verses teach us, firstly, *the uselessness of attempting to serve God with a divided heart.* Our Lord Jesus Christ says, 'No servant can serve two masters: for either he will hate the one and love the other; or else he will hold to the one and despise the other. Ye cannot serve God and mammon.'

The truth here propounded by our Lord appears, at first sight, too obvious to admit of being disputed. And yet the very attempt which is here declared to be useless is constantly being made by many in the matter of their souls. Thousands on every side are continually trying to do the thing which Christ pronounces impossible. They are endeavouring to be friends of the world and friends of God at the same time. Their consciences are so far enlightened, that they feel they must have *some* religion. But their affections are so chained down to earthly things, that they never come up to the mark of being true Christians. And hence they live in a state of constant discomfort. They have too much religion to be happy in the world, and they have too much of the world in their hearts to be happy in their religion. In short, they waste their time in labouring to do that which cannot be done. They are striving to 'serve God and mammon.'

He that desires to be a happy Christian, will do well to ponder our Lord's sayings in this verse. There is perhaps no point on which the experience of all God's saints is more uniform than this, that *decision* is the secret of comfort in Christ's service. It is the half-hearted Christian who brings up an evil report of the good land. The more thoroughly we give ourselves to Christ, the more sensibly shall we feel within 'the peace of God which passeth all understanding' (*Phil.* 4:7). The more entirely we live, not to ourselves, but to him who died for us, the more powerfully shall we realize what it is to have 'joy and peace in believing' (*Rom.* 15:13). If it is worthwhile to serve Christ at all, let us serve him with all our heart, and soul, and mind, and strength. Life, eternal life, after all, is the matter at stake, no less than happiness. If we cannot make up our minds to give up everything for Christ's sake, we must not expect Christ to own us at the last day. He will have all our hearts or none. 'Whosoever will be a friend of the world is the enemy of God' (*James* 4:4). The end of undecided and half-hearted Christians will be to be cast out for ever.

These verses teach us, secondly, *how widely different is the estimate set on things by man from that which is set on things by God.* Our Lord Jesus Christ declares this in a severe rebuke which he addresses to the covetous Pharisees who derided him. He says, 'Ye are they which justify yourselves before men; but God knoweth your hearts: for that which is highly esteemed among men is abomination in the sight of God.'

The truth of this solemn saying appears on every side of us. We have only to look round the world and mark the things on which most men set their affections, in order to see it proved in a hundred ways. Riches, and honours, and rank, and pleasure, are the chief objects for which the greater part of mankind are living. Yet these are the very things which God declares to be 'vanity,' and of the love of which he warns us to beware! Praying, and Bible-reading, and holy living, and repentance, and faith, and grace, and communion with God, are things for which few care at all. Yet these are the very things which God in his Bible is ever urging on our attention!—The disagreement is glaring, painful, and appalling. What God calls good, that man calls evil! What God calls evil, that man calls good!

Whose words, after all, are true? Whose estimate is correct? Whose judgment will stand at the last day? By whose standard will all be tried, before they receive their eternal sentence? Before whose bar will the current opinions of the world be tested and weighed at last? These are the only questions which ought to influence our conduct; and to these questions the Bible returns a plain answer. The counsel of the Lord,—it alone shall stand for ever. The word of Christ,—it alone shall judge man at the last day. By that word let us live. By that word let us measure everything, and every person in this evil world. It matters nothing what man thinks. 'What saith the Lord?'—It matters nothing what it is fashionable or customary to think. 'Let God be true, but every man a liar' (*Rom.* 3:4). The more entirely we are of one mind with God, the better we are prepared for the judgment day. To love what God loves, to hate what God hates, and to approve what God approves, is the highest style of Christianity. The moment we find ourselves honouring anything which in the sight of God is lightly esteemed, we may be sure there is something wrong in our souls.

These verses teach us, lastly, *the dignity and sanctity of the law of God*. Our Lord Jesus Christ declares that 'it is easier for heaven and earth to pass, than for one tittle of the law to fail.'

The honour of God's holy law was frequently defended by Christ during the time of his ministry on earth. Sometimes we find him defending it against man-made additions, as in the case of the fourth commandment. Sometimes we find him defending it against those who would lower the standard of its requirements, and allow it to be transgressed, as in the case of the law of marriage. But never do we find him speaking of the law in any terms but those of respect. He always 'magnified the law and made it honourable' (*Isa.* 42:21). Its ceremonial part was a type of his own gospel, and was to be fulfilled to the last letter. Its moral part was a revelation of God's eternal mind, and was to be perpetually binding on Christians.

The honour of God's holy law needs continually defending in the present day. On few subjects does ignorance prevail so widely among professing Christians. Some appear to think that Christians have nothing to do with the law,—that its moral and ceremonial parts were both of only temporary obligation,—and that the daily sacrifice and the Ten Commandments were both alike put aside by the gospel. Some on the other hand think that the law is still binding on us, and that we are to be saved by obedience to it,—but that its requirements are lowered by the gospel, and can be met by our imperfect obedience. Both these views are erroneous and unscriptural. Against both let us be on our guard.

Let us settle it in our minds that 'the law is good if man use it lawfully' (*1 Tim.* 1:8). It is intended to show us God's holiness and our sinfulness,—to convince us of sin and to lead us to Christ,—to show us how to live after we have come to Christ, and to teach us what to follow and what to avoid. He that so uses the law will find it a true friend to his soul. The established Christian will always say, 'I delight in the law of God after the inward man' (*Rom.* 7:22).

Notes—Luke 16:13-18

13.—[*No servant can serve two masters.*] These words are evidently connected with the preceding verses, in which our Lord had taught the duty of faithfulness in money matters. They were intended to answer the secret objection of some, that a man might divide his diligence between the things of this world and the things of the world to come, and so reap the full benefit of both. Against this secret thought the proverbial saying of this verse is a testimony.

[*Hate the one and love the other.*] The remark made on a similar expression about 'hating,' in a former chapter (*Luke* 14:26), applies to this expression. The meaning appears to be that the man will love one more than the other.

14.—[*Derided.*]—This word is only found in one other place in the New Testament (*Luke* 23:35). Our English word 'sneered' answers to it more closely than any other.

The consciences of the Pharisees were evidently pricked by our Lord's remarks about money, and the necessity of faithfulness in the management of it.

15.—[*Justify yourselves before men.*] The Pharisees made great professions of righteousness and holiness before men, while their hearts were full of wickedness and covetousness. Our Lord warns them solemnly of the uselessness of all such professions, while the heart is unrenewed and cleaving to the world. And the state of their hearts, he reminds them, is known to God. They might deceive the eye of man, but they could not deceive God.

[*Highly esteemed.*] The Greek word so translated means literally, 'high.' This is the only place in the New Testament where it is rendered as it is here.

16.—[*The law and the prophets were until John.*] This verse seems rather elliptical. Its connection with the preceding verse is not at first sight very clear. It is probably something like this.

'You make your boast of the law and the prophets, O ye Pharisees, and you do well to give them honour. But you forget that the dispensation of the law and prophets was only intended to pave the way for the better dispensation of the kingdom of God, which was to be ushered in by John the Baptist. That dispensation has come. John the Baptist has appeared. The kingdom of God is among you. While you are ignorantly deriding me and my doctrine, multitudes of publicans and sinners are pressing into it. Your boasting is not good. With all your professed zeal for the law and the prophets, you are utterly blind to that kingdom into which the law and the prophets were meant to guide you.'

[*Every man presseth into it.*] The Greek word translated 'presseth,' is only found in one other place in the New Testament. It is there rendered, 'suffereth violence' (*Matt.* 11:12).

By 'every man,' we must of course not understand literally every Jew. It either means, 'a very large number press in while you stand still deriding;'—or else, 'Everyone who enters the kingdom, enters it with much exertion and labour, under a conviction that it is worthwhile to use exertion. And yet you stand still.'

17.—[*Easier … heaven and earth to pass.*] This is a proverbial expression, indicating the perpetual dignity and obligation of God's law.

[*One tittle.*] The Greek word so translated means the slight mark which distinguishes some Hebrew letters which are much alike, one from another.

[*To fail.*] The word here means literally 'to fall.' It is like the expression about the words of Samuel, 'The Lord did not let any of them fall to the ground' (*1 Sam.* 3:19).

The connection between this verse and the preceding one is somewhat abrupt at first sight. The chain of thought is probably this:—'Think not because I say that the law and the prophets have introduced a better dispensation, the kingdom of God, that I count the law and the prophets of no value. On the contrary, I tell you that they are of eternal dignity and obligation. They have paved the way to a clearer revelation, but they have not been cast aside.'

18.—[*Whosoever putteth away his wife, etc.*] The connection of this verse with the preceding is again somewhat abrupt. The chain of thought seems as follows:—'So far from coming to destroy the law, O ye Pharisees, I would have you know that I am come to magnify it, and reassert its righteous demands. With all your boasted reverence for the law, you are yourselves breakers of it in the law of marriage. You have lowered the standard of the law of divorce. You have allowed divorce for trivial and insufficient causes. And hence while you make your boast of the law, you are by your unfair dealing with it, encouraging adultery.'

We must take care that we do not misinterpret the language used about divorce and remarriage in this verse. It is perfectly clear from another passage that our Lord allowed divorce in cases of adultery (*Matt.* 5:32). The act of adultery dissolves the marriage tie, and makes those who were one, become again two. Neither here nor elsewhere can I see that our Lord regards the remarriage of one who has been divorced for the cause of fornication, as adultery. It is divorce for frivolous causes which he denounces, and marriage after such frivolous divorce which he pronounces to be adultery.

LUKE 16:19-31

19 There was a certain rich man, which was clothed in purple and fine linen, and fared sumptuously every day:

20 And there was a certain beggar named Lazarus, which was laid at his gate, full of sores,

21 And desiring to be fed with the crumbs which fell from the rich man's table: moreover the dogs came and licked his sores.

22 And it came to pass, that the beggar died, and was carried by the angels into Abraham's bosom: the rich man also died, and was buried;

23 And in hell he lift up his eyes, being in torments, and seeth Abraham afar off, and Lazarus in his bosom.

24 And he cried and said, Father Abraham, have mercy on me, and send Lazarus, that he may dip the tip of his finger in water, and cool my tongue; for I am tormented in this flame.

25 But Abraham said, Son, remember that thou in thy lifetime receivedst thy good things, and likewise Lazarus evil things: but now he is comforted, and thou art tormented.

26 And beside all this, between us and you there is a great gulf fixed: so that they which would pass from hence to you cannot; neither can they pass to us, that *would come* from thence.

27 Then he said, I pray thee therefore, father, that thou wouldest send him to my father's house:

28 For I have five brethren; that he may testify unto them, lest they also come into this place of torment.

29 Abraham saith unto him, They have Moses and the prophets; let them hear them.

30 And he said, Nay, father Abraham: but if one went unto them from the dead, they will repent.

31 And he said unto him, If they hear not Moses and the prophets, neither will they be persuaded, though one rose from the dead.

THE parable we have now read, in one respect stands alone in the Bible. It is the only passage of Scripture which describes the feelings of the unconverted after death. For this reason, as well as for many others, the parable deserves especial attention.

We learn, firstly, from this parable, *that a man's worldly condition is no test of his state in the sight of God.* The Lord Jesus describes to us two men, of whom one was very rich, and the other very poor. The one 'fared sumptuously every day.' The other was a mere 'beggar,' who had nothing that he could call his own. And yet of these two the poor man had grace, and the rich had none. The poor man lived by faith, and walked in the steps of Abraham. The rich man was a thoughtless, selfish worldling, dead in trespasses and sins.

Let us never give way to the common idea that men are to be valued according to their income, and that the man who has most money is the one who ought to be the most highly esteemed. There is no authority for this notion in the Bible. The general teaching of Scripture is flatly opposed to it. 'Not many wise men after the flesh, not many mighty, not many noble are called' (*1 Cor.* 1:26). 'Let not the rich man glory in his riches. But let him that glorieth glory in this, that he knoweth and understandeth me' (*Jer.* 9:24). Wealth is no mark of God's favour. Poverty is no mark of God's displeasure. Those whom God justifies and glorifies are seldom the rich of this world. If we would measure men as God measures them, we must value them according to their grace.

We learn, secondly, from this parable, that *death is the common end to which all classes of mankind must come.* The trials of the 'beggar,' and the sumptuous faring of the 'rich man,' alike ceased at last. There came a time when both of them died. 'All go to one place' (*Eccles.* 3:20).

Death is a great fact that all acknowledge, but very few seem to realize. Most men eat, and drink, and talk, and plan, as if they were going to live upon earth for ever. The true Christian must be on his guard against this spirit. 'He that would live well,' said a great divine, 'should often think of his last day, and make it his company-keeper.' Against murmuring, and discontent, and envy, in the state of poverty,—against pride, and self-sufficiency, and arrogance, in the possession of wealth,—there are few better antidotes than the remembrance of death. 'The beggar died,' and his bodily wants were at an end. 'The rich man died,' and his feasting was stopped for evermore.

We learn, thirdly, from this parable, that *the souls of believers are specially cared for by God in the hour of death.* The Lord Jesus tells us that when the beggar died he 'was carried by angels to Abraham's bosom.'

There is something very comforting in this expression. We know little or nothing of the state and feelings of the dead. When our own last hour comes, and we lie down to die, we shall be like those who journey into an unknown country. But it may satisfy us to know that all who fall asleep in Jesus are in good keeping. They are not houseless, homeless wanderers between the hour of death and the day of resurrection. They are at rest in the midst of friends, with all who have had like faith with Abraham. They have no lack of anything. And, best of all, St Paul tells us they are 'with Christ' (*Phil.* 1:23).

We learn, fourthly, from this parable, *the reality and eternity of hell.* The Lord Jesus tells us plainly, that after death the rich man was 'in hell,—tormented with flame.' He gives us a fearful picture of his longing for a drop of 'water to cool his tongue,' and of 'the gulf' between him and Abraham, which could not be passed. There are few more awful passages perhaps in the whole Bible than this. And he from whose lips it came, be it remembered, was one who delighted in mercy!

The certainty and endlessness of the future punishment of the wicked, are truths which we must hold fast and never let go. From the day when Satan said to Eve, 'Ye shall not surely die,' there never have been wanting men who have denied them. Let us not be deceived. There is a hell for the impenitent, as well as a heaven for believers. There is a wrath to come for all who 'obey not the gospel of Christ' (*2 Thess.* 1:8). From that wrath let us flee betimes to the great hiding-place, Jesus Christ the Lord. If men find themselves 'in torment' at last, it will not be because there was no way of escape.

We learn, fifthly, from this parable, that *unconverted men find out the value of a soul, after death, when it is too late.* We read that the rich man desired Lazarus might be sent to his five brethren who were yet alive, 'lest they also should come to the place of torment.' While he lived he had never done anything for their spiritual good. They had probably been his companions in worldliness, and, like him, had neglected their souls entirely. When he is dead he finds out too late the folly of which they had all been guilty, and desires that, if possible, they might be called to repentance.

The change that will come over the minds of unconverted men after death is one of the most fearful points in their future condition. They will see, and know, and understand a hundred things to which they were obstinately blind while they were alive. They will discover that, like Esau, they have bartered away eternal happiness for a mere mess of pottage. There is no infidelity, or scepticism, or unbelief after death. It is a wise saying of an old divine that 'hell is nothing more than truth known too late.'

We learn, lastly, from this parable, *that the greatest miracles would have no effect on men's hearts, if they will not believe God's Word.* The rich man thought that 'if one went to his brethren from the dead they would repent.' He argued that the sight of one who came from another world must surely make them feel, though the old familiar words of Moses and the prophets had been heard in vain. The reply of Abraham is solemn and instructive,—'If they hear not Moses and the prophets, neither will they be persuaded though one rose from the dead.'

The principle laid down in these words is of deep importance. The Scriptures contain all that we need to know in order to be saved, and a messenger from the world beyond the grave could add nothing to them. It is not more evidence that is wanted in order to make men repent, but more heart and will to make use of what they already know. The dead could tell us nothing more than the Bible contains, if they rose from their graves to instruct us. After the first novelty of their testimony was worn away, we should care no more for their words than the words of any other. This wretched waiting for something which we have not, and neglect of what we have, is the ruin of thousands of souls. Faith, simple faith in the Scriptures which we already possess, is the first thing needful to salvation. The man who has the Bible, and can read it, and yet waits for more evidence before he becomes a decided Christian, is deceiving himself. Except he awakens from his delusion he will die in his sins.

Notes—Luke 16:19-31

19.—[*There was a certain rich man.*] The parable of the rich man and Lazarus has occasioned some diversity of opinion among commentators, and called forth some strange allegorical interpretations.

From the very earliest days it has been matter of dispute whether it ought to be regarded as a parable or a real history. The truth seems to me to lie between the two extremes. I see no reason why it should not be regarded as a real history. And yet it may be a history employed to point a lesson, after the manner of all our Lord's parables. The whole subject will be found fully discussed in Suicer's Thesaurus, under the word Lazarus.

I cannot see in it the allegorical meanings which some have discovered. I cannot hold, with Tertullian and Schleiermacher, that the rich man meant Herod Antipas, and Lazarus John the Baptist.—I cannot see, with Vitringa, that the rich man represents the Jewish nation,—Lazarus our Lord Jesus Christ,—his sores the sins of man which he bore,—the death of the rich man the downfall of the Jewish polity,—the request for sending Lazarus the Jew's vain desire of a Messiah,—the five brethren the Babylonish Jews,—the licking of the dogs the conversion of the Gentiles.—I cannot see, with Theophylact, that the rich man is a type of the proud and self-righteous Jewish nation, and Lazarus a type of the Gentile world.—All such interpretations appear to me unsatisfactory.

I believe the parable was specially intended by our Lord for the benefit of the Pharisees, to whom he was speaking when he delivered it. I believe the connecting link is to be found in the 9th verse, where Jesus said, 'Make to yourselves friends of the mammon of unrighteousness,' and in the 14th verse, where it is said, 'The Pharisees, who were covetous, heard all these things, and derided him.' And I believe that our Lord's principal object was to rebuke the selfishness, worldliness, want of charity, and general forgetfulness of their responsibilities, of which the Pharisees were guilty, and to expose the fearful end to which their unbelief and neglect of their own Scriptures were rapidly bringing them.

[*Clothed in purple.*] Purple was a peculiarly rich and expensive dye, and clothes dyed with it were worn by none but the rich and noble. Lydia in the 16th chapter of Acts, is mentioned as a 'seller of purple.'

[*Fared sumptuously.*] The Greek word rendered 'fared,' is only translated so in this place in the New Testament. In other places the verb is rendered 'to be merry,—make merry,—rejoice,—or be glad.'

Let it be noted, that we are not told that the rich man was an open breaker of any one of the Ten Commandments. It is not said that he was an idolater, blasphemer, murderer, adulterer, or thief. But he was one who lived only for himself. This was the ruin of his soul.

20.—[*A certain beggar named Lazarus.*] The Greek word rendered 'beggar' does not necessarily mean what our English word implies, a mendicant. In thirty-one out of thirty-two other places where it is used in the New Testament, beside this parable, it is translated 'poor.'

We know nothing of this Lazarus, excepting that he was not the brother of Martha and Mary. Several of the Fathers call attention to the fact that the beggar's name is given, but not the name of the rich man. It is thought to imply that the rich man's name was not in the book of life, while that of Lazarus was. Let us add to this, that to mention the name of the rich man in such a history as that before us, would have been most invidious, and most offensive to his relatives and friends.

21.—[*Desiring to be fed.*] This does not imply that he was not fed, though he desired it. It rather signifies, as in the case of the prodigal son with the husks (*Luke* 15:16), that he was 'only too glad to have' the crumbs. That which fell from the rich man's table, as refuse, was food for Lazarus.

[*The dogs came and licked ... sores.*] Some have thought that this is mentioned as an aggravation of Lazarus' misery, and that the dogs added to his sufferings. I cannot see this. To me it seems rather to imply that the dogs cared more for Lazarus than man did. It was an act of kindness.

22.—[*Into Abraham's bosom.*] This expression is most probably a proverbial one. It signifies the place of rest and safety to which all believing Jews were carried after death. Abraham was the father of the faithful, and the head of the whole Jewish family, and to be with him after death implied happiness. The expression, 'to sit down with Abraham, and Isaac, and Jacob in the kingdom of heaven,' is somewhat like it (*Matt.* 8:11).

23.—[*In hell ... in torments.*] In interpreting the expressions of this verse, and several of those which follow, we must carefully remember that we are reading a parabolical narrative. Our Lord's language is adapted to our understandings. How a lost soul can be susceptible of *bodily* suffering before the resurrection of the body, we cannot explain. The whole subject of the sensations of a disembodied spirit is far too deep for us to dogmatize about it. Let it suffice us to believe that lost souls can suffer intensely before the resurrection, and that they are conscious of their own lost condition, and of the happier condition of those who are saved.

24.—[*Father Abraham, have mercy.*] It is highly probable that this description of the rich man crying to Abraham to help him, was intended to rebuke the superstitious reverence of the Jews, and specially of the Pharisees, for Abraham. 'Think not,' says our Lord, in another place, 'to say, We have Abraham to our father' (*Matt.* 3:9). He would have them learn from this parable that Abraham himself could do nothing for those who died in sin, and that connection with Abraham would save no one from hell.

[*Lazarus ... water ... cool my tongue.*] The Fathers, and all commentators have justly dwelt here on the awful contrast between the state of the rich man before death and after death, and the complete change between his condition and that of Lazarus in another world.

[*I am tormented in this flame.*] Let that expression be noted. Few sayings in the Bible prove more strongly the reality of future punishment.

25.—[*But Abraham said, Son.*] In this, and the following verse, the dignity and solemnity of Abraham's language should specially be noted. On the one hand, there is nothing about it of severity, harshness, or unkindness. On the other, there is nothing of affected pity or compassion.

[*Remember.*] This word should be noted. The recollection of former things will be one of the worst parts of hell.

[*Thy good things.*] This expression deserves notice. It is not merely 'good things,' in contradistinction to 'evil things,' which Lazarus received. It is '*thy* good things,'—'Things which thou didst consider good, and care for as thy only good, to the utter neglect of thy soul, and its everlasting interests. Thou didst choose

thy portion and wast content with a mere earthly possession. Thou must now reap according as thou hast sown.'

26.—[*A great gulf fixed, etc.*] The language of this verse teaches plainly, if words have any meaning, that there is no hope of deliverance from hell for those who die in sin. Once in hell, men are in hell for ever. The doctrines of purgatory, or of a limited duration of punishment, are both incapable of reconciliation with this text.

27.—[*Send him to my father's house.*] It has been argued by some that the rich man's anxiety about his five brethren was a sign of improvement in him, and that his punishment had already purified his heart, and made him love his brethren, and that the notion of purgatory is consequently not without truth. Both these ideas appear to me destitute of foundation. That the rich man's state was hopeless is clear from the preceding verse. That he felt anything like true love, or spiritual affection for his five brethren is mere gratuitous assumption. It might easily be argued that his desire to have Lazarus sent to them arose from a selfish dread of their following him to the place of torment. Their company would doubtless add greatly to his misery. But it must not be forgotten that we are reading a parable, and that particular expressions in parables must not be stretched too far.

28.—[*Testify.*] The Greek word so rendered is a very strong and intensive one. It is the same that is used in Acts 2:40; 18:5; 20:21; 1 Timothy 5:21.

29.—[*Moses and the prophets.*] This expression doubtless means the writings of Moses and the prophets, and the instruction contained in them. It is a strong evidence of the sufficiency of Scripture for man's salvation. If the Old Testament alone was better than a dead man's testimony, how much better must the whole Bible be!

30.—[*They will repent.*] This is the reasoning of ignorant natural man. He knows neither the difficulty of repentance, nor the foolishness of expecting results from miraculous visions which have not been produced by the Word.

31.—[*Though one rose from the dead.*] Let the striking fact be noted that after this a man named 'Lazarus' did rise from the dead, yet the Jews remained unbelieving! Above all let it be remembered that Christ himself rose from the dead, and yet the Jewish nation would not believe!

Baxter remarks on this verse,—'God will bless his own means. Affrighting men will not renew their natures, and kindle in them a love to God and holiness. How little should we know whether one from the dead was a devil or a credible messenger? and whether he said true or false? Should he dwell with us as long as ministers, men would again despise and persecute him. Should he come but once, it would not equal the daily solicitations of God's ministers.

'Would not the rich man's guilty brethren accuse him of scandalizing and slandering the soul of their noble deceased brother, for telling them he was in hell,—and persecute him, if he was within their power?'

LUKE 17:1-4

1 Then said he unto the disciples, It is impossible but that offences will come: but woe *unto him*, through whom they come!

2 It were better for him that a millstone were hanged about his neck, and he cast into the sea, than that he should offend one of these little ones.

3 Take heed to yourselves: If thy brother trespass against thee, rebuke him; and if he repent, forgive him.

4 And if he trespass against thee seven times in a day, and seven times in a day turn again to thee, saying, I repent; thou shalt forgive him.

WE are taught for one thing in these verses, *the great sinfulness of putting stumbling-blocks in the way of other men's souls.* The Lord Jesus says, 'Woe unto him through whom offences come! It were better for him that a millstone were hanged about his neck, and he cast into the sea, than that he should offend one of these little ones.'

When do men make others stumble? When do they cause 'offences' to come? They do it, beyond doubt, whenever they persecute believers, or endeavour to deter them from serving Christ.—But this, unhappily, is not all. Professing Christians do it whenever they bring discredit on their religion by inconsistencies of temper, of word, or of deed. We do it whenever we make our Christianity unlovely in the eyes of the world, by conduct not in keeping with our profession. The world may not understand the doctrines and principles of believers. But the world is very keen-sighted about their practice.

The sin against which our Lord warns us was the sin of David. When he had broken the seventh commandment, and taken the wife of Uriah to be his wife, the prophet Nathan said to him, 'Thou hast given great occasion to the enemies of the Lord to blaspheme' (*2 Sam.* 12:14). It was the sin which St Paul charges on the Jews, when he says, 'the name of God is blasphemed among the Gentiles through you' (*Rom.* 2:24). It is the sin of which he frequently entreats Christians to beware:—'Give none offence, neither to the Jews nor to the Gentiles, nor to the church of God' (*1 Cor.* 10:32).

The subject is a deeply searching one. The sin which our Lord brings before us is unhappily very common. The inconsistencies of professing Christians too often supply the men of the world with an excuse for neglecting religion altogether. An inconsistent believer, whether he knows it or not, is daily doing harm to souls. His life is a positive injury to the gospel of Christ.

Let us often ask ourselves whether we are doing good or harm in the world. We cannot live to ourselves, if we are Christians. The eyes of many will always be upon us. Men will judge by what they see, far more than by what they hear. If they see the Christian contradicting by his practice what he professes to believe, they are justly stumbled and offended. For the world's sake, as well as for our own, let us labour to be eminently holy. Let us endeavour to make our religion beautiful in the eyes of men, and to adorn the doctrine of Christ in all things. Let us strive daily to lay aside every weight, and the sin which most easily besets us, and so to live that men can find no fault in us, except concerning the law of our God. Let us watch jealously over our tempers and tongues, and the discharge of our social duties. Anything is better than doing harm to souls. The cross of Christ will always give offence. Let us not increase that offence by carelessness in our daily life. The natural man cannot be expected to love the gospel. But let us not disgust him by inconsistency.

We are taught, for another thing, in these verses, *the great import-ance of a forgiving spirit*. The Lord Jesus says, 'if thy brother trespass against thee, rebuke him; and if he repent, forgive him. And if he trespass against thee seven times in a day, and seven times in a day turn again to thee, saying, I repent; thou shalt forgive him.'

There are few Christian duties which are so frequently and strongly dwelt upon in the New Testament as this of forgiving injuries. It fills a prominent place in the Lord's Prayer. The only profession we make in all that prayer, is that of forgiving 'those who trespass against us.'—It is a test of being forgiven ourselves. The man who cannot forgive his neighbour the few trifling offences he may have committed against him, can know nothing experimentally of that free and full pardon which is offered us by Christ (*Matt.* 18:35; *Eph.* 4:32).—Not least, it is one leading mark of the indwelling of the Holy Ghost. The presence of the Spirit in the heart may always be known by the fruits he causes to be brought forth in the life. Those fruits are both active and passive. The man who has not learned to bear and forbear, to put up with much and look over much, is not born of the Spirit (*1 John* 3:14; *Matt.* 5:44, 45).

The doctrine laid down by our Lord in this place is deeply humbling. It shows most plainly the wide contrariety which exists between the ways of the world and the gospel of Christ. Who does not know that pride, and haughtiness, and high-mindedness, and readiness to take offence, and implacable determination never to forget and never to forgive, are common among baptized men and women? Thousands will go to the Lord's table, and even profess to love the gospel, who fire up in a moment at the least appearance of what they call 'offensive' conduct, and make a quarrel out of the merest trifles. Thousands are perpetually quarrelling with all around them, always complaining how ill other people behave, and always forgetting that their own quarrelsome disposition is the spark which causes the flame. One general remark applies to all such persons. They are making their own lives miserable and showing their unmeetness for the kingdom of God. An unforgiving and quarrelsome spirit is the surest mark of an unregenerate heart. What says the Scripture? 'Whereas there is among you envying, and strife, and divisions, are ye not carnal, and walk as men?' (*1 Cor.* 3:3; *1 John* 3:18-20; 4:20).

Let us leave the whole passage with jealous self-inquiry. Few passages ought to humble Christians so much, and to make them feel so deeply their need of the blood of atonement and the mediation of Christ. How often we have given offence, and caused others to stumble! How often we have allowed unkind, and angry, and revengeful thoughts to nestle undisturbed in our hearts! These things ought not so to be. The more carefully we attend to such practical lessons as this passage contains, the more shall we recommend our religion to others, and the more inward peace shall we find in our own souls.

Notes—Luke 17:1-4

1.—[*Then said he unto the disciples.*] Let it be observed that our Lord here turns again to his disciples and specially addresses them, as he had done at the beginning of the last chapter. The parable of the rich man and Lazarus had been specially spoken to the Pharisees. Christ now turns away from them to his own followers.

It is not easy to trace the connection between the beginning of this chapter and the end of the last. Yet the two chapters seem to contain a continuous discourse of our Lord's without any pause, break, or intermission.—It is possible that our Lord may have had in his mind the stumbling-block, that conduct like that of the rich man towards Lazarus put in the way of weak believers, and meant to warn his disciples not to be discouraged if they met with similar treatment.—It is possible that our Lord may be referring again to his lesson about 'faithfulness in little things' in the parable of the unjust steward, and be warning his disciples not to give occasion to the enemy to blaspheme.—Both these conjectures, however, may perhaps be needless. A great teacher, like our Lord, has an undoubted right to open up entirely new subjects at his discretion. Perhaps this is the case here.

[*It is impossible … will come.*] This expression means, that human nature is such, and the world is such, that it is useless to expect there will be no offences. There will be, as long as the world stands.

Yet this does not lessen the guilt of those who cause them. Human infirmities are no excuse for the evil that is in the world, though they may explain its presence.

[*Offences.*] The Greek word so translated is rendered elsewhere in the New Testament, 'stumbling-block,'—'occasion to fall,'—and 'occasion of stumbling' (*Rom.* 11:9; 14:13; *1 John* 2:10).

[*Woe unto him, etc.*] This woe has probably a wide application. It includes all who cause Christ's people to stumble and be discouraged, from the fiercest persecutor, like Nero, down to the least inconsistent believer.

2.—[*A millstone hanged about his neck, etc.*] This is a proverbial expression. Anything is better than to give offence to a believer and make him stumble.

[*These little ones.*] This expression means here 'believers.' They are God's children, and as tenderly cared for by him, as the little infants in a man's family. (See *Mark* 9:42). It is probable that our Lord pointed to some of the weak and unestablished followers who accompanied him and the twelve apostles. There are always many who are 'babes in Christ' (*1 Cor.* 3:1).

3.—[*Take heed to yourselves, etc.*] The connection of this verse with that which precedes it is, again, not very clear. It would seem to imply that the 'offences' of which our Lord had just been speaking, were such as are specially occasioned by the want of a charitable and forgiving spirit among

Christians. It is like St John's expression, 'he that loveth his brother abideth in the light, and there is none occasion of stumbling in him' (*1 John* 2:10).

[*Rebuke him.*] This expression shows the Christian duty of plain, straightforward, faithful dealing with those who injure us. To say that of a brother behind his back which we are not prepared, if needful, to say before his face, is not the conduct of a true servant of Christ.

[*If he repent, forgive him.*] This expression is remarkable. It doubtless cannot mean, that we are not to forgive men unless they do repent. At this rate there would be much bitterness constantly kept alive. But it does mean that when there is no repentance or regret for an injury done, there can be no renewal of cordial friendship, or complete reconciliation between man and man.

4.—[*Seven times in a day.*] Here, as in other places, we cannot doubt that the number 'seven' must be taken indefinitely. It means, 'very frequently,' 'very often' (see *Matt* 12:45; 18:22; and *Luke* 8:2; 11:26. See also *1 Sam.* 2:5; *Ruth* 4:15; *Isa.* 4:1; *Psa.* 12:6; *Mic.* 5:5).

LUKE 17:5-10

5 And the apostles said unto the Lord, Increase our faith.

6 And the Lord said, If ye had faith as a grain of mustard seed, ye might say unto this sycamine tree, Be thou plucked up by the root, and be thou planted in the sea; and it should obey you.

7 But which of you, having a servant plowing or feeding cattle, will say unto him by and by, when he is come from the field, Go and sit down to meat?

8 And will not rather say unto him, Make ready wherewith I may sup, and gird thyself, and serve me, till I have eaten and drunken; and afterward thou shalt eat and drink?

9 Doth he thank that servant because he did the things that were commanded him? I trow not.

10 So likewise ye, when ye shall have done all those things which are commanded you, say, We are unprofitable servants: we have done that which was our duty to do.

LET us notice, in these verses, *the important request which the apostles made.* They said unto the Lord, 'Increase our faith.'

We know not the secret feelings from which this request sprung. Perhaps the hearts of the apostles failed within them, as they heard one weighty lesson after another fall from our Lord's lips. Perhaps the thought rose up in their minds, 'Who is sufficient for these things? Who can receive such high doctrines? Who can follow such a lofty standard of practice?' These, however, are only conjectures. One thing, at any rate, is clear and plain. The request which they made was most deeply important: 'Increase our faith.'

Faith is the root of saving religion. 'He that cometh unto God must believe that he is, and that he is a rewarder of them that diligently seek him' (*Heb.* 11:6). It is the hand by which the soul lays hold on Jesus Christ, and is united to him and saved. It is the secret of all Christian comfort, and spiritual prosperity. According to a man's faith will be his peace, his hope, his strength, his courage, his decision, and his victory over the world. When the apostles made request about faith, they did wisely and well.

Faith is a grace which admits of degrees. It does not come to full strength and perfection as soon as it is planted in the heart by the Holy Ghost. There is 'little' faith and 'great' faith. There is 'weak' faith and 'strong' faith. Both are spoken of in the Scriptures. Both are to be seen in the experience of God's people. The more faith a Christian has, the more happy, holy, and useful will he be. To promote the growth and progress of faith should be the daily prayer and endeavour of all who love life. When the apostles said, 'increase our faith,' they did well.

Have we any faith at all? This, after all, is the first question which the subject should raise in our hearts. Saving faith is not mere repetition of the creed, and saying, 'I believe in God the Father,—and in God the Son,—and in God the Holy Ghost.' Thousands are weekly using these words, who know nothing of real believing. The words of St Paul are very solemn, 'All men have not faith' (2 *Thess.* 3:2). True faith is not natural to man. It comes down from heaven. It is the gift of God.

If we have any faith let us pray for more of it. It is a bad sign of a man's spiritual state when he is satisfied to live on old stock, and does not hunger and thirst after growth in grace. Let a prayer for more faith form part of our daily devotions. Let us covet earnestly the best gifts. We are not to despise 'the day of small things' in a brother's soul, but we are not to be content with it in our own.

Let us notice, for another thing, in these verses, *what a heavy blow our Lord gives to self-righteousness.* He says to his apostles, 'When ye shall have done all these things which are commanded you, say, We are unprofitable servants: we have done that which was our duty to do.'

We are all naturally proud and self-righteous. We think far more highly of ourselves, our deserts, and our character, than we have any right to do. It is a subtle disease, which manifests itself in a hundred different ways. Most men can see it in other people. Few will allow its presence in themselves. Seldom will a man be found, however wicked, who does not secretly flatter himself that there is somebody else worse than he is. Seldom will a saint be found who is not at seasons tempted to be satisfied and pleased with himself. There is such a thing as a pride which wears the cloak of humility. There is not a heart upon earth which does not contain a piece of the Pharisee's character.

To give up self-righteousness is absolutely needful to salvation. He that desires to be saved must confess that there is no good thing in him, and that he has no merit, no goodness, no worthiness of his own. He must be willing to renounce his own righteousness, and to trust in the righteousness of another, even Christ the Lord. Once pardoned and forgiven, we must travel the daily journey of life under a deep conviction that we are 'unprofitable servants.' At our best we only do our duty, and have nothing to boast of. And even when we do our duty, it is not by our own power and might that we do it, but by the strength which is given to us from God. Claim upon God we have none. Right to expect anything from God we have none. Worthiness to deserve anything from God we have none. All that we have we have received. All that we are we owe to God's sovereign, distinguishing grace.

What is the true cause of self-righteousness? How is it that such a poor, weak, erring creature as man can ever dream of deserving anything at God's hands? It all arises from ignorance. The eyes of our understandings are naturally blinded. We see neither ourselves, nor our lives, nor God, nor the law of God, as we ought. Once let the light of grace shine into a man's heart, and the reign of self-righteousness is over. The roots of pride may remain, and often put forth bitter shoots. But the power of pride is broken when the Spirit comes into the heart, and shows the man himself, and God. The true Christian will never trust in his own goodness. He will say with St Paul, 'I am the chief of sinners.'—'God forbid that I should glory, save in the cross of our Lord Jesus Christ' (*1 Tim.* 1:15; *Gal.* 6:14).

Notes—Luke 17:5-10

5.—[*The apostles said.*] Both Stier and Alford remark, that this is the only instance we have of the 'apostles,' as a body, saying anything to our Lord, or making any request. Yet I venture to doubt the correctness of the remark. I think it a high probability that in Matthew 17:19, and Acts 1:6, those who spoke to our Lord together were the 'apostles.'

[*Increase our faith.*] The literal rendering of the Greek word here would be, 'add to us faith,'—that is 'give us more faith.' The reason why this request was made, I have given in the exposition. It follows a discourse extending from the beginning of the fifteenth chapter, and containing no less than five most important parables, beside other things. No wonder that the disciples said, 'Increase our faith.'

6.—[*As a grain of mustard seed.*] This is a proverbial expression for something very small and insignificant in size.

[*Say ... sycamine tree ... plucked up.*] This is a proverbial expression, apparently common among the Jews, for doing great works, and overcoming apparently insuperable difficulties. St Paul's expression is like it, 'though I have all faith, so that I could remove mountains' (*1 Cor.* 13:2). Major remarks, 'When the Jews intended to extol any of their doctors, they said of him, that he plucked up mountains by the roots.' Whether the tree mentioned is a mulberry tree, or a sycamine, commentators are not agreed.

7.—[*Which of you, etc.*] Our Lord's object in this and the three following verses appears to be, to check any idea of merit or worthiness in the disciples' minds. However great their faith might be, and however mighty their works, they were not to suppose they would have any claim on God, or any right to his favour.

[*Feeding cattle.*] The Greek word so rendered does not necessarily mean feeding *cattle.* It might as well have been *sheep.* The Greek word for 'shepherd' is the substantive from which it is taken.

[*By and by.*] The Greek word so rendered is translated in seventy-five other places in the New Testament, 'immediately,'—'straightway,'—'forthwith,' and in only one place 'by and by' (*Luke* 21:9). It admits of doubt whether the expression 'by and by' did not mean something more immediate, at the time of our own Bible translation, than it does now. It certainly seems so in the expression, 'The end is not by and by' (*Luke* 21:9).

It is questionable whether the verse altogether is rightly stopped in our version, or whether the word 'by and by' or 'immediately,' should not be connected with the expression 'go and sit down,' etc. It would then be, 'which of you will say unto him, when he is come from the fields, immediately go and sit down to meat?' This construction seems more natural and in keeping with the next verse.—The expressions 'immediately,' or 'by and by,' and 'afterward,' are evidently meant to be in contrast to the other.

8.—[*Gird thyself.*] The garments of people in Eastern countries are generally loose and flowing. Before doing anything requiring bodily exertion, the first thing necessary was to 'gird up the loins,' or tie the garments tightly round the waist, after gathering them up.

9.—[*I trow.*] The Greek word so rendered is generally translated, 'think,' or 'suppose,' in a sentence like that before us.

The word which our translators have used here they have not used anywhere else in the Bible.

10.—[*Say, We are unprofitable servants, etc.*] The doctrine laid down by our Lord in this verse is plain and evident to any impartial reader. He overthrows entirely all idea of creature-merit. When we have done all that Christ commands, we have done no more than our duty. Yet even what we do is only from grace given to us, and not from natural strength. And even then in what we do there are countless imperfections. To talk therefore of merit or claim to God's favour, in the face of such a verse as this, is absurd and preposterous.

In the fourteenth article of the Church of England this verse is very properly used as an argument against the Romish doctrine of works of supererogation.

The Greek word translated 'unprofitable,' is only used in one other place,—in the parable of the talents (*Matt.* 25:30). Major renders it, 'Servants who have conferred no benefit.' It may be doubted whether it does not mean even more, 'worthless, valueless.'

The words of Hooker are worth reading on the doctrine of this verse. 'We acknowledge a dutiful necessity of doing well: but the meritorious dignity of doing well we utterly renounce. We see how far we are from the perfect righteousness of the law. The little fruit which we have in holiness, it is, God knoweth, corrupt and unsound. We put no confidence in it at all. We challenge nothing in the world for it. We dare not call God to reckoning, as if we had him in our debt book. Our continual suit to him is, and must be, to bear with our infirmities, and pardon our offences.' (*Discourse on Justification, s. 7.*)

The contrast between what we must say of ourselves, 'we are unprofitable,' and what Christ will be graciously pleased to say at the last day (*Matt.* 25:21, 34-40), is very striking.

LUKE 17:11-19

11 And it came to pass, as he went to Jerusalem, that he passed through the midst of Samaria and Galilee.

12 And as he entered into a certain village, there met him ten men that were lepers, which stood afar off:

13 And they lifted up *their* voices, and said, Jesus, Master, have mercy on us.

14 And when he saw *them*, he said unto them, Go shew yourselves unto the priests. And it came to pass, that, as they went, they were cleansed.

15 And one of them, when he saw that he was healed, turned back, and with a loud voice glorified God,

16 And fell down on *his* face at his feet, giving him thanks: and he was a Samaritan.

17 And Jesus answering said, Were there not ten cleansed? But where *are* the nine?

18 There are not found that returned to give glory to God, save this stranger.

19 And he said unto him, Arise, go thy way: thy faith hath made thee whole.

LET us mark, firstly, in this passage, *how earnestly men can cry for help when they feel their need of it.* We read that 'as our Lord entered into a certain village there met him ten men that were lepers.' It is difficult to conceive any condition more thoroughly miserable than that of men afflicted with leprosy. They were cast out from society. They were cut off from all communion with their fellows. The men described in the passage before us appear to have been truly sensible of their wretchedness. They 'stood afar off;'—but they did not stand idly doing nothing. 'They lifted up their voices and said, Jesus, Master, have mercy on us.' They felt acutely the deplorable state of their bodies. They found words to express their feelings. They cried earnestly for relief when a chance of relief appeared in sight.

The conduct of the ten lepers is very instructive. It throws light on a most important subject in practical Christianity, which we can never understand too well. That subject is prayer.

How is it that many never pray at all? How is it that many others are content to repeat a form of words, but never pray with their hearts? How is it that dying men and women, with souls to be lost or saved, can know so little of real, hearty, businesslike prayer? The answer to these questions is short and simple. The bulk of mankind have no sense of sin. They do not feel their spiritual disease. They are not conscious that they are lost, and guilty, and hanging over the brink of hell. When a man finds out his soul's ailment, he soon learns to pray. Like the leper, he finds words to express his want. He cries for help.

How is it, again, that many true believers often pray so coldly? What is the reason that their prayers are so feeble, and wandering, and lukewarm, as they frequently are? The answer once more is very plain. Their sense of need is not so deep as it ought to be. They are not truly alive to their own weakness and helplessness, and so they do not cry fervently for mercy and grace. Let us remember these things. Let us seek to have a constant and abiding sense of our real necessities. If saints could only see their souls as the ten afflicted lepers saw their bodies, they would pray far better than they do.

Let us mark, secondly, in these verses, *how help meets men in the path of obedience.* We are told that when the lepers cried to our Lord, he only replied, 'Go shew yourselves to the priests.' He did not touch them and command their disease to depart. He prescribed no medicine, no washing, no use of outward material means. Yet heal-ing power accompanied the words which he spoke. Relief met the afflicted company as soon as they obeyed his command. 'It came to pass that as they went they were cleansed.'

A fact like this is doubtless intended to teach us knowledge. It shows us the wisdom of simple, childlike obedience to every word which comes from the mouth of Christ. It does not become us to stand still, and reason, and doubt, when our Master's commands are plain and unmistakable. If the lepers had acted in this way they would never have been healed. We must read the Scriptures diligently. We must try to pray. We must attend on the public means of grace. All these are duties which Christ requires at our hands, and to which, if we love life, we must attend, without asking vain and captious questions. It is just in the path of unhesitating obedience that Christ will meet and bless us. 'If any man will do his will, he shall know of the doctrine' (*John* 7:17).

Let us mark, lastly, in these verses, *what a rare thing is thankfulness*. We are told that of all the ten lepers whom Christ healed, there was only one who turned back and gave him thanks. The words that fell from our Lord's lips upon this occasion are very solemn: 'Were there not ten cleansed? But where are the nine?'

The lesson before us is humbling, heart-searching, and deeply instructive. The best of us are far too like the nine lepers. We are more ready to pray than to praise, and more disposed to ask God for what we have not, than to thank him for what we have. Murmurings, and complainings, and discontent abound on every side of us. Few indeed are to be found who are not continually hiding their mercies under a bushel, and setting their wants and trials on a hill. These things ought not so to be. But all who know the church and the world must confess that they are true. The widespread thanklessness of Christians is the disgrace of our day. It is a plain proof of our little humility.

Let us pray daily for a thankful spirit. It is the spirit which God loves and delights to honour. David and St Paul were eminently thankful men.—It is the spirit which has marked all the brightest saints in every age of the church. M'Cheyne, and Bickersteth, and Haldane Stewart, were always full of praise.—It is the spirit which is the very atmosphere of heaven. Angels and 'just men made perfect' are always blessing God.—It is the spirit which is the source of happiness on earth. If we would be careful for nothing, we must make our request known to God not only with prayer and supplication, but with thanksgiving (*Phil.* 4:6).

Above all, let us pray for a deeper sense of our own sinfulness, guilt, and undeserving. This, after all, is the true secret of a thankful spirit. It is the man who daily feels his debt to grace, and daily remembers that in reality he deserves nothing but hell,—this is the man who will be daily blessing and praising God. Thankfulness is a flower which will never bloom well excepting upon a root of deep humility.

Notes—Luke 17:11-19

11.—[*Passed ... midst ... Samaria ... Galilee.*] There is some difficulty about this expression. The usual road in travelling from the north of Palestine to Jerusalem, would be through Galilee first and *then* through Samaria. The most probable solution is that our Lord travelled along the boundary between Samaria and Galilee, to the river Jordan, and then followed the course of that river down to Jericho, at which city we find him in the next chapter.

12.—[*Lepers, which stood afar off.*] It should be remembered that, by the law of Moses, lepers were cast off from all society, and regarded as outcasts, who might not dwell with others. We read in Leviticus, 'he shall dwell alone; without the camp shall his habitation be' (*Lev.* 13:46).

13.—[*Jesus, Master, have mercy on us.*] We know not what degree of knowledge or faith these lepers possessed. It is probable that they only knew our Lord as a worker of mighty miracles of healing, whose fame was spread over the land.

14.—[*Shew yourselves to priests.*] The meaning of this direction will be obvious to all who are familiar with the thirteenth and fourteenth chapters of Leviticus. The priests were specially appointed by God to be the judges of all leprous cases, and to decide whether the leper was clean or unclean, cured or uncured. Moreover there was a special injunction to attend to the rules laid down in Leviticus about leprosy in the book of Deuteronomy: 'Take heed in the plague of leprosy, that thou observe diligently, and do according to all that the priests the Levites shall teach you' (*Deut.* 24:8).

A Jewish leper would doubtless catch at our Lord's direction to 'go to the priests,' and accept it as a hint that he would hear good tidings on showing himself to them.

It has been doubted whether our Lord meant only the Jewish priests, in giving this direction. Some have thought that he meant the Samaritan leper to go to the Samaritan priests on Mount Gerizim. This however appears exceedingly improbable. There is no clear proof that the Samaritan priests undertook the decision of leprous cases. Above all, there is nothing in the Gospels to show that our Lord ever recognized the Samaritan priests.—His words addressed to the Samaritan woman, 'Salvation is of the

Jews,—we know what we worship,—ye worship ye know not what' (*John* 4:22), appear to contradict the idea.

The Roman Catholic inference from this verse, that our Lord intended there should be a Christian priesthood, and that sinners deriving spiritual relief were always meant to go to a priest, is utterly baseless. There is nothing whatever in the verse to warrant it. So long as the ceremonial law lasted, and the Levitical priesthood continued, all its requirements were to be observed. The veil was not yet rent. The true sacrifice was not yet offered. The Old Testament dispensation had not yet passed away. In commanding lepers to go to the priests, our Lord simply declared his respect for the ceremonial law, so long as it lasted.

15.—[*One of them ... turned back ... glorified God.*] Let the likeness between this man's conduct and that of Naaman the Syrian, when he was healed, be carefully noted (2 *Kings* 5:15). Burgon gives the following apt quotation: 'The nine others were already healed and hastening to the priests, that they might be restored to the society of men, and their life in the world: but the first thoughts of the Samaritan are turned to his deliverer. He had forgotten all,

in the sense of God's mercy, and of his own unworthiness.'

16.—[*He was a Samaritan.*] Let it be noted that though a Samaritan, this man had been allowed to associate with Jewish lepers. Affliction, misfortune, and persecution drive men together, and make them forget points of difference, which in time of prosperity and ease are thought very important.

17.—[*But where are the nine?*] The Greek words so rendered might perhaps be translated more literally, 'But the nine,—where are they?'

18.—[*This stranger.*] The Greek word used here, means literally 'one of another nation,' and only occurs here. It is a strong expression, and shows clearly that our Lord did not recognize the Samaritans as anything more than Gentiles.

19.—[*Thy faith hath made thee whole.*] Alford remarks here, that this making whole was 'in a higher sense than the mere cleansing of his leprosy. The making whole of the nine was merely the beholding of the brazen serpent with the outward eye. He beheld with the eye of inward faith. This faith saved him;—not only healed his body, but his soul.'

LUKE 17:20-25

20 And when he was demanded of the Pharisees, when the kingdom of God should come, he answered them and said, The kingdom of God cometh not with observation:

21 Neither shall they say, Lo here! or, lo there! for, behold, the kingdom of God is within you.

22 And he said unto the disciples, The days will come, when ye shall desire to see

one of the days of the Son of man, and ye shall not see *it.*

23 And they shall say to you, See here; or, see there: go not after *them*, nor follow *them.*

24 For as the lightning, that lighteneth out of the one *part* under heaven, shineth unto the other *part* under heaven; so shall also the Son of man be in his day.

25 But first must he suffer many things, and be rejected of this generation.

WE are taught, firstly, in this passage, that *the kingdom of God is utterly unlike the kingdoms of this world.* The Lord Jesus tells the Pharisees that 'it cometh not with observation.' He meant by this that its approach and presence were not to be marked by outward signs of dignity. Those who expected to observe anything of this kind would be disappointed. They would wait and watch for such a kingdom in vain, while the real kingdom would be in the midst of them without their knowing it. 'Behold,' he says, 'the kingdom of God is within you.'

The expression which our Lord here uses describes exactly the beginning of his spiritual kingdom. It began in a manger at Bethlehem, without the knowledge of the great, the rich, and the wise. It appeared suddenly in the temple at Jerusalem, and no one but Simeon and Anna recognized its King. It was received thirty years after by none but a few fishermen and publicans in Galilee. The rulers and Pharisees had no eyes to see it. The King came to his own, and his own received him not. All this time the Jews professed to be waiting for the kingdom. But they were looking in the wrong direction. They were waiting for signs which they had no warrant for expecting. The kingdom of God was actually in the midst of them! Yet they could not see it!

The literal kingdom which Christ shall set up one day will begin in some respects very like his spiritual one. It will not be accompanied by the signs, and marks, and outward manifestations which many are expecting to see. It will not be ushered in by a period of universal peace and holiness. It will not be announced to the church by such unmistakable warnings, that everybody will be ready for it, and prepared for its appearing. It shall come suddenly, unexpectedly, and without note of warning to the immense majority of mankind. The Simeons and Annas will be as few in the last day as they were at the beginning of the gospel. The most shall awake one day, like men out of sleep, and find, to their surprise and dismay, that the kingdom of God is actually come.

We shall do well to lay these things to heart, and ponder them well. The vast majority of men are utterly deceived in their expectations with respect to the kingdom of God. They are waiting for signs which will never appear. They are looking for indications which they will never discover. They are dreaming of universal conversion in the day of election. They are fancying that missionaries, and ministers, and schools, will change the face of the world before the end comes. Let us beware of such mistakes. Let us not sleep as do others. The kingdom of God will be upon men much sooner than many expect. 'It cometh not with observation.'

We are taught, secondly, in this passage, that *the second coming of Jesus Christ will be a very sudden event*. Our Lord describes this by a striking figure. He says, 'As the lightning, that lighteneth out of the one part under heaven, shineth unto the other part under heaven; so shall also the Son of man be in his day.'

The second personal advent of Christ is the real fulfilment of these words. Of the precise day and hour of that advent we know nothing. But whenever it may take place, one thing at least is clear,—it will come on the church and the world suddenly, instantaneously, and without previous notice. The whole tenor of Scripture points this way. It shall be 'in such an hour as ye think not.'—It shall come 'as a thief in the night' (*Matt.* 24:44; *1 Thess.* 5:2).

This suddenness of Christ's second advent is a solemn thought. It ought to make us study a continual preparedness of mind. Our heart's desire and endeavour should be to be always ready to meet our Lord. Our life's aim should be to do nothing, and say nothing, which could make us ashamed if Christ were suddenly to appear. 'Blessed,' says the apostle John, 'is he who watcheth, and keepeth his garments' (*Rev.* 16:15). Those who denounce the doctrine of the second advent as speculative, fanciful, and unpractical, would do well to reconsider the subject. The doctrine was not so regarded in the days of the apostles. In their eyes patience, hope, diligence, moderation, personal holiness, were inseparably connected with an expectation of the Lord's return. Happy is the Christian who has learned to think with them! To be ever looking for the Lord's appearing is one of the best helps to a close walk with God.

We are taught, lastly, in this passage, *that there are two personal comings of Christ revealed to us in Scripture*. He was appointed to come the first time in weakness and humiliation, to suffer and to die. He was appointed to come the second time in power and great glory, to put down all enemies under his feet, and to reign.—At the first coming he was to be 'made sin for us,' and to bear our sins upon the cross. At the second coming he was to appear without sin, for the complete salvation of his people (2 *Cor.* 5:21; *Heb.* 9:28). Of both these comings our Lord speaks expressly in the verses before us. Of the first he speaks when he says that the Son of man 'must suffer, and be rejected.' Of the second he speaks when he says the Son of man shall be as the lightning which lighteneth out of one part of heaven unto another.

To see these two comings of Christ distinctly is of great importance to a right understanding of Scripture. The disciples, and all the Jews of our Lord's time, appear to have seen only one personal advent. They expected a Messiah who would come to reign, but not one who would come to suffer.—The majority of Christians, in like manner, appear to see only one personal advent. They believe that Christ came the first time to suffer. But they seem unable to understand that Christ is coming a second time to reign. Both parties have got hold of the truth, but neither, unhappily, has embraced the whole truth. Both are more or less in error, and the Christian's error is only second in importance to that of the Jew.

He that strives to be a well-instructed and established Christian, must keep steadily before his mind both the advents of Jesus Christ. Clear views on the subject are a great help to the profitable reading of the Bible. Without them we shall constantly find statements in prophecy which we can neither reconcile with other statements, nor yet explain away. Jesus coming in person the first time to suffer, and Jesus coming in person the second time to reign, are two landmarks of which we should never lose sight. We stand between the two. Let us believe that both are real and true.

Notes—Luke 17:20-25

20.—[*Demanded of the Pharisees.*] Euthymius thinks that this question was asked in derision. It is as if the Pharisees said, 'where is this kingdom you so often speak of? what likelihood is there of one so poor and lowly as you setting up a kingdom? how long are we to wait before this kingdom of yours shall appear?'

I am not satisfied that this view is correct. Messiah's kingdom was looked for by all Jews at the time when our Lord was upon earth. They expected the kingdom foretold by Daniel to appear (*Dan.* 2:44). The question before us appears to me nothing more than the natural question, which was uppermost in all Jews' minds at the time when it was asked.

[*Cometh not with observation.*] This expression is interpreted two ways.—Some think, with Schleusner and our marginal reading, that our Lord meant, 'it cometh not with outward pomp or show.'—Others think, with Parkhurst and our own translators, that our Lord meant, 'it cometh not in such a way that men shall be able to observe it.'—It comes quietly, noiselessly, and unnoticed, except by those who, like Simeon and Anna, are waiting for it in a right state of mind. I decidedly incline to this last view.

One word of caution must be added. Our Lord did not mean us to understand, that there were no 'signs' whatever of this kingdom, which any intelligent believer could perceive, and that it was useless to observe the signs of the times. In another place he rebukes the Jews for 'not discerning the signs of the times' (*Matt.* 16:3). He only meant that such signs as the carnal Jews expected, would never be seen. Those who waited for such signs would wait in vain.

The kingdom of which our Lord speaks here, evidently includes both his present spiritual kingdom and his future glorious kingdom.

21.—[*Neither shall they say, Lo here! etc.*] This expression is only an amplification of the preceding one. There were to be no signs of the kingdom of God so clear, plain, and unmistakable, that all men would be able to point at them and say,

'Behold, the kingdom of God is come.'—Neither the first spiritual kingdom which began under the gospel, nor the second glorious kingdom which shall begin at the second advent, were intended by God to be ushered in by such clear unmistakable signs, that no one could fail to see them, and no room be left for unbelief.

Those who maintain that all prophecies in the book of Revelation, were meant to be fulfilled so manifestly that no one could doubt their fulfilment,—and that Revelation is therefore entirely unfulfilled as yet, because interpreters of it have hitherto not explained it satisfactorily, would do well to mark our Lord's language in this verse. It appears somewhat damaging to their theory.

[*The kingdom of God is within you.*] This expression again is interpreted two ways. Some hold with our translators, that the word 'within' means, 'in your hearts and consciences. The kingdom of God is an inward and spiritual thing, and not an external and visible thing.'—Others hold with our marginal reading, that 'within,' means 'among you.' The kingdom has already begun in the midst of your nation. My disciples have already joined it and become its first subjects. While you are waiting, my spiritual kingdom has already been set up. I decidedly adhere to this last view.

22.—[*He said unto the disciples.*] Let it be noted that our Lord here turns away from the Pharisees and addresses his own disciples.

[*The days will come, etc.*] This expression is somewhat obscure. Stella thinks it refers to the time of our Lord's second advent, and that it describes the misery of the unconverted in that day, desiring to have one day of gospel offers granted to them, when it is too late.—I rather regard it as describing the whole state of the believing church, during the interval between the first and second advents of Christ, and specially the state of the apostles, and our Lord's immediate followers after his ascension. How much they would long for one of the happy days, when they had their Master visibly among them, we can easily conceive.

The expression is like that in Matthew, 'The days will come, when the bridegroom shall be taken from them, and then shall they fast' (*Matt.* 9:15).

23.—[*They shall say, See here, etc.*] This verse contains a warning to the disciples not to be moved by rumours of Messiah having come in glory, and the kingdom having been set up. Such rumours we know from history, abounded from the time of our Lord's ascension till the taking of Jerusalem. False christs and false prophets were continually arising. The warning is unquestionably meant to apply to the times immediately preceding the second advent. False christs, false prophets, and pretenders to divine commission may be expected in the latter days, and believers must be on their guard against them.

24.—[*For as the lightning, etc.*] In this verse our Lord declares distinctly that his second advent, when it does take place, will be so sudden, so clearly marked, and so unmistakable, that true believers shall at once recognize it as the coming of their King. It will not be a slow, gradual event. It will come on men in a moment.

That our Lord in this verse meant nothing more than the march of the Roman armies to destroy Jerusalem, is, to my mind, an unsatisfactory and improbable interpretation.

25.—[*First must he suffer.*] Our Lord here asserts that great truth which his disciples and all the Jews were so exceedingly slow to see. He must first suffer and afterwards reign. He must first endure the cross, and afterwards, at his second advent, wear the crown.

[*Rejected of this generation.*] I am strongly disposed to think, that both here and in Luke 21:32; Mark 13:30 and Matthew 24:34, the word translated, 'generation,' means this *nation* or people of the Jews, and not merely the men who were living when our Lord spoke. Those who wish to see this view, and the quotations in favour of it, will find it set forth in Ravanelli's Thesaurus, under the word 'generatio.'

LUKE 17:26-37

26 And as it was in the days of Noe, so shall it be also in the days of the Son of man.

27 They did eat, they drank, they married wives, they were given in marriage, until the day that Noe entered into the ark, and the flood came and destroyed them all.

28 Likewise also as it was in the days of Lot; they did eat, they drank, they bought, they sold, they planted, they builded;

29 But the same day that Lot went out of Sodom it rained fire and brimstone from heaven, and destroyed *them* all.

30 Even thus shall it be in the day when the Son of man is revealed.

31 In that day, he which shall be upon the housetop, and his stuff in the house, let him not come down to take it away: and he that is in the field, let him likewise not return back.

32 Remember Lot's wife.

33 Whosoever shall seek to save his life shall lose it; and whosoever shall lose his life shall preserve it.

34 I tell you, in that night there shall be two *men* in one bed; the one shall be taken, and the other shall be left.

35 Two *women* shall be grinding together; the one shall be taken, and the other left.

36 Two *men* shall be in the field; the one shall be taken, and the other left.

37 And they answered and said unto him, Where, Lord? And he said unto them, Wheresoever the body *is*, thither will the eagles be gathered together.

THE subject of these verses is one of peculiar solemnity. It is the second advent of our Lord Jesus Christ. That great event, and the things immediately connected with it, are here described by our Lord's own lips.

We should observe, for one thing, in these verses, *what a fearful picture our Lord gives of the state of the professing church at his second coming.* We are told that as it was in the 'days of Noah,' and in the 'days of Lot,' 'so shall it be in the day when the Son of man is revealed.' The character of those days we are not left to conjecture. We are told distinctly, that men were entirely taken up with eating, drinking, marrying, buying, selling, planting, building,—and would attend to nothing else. The flood came at last in Noah's day, and drowned all except those who were in the ark. The fire fell from heaven at last in Lot's day, and destroyed all except Lot, his wife, and his daughters. And our Lord declares most plainly that like things will happen when he comes again at the end of the world. 'When they shall say, Peace and safety; then sudden destruction cometh upon them' (*1 Thess.* 5:3).

It is hard to imagine a passage of Scripture which more completely overthrows the common notions that prevail among men about Christ's return. The world will not be converted when Jesus comes again. The earth will not be full of the knowledge of the Lord. The reign of peace will not have been established. The millennium will not have begun. These glorious things will come to pass *after* the second advent, but not before. If words have any meaning, the verses before us show that the earth will be found full of wickedness and worldliness in the day of Christ's appearing. The unbelievers and the unconverted will be found very many. The believers and the godly, as in the days of Noah and Lot, will be found very few.

Let us take heed to ourselves, and beware of the spirit of the world. It is not enough to do as others, and buy, and sell, and plant, and build, and eat, and drink, and marry, as if we were born for nothing else. Exclusive attention to these things may ruin us as thoroughly as open sin. We must come out from the world and be separate. We must dare to be peculiar. We must escape for our lives like Lot. We must flee to the ark like Noah. This alone is safety. Then, and then only, we shall be hid in the day of the Lord's anger, and avoid destruction when the Son of man is revealed (*Zeph.* 2:3).

We should observe, for another thing, in these verses, *what a solemn warning our Lord gives us against unsound profession.* He says to us, in immediate connection with the description of his second advent, 'Remember Lot's wife.'

Lot's wife went far in religious profession. She was the wife of a 'righteous man.' She was connected through him with Abraham, the father of the faithful. She fled with her husband from Sodom in the day when he escaped for his life by God's command. But Lot's wife was not really like her husband. Though she fled with him, she had left her heart behind her. She wilfully disobeyed the strict injunction which the angel had laid upon her. She looked back towards Sodom, and was at once struck dead. She was turned into a pillar of salt, and perished in her sins. 'Remember' her, says our Lord,—'Remember Lot's wife.'

Lot's wife is meant to be a beacon and a warning to all professing Christians. It may be feared that many will be found like her in the day of Christ's second advent. There are many in the present day who go a certain length in religion. They conform to the outward ways of Christian relatives and friends. They speak the 'language of Canaan.' They use all the outward ordinances of religion. But all this time their souls are not right in the sight of God. The world is in their hearts, and their hearts are in the world. And by and by, in the day of sifting, their unsoundness will be exposed to all the world. Their Christianity will prove rotten at the core. The case of Lot's wife will not stand alone.

Let us remember Lot's wife, and resolve to be *real* in our religion. Let us not profess to serve Christ for no higher motive than to please husbands, or wives, or masters, or ministers. A mere *lean-to* religion like this will never save our souls. Let us serve Christ for his own sake. Let us never rest till we have the true grace of God in our hearts, and have no desire to look back to the world.

We should observe, lastly, in these verses, *what an awful separation there will be in the professing church when Christ comes again.* Our Lord describes this separation by a very striking picture. He says, 'In that night there shall be two men in one bed; the one shall be taken, and the other shall be left. Two women shall be grinding together; the one shall be taken, and the other left.'

The meaning of these expressions is clear and plain. The day of Christ's second advent shall be the day when good and evil, converted and unconverted, shall at length be divided into two distinct bodies. The visible church shall no longer be a mixed body. The wheat and the tares shall no longer grow side by side. The good fish and the bad shall at length be sorted into two bodies. The angels shall come forth, and gather together the godly, that they may be rewarded; and leave the wicked behind to be punished. 'Converted or unconverted,' will be the only subject of enquiry. It will matter nothing that people have worked together, and slept together, and lived together for many years. They will be dealt with at last according to their religion. Those members of the family who have loved Christ, will be taken up to heaven; and those who have loved the world, will be cast down to hell. Converted and unconverted shall be separated for evermore when Jesus comes again.

Let us lay to heart these things. He that loves his relatives and friends is specially bound to consider them. If those whom he loves are true servants of Christ, let him know that he must cast in his lot with them, if he would not one day be parted from them for ever.—If those whom he loves are yet dead in trespasses and sins, let him know that he must work and pray for their conversion, lest he should be separated from them by and by to all eternity. Life is the only time for such work. Life is fast ebbing away from us all. Partings, and separations, and the breaking up of families are at all times painful things. But all the separations that we see now are nothing compared to those which will be seen when Christ comes again.

Notes—Luke 17:26-37

26.—[*As it was in the days of Noe, etc.*] The whole passage, from this verse down to the end, applies exclusively to the second personal advent of Christ, when he shall come to set up his glorious kingdom. The Pharisees had inquired about Messiah's kingdom. The disciples themselves thought much of it, and were full of ignorant expectations. Our Lord thought it good to show them that Messiah's kingdom in glory would be a far more solemn event than they supposed, and that it would find the vast majority of mankind utterly unprepared. Instead of indulging in carnal speculations, and looking for carnal rewards, they would do well to study an unworldly frame of mind, and to take heed that they were ready for the kingdom in heart and life. Its setting up would be attended by such a sifting and separation as they had not considered. For that day of sifting they would do well to prepare.

Let it be noted, that our Lord speaks of Noah's days as an illustration of the days of his own second advent, in the twenty-fourth chapter of St Matthew. But the discourse which he delivered then was delivered on a totally different occasion from that before us. It is plain therefore that he used the illustration twice.

To apply the conclusion of this chapter, as many do, to the destruction of Jerusalem by the Romans, appears to me an unwarrantable, and violent straining of Scripture.

27.—[*They did eat, they drank, etc.*] These expressions would perhaps be more literally translated, 'They were eating, they were drinking,' etc. It was the habit of living, in which they were absorbed.

[*Noe entered into the ark, etc.*] Let it be noted, that both here and in the two following verses, our Lord speaks of the history of Noah's ark, and of Lot and the destruction of Sodom, and of Lot's wife, as real, true historical facts. The idea of modern sceptics, that the events recorded in Genesis are nothing better than myths and fables, finds no countenance here. Specially let it be observed, that the modern notion of Neologians, that Sodom was destroyed by an earthquake, is completely overturned

here. Our Lord expressly asserts, that 'It rained fire and brimstone from heaven.' It is a dangerous thing to be wise above that which is written.

31.—[*He which shall be upon the housetop, etc.*] This expression is remarkable. It is exactly like that which our Lord uses upon another occasion, where he is foretelling the destruction of Jerusalem, and the miseries of its sieges, both the siege when the Romans took it, and the siege foretold by Zechariah (*Zech.* 14), which is yet to come. Yet in the passage before us there is no reference whatever to the destruction of Jerusalem by the Romans. The whole passage is exclusively confined to the second advent of Christ, and the circumstances attending it.

What then are we to understand by the language which our Lord uses, both in this verse and the five which follow it?

The most probable solution appears to me to be this. Our Lord desired to teach his disciples that his own second advent in glory would not be a time of carnal ease to everybody, as the Jews thought, but a time of trial to men's religion, and of sifting and separation to the visible church.—It would be ushered in by such a period of tribulation and suffering, that none but those who were sitting loose to the world, and ready to give up everything for Christ's sake, would come out of it unscathed.—It would be a time when believers must give up all thought of worldly goods, and beware of lingering and looking back to the world. Nothing but singleness of eye, wholeness of heart, and unworldliness of spirit would abide the fire of that day.

The verse before us, in short, appears to me a proverbial expression. It shows the sort of thing which Christians must not do, and the sort of spirit which they must beware of, if they would come safely through the day of the Lord's appearing.

The housetops in Eastern countries, be it remembered, are generally flat, and much used by the inhabitants. The stairs were often outside, and a man need not come down through the house to flee away. Moreover he might flee over the flat roofs of his neighbours' houses, and thus escape, in any sudden time of danger.

Whether in all this there may not be some reference to that future siege of Jerusalem, which is so closely connected with our Lord's second advent (*Zech.* 14), I am not prepared to decide. There is perhaps a deeper and fuller meaning in the verse than has yet been discovered. There are to be circumstances attending the second advent of Christ, in all probability, of which at present we have very inadequate conceptions, and which perhaps are mercifully withheld from us now, because we could not bear them.

33.—[*Whosoever shall seek, etc.*] This verse appears to point out that there will be a fiery trial of men's religion at the time of Christ's second advent, and that none will come through it safely, but those who are prepared to give up everything, even life itself, for Christ's sake.

[*Preserve it.*] The word so rendered is very peculiar. It means literally 'to bring forth alive.' It is only found in one other place in the New Testament (*Acts* 7:19).

35.—[*Two women ... grinding together.*] This expression may seem strange to an English ear at first hearing. It is an exact description of what may commonly be seen in Eastern countries. Major quotes the following passage from Dr Clarke. 'Scarcely had we reached our apartments at Nazareth, than we beheld two women grinding at the mill, in a manner most fully illustrating the saying of our Saviour. They were preparing flour to make bread, as is always customary when strangers arrive. The two women seated on the ground held between them two round flat stones. In the centre of the upper stone was a cavity for pouring in corn, and by the side of this an upright wooden handle for moving the stone. One of the women with her right hand pushed this handle to the women opposite, who again sent it to her companion, thus giving a rotatory and very rapid motion to the upper stone. Their left hand was all the while employed in supplying fresh corn, as fast as the bran and corn escaped from the sides of the machine.' See Exodus 11:5; Isaiah 47:1-3.

37.—[*Where, Lord?*] The question of the disciples appears to show that they were entirely perplexed by the words which our Lord had just spoken. The answer they received seems intended to keep them purposely in ignorance of our Lord's full meaning. At present they were not able to bear it.

[*Wheresoever ... body ... eagles ... together.*] This is a dark and mysterious saying, and has greatly perplexed all commentators. That it refers to the well-known power of the vulture-tribe, to discern carcases, whether by eye or by smell, is allowed by all (*Job* 39:30). That it is a proverbial saying, signifying the gathering of things which from any cause have an attraction one to another, is also allowed.—But when we come to the precise application of the saying, we find great variety of opinions. The parallel expression in St Matthew (*Matt.* 24:28) contains a Greek word for the body, which means a 'dead body.' The word used in the verse before us, does not necessarily mean a dead body. In other respects the two passages are alike.

1. Some think that 'the eagles' mean the saints. This is by far the commonest opinion. It is held by Chrysostom, Ambrose, Jerome, Theophylact, Euthymius, Luther, Calvin, Brentius, Bullinger, Bucer, Gualter, Beza, Pellican, Flacius, Musculus, Paraeus, Piscator, Cocceius, Jansenius, Quesnel, Du Veil, Cornelius à Lapide, Calovius, Suicer, Ravanell, Poole, Trapp, Cartwright, Pearce, Leigh, Wordsworth, and Burgon.

The meanings these writers attach to 'the body,' are exceedingly various. Suffice it to say that some think it means 'heaven,'—some 'Christ,'—some 'the church,'—some 'the Lord's supper,'—and some 'the judgment.'

2. Some think that 'the eagles' mean the Roman armies, whose military ensign was the eagle, and 'the body,' Jerusalem and the Jewish nation. This is the view of Hammond, Lightfoot, Whitby, Doddridge, Burkitt, Bengel, Gill, Parkhurst, Scott, A. Clarke, Major, Davidson, Stier, and Barnes.

Matthew Henry, with characteristic kindliness, seems to think that this interpretation and the former one may both be correct at the same time.

3. Some think that 'the eagles' means false prophets. This is the view of Aretius and Arias Montanus.

4. Some think that 'the eagles' mean all mankind, and 'the body,' the judgment day. This is the view of Barradius, Stella, and Maldonatus.

5. Origen thinks that 'the body' means the church, and 'the eagles gathered together,' the unanimous consent of doctors and early Fathers.

6. Chemnitius thinks that 'the eagles' mean Christ himself.

7. Heinsius thinks that the whole sentence is only a figurative prediction of the extreme rapidity of Christ's second advent. He shall come as rapidly as eagles come to a carcase.

8. Alford thinks that 'the eagles' mean the angels of vengeance, and 'the body' the whole world.

I cannot undertake to decide amidst so many conflicting judgments. I only venture the opinion, that, looking at the context, the eagles are more likely to be emblems of the angels who will be employed at our Lord's second coming, than of anything else. The verse immediately preceding that before us speaks of the separation between the just and the unjust which shall take place at our Lord's appearing. In that separation we are distinctly told elsewhere, the agents employed shall be the angels (*Matt.* 13:49). Is it too much then, to conjecture that our Lord's simple meaning is, that wherever 'his body' is, his professing church, there the angels shall gather together at the last day, and sever the wicked from the just, in order to give to each his appointed place?

It is, however, very probable that all the interpretations hitherto proposed will prove at last incorrect, and that the true one may yet remain to be discovered at the second advent. That our Lord purposely meant it to be regarded as a mysterious saying is very evident.

LUKE 18:1-8

1 And he spake a parable unto them *to this end*, that men ought always *to* pray, and not to faint;

2 Saying, There was in a city a judge, which feared not God, neither regarded man:

3 And there was a widow in that city; and she came unto him saying, Avenge me of mine adversary.

4 And he would not for a while: but afterward he said within himself, Though I fear not God, nor regard man;

5 Yet because this widow troubleth me, I will avenge her, lest by her continual coming she weary me.

6 And the Lord said, Hear what the unjust judge saith.

7 And shall not God avenge his own elect, which cry day and night unto him, though he bear long with them?

8 I tell you that he will avenge them speedily. Nevertheless when the Son of man cometh, shall he find faith on the earth?

THE object of the parable before us, is explained by Christ himself. To use the words of an old divine, 'The key hangs at the door.'—'He spake a parable to this end; that men ought always to pray, and not to faint.' These words, be it remembered, are closely connected with the solemn doctrine of the second advent, with which the preceding chapter concludes. It is prayer without fainting, during the long weary interval between the first and second advents, which Jesus is urging his disciples to keep up. In that interval we ourselves are standing. The subject therefore is one which ought to possess a special interest in our eyes.

These verses teach us, firstly, *the great importance of perseverance in prayer.* Our Lord conveys this lesson by telling the story of a friendless widow, who obtained justice from a wicked magistrate, by dint of sheer importunity.—'Though I fear not God, nor regard man,' said the unjust judge, 'yet because this widow troubleth me, I will avenge her, lest by her continual coming she weary me.'—Our Lord himself supplies the application of the parable: 'Hear what the unjust judge saith. Shall not God avenge his own elect, which cry day and night unto him, though he bear long with them?' If importunity obtains so much from a wicked man, how much more will it obtain for the children of God from the Righteous Judge, their Father in heaven!

The subject of prayer ought always to be interesting to Christians. Prayer is the very life-breath of true Christianity. Here it is that religion begins. Here it flourishes. Here it decays. Prayer is one of the first evidences of conversion (*Acts* 9:11). Neglect of prayer is the sure road to a fall (*Matt.* 26:40, 41). Whatever throws light on the subject of prayer is for our soul's health.

Let it then be graven deeply in our minds, that it is far more easy to begin a habit of prayer than it is to keep it up. The fear of death,— some temporary prickings of conscience,—some excited feelings, may make a man begin praying after a fashion. But to go on praying requires faith. We are apt to become weary, and to give way to the suggestion of Satan, that 'it is of no use.' And then comes the time when the parable before us ought to be carefully remembered. We must recollect that our Lord expressly told us 'always to pray and not to faint.'

Do we ever feel a secret inclination to hurry our prayers, or shorten our prayers, or become careless about our prayers, or omit our prayers altogether? Let us be sure, when we do, that it is a direct temptation from the devil. He is trying to sap and undermine the very citadel of our souls, and to cast us down to hell. Let us resist the temptation, and cast it behind our backs. Let us resolve to pray on steadily, patiently, perseveringly, and let us never doubt that it does us good. However long the answer may be in coming, still let us pray on. Whatever sacrifice and self-denial it may cost us, still let us pray on, 'pray always,'—'pray without ceasing,'—and 'continue in prayer' (1 Thess. 5:17; Col. 4:2). Let us arm our minds with this parable, and while we live, whatever we make time for, let us make time for prayer.

These verses teach us, secondly, that *God has an elect people upon earth, who are under his special care.* The Lord Jesus declares that God will 'avenge his own elect, which cry day and night unto him.'—'I tell you,' he says, 'that he will avenge them speedily.'

Election is one of the deepest truths of Scripture. It is clearly and beautifully stated in the seventeenth Article of the Church of England. It is 'the everlasting purpose of God, whereby, before the foundations of the world were laid, he hath decreed by his counsel, secret to us, to deliver from curse and damnation those whom he hath chosen in Christ out of mankind, and to bring them by Christ to everlasting salvation.' This testimony is true. This is 'sound speech which cannot be condemned' (*Titus* 2:8).

Election is a truth which should call forth praise and thanksgiving from all true Christians. Except God had chosen and called them, they would never have chosen and called on him. Except he had chosen them of his own good pleasure, without respect to any good-ness of theirs, there would never have been anything in them to make them worthy of his choice. The worldly and the carnal-minded may rail at the doctrine of election. The false professor may abuse it, and 'turn the grace of God into lasciviousness' (*Jude* 4). But the believer who knows his own heart will ever bless God for election. He will confess that without election there would be no salvation.

But what are the marks of election? By what tokens shall a man know whether he is one of God's elect? These marks are clearly laid down in Scripture. Election is inseparably connected with faith in Christ, and conformity to his image (*Rom.* 8:29, 30). It was when St Paul saw the working 'faith,' and patient 'hope,' and labouring 'love' of the Thessalonians, that he knew their 'election of God' (*1 Thess.* 1:3, 4). Above all, we have a plain mark, described by our Lord, in the passage before us. God's elect are a people who 'cry unto him night and day.' They are essentially a praying people. No doubt there are many persons whose prayers are formal and hypocritical. But one thing is very clear,—a prayerless man must never be called one of God's elect. Let that never be forgotten.

These verses teach us, lastly, that *true faith will be found very scarce at the end of the world.* The Lord Jesus shows this, by asking a very solemn question, 'When the Son of man cometh, shall he find faith on the earth?'

The question before us is a very humbling one. It shows the uselessness of expecting that all the world will be converted before Christ comes again. It shows the foolishness of supposing that all persons are 'good,' and that though differing in outward matters, they are all right at heart, and all going to heaven. Such notions find no countenance in the text before us.

Where is the use, after all, of ignoring facts under our own eyes,— facts in the world,—facts in the churches,—facts in the congregations we belong to,—facts by our own doors and firesides? Where is faith to be seen? How many around us really believe what the Bible contains? How many live as if they believed that Christ died for them, and that there is a judgment, a heaven, and a hell?—These are most painful and serious inquiries. But they demand and deserve an answer.

Have we faith ourselves? If we have, let us bless God for it. It is a great thing to believe all the Bible. It is matter for daily thankfulness if we feel our sins, and really trust in Jesus. We may be weak, frail, erring, short-coming sinners. But do we believe? That is the grand question. If we believe, we shall be saved. But he that believeth not, shall not see life, and shall die in his sins (*John* 3:36; 8:24).

Notes—Luke 18:1-8

1.—[*And he spake a parable, etc.*] Let it be noted that this parable is closely connected with the preceding chapter. After giving a fearful account of the sifting and tribulations which shall attend his own second advent, our Lord proceeds to urge on his people the importance of the habit of persevering in prayer as a preparation for the advent, and of not fainting under trial and giving up prayer in despair.

[*Always to pray.*] This expression does not mean that a man should be incessantly performing the act of prayer. It means that a man should constantly keep up the habit of prayer, and endeavour to be always in a prayerful frame of mind.

2.—[*There was in a city, etc.*] As usual, there are various opinions about the primary purpose and application of this parable.

It is the opinion of many that the 'widow' in the parable represents the church, and the 'adversary' the devil, or Antichrist; the widow's distressed state the whole condition of the church between the first and second advents of Christ,—and her crying for help the groaning of creation for the manifestation of the sons of God (*Rom.* 8:19).

Trench mentions a strange view of Vitringa's, that the unjust judge represents the Roman emperors, and the widow the early church;—and a still stranger view of Irenæus and Hippolytus, that the widow is the earthly Jerusalem, and the unjust judge Antichrist.

My own impression is that the parable was meant simply to describe the duty of individual believers during the whole period of the present dispensation, and to encourage them to persevering prayer, by holding out the hope that God will at length plead their cause, when things seem at the worst.

[*Which feared not God ... regarded man.*] This is a proverbial description of a thoroughly bad man in high office. Our Lord Jesus Christ, be it observed, knows that there are such men in high places, and will one day reckon with them.

The description has stumbled some commentators, and has been treated as a great difficulty. They have been offended at the idea of such a man as this judge standing in the position of a type and emblem of God. To avoid this seeming inconsistency, Theophylact mentions a strange and monstrous view held by some, that the words exactly describe God, since he is one who need not fear God, and is no respecter of men's persons!

The difficulty raised appears to me thoroughly unreasonable. Both here, and in other places, we are not meant to draw an exact parallel between the person described and God. The one single point we are meant to notice is, that even an unjust and wicked man can be moved by importunity. And the inference pressed on us, is simply this, that if a wicked man is to be moved by importunity, much more is God.

Quesnel says, 'We may make a good use even of the worst examples. Everything serves to display the justice and goodness of God, either by way of conformity or opposition, either as lines which form the resemblance thereof, or as shadows which heighten the lustre and liveliness of the colours.'

3.—[*A widow.*] The helpless and friendless condition of a widow in Eastern countries and Bible times, should be carefully remembered. See Exodus 22:22; Deuteronomy 10:18; Job 29:13; 1 Kings 17:9, 12.

5.—[*Weary me.*] The Greek word translated 'weary,' is very peculiar. It signifies literally 'to strike under the eyes.' Some have thought it very strange that a man in the judge's position should use such language, and express any fear that a poor weak, defenceless woman could trouble him so much as to require such a strong phrase. Yet a moment's reflection will show us, that selfish, worldly, wicked men, are just exactly the persons who employ such violent expressions, in order to express their sense of annoyance even on trifling occasions. How often for instance people talk of being 'tired to death,' or 'worried out of their lives,' when there is nothing to justify the use of such language.

6.—[*The unjust judge.*] The Greek words here mean literally 'the judge of injustice.' It is precisely the same form of language, that is used in a previous chapter describing 'the unjust steward' (*Luke* 16:8).

7.—[*Which cry day and night.*] This is doubtless a proverbial expression, signifying a habit of continual prayer.

[*Bear long.*] The Greek word so translated is generally rendered 'have patience,' 'is longsuffering.' The remark of Pearce on the passage is worth reading. 'The word is commonly used for delaying to punish a bad man. Here it has another sense, and signifies the delaying to help a good man. So Peter seems to use the expression, "longsuffering," when he says, "account that the longsuffering of God is salvation," that is, that though he delays long to save you, yet he will save you at the last' (*2 Pet.* 3:15).

8.—[*He will avenge them speedily.*] This sentence points to the second advent of Christ. To our eyes it seems long delayed. But a thousand years in God's sight are but as one day.

[*When ... Son of man ... faith ...earth.*] These words are differently interpreted.

Some, as usual, can see in the 'coming of the Son of man,' nothing but the destruction of Jerusalem by the Romans. They think the sentence means, when the Jewish polity is overthrown, the number of believers will be found very small.

Wordsworth maintains that 'the earth' means the 'world,' in contradiction to the children of light.

I am unable to see either view to be correct. I believe the view given in the exposition is the true one. Our Lord teaches that there will be comparatively few true believers upon earth when he comes again. True faith will be found as rare as it was in the days of Noah, when only eight persons entered the ark, and in the days of Lot, when only four persons left Sodom. He is speaking, we must remember, in close connection with the account of the second advent, and his own vivid comparison of the day of Noah and Lot, with the day when the Son of man shall be revealed.

There is doubtless an implied lesson here, that persevering prayer is the secret of keeping up faith. Augustine says, 'When faith fails, prayer dies. In order to pray, then, we must have faith; and that our faith fail not, we must pray. Faith pours forth prayer; and the pouring forth of the heart in prayer, gives steadfastness to faith.'

The unbelief of man on the subject of both advents is strikingly shown in the beginning of Isaiah 53 and of 2 Peter 3.

LUKE 18:9-14

9 And he spake this parable unto certain which trusted in themselves that they were righteous, and despised others:

10 Two men went up into the temple to pray; the one a Pharisee, and the other a publican.

11 The Pharisee stood and prayed thus with himself, God, I thank thee that I am not as other men are, extortioners, unjust, adulterers, or even as this publican.

12 I fast twice in the week, I give tithes of all that I possess.

13 And the publican, standing afar off, would not lift up so much as *his* eyes unto heaven, but smote upon his breast, saying, God be merciful to me a sinner.

14 I tell you, this man went down to his house justified *rather* than the other: for every one that exalteth himself shall be abased; and he that humbleth himself shall be exalted.

T HE parable we have now read is closely connected with the one which immediately precedes it. The parable of the persevering widow teaches the value of importunity in prayer. The parable of the Pharisee and publican teaches the spirit which should pervade our prayers.—The first parable encourages us to pray and faint not. The second parable reminds us how and in what manner we ought to pray.—Both should be often pondered by every true Christian.

Let us notice, firstly, *the sin against which our Lord Jesus Christ warns us in these verses.* There is no difficulty in finding out this. St Luke tells us expressly, that 'he spake this parable unto certain which trusted in themselves that they were righteous and despised others.' The sin which our Lord denounces is 'self-righteousness.'

We are all naturally self-righteous. It is the family-disease of all the children of Adam. From the highest to the lowest we think more highly of ourselves than we ought to do. We secretly flatter ourselves that we are not so bad as some, and that we have something to recommend us to the favour of God. 'Most men will proclaim every one his own goodness' (*Prov.* 20:6). We forget the plain testimony of Scripture, 'In many things we offend all.'—'There is not a just man upon earth, that doeth good and sinneth not.'—'What is man, that he should be clean? and he that is born of a woman, that he should be righteous?' (*James* 3:2; *Eccles.* 7:20; *Job* 15:14).

The true cure for self-righteousness is self-knowledge. Once let the eyes of our understanding be opened by the Spirit, and we shall talk no more of our own goodness. Once let us see what there is in our own hearts, and what the holy law of God requires, and self-conceit will die. We shall lay our hands on our mouths, and cry with the leper, 'Unclean, unclean' (*Lev.* 13:45).

Let us notice, secondly, in these verses, *the prayer of the Pharisee, which our Lord condemns.* We read that he said, 'God, I thank thee that I am not as other men are, extortioners, unjust, adulterers, or even as this publican. I fast twice in the week, I give tithes of all that I possess.'

One great defect stands out on the face of this prayer,—a defect so glaring that even a child might mark it. It exhibits no sense of sin and need. It contains no confession and no petition,—no acknowledgment of guilt and emptiness,—no supplication for mercy and grace. It is a mere boasting recital of fancied merits, accompanied by an uncharitable reflection on a brother sinner. It is a proud, high-minded profession, destitute alike of penitence, humility, and charity. In short, it hardly deserves to be called a prayer at all.

No state of soul can be conceived so dangerous as that of the Pharisee. Never are men's bodies in such desperate plight, as when mortification and insensibility set in. Never are men's hearts in such a hopeless condition, as when they are not sensible of their own sins. He that would not make shipwreck on this rock, must beware of measuring himself by his neighbours. What does it signify that we are more moral than 'other men?' We are all vile and imperfect in the sight of God.—'If we contend with him, we cannot answer him one of a thousand' (*Job* 9:3). Let us remember this. In all our self-examination let us not try ourselves by comparison with the standard of men. Let us look at nothing but the requirements of God. He that acts on this principle will never be a Pharisee.

Let us notice, thirdly, in these verses, *the prayer of the publican, which our Lord commends.* That prayer was in every respect the very opposite of that of the Pharisee. We read that he 'stood afar off, and smote upon his breast, and said, God be merciful to me a sinner.' Our Lord himself stamps this short prayer with the seal of his approbation. He says, 'I tell you, this man went down to his house justified rather than the other.'

The excellence of the publican's prayer consists in five points, each of which deserves attention. For one thing, it was a real *petition.* A prayer which only contains thanksgiving and profession, and asks nothing, is essentially defective. It may be suitable for an angel, but it is not suitable for a sinner.—For another thing, it was a direct *personal* prayer. The publican did not speak of his neighbours, but himself. Vagueness and generality are the great defects of most men's religion. To get out of 'we,' and 'our,' and 'us,' into 'I,' and 'my,' and 'me,' is a great step toward heaven.—For another thing, it was a *humble* prayer,—a prayer which put self in the right place. The publican confessed plainly that he was a sinner. This is the very ABC of saving Christianity. We never begin to be good till we can feel and say that we are bad.—For another thing, it was a prayer in which *mercy* was the chief thing desired, and faith in God's covenant mercy, however weak, displayed. Mercy is the first thing we must ask for in the day we begin to pray. Mercy and grace must be the subject of our daily petitions at the throne of grace till the day we die.—Finally, the publican's prayer was one which came from his *heart*. He was deeply moved in uttering it. He smote upon his breast, like one who felt more than he could express. Such prayers are the prayers which are God's delight. A broken and a contrite heart he will not despise (*Psa.* 51:17).

Let these things sink down into our hearts. He that has learned to feel his sins has great reason to be thankful. We are never in the way of salvation until we know that we are lost, ruined, guilty, and helpless. Happy indeed is he who is not ashamed to sit by the side of the publican! When our experience tallies with his, we may hope that we have found a place in the school of God.

Let us notice, lastly, in these verses, *the high praise which our Lord bestows on humility.* He says, 'Every one that exalteth himself shall be abased, and he that humbleth himself shall be exalted.'

The principle here laid down is so frequently found in the Bible, that it ought to be deeply graven in our memories. Three times we find our Lord using the words before us in the Gospels, and on three distinct occasions. Humility, he would evidently impress upon us, is among the first and foremost graces of the Christian character. It was a leading grace in Abraham, Jacob, Moses, David, Job, Isaiah, and Daniel. It ought to be a leading grace in all who profess to serve Christ. All the Lord's people have not gifts or money. All are not called to preach, or write, or fill a prominent place in the church. But all are called to be humble. One grace at least should adorn the poorest and most unlearned believer. That grace is humility.

Let us leave the whole passage with a deep sense of the great encouragement it affords to all who feel their sins, and cry to God for mercy in Christ's name. Their sins may have been many and great. Their prayers may seem weak, faltering, unconnected, and poor. But let them remember the publican, and take courage. That same Jesus who commended his prayer is sitting at the right hand of God to receive sinners. Then let them hope and pray on.

Notes—Luke 18:9-14

9.—[*Unto certain which trusted, etc.*] It seems probable that this parable was not addressed to the Pharisees, so much as to certain of our Lord's own followers and disciples. Our Lord knew all hearts, and he probably saw in some of his own immediate adherents a tendency to value themselves too highly because they were his disciples. He checks it by speaking this parable.

Pride, self-conceit, and a disposition to look down on others as ignorant, blind, and inferior to ourselves, are faults to which many converted people are peculiarly liable.

10.—[*A Pharisee … a publican.*] These two are mentioned as types of opposite classes of character. The Pharisee represents the moral, the respectable, and the externally correct. The publican represents the wicked, the profligate, and the utterly irreligious.

The theory held by some, that the Pharisee represents the Jewish nation, and the publican the Gentile world, appears to me destitute of foundation.

11.—[*Stood and prayed thus with himself.*] Some have thought that the Greek words should have been rendered, 'stood by himself and prayed thus.' It is probable, however, that our English version gives the sense correctly.

It is a mistake to suppose, as some have done, that there was anything to be blamed, as indicative of pride, in the Pharisee's attitude. Standing was as common a position for prayer as kneeling, among the Jews. See Matthew 6:5; Mark 11:25; 2 Chronicles 6:12.

[*I thank thee.*] Gill gives some singular instances from rabbinical writers of the thanksgivings, which commonly formed part of Jewish prayers. One quotation will suffice. 'It is a tradition of Rabbi Juda saying three things a man ought to say every day,—Blessed be thou that thou hast not made me a gentile.—Blessed be thou that thou hast not made me an unlearned man.—Blessed be thou that thou hast not made me a woman.'

It needs hardly be noted, that we are not to infer that thankfulness is wrong in our prayers. It is thankfulness accompanied by self-conceit, and uncharitable comparisons of ourselves with other men, and unaccompanied by confession of unworthiness, and prayer for mercy and grace, which our Lord condemns.

12.—[*I fast twice … give tithes of all … etc.*] Here the Pharisee, let it be noted, exalts his own works of supererogation. He fasted even more than God required. He gave tithes even of things which God did not command to be tithed,—not of his corn and his fruits only, but of all his possessions.

A more miserable and defective righteousness than this Pharisee's, it is hard to conceive. His negative goodness consisted in not being so bad as some! His positive goodness consisted in fasting and paying tithes with excessive scrupulosity! Of heart-holiness, we do not hear a word!

13.—[*Would not lift up.*] The Greek words mean literally, 'was not willing to lift,'—had no mind, or will, or inclination.

[*Be merciful to.*] It is not improbable that the idea of mercy through a propitiation, enters into this prayer. The Greek word rendered, 'be merciful to,' is only found in one other place, and is there applied to our Lord Jesus Christ, as a High Priest, 'making reconciliation' for the sins of the people (*Heb.* 2:17).

[*A sinner.*] The Greek words are here even stronger than our version, if literally translated. They signify '*the* sinner,' that is 'the great sinner.'

14.—[*Justified rather than the other.*] We must not suppose that this means that the Pharisee was a little justified, and the publican very much, and that the difference between them was only one of degree. There are no degrees in justification. The words mean that the Pharisee was not justified at all, or accepted with God, and that the publican went home pardoned, forgiven, and counted righteous before God.

[*Every one ... exalteth ... abased.*] The truth of this great principle admits of illustration at every step of Bible history. Pharaoh, Goliath, Haman, Sennacherib, Nebuchadnezzar, Herod, are all cases in point.

LUKE 18:15-17

15 And they brought unto him also infants, that he would touch them: but when his disciples saw it, they rebuked them.

16 But Jesus called them *unto him*, and said, Suffer little children to come unto me, and forbid them not: for of such is the kingdom of God.

17 Verily I say unto you, Whosoever shall not receive the kingdom of God as a little child shall in no wise enter therein.

L ET us observe, for one thing, in this passage, *how ignorantly people are apt to treat children, in the matter of their souls.* We read that there were some who 'brought infants to Jesus that he would touch them: but when his disciples saw it, they rebuked them.' They thought most probably that it was mere waste of their Master's time, and that infants could derive no benefit from being brought to Christ. They drew from our Lord a solemn rebuke. We read that 'Jesus called them unto him, and said, Suffer little children to come unto me, and forbid them not.'

The ignorance of the disciples does not stand alone. On few subjects, perhaps, shall we find such strange opinions in the churches, as on the subject of the souls of children. Some think that children ought to be baptized, as a matter of course, and that if they die unbaptized they cannot be saved. Others think that children ought not to be baptized, but can give no satisfactory reason why they think so.—Some think that all children are regenerate by virtue of their baptism. Others seem to think that children are incapable of receiving any grace, and that they ought not to be enrolled in the church till they are grown up.—Some think that children are naturally innocent, and would do no wickedness unless they learned it from others. Others think that it is no use to expect them to be converted when young, and that they must be treated as unbelievers till they come to years of discretion.—All these opinions appear to be errors, in one direction or another. All are to be deprecated, for all lead to many painful mistakes.

We shall do well to get hold of some settled scriptural principles about the spiritual condition of children. To do so may save us much perplexity, and preserve us from grave false doctrine.

The souls of young children are evidently precious in God's sight. Both here and elsewhere there is plain proof that Christ cares for them no less than for grown-up people.—The souls of young children are capable of receiving grace. They are born in sin, and without grace cannot be saved. There is nothing, either in the Bible or experience, to make us think that they cannot receive the Holy Ghost, and be justified, even from their earliest infancy.—The baptism of young children seems agreeable to the general tenor of Scripture, and the mind of Christ in the passage before us. If Jewish children were not too young to be circumcised in the Old Testament dispensation, it is exceedingly hard to understand why Christian children should be too young to be baptized under the gospel. Thousands of children, no doubt, receive no benefit from baptism. But the duty of baptizing them remains the same.—The minds of young children are not unequal to receiving religious impressions. The readiness with which their minds receive the doctrines of the gospel, and their consciences respond to them, is matter of fact well known to all who have anything to do with teaching.—Last, but not least, the souls of children are capable of salvation, however young they may die. To suppose that Christ will admit them into his glorified church, and yet maintain that he would not have them in his professing church on earth, is an inconsistency which can never be explained.

These points deserve calm consideration. The subject is unquestionably difficult, and one on which good men disagree. But in every perplexity about it we shall find it good to return again and again to the passage before us. It throws a strong light on the position of children before God. It shows us in general terms the mind of Christ.

Let us observe, for another thing, in this passage, *the strong declaration which our Lord Jesus Christ makes about infants.* He says, 'Of such is the kingdom of God.'

The meaning of these words no doubt is a matter of dispute. That they were not meant to teach that children are born sinless and innocent, is abundantly clear from other parts of Scripture. 'That which is born of the flesh is flesh' (*John* 3:6). A three-fold lesson is probably contained in our Lord's words. To that three-fold lesson we shall do well to take heed.

'Like such as little children,' all saints of God should strive to live. Their simple faith and dependence on others,—their unworldliness and indifference to earthly treasures,—their comparative humility, harmlessness, and freedom from deceit,—are points in which they furnish believers with an excellent example. Happy is he who can draw near to Christ and the Bible in the spirit of a little child!

'Out of such as little children,' the church of God on earth ought to be constantly recruited. We should not be afraid to bring them to baptism even in their earliest infancy, and to dedicate them to Christ from the beginning of their days. Useless and formal as baptism often is, it is an ordinance appointed by Christ himself. Those who use it with prayer and faith may confidently look for a blessing.

'Of such as little children,' the kingdom of God in glory will be largely composed. The salvation of all who die in infancy may confidently be expected. Though sin has abounded, grace has much more abounded (*Rom.* 5:20). The number of those in the world who die before they 'know good from evil' is exceedingly great. It is surely not too much to believe that a very large proportion of the glorified inhabitants of heaven, will be found at length to be little children.

Let us leave the whole passage with a deep sense of the value of children's souls, and with a settled resolution to 'put on the mind of Christ' in all our dealings with them. Let us regard children as a most important part of Christ's professing church, and a part which the great Head of the church does not like to see neglected. Let us train them from their earliest infancy in godly ways, and sow the seed of Scripture truth in their minds, with strong confidence that it will one day bear fruit. Let us believe that they think more, and feel more, and consider more, than at first sight appears; and that the Spirit is often working in them, as really and truly as in old people. Above all, let us often name them before Christ in prayer, and ask him to take them under his special charge. He never changes. He is always the same. He cared for boys and girls when he was upon earth. Let us not doubt that he cares for them at the right hand of God in heaven.

Notes—Luke 18:15-17

15.—[*And they brought, etc.*] The connection between this passage and the parable preceding it should not be overlooked. Our Lord had just been speaking of humility. He now gives a practical illustration of his delight in humility, by his treatment of little children.

[*Infants.*] Let this word be carefully noted. The Greek word admits of only one sense. It is children of the youngest and tenderest age. It is the same word used in Luke 1:41, 44; 2:12, 16; 1 Peter 2:2. It is impossible to interpret the expression as meaning young persons come to years of discretion.

[*Touch them.*] There is reference here in all probability to the Jewish habit of laying hands on a child and blessing it. We have an instance in the case of Jacob blessing Joseph's children (*Gen.* 48:14).

[*They rebuked them.*] Comparing this passage with the parallel one in St Mark, we see that it was the persons who brought the children who were rebuked by the disciples.

16.—[*Jesus called them.*] The word 'them' in this place applies to the infants, and not to their parents and friends. Our Lord specially addressed himself to the children.

[*Of such is the kingdom of God.*] Considering the verse which follows these words, and the parable which precedes it, it seems probable that the principal idea in our Lord's mind was to set before us the beauty of a humble and childlike spirit, and to commend such a spirit to his disciples for imitation. We need not however exclude from this sentence the other and further meanings which I have mentioned in the exposition.

Undoubtedly the expression is not a proof of infant baptism. To establish the right of infants we must look elsewhere,—to the circumcision of children under the law,—to the baptism of whole families in the

Acts,—to the striking absence of any hint in the New Testament, that children were not to be formally admitted into the church by an outward ordinance under the gospel, as they had been under the law,—and not least to the remarkable fact mentioned by Lightfoot, that the children of all proselytes admitted into the Jewish church by baptism before our Lord's time, were always baptized together with their parents.

Nevertheless the passage before us will always remain a strong testimony of our Lord Jesus Christ's care for little children. There is a deep significance in his rebuke of those who would have kept infants from him, which deserves serious consideration.

17.—[*Verily I say unto you, etc.*] The lesson of this verse admits of only one interpretation. It describes the spirit and frame of mind which are absolutely necessary to salvation. Pride, high thoughts, and self-righteousness, must be laid aside. We must be converted and become as little children (*Matt.* 18:3).

LUKE 18:18-27

18 And a certain ruler asked him, saying, Good Master, what shall I do to inherit eternal life?

19 And Jesus said unto him, Why callest thou me good? none *is good*, save one, *that is*, God.

20 Thou knowest the commandments, Do not commit adultery, Do not kill, Do not steal, Do not bear false witness, Honour thy father and thy mother.

21 And he said, All these have I kept from my youth up.

22 Now when Jesus heard these things, he said unto him, Yet lackest thou one thing: sell all that thou hast, and distribute unto the poor, and thou shalt have treasure in heaven: and come, follow me.

23 And when he heard this, he was very sorrowful: for he was very rich.

24 And when Jesus saw that he was very sorrowful, he said, How hardly shall they that have riches enter into the kingdom of God!

25 For it is easier for a camel to go through a needle's eye, than for a rich man to enter into the kingdom of God.

26 And they that heard *it* said, Who then can be saved?

27 And he said, The things which are impossible with men are possible with God.

THE story we have now read is three times reported in the Gospels. Matthew, Mark, and Luke were all moved by the Holy Ghost to record the history of the rich man who came to Christ. This fact should be noticed. It shows us that there are lessons before us which demand special attention. When God would impress on Peter his duty towards the Gentiles, he sent him a vision which was repeated 'three times' (*Acts* 10:16).

We learn, firstly, from these verses, *to what lengths men may go in self-ignorance.* We are told of 'a certain ruler,' who asked our Lord what he should 'do to inherit eternal life.' Our Lord knew the ruler's heart, and gave him the answer which was most likely to bring to light the real state of his soul. He reminds him of the Ten Commandments. He recites some of the principal requirements of the second table of the law. At once the spiritual blindness of the inquirer was detected. 'All these,' said the man, 'I have kept from my youth up.'—An answer more full of darkness and self-ignorance it is impossible to conceive! He who made it could have known nothing rightly, either about himself, or God, or God's law.

Does the case of this rich ruler stand alone? Do we suppose there are none like him at the present day?—If we do, we are greatly deceived. There are thousands, it may be feared, in all our congregations, who have not the least idea of the spiritual nature of God's law, and consequently know nothing of their own sinfulness. They do not see that God requires 'truth in the inward parts,' and that we may break commandments in our heart and thoughts, even when we do not break them in outward actions (*Psa.* 51:6; *Matt.* 5:21-28). To be delivered from such blindness is one of the first things needful to our salvation. The eyes of our understandings must be enlightened by the Holy Ghost (*Eph.* 1:18). We must learn to know ourselves. No man really taught of the Spirit will ever talk of having 'kept all God's commandments from his youth.' He will rather cry with St Paul, 'The law is spiritual: but I am carnal.' 'I know that in me dwelleth no good thing' (*Rom.* 7:14-18).

We learn, secondly, from these verses, *what harm one master-sin may do to a soul.* The desires which the rich ruler expressed were right and good. He wanted 'eternal life.' There seemed at first sight no reason why he should not be taught the way of God, and become a disciple. But there was one thing, unhappily, which he loved better than 'eternal life.' That thing was his *money.* When invited by Christ, to give up all that he had on earth, and seek treasure in heaven, he had not faith to accept the invitation. The love of money was his master-sin.

Shipwrecks like this are sadly common in the church of Christ. Few are the ministers who could not put their finger on many cases like that of the man before us. Many are ready to give up everything for Christ's sake, excepting one darling sin, and for the sake of that sin are lost for evermore. When Herod heard John the Baptist, he 'heard him gladly, and did many things.' But there was one thing he could not do. He could not part with Herodias. That one thing cost Herod his soul (*Mark* 6:20).

There must be no reserve in our hearts, if we would receive anything at Christ's hands. We must be willing to part with anything, however dear it may be, if it stands between us and our salvation. We must be ready to cut off the right hand and pluck out the right eye, to make any sacrifice, and to break any idol. Life, we must remember, eternal life is at stake! One leak neglected, is enough to sink a mighty ship. One besetting sin, obstinately clung to, is enough to shut a soul out of heaven. The love of money, secretly nourished in the heart, is enough to bring a man, in other respects moral and irreproachable, down to the pit of hell.

We learn, thirdly, from these verses, *how great is the difficulty of a rich man being saved.* Our Lord declares this in the solemn comment which he makes on the ruler's case: 'How hardly shall they that have riches enter into the kingdom of God! It is easier for a camel to go through a needle's eye, than for a rich man to enter into the kingdom of God.'

The truth which our Lord lays down in this place, is one which we may see confirmed on every side. Our own eyes will tell us that grace and riches seldom go together. 'Not many mighty, not many noble, are called' (*1 Cor.* 1:26). It is plain matter of fact, that comparatively few rich men are to be found in the way of life. For one thing, riches incline their possessors to pride, self-will, self-indulgence, and love of the world. For another thing, the rich man is seldom dealt with faithfully about his soul. He is generally flattered and fawned upon. 'The rich hath many friends' (*Prov.* 14:20). Few persons have the courage to tell him the whole truth. His good points are grossly exaggerated. His bad points are glossed over, palliated, and excused. The result is, that while his heart is choked up with the things of the world, his eyes are blinded to his own real condition. What right have we to wonder if a rich man's salvation is a hard thing?

Let us beware of envying rich men and coveting their possessions. We little know what we might come to if our desires were granted. Money, which thousands are constantly wanting and longing for,—money, which many make their god,—money keeps myriads of souls out of heaven! 'They that will be rich fall into temptation and a snare.' Happy is he who has learned to pray, 'Give me neither poverty nor riches,' and is really 'content with such things as he has' (*1 Tim.* 6:9; *Prov.* 30:8; *Heb.* 13:5).

We learn, lastly, from these verses, *how mighty is the power of God's grace.* We see this in the words which our Lord addressed to those who heard him speaking of the rich man's danger. They said, 'who then can be saved?' Our Lord's reply is broad and full: 'The things which are impossible with men are possible with God.' By grace a man may serve God and reach heaven in any condition of life.

The Word of God contains many striking instances in illustration of this doctrine. Abraham, and David, and Hezekiah, and Jehoshaphat, and Josiah, and Job, and Daniel, were all great and rich. Yet they all served God and were saved. They all found grace sufficient for them, and overcame the temptations by which they were surrounded. Their Lord and Master still lives, and what he did for them he can do for others. He can give power to rich Christians to follow Christ in spite of their riches, as well as he did to rich Jews.

Let us beware of allowing ourselves to suppose that our own salvation is impossible, because of the hardness of our position. It is too often a suggestion of the devil and our own lazy hearts. We must not give way to it. It matters not where we live, so long as we are not following a sinful calling. It matters not what our income may be, whether we are burdened with riches or pinched with poverty. *Grace*, and not *place*, is the hinge on which our salvation turns. Money will not keep us out of heaven if our hearts are right before God. Christ can make us more than conquerors. Christ can enable us to win our way through every difficulty. 'I can do all things,' said St Paul, 'through Christ which strengtheneth me' (*Phil.* 4:13).

Notes—Luke 18:18-27

18.—[*A certain ruler asked him, etc.*] The connection between the history of the rich ruler and the verses which immediately precede it ought not to be overlooked. Matthew, Mark, and Luke all relate it as following the account of our Lord's sayings about little children. It seems intended to show us how a man may miss heaven for want of a childlike indifference to worldly riches.

The man before us appears to have been one of a far better spirit than the scribes, and Pharisees, and Sadducees. He was anxious about salvation. He had evidently a feeling of respect for our Lord. Yet through love of money, his one besetting sin, he lost his soul.

[*What shall I do to inherit?*] The literal rendering of the Greek words in this place brings out the legality of the ruler's mind more forcibly than our translation. It would be literally translated, 'What, having done, shall I inherit?'

19.—[*Why callest thou me good?*] The paraphrase of Whitby on this verse is worth noticing:—'Why givest thou me a title not ascribed to your reverent rabbins, nor due to any mere man? Thinkest thou there is anything in me more human, or that the Father dwelleth in me? This thou oughtest to believe if thou conceivest the title "good" doth truly belong to me, seeing there is none good but one, that is God.'

20.—[*Thou knowest the commandments.*] Gualter here remarks, that our Lord treats the ruler as a wise physician treats a sick patient. He administers the medicine most likely ultimately to conduce to his spiritual health. He addresses him in the way most likely to bring him to self-knowledge. As the ruler spoke of 'doing,' Jesus begins by speaking of God's commandments.

[*Do not commit adultery, etc.*] Let it be noted that our Lord does not recite the commandments in the exact order in which they are given in Exodus. It is a singular fact that in the Septuagint version of the Old Testament the seventh commandment is put before the sixth.

22.—[*Yet lackest thou one thing.*] The process by which our Lord convinces the ruler of sin should not be overlooked. He shows him that whatever he might think of his obedience to the second table of the law, he was certainly a breaker of the first table. He did not keep either the first commandment or the second. His money was his God, and he was guilty of covetousness, which is idolatry.

[*Sell all ... distribute ... poor.*] We are not to understand that our Lord meant all Christians to do what he here enjoins the rich ruler to do. The language of Peter to Ananias contradicts the idea (*Acts* 5:4). Reason itself shows that if all acted on this system idleness would be encouraged, and all men would ultimately come to poverty. 'If any man will not work,' says St Paul, 'neither shall he eat' (2 *Thess.* 3:10).

Our Lord prescribed according to the disease before him. It was a case of desperate and idolatrous love of money. There was but one remedy,—'Sell all and distribute.' Like St Paul and his companions on board ship, he must cast overboard the lading of the ship if he would save his life.

23.—[*When he heard ... very sorrowful.*] We hear of this ruler no more. Some have conjectured that after all he obeyed our Lord's commands, and became a disciple. It seems far more probable that he could not stand the test which our Lord imposed on him, and lost his soul. St Mark says, 'he went away' (*Mark* 10:22).

24.—[*They that have riches.*] These words should always be compared with the fuller account of this history which St Mark gives. He says that our Lord repeated this saying twice, and on the second occasion said, 'How hard is it for them that *trust in* riches to enter into the kingdom.'

25.—[*It is easier for a camel, etc.*] Some commentators have laboured to prove that the word we translate 'camel' ought to be rendered 'a cable.' The alteration wished for seems needless. The expression used by our Lord was probably proverbial, and familiar to his hearers. The camel was the largest animal which the Jews were accustomed to use, and a 'camel passing through a needle's eye,' according to some rabbinical writings, signified a thing absolutely impossible. Michaelis says, that a similar proverb about

an elephant passing through a needle's eye is in use in India.

Harmer remarks, 'In the East the doors are frequently made extremely low, sometimes not more than three or four feet high, to prevent the plundering Arab from riding into the inner court. Still they train their camels to make their way, though with difficulty, through these doorways. It was probably in allusion to this practice that this proverbial expression was formed.'

27.—[*Things ... impossible, etc.*] This is a general proverbial expression. But the application is clear and plain. The salvation even of a rich man is possible with the grace of God.

LUKE 18:28-34

28 Then Peter said, Lo, we have left all, and followed thee.

29 And he said unto them, Verily I say unto you, There is no man that hath left house, or parents, or brethren, or wife, or children, for the kingdom of God's sake,

30 Who shall not receive manifold more in this present time, and in the world to come life everlasting.

31 Then he took *unto him* the twelve, and said unto them, Behold, we go up to Jerusalem, and all things that are written

by the prophets concerning the Son of man shall be accomplished.

32 For he shall be delivered unto the Gentiles, and shall be mocked, and spitefully entreated, and spitted on:

33 And they shall scourge *him*, and put him to death: and the third day he shall rise again.

34 And they understood none of these things: and this saying was hid from them, neither knew they the things which were spoken.

LET us observe, firstly, in these verses, what *a glorious and satisfying promise our Lord holds out to all believers who make sacrifices for his sake.* He says, 'There is no man that hath left house, or parents, or brethren, or wife, or children, for the kingdom of God's sake, who shall not receive manifold more in this present time, and in the world to come life everlasting.'

The promise before us is a very peculiar one. It does not refer to the believer's reward in another world, and the crown of glory which fadeth not away. It refers distinctly to the life that now is. It is spoken of 'this present time.'

The 'manifold more' of the promise must evidently be taken in a spiritual sense. The meaning is, that the believer shall find in Christ a full equivalent for anything that he is obliged to give up for Christ's sake. He shall find such peace, and hope, and joy, and comfort, and rest, in communion with the Father and the Son, that his losses shall be more than counterbalanced by his gains. In short, the Lord Jesus Christ shall be more to him than property, or relatives, or friends.

The complete fulfilment of this wonderful promise has been often seen in the experience of God's saints. Hundreds could testify in every age of the church, that when they were obliged to give up everything for the kingdom of God's sake, their losses were amply supplied by Christ's grace. They were kept in perfect peace, staying their souls on Jesus (*Isa.* 26:3). They were enabled to glory in tribulation, and to take pleasure in infirmities, in reproaches, in necessities, in distresses for Christ's sake (*Rom.* 5:3; *2 Cor.* 12:10). They were enabled in the darkest hour to rejoice with joy unspeakable and full of glory, and to count it an honour to suffer shame for their Master's name (*1 Pet.* 1:8; *Acts* 5:41). The last day will show that in poverty and in exile,—in prisons and before judgment seats,—in the fire and under the sword,—the words of Christ before us have repeatedly been made good. Friends have often proved faithless. Royal promises have often been broken. Riches have made themselves wings. But Christ's engagements have never been known to fail.

Let us grasp this promise firmly. Let us go forward in the way of life with a firm conviction that it is a promise which is the property of all God's people. Let us not give way to doubts and fears because of difficulties that cross our path. Let us press onward with a strong persuasion, that if we lose anything for Christ's sake, Christ will make it up to us even in this present world. What believers need is more daily practical faith in Christ's words. The well of living water is always near us, as we travel through the wilderness of this world. Yet for want of faith, we often fail to see it, and faint by the way (*Gen.* 21:19).

Let us observe, secondly, in these verses, *the clear and plain prediction which our Lord makes about his own death.* We see him telling the disciples that he would be 'delivered to the Gentiles, mocked, spitefully entreated, spitted on, scourged, and put to death.'

The importance of our Lord's death appears in the frequency with which he foretold it, and referred to it during his life. He knew well that it was the principal end for which he came into the world. He was to give his life a ransom for many. He was to make his soul an offering for sin, and to bear our transgressions in his own body on the tree. He was to give his body and blood for the life of the world. Let us seek to be of the same mind with Christ in our estimate of his death. Let our principal thoughts about Jesus be inseparably bound up with his crucifixion. The cornerstone of all truth concerning Christ is this,—that 'While we were yet sinners, he died for us' (*Rom.* 5:8).

The love of our Lord Jesus Christ towards sinners is strikingly shown in his steady purpose of heart to die for them. All through his life he knew that he was about to be crucified. There was nothing in his cross and passion which he did not foresee distinctly, even to the minutest particular, long before it came upon him. He tasted all the well-known bitterness of anticipated suffering. Yet he never swerved from his path for a moment. He was straitened in spirit till he had finished the work he came to do (*Luke* 12:50). Such love passeth knowledge. It is unspeakable, unsearchable. We may rest on that love without fear. If Christ so loved us before we thought of him, he will surely not cease to love us after we have believed.

The calmness of our Lord Jesus Christ in the prospect of certain death ought to be a pattern to all his people. Like him, let us drink the bitter cup which our Father gives us, without a murmur, and say 'not my will but thine be done.' The man that has faith in the Lord Jesus has no reason to be afraid of the grave. 'The sting of death is sin; and the strength of sin is the law. But thanks be to God, which giveth us the victory through our Lord Jesus Christ' (*1 Cor.* 15:56, 57).

The grave is no longer what it once was. It is the place where the Lord lay. If the great Head of the body looked forward to the grave with calmness, much more may all his believing members. For them he has overcome death. The king of terrors at the worst is a conquered foe.

Let us observe, lastly, in these verses, *the slowness of the disciples to understand Christ's death.* We find that when our Lord described his coming sufferings, the disciples 'understood none of these things: and this saying was hid from them, neither knew they the things which were spoken.'

We read such passages as these, perhaps, with a mixture of pity and surprise. We wonder at the darkness and blindness of these Jews. We marvel that in the face of plain teaching, and in the light of plain types of the Mosaic law, the sufferings of Messiah should have been lost sight of in his glory, and his cross hidden behind his crown.

But are we not forgetting that the vicarious death of Christ has always been a stumbling-block and an offence to proud human nature?—Do we not know that even now, after Christ has risen from the dead and ascended into glory, the doctrine of the cross is still foolishness to many, and that Christ's substitution for us on the cross is a truth which is often denied, rejected, and refused?—Before we wonder at these first weak disciples, for not understanding our Lord's words about his death, we should do well to look around us. It may humble us to remember that thousands of *so-called* Christians neither understand nor value Christ's death at the present day.

Let us look well to our own hearts. We live in a day when false doctrines about Christ's death abound on every side. Let us see that Christ crucified is really the foundation of our own hopes, and that Christ's atoning death for sin is indeed the whole life of our souls. Let us beware of adding to Christ's sacrifice, as the Roman Catholic does. Its value was infinite. It admits of no addition.—Let us beware of taking away from Christ's sacrifice, as the Socinian does. To suppose that the Son of God only died to leave us an example of self-denial, is to contradict a hundred plain texts of Scripture.—Let us walk in the old paths. Let us say with St Paul, 'God forbid that I should glory, save in the cross of our Lord Jesus Christ' (*Gal.* 6:14).

Notes—Luke 18:28-34

28.—[*We have left all.*] The remark has often been made, that Peter and his fellow-disciples had left little or nothing for Christ's sake. A few boats and fishing nets were probably the whole amount of their worldly goods. Yet it must never be forgotten that a poor man's 'all' is as dear to him, in a certain sense, as the rich man's palace. He knows nothing higher or better excepting by report. In giving up everything for Christ's sake, he makes, at any rate, the greatest sacrifice in his power.

29.—[*There is no man that hath left, etc.*] The cases which our Lord here describes are undoubtedly cases which can seldom occur in England. We can hardly conceive a case among ourselves in which religion could oblige a man to separate from his 'wife and children.'

But there can be no doubt that sacrifices like this were often necessary when the gospel was first preached, and was bitterly opposed by prejudiced Jews and ignorant heathen. Moreover, it is a striking fact that at the present day a converted Jew is often obliged to separate from his nearest and dearest relatives, and a converted Hindoo is cast off by all his family.

There can be no doubt that our Lord spoke with foresight of cases like these. In this point of view, his words are singularly full of comfort.

30.—[*Manifold more ... this present time.*] It is the safest course to give a spiritual sense to this glorious promise. A converted man will no doubt often find new friends among converted people, who shall amply make up to him for the loss of his former worldly acquaintances.—But it is not always so. The wisdom of God is sometimes pleased to allow a converted man to be a loser in temporal things by his conversion. Christ himself, and all the inward comforts of heart, conscience, and soul which Christ alone can bestow, and the world can neither give nor take away, must be regarded as the real substance of the promise.

31.—[*All things ... written, etc.*] If we confine this expression to the sufferings and passion of our Lord, the reference must of course be to Psalm 22; Isaiah 53; and Daniel 9:26. But it admits of question whether our Lord did not refer to all that was to happen at Jerusalem from the time when he rode into the city upon an ass until his resurrection. The passages referred to would then be more numerous. In any case, let it be noted, the book of Psalms is classed among 'the prophets.' There is far more of prophetical matter in the Psalms than most readers suppose.

32, 33.—[*He shall be delivered, etc.*] The following passage from Doddridge is worth reading: 'This prediction is a strong instance of the spirit of prophecy exerted by our Lord. It was more probable that he would be privately slain, or stoned to death in a tumult. And when he was delivered back to the Jews by Pilate, with permission to judge him according to their law, it is wonderful that he was not stoned. But all was done that the Scriptures might be fulfilled.'

34.—[*They understood none, etc.*] The blindness of the disciples about our Lord's crucifixion and sufferings is, at first sight, very extraordinary. But we must remember that they were all Jews, and trained from their infancy to expect a Messiah in glory and majesty, but not in suffering and humiliation. The influence of early training, and incessant indoctrinating with one set of ideas, is exceedingly great.

Pellican has a clever and ingenious note on this passage, in which he shows how the disciples would probably interpret our Lord's predictions of his own sufferings, and explain away a sense which was offensive and painful to their own feelings.

He thinks that they would call to mind the many figurative and parabolical expressions which our Lord used in his teaching, such as 'eating his flesh and blood,'—'taking heed of the leaven of the Pharisees,'—and would persuade themselves that his strong language about his own death might yet receive some figurative fulfilment without their Master really dying.

After all, we have no right to wonder at the disciples being slow to understand the first advent of Christ in humiliation, when we see how many Christians refuse to acknowledge the second advent in glory, although the texts about Messiah's glory are far more numerous than those about his sufferings. Above all, we have no right to wonder when we see how many, even, now, are utterly in the dark about the true purpose of Christ's death upon the cross.

LUKE 18:35-43

35 And it came to pass, that as he was come nigh unto Jericho, a certain blind man sat by the way side begging:

36 And hearing the multitude pass by, he asked what it meant.

37 And they told him, that Jesus of Nazareth passeth by.

38 And he cried, saying, Jesus, *thou* Son of David, have mercy on me.

39 And they which went before rebuked him, that he should hold his peace: but he cried so much the more, *Thou* Son of David, have mercy on me.

40 And Jesus stood, and commanded him to be brought unto him: and when he was come near, he asked him,

41 Saying, What wilt thou that I shall do unto thee? And he said, Lord, that I may receive my sight.

42 And Jesus said unto him, Receive thy sight: thy faith hath saved thee.

43 And immediately he received his sight, and followed him, glorifying God: and all the people, when they saw *it*, gave praise unto God.

THE miracle described in these verses is rich in instruction. It was one of the great works which witnessed that Christ was sent of the Father (*John* 5:36). But this is not all. It contains also some lively patterns of spiritual things which deserve attentive study.

We see, for one thing, in this passage, *the importance of diligence in the use of means.* We are told of 'a certain blind man who sat by the wayside begging.' He sought the place where his pitiful condition was most likely to attract notice. He did not sit lazily at home, and wait for relief to come to him. He placed himself by the roadside, in order that travellers might see him and give him help. The story before us shows the wisdom of his conduct. Sitting by the wayside, he heard that 'Jesus was passing by.' Hearing of Jesus he cried for mercy, and was restored to sight. Let us mark this well! If the blind man had not sat by the wayside that day, he might have remained blind to the hour of his death.

He that desires salvation should remember the example of this blind man. He must attend diligently on every means of grace. He must be found regularly in those places where the Lord Jesus is specially present. He must sit by the wayside, wherever the Word is read and the gospel preached, and God's people assemble together. To expect grace to be put into our hearts, if we sit idling at home on Sundays, and go to no place of worship, is presumption and not faith. It is true that 'God will have mercy on whom he will have mercy;'—but it is no less true that he ordinarily has mercy on those who use means. It is true that Christ is sometimes 'found of those who seek him not;'—but it is also true that he is always found of those who really seek him. The sabbath-breaker, the Bible-neglecter, and the prayerless man are forsaking their own mercies and digging graves for their own souls. They are not sitting 'by the wayside.'

We see, for another thing, in this passage, *an example of our duty in the matter of prayer.* We are told that when this blind man heard that Jesus of Nazareth was passing by, he 'cried, saying, Jesus, thou Son of David, have mercy on me.' We are told further, that when some rebuked him, and bade him hold his peace, he would not be silenced. He only 'cried so much the more.' He felt his need, and found words to tell his story. He was not to be stopped by the rebukes of people who knew nothing of the misery of blindness. His sense of wretchedness made him go on crying. And his importunity was amply rewarded. He found what he sought. That very day he received sight.

What the blind man did on behalf of his bodily ailment, it is surely our bounden duty to do on behalf of our souls. Our need is far greater than his. The disease of sin is far more grievous than the want of sight. The tongue that can find words to describe the necessities of the body, can surely find words to explain the wants of the soul. Let us begin praying if we never prayed yet. Let us pray more heartily and earnestly, if we have prayed in time past. Jesus, the Son of David, is still passing by, and not far from every one of us. Let us cry to him for mercy and allow nothing to stop our crying. Let us not go down to the pit speechless and dumb, without so much as a cry for help. None will be so excuseless at the last day as baptized men and women who never tried to pray.

We see, for another thing, in this passage, *an encouraging instance of Christ's kindness and compassion.* We are told that when the blind man continued crying for mercy, our Lord 'stood, and commanded him to be brought unto him.' He was going up to Jerusalem to die, and had weighty matters on his mind, but he found time to stop to speak kindly to this poor sufferer. He asked him what he would have done to him? 'Lord,' was the eager reply, 'that I may receive my sight.' At once we are told, 'Jesus said unto him, Receive thy sight: thy faith hath saved thee.' That faith perhaps was weak, and mixed with much imperfection. But it had made the man cry to Jesus, and go on crying in spite of rebukes. So coming with faith, our blessed Lord did not cast him out. The desire of his heart was granted, and 'immediately he received sight.'

Passages like these in the Gospels are intended for the special comfort of all who feel their sins and come to Christ for peace. Such persons may be sensible of much infirmity in all their approaches to the Son of God. Their faith may be very feeble,—their sins many and great,—their prayers very poor and stammering,—their motives far short of perfection. But after all, do they really come to Christ with their sins? Are they really willing to forsake all other confidence, and commit their souls to Christ's hands? If this be so, they may hope and not be afraid. That same Jesus still lives who heard the blind man's cry, and granted his request. He will never go back from his own words,—'Him that cometh to me I will in no wise cast out' (*John* 6:37).

We see, lastly, in this passage, *a striking example of the conduct which becomes one who has received mercy from Christ*. We are told that when the blind man was restored to sight, 'he followed Jesus, glorifying God.' He felt deeply grateful. He resolved to show his gratitude by becoming one of our Lord's followers and disciples. Pharisees might cavil at our Lord. Sadducees might sneer at his teaching. It mattered nothing to this new disciple. He had the witness in himself that Christ was a Master worth following. He could say 'I was blind, and now I see' (*John* 9:25).

Grateful love is the true spring of real obedience to Christ. Men will never take up the cross and confess Jesus before the world, and live to him, until they feel that they are indebted to him for pardon, peace, and hope. The ungodly are what they are, because they have no sense of sin, and no consciousness of being under any special obligation to Christ. The godly are what they are, because they love him who first loved them, and washed them from sin in his own blood. Christ has healed them, and therefore they follow Christ.

Let us leave the passage with solemn self-inquiry. If we would know whether we have any part or lot in Christ, let us look at our lives. Whom do we follow? What are the great ends and objects for which we live? The man who has a real hope in Jesus, may always be known by the general bias of his life.

Notes—Luke 18:35-43

35.—[*As he was come nigh, etc.*] The miracle described in this passage is recorded by all the three first Gospel writers, but with some variations. Matthew speaks of two blind men. Mark and Luke speak of only one. Matthew and Mark say that the miracle was wrought when our Lord was 'departing' from Jericho. Luke says that it happened, 'as he was come nigh.'

With regard to the variation in the reports of the number of blind men, there is little difficulty. There were doubtless two blind persons healed. Mark and Luke, however, only report one case, which was probably that of the man best known at Jericho. Mark tells us that his name was Bartimæus.—Precisely the same variation may be observed in the accounts given by the three Gospel writers of the casting out of the devils in the country of the Gadarenes. Matthew says that two men were cured. Mark and Luke say that there was one. That one was evidently the most remarkable case, because he was the one who asked to be allowed to follow our Lord.—The same remark applies to both miracles. Two persons were healed, as Matthew says. One case only was reported by Mark and Luke, because it was for some reason the more noticeable of the two. In either miracle, to suppose that only one person was healed, because Mark and Luke were inspired to single out and report only one cure, is surely unreasonable and unfair. There was another cure, but for some wise reason, Mark and Luke did not report it.

The other variation is undoubtedly more difficult of explanation. Why Matthew and Mark should say that the miracle before us was wrought when our Lord was 'going out of' Jericho, and Luke, that it was wrought as he 'came near' to Jericho, is a hard knot to untie. At any rate the reconciliation of the apparent discrepancy between the two accounts, has occasioned much difference of opinion among commentators.

1. Some think that there were two cases of blind men cured, and that they were cured at two different times,—one as our Lord entered into Jericho, the other as our Lord departed from Jericho,—and that Luke reported one case, and Matthew and Mark another. This is the opinion of Augustine, Chemnitius, Barradius, Stella, Lightfoot, Gill, and Greswell.—Euthymius goes so far as to think that there were four altogether healed, and that the two in Matthew, the one in Mark, and the one in Luke, were four distinct cases!

2. Some think that the words of St Luke, 'as he was come nigh,' only mean, 'as he was in the neighbourhood of Jericho,' and that they do not necessarily mean, 'as he was approaching or coming to.' This is the opinion of Grotius, Doddridge, and Scott.

3. Some think that the blind man began crying to our Lord as he was approaching Jericho, but was not healed until our Lord was leaving Jericho, and was accompanied by the second blind man at the time of his healing, though he was alone when he first cried. This is the opinion of Poole, Paræus, Bengel, Jansenius, Maldonatus, and Wordsworth.

4. Macknight thinks that Jericho consisted of two quarters, an old and a new town, situated at a little distance one from the other, and that the blind men were sitting on the road between the two towns. Our Lord might then be truly reported as 'going out' of one town, and 'coming nigh' to another.

5. Markland thinks that 'as he came nigh,' means, 'as he came nigh to Jerusalem,' and St Luke only means that Jesus on his journey to Jerusalem was somewhere *near* or *about* Jericho, without determining whether he was leaving or entering.

I must frankly confess that none of the above explanations is altogether and completely satisfactory. The third appears to me by far the most probable. The other four seem to be either contradictory to grammar, or to common sense.—I have no doubt whatever that the apparent discrepancy admits of thorough explanation, and is no fair argument against the plenary inspiration of Scripture. Some difficulties of this nature we might reasonably expect to find in such a book as the Bible. If we learn nothing else from them, they may teach us humility.

Everyone must allow that it is perfectly possible for two independent reporters of an event to differ slightly in their account of its details, without the slightest intention to deceive, and without any departure from truth. Occasional differences on slight points of detail are strong evidences that the Gospel writers are independent witnesses, and that in writing the Gospels they did not copy one another, but were independently guided by the Holy Ghost.

36.—[*What it meant.*] This would be rendered more literally, 'What this thing might be.'

38.—[*Thou Son of David.*] This expression is remarkable, because the preceding verse informs us distinctly that the blind man was told that 'Jesus of Nazareth' was passing by. To call our Lord the 'Son of David' was a sign of faith, and showed that the blind man had some idea that Jesus was the Messiah. When the Pharisees were asked whose son Christ would be, they replied at once, 'The Son of David.' Matthew 22:42. The fame of our Lord as a mighty worker of miracles, had probably reached the blind man's ears, and made him believe that he who could do such great miracles, must be one sent from God.

41.—[*Receive my sight.*] Both here, and in the two following verses, the Greek word so rendered means literally, 'look up,' or 'see again.'

42.—[*Thy faith.*] This expression seems to indicate very plainly, that the blind man did not call our Lord, 'Son of David,' as a mere appellation of dignity, and that he had some vague but real belief that our Lord was the Messiah.

LUKE 19:1-10

1 And *Jesus* entered and passed through Jericho.

2 And, behold, *there was* a man named Zacchæus, which was the chief among the publicans, and he was rich.

3 And he sought to see Jesus who he was; and could not for the press, because he was little of stature.

4 And he ran before, and climbed up into a sycamore tree to see him: for he was to pass that *way*.

5 And when Jesus came to the place, he looked up, and saw him, and said unto him, Zacchæus, make haste, and come down; for to day I must abide at thy house.

6 And he made haste, and came down, and received him joyfully.

7 And when they saw *it*, they all murmured, saying, That he was gone to be guest with a man that is a sinner.

8 And Zacchæus stood, and said unto the Lord; Behold, Lord, the half of my goods I give to the poor; and if I have taken any thing from any man by false accusation, I restore *him* fourfold.

9 And Jesus said unto him, This day is salvation come to this house, forsomuch as he also is a son of Abraham.

10 For the Son of man is come to seek and to save that which was lost.

THESE verses describe the conversion of a soul. Like the stories of Nicodemus, and the Samaritan woman, the story of Zacchæus should be frequently studied by Christians. The Lord Jesus never changes. What he did for the man before us, he is able and willing to do for any one of ourselves.

We learn, firstly, from these verses, that *no one is too bad to be saved, or beyond the power of Christ's grace.* We are told of a wealthy publican becoming a disciple of Christ. A more unlikely event we cannot well imagine! We see the 'camel passing through the eye of a needle,' and the 'rich man entering the kingdom of God.' We behold a plain proof that 'all things are possible with God.' We see a covetous tax-gatherer transformed into a liberal Christian!

The door of hope which the gospel reveals to sinners is very wide open. Let us leave it open as we find it. Let us not attempt, in narrow-minded ignorance, to shut it. We should never be afraid to maintain that Christ is 'able to save to the uttermost,' and that the vilest of sinners may be freely forgiven if they will only come to him. We should offer the gospel boldly to the worst and wickedest, and say, 'There is hope. Only repent and believe. Though your sins be as scarlet they shall be as white as snow; though they be red like crimson they shall be as wool' (*Isa.* 1:18). Such doctrine may seem to worldly people foolishness and licentiousness. But such doctrine is the gospel of him who saved Zacchæus at Jericho. Hospitals discharge many cases as incurable. But there are no incurable cases under the gospel. Any sinner may be healed, if he will only come to Christ.

We learn, secondly, from these verses, *how little and insignificant are the things on which a soul's salvation often turns.* We are told that Zacchæus 'sought to see Jesus who he was; and could not, because he was little of stature.' Curiosity, and nothing but curiosity, appears to have been the motive of his mind. That curiosity once roused, Zacchæus was determined to gratify it. Rather than not see Jesus he ran on before along the road, and 'climbed up into a tree.' Upon that little action, so far as man's eyes can see, there hinged the salvation of his soul. Our Lord stopped under the tree, and said, 'Come down, I must abide at thy house.' From that very moment Zacchæus was an altered man. That very night he lay down a Christian.

We must never 'despise the day of small things' (*Zech.* 4:10). We must never reckon anything little that concerns the soul. The ways by which the Holy Ghost leads men and women to Christ are wonderful and mysterious. He is often beginning in a heart a work which shall stand to eternity, when a looker-on observes nothing remarkable. In every work there must be a beginning, and in spiritual work that beginning is often very small. Do we see a careless brother beginning to use means of grace, which in time past he neglected? Do we see him coming to church and listening to the gospel after a long course of sabbath-breaking? When we see such things let us remember Zacchæus and be hopeful. Let us not look coldly on him because his motives are at present very poor and questionable. Let us believe that it is far better to hear the gospel out of mere curiosity, than not to hear it at all. Our brother is with Zacchæus in the tree! For anything we know he may go further. Who can tell but that he may one day receive Christ joyfully?

We learn, thirdly, from these verses, *Christ's free compassion towards sinners, and Christ's power to change hearts.* A more striking instance than that before us it is impossible to conceive. Unasked, our Lord stops and speaks to Zacchæus. Unasked, he offers himself to be a guest in the house of a sinner. Unasked, he sends into the heart of a publican the renewing grace of the Spirit, and puts him that very day among the children of God (*Jer.* 3:19).

It is impossible, with such a passage as this before us, to exalt too highly the grace of our Lord Jesus Christ. We cannot maintain too strongly that there is in him an infinite readiness to receive, and an infinite ability to save sinners. Above all, we cannot hold too firmly that salvation is not of works, but of grace. If ever there was a soul sought and saved, without having done anything to deserve it, that soul was the soul of Zacchæus. Let us grasp these doctrines firmly and never let them go. Their price is above rubies. Grace, free grace, is the only thought which gives men rest in a dying hour.—Let us proclaim these doctrines confidently to everyone to whom we speak about spiritual things. Let us bid them come to Jesus Christ, just as they are, and not wait in the vain hope that they can make themselves fit and worthy to come. Not least, let us tell them that Jesus Christ waits for them, and would come and dwell in their poor sinful hearts, if they would only receive him. 'Behold,' he says, 'I stand at the door and knock: if any man hear my voice, and open the door, I will come in to him and will sup with him, and he with me' (*Rev.* 3:20).

We learn, lastly, from these verses, that *converted sinners will always give evidence of their conversion.* We are told that Zacchæus 'stood, and said unto the Lord, the half of my goods I give to the poor; and if I have taken anything from any man by false accusation, I restore him fourfold.' There was *reality* in that speech. There was unmistakable proof that Zacchæus was a new creature. When a wealthy Christian begins to distribute his riches, and an extortioner begins to make restitution, we may well believe that old things have passed away, and all things become new (2 Cor. 5:17).—There was *decision* in that speech. 'I give,' says Zacchæus,—'I restore.' He does not speak of future intentions. He does not say, 'I will,' but 'I do.' Freely pardoned, and raised from death to life, Zacchæus felt that he could not begin too soon to show whose he was and whom he served.

He that desires to give proof that he is a believer should walk in the steps of Zacchæus. Like him, let him thoroughly renounce the sins which have formerly most easily beset him. Like him, let him follow the Christian graces which he has formerly most habitually neglected. In any case a believer should so live that all may know that he is a believer. Faith that does not purify the heart and life, is not faith at all. Grace that cannot be seen, like light, and tasted, like salt, is not grace, but hypocrisy. The man who professes to know Christ and trust him, while he cleaves to sin and the world, is going down to hell with a lie in his right hand. The heart that has really tasted the grace of Christ, will instinctively hate sin.

Let us turn from the whole passage with the last verse ringing in our ears,—'The Son of man is come to seek and to save that which was lost.' It is as a Saviour, more than as a Judge, that Christ desires to be known. Let us see that we know him as such. Let us take heed that our souls are saved. Once saved and converted, we shall say, 'What shall I render to the Lord for all his benefits?' (*Psa.* 116:12). Once saved, we shall not complain that self-denial, like that of Zacchæus, is a grievous requirement.

Notes—Luke 19:1-10

1.—[*Entered and passed through.*] It is probable that our version does not exactly give the sense of the Greek here. It would be more literally rendered, 'was passing through.'

2.—[*And, behold.*] It is worthy of remark that this expression is frequently found in the New Testament, when something wonderful is about to be narrated. Thus it indicates that the conversion of Zacchæus was a peculiarly marvellous thing.

The connection between the story of Zacchæus and the preceding chapter, ought not to be overlooked. The difficulty of a rich man's salvation had been strongly set forth there. The Holy Ghost now proceeds to show us, by the example of Zacchæus, that nothing is impossible with God.

Whether Zacchæus was by birth a Jew or a Gentile, is a point upon which commentators are not agreed. Cyprian, Tertullian, Chrysostom, Ambrose, Bede, and Maldonatus, think that he was a Gentile.—The more common and probable opinion is that he was a Jew. The publicans were generally Jews. Moreover his name seems a Hebrew name. Doddridge thinks it was Zaccai.

3.—[*He sought to see Jesus.*] Pellican considers that Zacchæus was under the influence of grace already, and compares him to old Simeon in the temple, rejoicing in the sight of the infant Jesus! This seems to me a very improbable opinion. I hold with Poole, Burkitt, and Scott, that Zacchæus only sought to see Jesus out of mere curiosity, although no doubt his curiosity was overruled by God to his conversion.

4.—[*Climbed up into a sycamore tree.*] The ridicule that such an action would entail on Zacchæus ought to be remembered. A wealthy publican climbing up into a tree, after running along a road, in order to see a religious teacher, would doubtless call forth mockery from all who saw him! Yet the circumstance, trifling as it seems, throws light on the character of Zacchæus. He was one who cared not for man's opinion. If he took up a thing he went through with it. If he wanted to see Christ, he would not be prevented by difficulties.

5.—[*Today I must abide at thy house.*] Let it be noted, that this is the only case in the Gospels, in which we find our Lord offering himself uninvited to be a man's guest. In this point of view the expression is a very precious one. Christ sometimes comes to those who seek him not (*Isa.* 65:1).

Our Lord's perfect knowledge is clearly shown in this case. He knew not only the name of the man in the sycamore tree, but the state of his heart (see *John* 1:48).

6.—[*Came down and received him.*] It is precisely at this point that the conversion of Zacchæus seems to have taken place.

The unexpected condescension of such a famous teacher of religion in offering to be a publican's guest, was made the means by which the Spirit changed his heart. Nothing is so frequently found to turn the hearts of great sinners, as the unexpected and undeserved tidings, that Christ loves them and cares for their souls. These tidings have often broken and melted hearts of stone.

7.—[*All murmured.*] The 'all' here mentioned must doubtless be the Pharisees, and the Pharisaical portion of the crowd which followed our Lord. It cannot of course mean his disciples.

[*Murmured.*] The Greek word used here is only found in one other place (*Luke* 15:2). It is there used in precisely the same connection to describe the feeling shown by self-righteous Pharisees, on seeing sinners received by Christ.

[*A man that is a sinner.*] This expression goes far to indicate that Zacchæus was not a Gentile but a Jew. If he had been a Gentile, that circumstance would surely have been cast in our Lord's teeth, as well as the fact that he was 'a sinner.'

8.—[*And Zacchæus stood.*] Some have thought that our Lord tarried a day or two at the house of Zacchæus, and that the speech here recorded was made at the end of his stay. There seems, however, no sufficient reason for supposing that this idea is correct. It is far more probable that our Lord accepted the hospitality of Zacchæus for a meal, and then passed on his journey.

[*My goods.*] We must, in reason, assume that Zacchæus first made restitution to those he had robbed, and *afterwards* gave half of what was justly and honestly his own to the poor. Otherwise he would have given away what was not his.

[*I give to the poor.*] The contrast between the readiness of Zacchæus to distribute to the poor, and the unwillingness of the rich ruler described in the last chapter, ought not to be overlooked. Our Lord had required of the ruler nothing but what grace can enable man to do.

The use of the present tense in the speech of Zacchæus ought to be noted. He says, 'I give,' and 'I restore.' There was no deferring and putting off in his conduct.

Ford on this verse quotes a fine passage from Basil, exposing the meanness of those who are only liberal to the poor in their wills, and give away their money in charity when they can no longer keep or enjoy it. Zacchæus gave away during his own lifetime.

[*Taken by false accusation.*] The word so translated is very peculiar. It is only found in one other place in the New Testament (*Luke* 3:14). It is there applied to the soldiers, and is rendered 'accuse falsely.'

The Greek word from which it is formed is the origin of our English word 'sycophant.' It is said to have been originally applied at Athens, to persons who informed against those who illegally exported figs. Afterwards the word seems to have been applied to everyone who wronged another by false, or frivolous, or vexatious information, and finally, to any extortion under pretence of law.

[*I restore fourfold.*] This expression deserves notice. It shows how thorough and complete was Zacchæus' repentance for his past life. It was restitution far exceeding what the law of Moses required.

Burgon remarks, 'Zacchæus imposed upon himself the severest measure enjoined by the law concerning anyone convicted of theft. It is written, "he shall restore four sheep for a sheep" (*Exod.* 22:1); but even this was exacted only of him who had made away with the property he had stolen. "If the theft be found in his hand alive, he was only to restore double" (*Exod.* 22:4). But with respect to him who confessed his crime it is only said, "he shall recompense his trespass with the principal thereof, and add unto it the fifth part thereof, and give it unto him against whom he hath trespassed" (*Num.* 5:7). Zacchæus therefore judged himself most severely.'—Let us do likewise, when we repent.

9.—[*Salvation come to this house.*] Some commentators maintain from this expression that Zacchæus' family were all converted together with himself. Such an interpretation appears needless and groundless. The simplest idea is, that salvation comes to a 'house' when the head and master of it is saved.

[*He is a son of Abraham.*] This expression was probably used with a reference to the sneers of Pharisees against publicans and sinners, as being unworthy of eternal life. Our Lord declares that however much the self-righteous Pharisees might despise Zacchæus, he was a genuine son of Abraham, if anyone was. He was one by natural descent. But better than that, he was a son of Abraham in a way the Pharisees were not. He walked in the steps of Abraham's faith and works, which they did not do. He was one in heart with Abraham as well as in blood.

10.—[*The Son of man is come, etc.*] This sentence seems to be a general reply to the uncharitable remarks of those who had wondered at Jesus, for going to be 'guest with a man that was a sinner.'

Our Lord declares that such persons had only displayed their ignorance of the great purpose for which he came into the world. He had come into the world to save sinners. He was not ashamed to visit such people as Zacchæus, and to receive them into the number of his disciples. In short, he had come 'to seek and save that which was lost.'

There is a close resemblance between our Lord's argument in this place, and that which we find him using in the fifteenth chapter of St Luke, where the scribes and Pharisees accused him of 'receiving sinners, and eating with them.'

LUKE 19:11-27

11 And as they heard these things, he added and spake a parable, because he was nigh to Jerusalem, and because they thought that the kingdom of God should immediately appear.

12 He said therefore, A certain nobleman went into a far country to receive for himself a kingdom, and to return.

13 And he called his ten servants, and delivered them ten pounds, and said unto them, Occupy till I come.

14 But his citizens hated him, and sent a message after him, saying, We will not have this *man* to reign over us.

15 And it came to pass, that when he was returned, having received the kingdom, then he commanded these servants to be called unto him, to whom he had given the money, that he might know how much every man had gained by trading.

16 Then came the first, saying, Lord, thy pound hath gained ten pounds.

17 And he said unto him, Well, thou good servant: because thou hast been faithful in a very little, have thou authority over ten cities.

18 And the second came, saying, Lord, thy pound hath gained five pounds.

19 And he said likewise to him, Be thou also over five cities.

20 And another came, saying, Lord behold, *here is* thy pound, which I have kept laid up in a napkin:

21 For I feared thee, because thou art an austere man: thou takest up that thou layedst not down, and reapest that thou didst not sow.

22 And he saith unto him, Out of thine own mouth will I judge thee, *thou* wicked servant. Thou knewest that I was an austere man, taking up that I laid not down, and reaping that I did not sow:

23 Wherefore then gavest not thou my money into the bank, that at my coming I might have required mine own with usury?

24 And he said unto them that stood by, Take from him the pound, and give *it* to him that hath ten pounds.

25 (And they said unto him, Lord, he hath ten pounds.)

26 For I say unto you, That unto every one which hath shall be given; and from him that hath not, even that he hath shall be taken away from him.

27 But those mine enemies, which would not that I should reign over them, bring hither, and slay *them* before me.

THE occasion of our Lord speaking the parable before us, is clear and plain. It was intended to correct the false expectations of the disciples on the subject of Christ's kingdom. It was a prophetical sketch of things present and things to come, which ought to raise solemn thoughts in the minds of all professing Christians.

We see, for one thing, in this parable, *the present position of our Lord Jesus Christ*. He is compared to 'a certain nobleman, who went into a far country, to receive for himself a kingdom, and to return.'

When the Lord Jesus left the world, he ascended up into heaven as a conqueror, leading captivity captive. He is there sitting at the right hand of God, doing the work of a High Priest for his believing people, and ever making intercession for them. But he will not sit there always. He will come forth from the holy of holies to bless his people. He will come again with power and glory to put down every enemy under his feet, and to set up his universal kingdom on earth. At present 'we see not all things put under him.' The devil is the 'prince of this world' (*Heb.* 2:8; *John* 14:30). But the present state of things shall be changed one day. When Christ returns, the kingdoms of the world shall become his.

Let these things sink down into our minds. In all our thoughts about Christ, let us never forget his second advent. It is well to know that he lived for us, and died for us, and rose again for us, and intercedes for us. But it is also well to know that he is soon coming again.

We see, for another thing, in this parable, *the present position of all professing Christians.* Our Lord compares them to servants who have been left in charge of money by an absent master, with strict directions to use that money well. They are to 'occupy till he comes.'

The countless privileges which Christians enjoy, compared to the heathen, are 'pounds' given to them by Christ, for which they must one day give account. We shall not stand side by side in the judgment day with the African and Chinese, who never heard of the Bible, the Trinity, and the crucifixion. The most of us, it may be feared, have little idea of the extent of our responsibility. To whomsoever much is given, of them much will be required.

Are we 'occupying?' Are we living like men who know to whom they are indebted, and to whom they must one day give account? This is the only life which is worthy of a reasonable being. The best answer we can give to those who invite us to plunge into worldliness and frivolity, is the Master's commandment which is before us. Let us tell them that we cannot consent, because we look for the coming of the Lord. We would fain be found 'occupying' when he comes.

We see, for another thing, in this parable, *the certain reckoning which awaits all professing Christians.* We are told that when the Master returned, he 'commanded his servants to be called, that he might know how much every man had gained.'

There is a day coming when the Lord Jesus Christ shall judge his people, and give to everyone according to his works. The course of this world shall not always go on as it does now. Disorder, confusion, false profession, and unpunished sin, shall not always cover the face of the earth. The great white throne shall be set up. The Judge of all shall sit upon it. The dead shall be raised from their graves. The living shall all be summoned to the bar. The books shall be opened. High and low, rich and poor, gentle and simple, all shall at length give account to God, and all shall receive an eternal sentence.

Let the thought of this judgment exercise an influence on our hearts and lives. Let us wait patiently when we see wickedness triumphing in the earth. The time is short. There is One who sees and notes down all that the ungodly are doing. 'There be higher than they' (*Eccles.* 5:8). Above all, let us live under an abiding sense, that we shall stand one day at the judgment seat of Christ. Let us 'judge ourselves,' that we be not condemned of the Lord. It is a weighty saying of St James, 'So speak ye, and so do, as they that shall be judged by the law of liberty' (*1 Cor.* 11:31; *James* 2:12).

We see, for another, thing, in this parable, *the certain reward of all true Christians.* Our Lord tells us that those who are found to have been faithful servants shall receive honour and dignity. Each shall receive a reward proportioned to his diligence. One shall be placed 'over ten cities,' and another 'over five.'

The people of God receive little apparent recompense in this present time. Their names are often cast out as evil. They enter the kingdom of God through much tribulation. Their good things are not in this world. The gain of godliness does not consist in earthly rewards, but in inward peace, and hope, and joy in believing. But they shall have an abundant recompense one day. They shall receive wages far exceeding anything they have done for Christ. They shall find, to their amazement, that for everything they have done and borne for their Master, their Master will pay them a hundred-fold.

Let us often look forward to the good things which are yet to come. The 'sufferings of this present time are not worthy to be compared' with the glory which shall be revealed' (*Rom.* 8:18). Let the thought of that glory cheer us in every time of need, and sustain us in every dark hour. Many, no doubt, are 'the afflictions of the righteous.' One great receipt for bearing them patiently is to 'have respect, like Moses, to the recompense of the reward' (*Psa.* 34:19; *Heb.* 11:26).

We see, lastly, in this parable, *the certain exposure of all unfaithful Christians at the last day.* We are told of one servant who had done nothing with his lord's money, but had 'laid it up in a napkin.'—We are told of his useless arguments in his own defence, and of his final ruin, for not using the knowledge which he confessedly possessed. There can be no mistake as to the persons he represents.—He represents the whole company of the ungodly; and his ruin represents their miserable end in the judgment day.

Let us never forget the end to which all ungodly people are coming. Sooner or later, the unbeliever and the impenitent will be put to shame before the whole world, stripped of the means of grace and hope of glory, and cast down to hell. There will be no escape at the last day. False profession and formality will fail to abide the fire of God's judgment. Grace, and grace only, shall stand. Men will discover at last, that there is such a thing as 'the wrath of the Lamb.' The excuses with which so many content their consciences now, shall prove unavailing at the bar of Christ. The most ignorant shall find that they had knowledge enough to be their condemnation. The possessors of buried talents and misused privileges will discover at last that it would have been good for them never to have been born.

These are solemn things. Who shall stand in the great day when the Master requires an account of 'his pounds?' The words of St Peter will form a fitting conclusion to the whole parable, 'Seeing that ye look for such things, be diligent that ye may be found of him in peace, without spot, and blameless' (2 *Pet.* 3:14).

Notes—Luke 19:11-27

11.—[*As they heard these things.*] Our Lord's hearers had just heard him speaking of himself as one who had come into the world for a great end, to seek and save that which was lost. Their minds were probably full of the idea that he was come to restore the kingdom to Israel, and save the Jews from the power of Rome. He proceeds to check their error.

[*Spake a parable.*] There is great resemblance between this parable and that of the talents in Matthew. Yet they are not the same. They were evidently spoken at different times, and differ in one important respect, namely, the sums given to the servants. In Matthew the servants receive different sums. In Luke all receive the same.

[*Nigh ... Jerusalem ... kingdom ... appear.*] The disciples evidently expected that our Lord was about to be proclaimed king, as soon as he arrived at Jerusalem, and to wind up his miracles by reigning on earth.

Our Lord undeceives them by showing in the parable of the pounds, the true nature of the position he was about to take up, and of the position which his disciples would soon have to fill. As for himself, he was going away from them, to receive a kingdom, and would not return for a long time. As for them, they would be left behind in charge of great privileges, and upon their faithfulness in the use of them their place in the final glorious kingdom would depend. There would be a kingdom one day in which he would be a King upon earth. But there was much to be done and borne by his people before that time came. He would have them think of their present duty rather than waste time in looking for a kingdom which was yet far distant.

12.—[*A certain nobleman.*] This clearly represents Jesus Christ himself.

[*Went into a far country.*] Augustine thinks this means that Christ left the Jews and went to the Gentiles. I prefer the opinion of Theophylact and Euthymius, that it means Christ's ascension into heaven.

[*To receive a kingdom.*] Most commentators agree in thinking that this part of the parable refers to a well-known custom in Eastern countries, in the time when our Lord was upon earth. The princes and kings of petty territories under the protection and supremacy of Rome, made journeys to Rome, in order to be invested with kingly authority at the hands of the Roman emperor. Josephus, for example, mentions that Archelaus, one of Herod's family, did so, and that the Jews sent after him a protest against his receiving the kingdom, to which Augustus would not listen. Alford observes that the place where our Lord spoke this parable, made this circumstance singularly appropriate. It was spoken at Jericho, where this very

Archelaus had built himself a royal palace of great magnificence.

13.—[*Ten servants.*] Chemnitius and others think that the 'servants' in this parable mean only the ministers of the gospel. I cannot take so narrow a view of the parable. I think that the expression means all who profess and call themselves Christians. By baptism they all profess to be Christ's soldiers and servants.

[*Ten pounds.*] The word translated 'pound,' means a sum much larger than an English pound. It was worth about £4 1s. 3d. of our money. In the kindred parable of the talents in Matthew, it should be noted, the servants receive much more. The talent was worth £243 15s.

[*Occupy.*] The Greek word so translated is only found here. It means literally, 'employ in business, or trading.' A substantive formed from it is found in 2 Timothy 2:4, and is rendered 'the affairs' of this life.

14.—[*His citizens hated him, etc.*] There can be no doubt that this verse describes the conduct of the Jews towards Christ, both while he was among them and after he had ascended into heaven. It is a lively emblem of their bitter hatred and obstinate unbelief.

[*We will not have this man, etc.*] Theophylact remarks the striking resemblance between this part of the parable and the cry of the Jews when Christ was before Pilate. They were asked, 'Shall I crucify your King?' They answered, 'We have no king but Cæsar.' They said, 'Away with him! Crucify him.'

15.—[*When he was returned ... kingdom.*] This part of the parable describes the second advent of Jesus Christ. The kingdom for which we pray in the Lord's Prayer is not yet come.

[*Commanded ... servants ... called.*] These words describe the judgment of all professing Christians, when Christ comes the second time. He will take account of every man's works.

16.—[*Thy pound.*] The humility of a true Christian is indicated in this expression. The servant does not say, 'By my skill I have gained,' but, 'thy pound hath gained.' We have nothing to boast of. All that we have we have received.

17.—[*Faithful in a very little.*] The sum given to each servant was undoubtedly very small. But our Lord would have us learn that however small a man's gifts and opportunities, he is as much accountable for using them rightly as if they were very great. And he would have us know that the poorest and the humblest Christian, if he uses his one pound well, shall be as carefully noticed and rewarded as the mightiest king. Faithfulness in the use of what we have, however little, is what Christ requires at our hands.

[*Over ten cities.*] Let it be noted, that the servant who had turned one pound into ten, was set over ten cities, and the servant who had turned one into five, was set over five cities. Each was rewarded according to his diligence. The doctrine of reward according to works seems to stand out here as well as in other places of Scripture. Our title to heaven is all of grace. Our degree of glory in heaven will be proportioned to our works. 'Every man shall receive his own reward according to his own labour.'

Henry remarks, 'There are degrees of glory in heaven. Every vessel will be alike full, but not alike large. And the degree of glory there will be according to the degrees of usefulness here' (*1 Cor.* 3:8).

20.—[*I have kept ... napkin.*] The ingenuity of commentators has discovered allegorical meanings here. Some have thought that as napkins were used for tying round the faces of dead persons, the whole expression represents a sleeping conscience and a dead soul. I am unable to see that there is anything more in the expression than a circumstance of the parable.

21.—[*I feared thee ... austere man.*] The heart of the unconverted man is figured in a very striking manner in this expression. Like Adam and Eve, when they had eaten the forbidden fruit, he is afraid of his Master in heaven, and does not love him. Like the murmuring Israelites in the wilderness, he finds fault with God's appointments and dealings, and charges him with hardness and injustice.

Hard thoughts of God are a common mark of all unconverted people. They first misrepresent him, and then try to excuse themselves for not loving and serving him.

22, 23.—[*Out of thine own mouth, etc.*]

The particular expressions in the concluding portion of the parable must not be pressed too closely. We are reading a story of an earthly lord's dealings with his servants, which illustrates Christ's dealings with men, and justifies his final condemnation of the wicked. We are not reading an exact account of what will be said and done in the day of judgment.

The turning point of the king's address to the unfaithful servant is the expression 'Thou knewest.' It is meant to teach us that those who are condemned at the last day will be found to have 'known' enough to guide them to salvation if they would have used their knowledge.

24.—[*Take from him ... give it.*] It should be observed, that we have no mention here of any positive punishment inflicted on the unfaithful servant, such as we find inflicted on the man who buried his talent. But we may not therefore suppose that unfaithful Christians will not be condemned to punishment at the last day. The privation of all privileges, and taking away of all gifts, described in the parable before us, evidently implies that unfaithful Christians will be cast out for ever from Christ's presence. We must once more remember that we are reading a parable, and not a history of the last day. The punishment of unfaithful Christians will doubtless answer to the punishment which a king will inflict on unfaithful servants.

25.—[*They said unto him, etc.*] This parenthetical expression is remarkable. It was either spoken by those at Jericho, who heard our Lord deliver this parable. (Such an interruption by interested hearers, would not be extraordinary in Eastern countries.) Or else it forms part of the parable itself, and was spoken by our Lord's own mouth. In either case, the lesson is the same. It shows that the honour placed on faithful Christians, at the last day, will be so great as to surprise and amaze all who behold it.

Some have thought that it means the angels, who will be the standers-by and ministering agents in all the proceedings of the last day. This, however, seems very improbable.

26.—[*Hath ... hath not.*] It is evident that these two expressions are elliptical.

'Everyone which hath,' signifies every Christian who not only has privileges, but improves them and turns them to good account. 'He that hath not,' signifies the professing Christian who is content with the idle possession of Christianity, and makes no effort to use it for his soul's good, or the glory of God.

The Gentile Christians who have not made a good use of the gospel, are very probably included prophetically in the latter part of the verse.

27.—[*Those mine enemies ... slay ... before me.*] The meaning of this verse appears to be, that the Jews, who persisted in unbelief when Christ came among them, and died in unbelief, will be fearfully punished in the last day. They will be raised and brought before the bar of Christ, and receive a punishment proportioned to their enormous sin, in killing the Lord of glory. Though triumphing apparently in the day of our Lord's crucifixion, Christ foretells in this parable, that

there will be a reckoning day. Annas and Caiaphas and their companions will yet be brought before Jesus of Nazareth and punished.

In leaving the parable, let us not forget that it shows us three sorts of people.

Firstly, there are open opposers of Christ and the gospel. Such were the Jews who refused to receive our Lord. Such are all infidels in the present day.

Secondly, there are faithful Christians. Such are all they who make a good use of the gospel, for their own good and for God's glory.

Thirdly, there are unfaithful, formal Christians, who have Christianity, but make no real use of it. Of these it should be always noted, that the parable does not charge them with being open enemies of Christ, or open breakers of God's commandments. But they 'hide their pound in a napkin.' They have a mighty gift from God, and make no use of it. This will prove at last their eternal ruin.

LUKE 19:28-40

28 And when he had thus spoken, he went before, ascending up to Jerusalem.

29 And it came to pass, when he was come nigh to Bethphage and Bethany, at the mount called *the mount* of Olives, he sent two of his disciples,

30 Saying, Go ye into the village over against *you*; in the which at your entering ye shall find a colt tied, whereon yet never man sat: loose him, and bring *him hither.*

31 And if any man ask you, Why do ye loose *him?* thus shall ye say unto him, Because the Lord hath need of him.

32 And they that were sent went their way, and found even as he had said unto them.

33 And as they were loosing the colt, the owners thereof said unto them, Why loose ye the colt?

34 And they said, The Lord hath need of him.

35 And they brought him to Jesus: and they cast their garments upon the colt, and they set Jesus thereon.

36 And as he went, they spread their clothes in the way.

37 And when he was come nigh, even now at the descent of the mount of Olives, the whole multitude of the disciples began to rejoice and praise God with a loud voice for all the mighty works that they had seen;

38 Saying, Blessed *be* the King that cometh in the name of the Lord: peace in heaven, and glory in the highest.

39 And some of the Pharisees from among the multitude said unto him, Master, rebuke thy disciples.

40 And he answered and said unto them, I tell you that, if these should hold their peace, the stones would immediately cry out.

L ET us mark, for one thing, in these verses, *the perfect knowledge of our Lord Jesus Christ.* We see him sending two of his disciples to a village, and telling them what they would find at the entrance of it, 'a colt tied, whereon yet never man sat.' We see him describing what they would see and hear, with as much confidence as if the whole transaction had been previously arranged. In short, he speaks like one to whom all things were naked and open, like one whose eyes were in every place,—like one who knew things unseen as well as things seen.

An attentive reader will observe the same thing in other parts of the gospel. We are told in one place that 'he knew the thoughts' of his enemies. We are told in another, that 'he knew what was in man.' We are told in another, that 'he knew from the beginning who they were that believed not, and who should betray him' (*Matt.* 12:25; *John* 2:25; *John* 6:64). Knowledge like this is the peculiar attribute of God. Passages like these are meant to remind us, that 'the man Christ Jesus' is not only man. He is also 'God blessed for ever' (*Rom.* 9:5).

The thought of Christ's perfect knowledge should alarm sinners and awaken them to repentance. The great Head of the church knows them and all their doings. The Judge of all sees them continually, and marks down all their ways. There is 'no darkness where the workers of iniquity can hide themselves' (*Job* 34:22). If they go into the secret chamber, the eyes of Christ are there. If they privately scheme villainy and plot wickedness, Christ knows it and observes it. If they speak secretly against the righteous, Christ hears. They may deceive men all their life long, but they cannot deceive Christ. A day comes when God 'will judge the *secrets* of men by Jesus Christ according to the gospel' (*Rom.* 2:16).

The thought of Christ's perfect knowledge should comfort all true-hearted Christians, and quicken them to increased diligence in good works. The Master's eye is always upon them. He knows where they dwell, and what are their daily trials, and who are their companions. There is not a word in their mouths, or a thought in their hearts, but Jesus knows it altogether. Let them take courage when they are slandered, misunderstood, and misrepresented by the world. It matters nothing so long as they can say, 'Thou, Lord, who knowest all things, knowest that I love thee' (*John* 21:17). Let them walk on steadily in the narrow way, and not turn aside to the right hand or the left. When sinners entice them, and weak brethren say 'spare thyself,' let them reply, 'My Master is looking at me. I desire to live and move as in the sight of Christ.'

Let us mark, for another thing, in this passage, *the publicity of our Lord's last entry into Jerusalem.* We are told of his riding in on an ass, like a king visiting his capital, or a conqueror returning in triumph to his native land. We read of a 'multitude of disciples' surrounding him, as he rode into the city, 'rejoicing and praising God with a loud voice.' The whole history is strikingly unlike the general tenor of our Lord's life. On other occasions, we see him withdrawing from public observation, retiring into the wilderness, charging those whom he healed to tell no man what was done. On the present occasion all is changed. Reserve is completely thrown aside. He seems to court public notice. He appears desirous that all should see him, and should mark, note, and observe what he did.

The reasons of our Lord's conduct at this crisis of his ministry, at first sight, may appear hard to discover. On calm reflection they are clear and plain. He knew that the time had come when he was to die for sinners on the cross. His work as the great Prophet, so far as his earthly ministry was concerned, was almost finished and completed. His work as the sacrifice for sin and substitute for sinners, remained to be accomplished. Before giving himself up as a sacrifice, he desired to draw the attention of the whole Jewish nation to himself. The Lamb of God was about to be slain. The great sin-offering was about to be killed. It was meet that the eyes of all Israel should be fixed upon him. This great thing was not to be done in a corner.

For ever let us bless God that the death of our Lord Jesus Christ was so widely known and so public an event. Had he been suddenly stoned in some popular tumult,—or privately beheaded like John the Baptist in prison, there never would have been wanting Jewish and Gentile unbelievers, who would have denied that the Son of God died at all. The wisdom of God so ordered events that such a denial was rendered impossible. Whatever men may think of the doctrine of Christ's atoning death, they never can deny *the fact* that Christ died. Publicly he rode into Jerusalem a few days before his death. Publicly he was seen and heard in the city until the day that he was betrayed. Publicly he was brought before the high priests and Pilate, and condemned. Publicly he was led forth to Calvary, and nailed to the cross. The cornerstone and crowning event in our Lord's ministry was his death for sinners. Of all the events of his ministry that death was the one most public, and the one witnessed by the greatest number of Jews. And that death was the 'life of the world' (*John* 6:51).

Let us leave the whole passage with the cheering reflection, that the joy of Christ's disciples at his entry into Jerusalem, when he came to be crucified, will prove as nothing compared to the joy of his people when he comes again to reign.—That first joy was soon broken off and exchanged for sorrow and bitter tears. The second joy shall be a joy for evermore.—That first joy was often interrupted by the bitter sneers of enemies, who were plotting mischief. The second joy shall be liable to no such rude interruptions. Not a word shall be said against the King when he comes to Jerusalem the second time. 'Before him every knee shall bow, and every tongue confess that he is Lord' (*Phil.* 2:10–11).

Notes—Luke 19:28-40

30.—[*Ye shall find a colt tied, etc.*] Let it be noted, that the public entry into Jerusalem which we read of here, is one of the few events in our Lord's history which all four Gospel writers relate. There is evidently an importance about it as a step in our Lord's earthly ministry, which we should not overlook.

The allegorical meanings which many commentators attach to the whole transaction, appear to me, to say the least, very questionable. I am unable to see that 'the colt' is a type of the Gentile church, and our Lord's riding on it a type of the Gentiles becoming obedient to the gospel. Those who wish to see instances of allegorical views of the subject, will find them in the commentaries of Pellican and Brentius, and in Luther's Exposition of the Gospel for the First Sunday in Advent.

It may be well to remark that there was nothing ignominious or unworthy of a great person in riding on an ass. In Eastern countries asses have in every age been used by persons of high rank (see *Judg.* 5:10).

31.—[*The Lord hath need of him.*] It is not quite clear whether these words were meant to have a miraculous constraining influence on the mind of the master of the colt, or whether he would simply regard it as a case of borrowing for some eminent person's use. The former of the two opinions seems the more probable. It is clear that throughout the whole transaction of this last entry into Jerusalem, a constraining miraculous influence was exercised over the minds of many persons, showing plainly what our Lord might have easily done, if he had been minded to take to himself a temporal dominion.

32.—[*Found as he had said.*] It is interesting to note here how many various minute circumstances were mentioned by our Lord when he sent his disciples for the colt, and how accurate his description proved.

37.—[*Multitude of the disciples.*] We must necessarily suppose that many of the disciples here mentioned were not really disciples in heart. They followed our Lord probably in much ignorance, and under very mistaken expectations.

38.—[*Peace in heaven.*] We can only conjecture what the multitude meant by this expression. It is possible that they intended to declare their belief that Messiah's reign of universal 'peace' and his advent in 'glory,' was on the point of beginning. In the mouths of many it was probably a scriptural phrase used at any period of great religious rejoicing, without any distinct application to Messiah's times.

39.—[*Rebuke thy disciples.*] This expression seems to show clearly that the Pharisees considered the multitude to be treating Jesus as the Messiah, and considered Jesus to be claiming the Messiahship by his not checking the language his attendants used. His riding on the colt would doubtless bring to their recollection the famous prophecy of Zechariah, which all Jews applied to the Messiah, and would add to their displeasure.

40.—[*The stones would cry out.*] This expression must evidently be regarded as a proverbial and figurative one. If men did not rejoice at Christ's advent, even inanimate nature would cry shame.

In leaving this passage, it is fair to remark, that the view I have set forth in the exposition, of our Lord's design in making his public entry into Jerusalem, is not that which is commonly given by commentators. It seems generally thought that our Lord's principal object was to manifest his kingly power, and his dominion, when he thought fit to exercise it, over the wills of men.

I cannot help thinking that this theory falls short of the true meaning of the event. I have a firm conviction that our Lord did what he did in anticipation of his approaching death on the cross. Before dying for our sins, he called public attention to himself, and filled Jerusalem with the report of his arrival. The consequence was, that when he was crucified a few days after, the attention of the whole multitude assembled at Jerusalem for the passover, was directed to him. He was offered up as a sacrifice with the greatest possible publicity, and with the eyes of the whole nation upon him. One of the greatest helps to this publicity, beyond doubt, was his remarkable entry into Jerusalem. Myriads of Jews from foreign parts came up to the holy city at the feast of the passover. There was probably not one among them who did not hear that a wonderful teacher had arrived, who claimed to be the Messiah, and rode into the city in the manner predicted by Zechariah. His death on the cross a few days after, would doubtless raise many thoughts in their minds, and in many cases would never be forgotten.

LUKE 19:41-48

41 And when he was come near, he beheld the city, and wept over it,

42 Saying, If thou hadst known, even thou, at least in this thy day, the things *which belong* unto thy peace! but now they are hid from thine eyes.

43 For the days shall come upon thee, that thine enemies shall cast a trench about thee, and compass thee round, and keep thee in on every side,

44 And shall lay thee even with the ground, and thy children within thee; and they shall not leave in thee one stone upon another; because thou knewest not the time of thy visitation.

45 And he went into the temple, and began to cast out them that sold therein, and them that bought;

46 Saying unto them, It is written, My house is the house of prayer: but ye have made it a den of thieves.

47 And he taught daily in the temple. But the chief priests and the scribes and the chief of the people sought to destroy him,

48 And could not find what they might do: for all the people were very attentive to hear him.

WE learn, firstly, from these verses, *how great is the tenderness and compassion of Christ towards sinners*. We are told that when he came near Jerusalem for the last time, 'he beheld the city and wept over it.' He knew well the character of the inhabitants of Jerusalem. Their cruelty, their self-righteousness, their stubbornness, their obstinate prejudice against the truth, their pride of heart were not hidden from him. He knew well what they were going to do to himself within a very few days. His unjust judgment, his delivery to the Gentiles, his sufferings, his crucifixion, were all spread out distinctly before his mind's eye. And yet knowing all this, our Lord pitied Jerusalem! 'He beheld the city and wept over it.'

We err greatly if we suppose that Christ cares for none but his own believing people. He cares for all. His heart is wide enough to take an interest in all mankind. His compassion extends to every man, woman, and child on earth. He has a love of general pity for the man who is going on still in wickedness, as well as a love of special affection for the sheep who hear his voice and follow him. He is not willing that any should perish, but that all should come to repentance. Hardened sinners are fond of making excuses for their conduct. But they will never be able to say that Christ was not merciful, and was not ready to save.

233

We know but little of true Christianity, if we do not feel a deep concern about the souls of unconverted people. A lazy indifference about the spiritual state of others, may doubtless save us much trouble. To care nothing whether our neighbours are going to heaven or hell, is no doubt the way of the world. But a man of this spirit is very unlike David, who said, 'rivers of waters run down mine eyes, because men keep not thy law.' He is very unlike Paul, who said, 'I have great heaviness and continual sorrow of heart for my brethren' (*Psa.* 119:136; *Rom.* 9:2). Above all, he is very unlike Christ. If Christ felt tenderly about wicked people, the disciples of Christ ought to feel likewise.

We learn, secondly, from these verses, that *there is a religious ignorance which is sinful and blameworthy.* We read that our Lord denounced judgments on Jerusalem, 'because she knew not the time of her visitation.' She might have known that the times of Messiah had fully come, and that Jesus of Nazareth was the Messiah. But she would not know. Her rulers were wilfully ignorant. They would not calmly examine evidences, and impartially consider great plain facts. Her people would not see 'the signs of the times.' Therefore judgment was soon to come upon Jerusalem to the uttermost. Her wilful ignorance left her without excuse.

The principle laid down by our Lord in this place is deeply important. It contradicts an opinion which is very common in the world. It teaches distinctly that all ignorance is not excusable, and that when men might know truth but refuse to know it, their guilt is very great in the sight of God. There is a degree of knowledge for which all are responsible, and if from indolence or prejudice we do not attain that knowledge, the want of it will ruin our souls.

Let us impress this great principle deeply on our own hearts. Let us urge it diligently on others, when we speak to them about religion. Let us not flatter ourselves that ignorance will excuse everyone who dies in ignorance, and that he will be pardoned because he knew no better!—Did he live up to the light he had? Did he use every means for attaining knowledge? Did he honestly employ every help within his reach, and search industriously after wisdom? These are grave questions. If a man cannot answer them, he will certainly be condemned in the judgment day. A wilful ignorance will never be allowed as a plea in a man's favour. On the contrary, it will rather add to his guilt.

We learn, thirdly, from these verses, that *God is sometimes pleased to give men special opportunities and invitations.* We are told by our Lord, that Jerusalem 'knew not the day of her visitation.' Jerusalem had a special season of mercy and privilege. The Son of God himself visited her. The mightiest miracles that man had ever seen were wrought around her. The most wonderful preaching that ever was heard was preached within her walls. The days of our Lord's ministry were days of the clearest calls to repentance and faith that any city ever received. They were calls so marked, peculiar, and unlike any previous calls Jerusalem had received, that it seemed impossible they should be disregarded. But they were disregarded! And our Lord declares that this disregard was one of Jerusalem's principal sins.

The subject before us is a deep and mysterious one. It requires careful stating and delicate handling, lest we should make one scripture contradict another. There seems no doubt that churches, nations, and even individuals are sometimes visited with special manifestations of God's presence, and that their neglect of such manifestations is the turning point in their spiritual ruin. Why this should take place in some cases and not in others we cannot tell. Facts, plain facts in history and biography, appear to prove that it is so. The last day will probably show the world, that there were seasons in the lives of many who died in sin, when God drew very near to them, when conscience was peculiarly alive, when there seemed but a step between them and salvation. Those seasons will probably prove to have been what our Lord calls their 'day of visitation.' The neglect of such seasons will probably be at last one of the heaviest charges against their souls.

Deep as the subject is, it should teach men one practical lesson. That lesson is the immense importance of not stifling convictions, and not quenching the workings of conscience. He that resists the voice of conscience may be throwing away his last chance of salvation. That warning voice may be God's 'day of visitation.' The neglect of it may fill up the measure of a man's iniquity, and provoke God to let him alone for ever.

We learn, lastly, from these verses, *how much Christ disapproves of the profanation of holy things.* We read that he cast the buyers and sellers out of the temple, and told them that they had made God's house 'a den of thieves.' He knew how formal and ignorant the ministers of the temple were. He knew how soon the temple and its services were to be destroyed, the veil to be rent, and the priesthood to be ended. But he would have us know that a reverence is due to every place where God is worshipped. The reverence he claimed for the temple, was not for the temple as the house of sacrifice, but as 'the house of prayer.'

Let us remember this conduct and language of our Lord, whenever we go to a place of public worship. Christian churches no doubt are not like the Jewish temples. They have neither altars, priesthood, sacrifices, nor symbolical furniture. But they are places where God's Word is read, where Christ is present, and where the Holy Ghost works on souls. These facts ought to make us grave, reverent, solemn, and decorous, whenever we enter them. The man who behaves as carelessly in a church as he would in an inn, or a private dwelling, has yet much to learn. He has not the 'mind of Christ.'

Notes—Luke 19:41-48

41.—[*Wept over it.*] This is a remarkable expression. Gualter and Gerhard call attention to it, as a conclusive argument against the doctrine of reprobation. Christ loves and pities all, even those who are his open enemies. None are hated, though none but believers are finally saved.

Wordsworth remarks, 'Christ here proves his two-fold nature by shedding tears as man, for what he foretold as God.'

42.—[*If thou hadst known.*] The Greek expression so translated is equivalent to saying, 'I wish that thou hadst known.'— 'Oh that thou hadst known.' It is like Isaiah 48:18.

[*Now they are hid.*] Poole remarks, 'God will not allow his Spirit always to strive with man, because he is but flesh, not fit to be always waited on by the Majesty of heaven. First, men shut their eyes against the things belonging to their peace, and then God hideth them from them.'

43.—[*The days shall come, etc.*] The predictions of this and the following verse were fulfilled with most literal completeness at the siege of Jerusalem under Titus. Not one word failed.

44.—[*The time of thy visitation.*] Poole remarks, 'God's visitations are either of wrath, or mercy;—of wrath, Exodus 32:34, of mercy, Jeremiah 29:10. It is plain that our Saviour useth the term here in its latter, not its former sense; and that by God's visitation is meant his visiting them by the prophets, John the Baptist, and himself.'

45.—[*He went into the temple.*] Let it be noted, that our Lord purified the temple from profane uses twice, once at the beginning of his ministry, and once at the end. Jerome considers it the greatest miracle that Christ ever wrought.

[*Them that sold ... and bought.*] To account for the presence of those buyers and sellers, we must remember that Jews came to Jerusalem at the passover from every part of the world, and required animals to offer as sacrifices. The buying and selling of these sacrifices, in the outward court of the temple, was doubtless the proceeding which called forth our Lord's righteous indignation.

We can hardly question that a mighty divine influence must have accompanied our Lord's action on this occasion. Otherwise it is difficult to understand the apparent ease with which one person succeeded in producing so great an effect on a multitude without resistance.

46.—[*Saying unto them, It is written.*] The remark has been made that even in purifying the temple from profane uses, our Lord supports his conduct by a text of Scripture. All reformation of abuses in churches should be built upon God's Word.

47.—[*He taught daily in the temple.*] The connection between this verse and the preceding one ought not to be overlooked. Our Lord had just called the temple 'the house of prayer.' Yet he proceeds to show, by his own example, that it is to be the house of 'teaching' as well as praying.

48.—[*Were very attentive.*] The Greek word so rendered is remarkable. It is only used in this place in the New Testament. The marginal reading is more literal. They 'hanged on him.'

LUKE 20:1-8

1 And it came to pass, *that* on one of those days, as he taught the people in the temple, and preached the gospel, the chief priests and the scribes came upon *him* with the elders,

2 And spake unto him, saying, Tell us, by what authority doest thou these things? or who is he that gave thee this authority?

3 And he answered and said unto them, I will also ask you one thing; and answer me:

4 The baptism of John, was it from heaven, or of men?

5 And they reasoned with themselves, saying, If we shall say, From heaven; he will say, Why then believed ye him not?

6 But and if we say, Of men; all the people will stone us: for they be persuaded that John was a prophet.

7 And they answered, that they could not tell whence *it was.*

8 And Jesus said unto them, Neither tell I you by what authority I do these things.

L ET us notice, firstly, in this passage, *the demand which the chief priests and scribes made upon our Lord.* 'Tell us,' they said, 'by what authority thou doest these things? and who gave thee this authority?'

The spirit which prompted this demand is too evident to be mistaken. These men hated and envied Christ. They saw his influence increasing. They saw their own power waning. They resolved, if possible, to stop the progress of this new teacher; and the point on which they made their assault was his authority. His mighty works they ought to have examined. His teaching they ought, in all fairness, to have compared with their own Scriptures. But they refused to take either one course or the other. They preferred to call in question his commission.

Every true-hearted Christian who tries to do good in the world, must make up his mind to be treated like his Master. He must never be surprised to find, that the self-righteous and the worldly-minded dislike his ways. The lawfulness of his proceedings will be constantly called in question. He will be regarded as meddlesome, disorderly, and self-conceited, a pestilent fellow, and a troubler of Israel (*Acts* 24:5; *1 Kings* 18:17). Scripture-readers, district-visitors, lay-agents, and unordained missionaries, are specially liable to meet with such treatment. And worst of all they will often meet with enemies, where they ought to find friends.

Let all who are attacked by the world for trying to do good, take comfort in the thought that they are only drinking of the cup which Christ drank. Their Master in heaven sympathizes with them. Let them work on patiently, and believe that, if they are faithful, their work will speak for itself. The world's opposition is sure to attend every really good work. If the servants of Christ are to cease from every movement which the world calls in question, they will soon come to an entire standstill. If we are to wait till the world approves our plans, and is satisfied with the propriety of our efforts, we shall never do anything on earth.

Let us notice, secondly, in this passage, *the manner in which our*

Lord speaks of John the Baptist's ministry. He refers those who questioned his authority to John's constant and unvarying testimony to himself. 'Ought they not to remember how John had spoken of him as the Lamb of God,—as One whose shoe-latchets he was not worthy to bear,—as One who had the fan in his hand, and had the Spirit without measure? Ought they not to recollect that they and all Jerusalem had gone out to John's baptism, and confessed that John was a prophet? Yet John had always told them plainly that Christ was the Messiah! Surely, if they were honest they would not come now to demand his authority. If they really believed John to be a prophet sent from God, they were bound to believe that Jesus was the Christ.'

It may reasonably be doubted whether the importance of John the Baptist's ministry is generally understood by Christians. The brightness of our Lord's history overshadows the history of his forerunner, and the result is that John's baptism and preaching do not receive the attention which they deserve. Yet it should never be forgotten, that the ministry of the Baptist was the only New Testament ministry foretold in the Old Testament, excepting that of Christ. It was a ministry which produced an immense effect on the Jewish mind, and aroused the expectation of Israel from one end of Palestine to the other. Above all, it was a ministry which made the Jews without excuse in their rejection of Christ, when Christ appeared. They could not say that they were taken by surprise when our Lord began to preach. Their minds had been thoroughly prepared for his appearing. To see the full sinfulness of the Jews, and the entire justice of the judgments which came on them after crucifying our Lord, we must remember the ministry of John the Baptist.

However little man may esteem the work of faithful ministers, there is One in heaven who sees it, and keeps account of all their labour. However little their proceedings may be understood, and however much they may be slandered and misrepresented, the Lord Jesus Christ writes all their doings in his book. He lives who testified to the importance of John the Baptist's ministry, when John was dead and buried. He will yet testify to the toil of every one of his faithful servants at the last day. In the world they may have tribulation and disappointment. But they are not forgotten by Christ.

Let us notice, lastly, in this passage, *the falsehood of which our Lord's enemies were guilty.* In reply to our Lord's question whether John's baptism was from heaven or men, 'they answered that they could not tell.' This was a downright untruth. They could have told, but they would not. They knew that if they said what they really believed they would condemn themselves. If they confessed that John was a prophet sent from God, they would be guilty of a gross inconsistency in not believing his testimony about Christ.

Falsehoods like this, it may be feared, are only too common among unconverted men. Thousands will say anything rather than acknowledge themselves to be in the wrong. Lying is just one of the sins to which the human heart is most naturally inclined, and one of the commonest sins in the world. Gehazi, Ananias and Sapphira have more followers and imitators than Peter and Paul. The number of lies which are constantly told by men, to save their own credit, and to cover over their own wickedness, is probably far greater than we are aware.

The true servant of Christ will do well to remember these things as he travels through this world. He must not believe all he hears, and especially in the matter of religion. He must not suppose that unconverted men really believe in their own hearts all that they say. They often feel more than they appear to feel. They often say things against religion and religious people, which they secretly know to be untrue. They often know the gospel is true, but have not the courage to confess it. They often know the Christian's life is right, but are too proud to say so. The chief priests and scribes are not the only people who deal dishonestly in religion, and say what they know to be false. Then let the servant of Christ go patiently on his way. Those who are now his enemies, will one day confess that he was right, though they used to cry loudly that he was wrong.

Notes—Luke 20:1-8

1.—[*And it came to pass, etc.*] The chapter we have now begun is remarkable because of the variety of attacks on our Lord which it describes. Whether the whole of the events here narrated took place on one day is a question on which commentators do not agree. If they did not all happen on one day, they must at any rate have happened on two successive days.

[*In the temple.*] This expression means 'in the outward courts of the temple,' to which all Jews were admitted.

4.—[*The baptism of John, etc.*] We must beware of supposing that this question which our Lord put was not pertinent to the one which had been put to himself, or was at all an evasion of a disagreeable query by a counter inquiry.

Our Lord's question was in reality an answer to the question of his inquirers. They had asked him 'by what authority' he did what he did. In reply, he asked them whether 'John the Baptist was a prophet sent from God.' His meaning evidently was that John the Baptist had expressly testified that he was the Messiah. They knew this. They could not deny it. Now if they really believed that John the Baptist was a prophet, they would see at once by 'what authority' he did what he did. He did all as the Messiah, whom John had proclaimed him to be.

[*From heaven.*] This expression means simply 'from God' (see *Dan.* 4:26; *Luke* 15:18, 21).

5.—[*Why then believed ye him not?*] The meaning of this of course must be, 'Why did ye not believe what he told you about me?'

6.—[*The people will stone us.*] Grotius remarks, 'They had themselves accustomed the people to this violence. When they could not legally convict their enemies, they incited the people to stone them. It was called the judgment of zeal.' See John 10:31; Acts 14:19.

7.—[*They could not tell.*] The Greek words here, when literally translated, are even more remarkable than our version, as a proof of the falsehood of our Lord's enemies. They are literally, 'they did not know.'

8.—[*Neither tell I you, etc.*] Our Lord's refusal was just, because those who asked him were not honest in their inquiry about his authority. Our Lord never refused to answer the question of any honest inquirer.

LUKE 20:9-19

9 Then began he to speak to the people this parable; A certain man planted a vineyard, and let it forth to husbandmen, and went into a far country for a long time.

10 And at the season he sent a servant to the husbandmen, that they should give him of the fruit of the vineyard: but the husbandmen beat him, and sent *him* away empty.

11 And again he sent another servant: and they beat him also, and entreated *him* shamefully, and sent *him* away empty.

12 And again he sent a third: and they wounded him also, and cast *him* out.

13 Then said the lord of the vineyard, What shall I do? I will send my beloved son: it may be they will reverence *him* when they see him.

14 But when the husbandmen saw him, they reasoned among themselves, saying, This is the heir: come, let us kill him, that the inheritance may be ours.

15 So they cast him out of the vineyard, and killed *him*. What therefore shall the lord of the vineyard do unto them?

16 He shall come and destroy these husbandmen, and shall give the vineyard to others. And when they heard *it*, they said, God forbid.

17 And he beheld them, and said, What is this then that is written, The stone which the builders rejected, the same is become the head of the corner?

18 Whosoever shall fall upon that stone shall be broken; but on whomsoever it shall fall, it will grind him to powder.

19 And the chief priests and the scribes the same hour sought to lay hands on him; and they feared the people: for they perceived that he had spoken this parable against them.

THE parable we have now read, is one of the very few which are recorded more than once by the Gospel writers. Matthew, Mark, and Luke, all give it at full length. The three-fold repetition is alone sufficient to point out the importance of its contents.

The parable, no doubt, was specially intended for the Jews to whom it was addressed. But we must not confine its application to them. It contains lessons which should be remembered in all churches of Christ as long as the world stands.

In the first place, the parable shows us *the deep corruption of human nature.* The conduct of the wicked 'husbandmen,' is a vivid representation of man's dealings with God.—It is a faithful picture of the history of the Jewish church. In spite of privileges, such as no nation ever had, in the face of warnings such as no people ever received, the Jews rebelled against God's lawful authority, refused to give him his rightful dues, rejected the counsel of his prophets, and at length crucified his only-begotten Son. It is a no less faithful picture of the history of all the Gentile churches. Called as they were out of heathen darkness by infinite mercy, they have done nothing worthy of the vocation wherewith they were called. On the contrary, they have allowed false doctrines and wicked practices to spring up rankly among them, and have crucified Christ afresh. It is a mournful fact that in hardness, unbelief, superstition, and self-righteousness, the Christian churches, as a whole, are little better than the Jewish church of our Lord's time. Both are described with painful correctness in the story of the wicked husbandmen. In both we may point to countless privileges misused, and countless warnings despised.

Let us often pray that we may thoroughly understand the sinfulness of man's heart. Few of us, it may be feared, have the least conception of the strength and virulence of the spiritual disease with which we are born. Few entirely realize that 'the carnal mind is enmity against God,' and that unconverted human nature, if it had the power, would cast its Maker down from his throne. The behaviour of the husbandmen before us, whatever we may please to think, is only a picture of what every natural man would do to God, if he only could. To see these things is of great importance. Christ is never fully valued, until sin is clearly seen. We must know the depth and malignity of our disease, in order to appreciate the great Physician.

In the second place, this parable shows us *the amazing patience and long-suffering of God.* The conduct of the 'lord of the vineyard' is a vivid representation of God's dealings with man.—It is a faithful picture of his merciful dealings with the Jewish church. Prophet after prophet was sent to warn Israel of his danger. Message after message was repeatedly sent, notwithstanding insults and injuries heaped on the messengers.—It is a no less faithful picture of his gracious treatment of the Gentile churches. For eighteen hundred years he has suffered their manners. They have repeatedly tried him by false doctrines, superstitions, and contempt of his Word. Yet he has repeatedly granted them seasons of refreshing, raised up for them holy ministers and mighty reformers, and not cut them off, notwithstanding all their persecutions. The churches of Christ have no right to boast. They are debtors to God for innumerable mercies, no less than the Jews were in our Lord's time. They have not been dealt with according to their sins, nor rewarded according to their iniquities.

We should learn to be more thankful for God's mercy. We have probably little idea of the extent of our obligations to it, and of the number of gracious messages which the Lord of the vineyard is constantly sending to our souls. The last day will unfold to our wondering eyes a long list of unacknowledged kindnesses, of which while we lived we took no notice. Mercy we shall find was indeed God's darling attribute. 'He delighteth in mercy' (*Mic.* 7:18). Mercies before conversion, mercies after conversion, mercies at every step of their journey on earth, will be revealed to the minds of saved saints, and make them ashamed of their own thanklessness. Sparing mercies, providential mercies, mercies in the way of warnings, mercies in the way of sudden visitations, will all be set forth in order before the minds of lost sinners, and confound them by the exhibition of their own hardness and unbelief. We shall all find that God was often speaking to us when we did not hear, and sending us messages which we did not regard. Few texts will be brought out so prominently at the last day as that of St Peter: 'The Lord is long-suffering to usward, not willing that any should perish' (2 *Pet.* 3:9).

In the last place, this parable shows us *the severity of God's judgments when they fall on obstinate sinners.* The punishment of the wicked husbandmen is a vivid representation of God's final dealings with such as go on still in wickedness.—At the time when our Lord spoke this parable, it was a prophetical picture of the approaching ruin of the Jewish church and nation. The vineyard of the Lord in the land of Israel, was about to be taken from its unfaithful tenants. Jerusalem was to be destroyed. The temple was to be burned. The Jews were to be scattered over the earth.—At the present time, it may be feared, it is a mournful picture of things yet to come on the Gentile churches in the latter days. The judgments of God will yet fall on unbelieving Christians, as they fell on unbelieving Jews. The solemn warning of St Paul to the Romans will yet receive an accomplishment: 'If thou continuest not in God's goodness, thou also shalt be cut off' (*Rom.* 11:22).

We must never flatter ourselves that God cannot be angry. He is indeed a God of infinite grace and compassion. But it is also written, that he is 'a consuming fire' (*Heb.* 12:29). His Spirit will not always strive with men (*Gen.* 6:3). There will be a day when his patience will come to an end, and when he will arise to judge terribly the earth. Happy will they be who are found hid in the ark in the day of the

Lord's anger! Of all wrath, none can be conceived so awful as 'the wrath of the Lamb.' The man on whom the 'stone cut out without hands' falls at his second coming, will indeed be crushed to powder (*Dan.* 2:34, 35).

Do we know these things, and do we live up to our knowledge? The chief priests and elders, we are told, 'perceived that this parable was spoken against them.' But they were too proud to repent, and too hardened to turn from their sins. Let us beware of doing likewise.

Notes—Luke 20:9-19

10.—[*Speak to ... people ... parable.*] Let it be noted, that our Lord addresses this parable to all the people who were listening to his teaching, and not to the priests and elders only.

The parable itself is a remarkable combination of figure, history, and prophecy. Cyril calls it 'the history of Israel in a compendium.' The parable of the sower, the parable of the mustard seed, and the parable of the wicked husbandmen, are the only parables which are three times recorded in the Gospels.

[*A vineyard.*] This expression is one which we find used parabolically in Isaiah: 'The vineyard of the Lord of hosts is the house of Israel' (*Isa.* 5:7 etc.). Here it seems to mean the land of Judæa, and the peculiar privileges of the Jewish nation.

[*Husbandmen.*] These are the Jewish people and their rulers and priests.

[*Went into a far country.*] This expression must not be pressed too closely. It signifies that as the lord of the vineyard left his vineyard to the occupation of the tenants, so God left the privileges of the Jews to be turned to good account by the nation.

10, 11, 12.—[*A servant.*] In all these three verses the 'servants' sent signify the prophets and others whom God sent to call the Jews to repentance, and rouse them to a sense of their privileges and responsibilities. The treatment the prophets received from the Jews is figured by the beating and wounding of the servants.

13.—[*My beloved Son.*] This part of the parable admits of only one interpretation. The Lord Jesus speaks of himself and the treatment which he was on the point of receiving at the hands of the priests and elders. He knew that while he spoke they were already plotting his death, and saying 'let us kill him.'

16.—[*He shall come and destroy.*] Here the parable passes into prophecy. Our Lord predicts the destruction of Jerusalem, the scattering of the Jews, and the calling of the Gentiles to enjoy their privileges.

[*They said, God forbid.*] These words would be rendered more literally 'may it not be.' The word 'God,' is not in the Greek. The exclamation appears to me to show clearly, that those who heard this parable saw the application of it.

17.—[*The stone.*] This means Christ. Though rejected by those who called themselves leaders and builders in the Jewish church, it was prophesied that he would become the headstone of the corner. And as it was foretold, so it would be (*Psa.* 118:22).

18.—[*Whosoever shall fall, etc.*] The meaning of this verse has perplexed some commentators. The distinction between the first and last parts of it has been thought a difficulty. Some have thought that the end of the verse refers to the taking of Jerusalem by the Romans. I venture to think that a better solution of the difficulty can be found.

'Whosoever shall fall upon this stone,' signifies everyone who stumbles at Christ and his gospel, and refuses to believe in him as his Saviour, during the present dispensation. Such a one shall be 'broken,' ruined, lost, and cast away.

'On whomsoever it shall fall,' signifies everyone who shall be found unbelieving when Christ comes again the second time in glory. Such a one shall be 'ground to powder,' and visited with the heaviest displeasure of God. The guilt of unbelief at the end of the gospel dispensation shall be far greater than the guilt of unbelief at the beginning.

Barradius says, that Augustine takes this view and refers the verse to the two advents of Christ. The ruin of the unbeliever at the first advent shall be miserable. But the ruin of the unbeliever at the second advent shall be even more miserable still.

Gerhard says, that Chrysostom, Theophylact, and Euthymius, all take the same view with regard to the stone grinding to powder him on whom it falls. They apply it to Christ's coming to judgment at the last day.

Some see in the verse a distinction between the punishment of the Jewish church for its unbelief at Christ's first advent, and the punishment of the Gentile churches at Christ's second advent. The Jewish church stumbled and was 'broken,' but shall yet be raised again, and restored to God's favour at the latter day. The Gentile churches, when God's judgments shall fall upon them at last, shall never be restored. Their ruin shall be complete and irretrievable. They shall be 'ground to powder.'

LUKE 20:20-26

20 And they watched *him*, and sent forth spies, which should feign themselves just men, that they might take hold of his words, that so they might deliver him unto the power and authority of the governor.

21 And they asked him, saying, Master, we know that thou sayest and teachest rightly, neither acceptest thou the person *of any*, but teachest the way of God truly:

22 Is it lawful for us to give tribute unto Cæsar, or no?

23 But he perceived their craftiness, and said unto them, Why tempt ye me?

24 Shew me a penny. Whose image and superscription hath it? They answered and said, Cæsar's.

25 And he said unto them, Render therefore unto Cæsar the things which be Cæsar's, and unto God the things which be God's.

26 And they could not take hold of his words before the people: and they marvelled at his answer, and held their peace.

LET us mark, for one thing, in this passage, *the cloak of goodness under which some of our Lord's enemies approached him.* We read that they 'sent forth spies, which should feign themselves just men.' We read further that they attempted to impose on him by flattering words: 'We know that thou sayest and teachest rightly, neither acceptest thou the person of any, but teachest the way of God truly.' Those words sounded well. An ignorant bystander would have said, 'These are sincere inquirers after truth!' But all was hollow and unreal. It was the wolf putting on the sheep's clothing, under the vain idea of deceiving the shepherd. Their words were 'smoother than butter,' yet there was 'war in their hearts' (*Psa.* 55:21).

The true servant of Christ must expect to meet persons of this description, as long as the world stands. There never will be wanting those, who from interested or sinister motives will profess with their lips to love Christ, while in heart they deny him. There will always be some, who 'by good words and fair speeches,' will attempt to deceive the heart of the simple. The union of 'burning lips and a wicked heart,' is far from uncommon. There are probably few congregations which do not contain some of those whom Solomon likens to 'potsherds, covered with silver dross' (*Rom.* 16:18; *Prov.* 26:23).

He that would not be often deceived in this wicked world, must carefully remember these things. We must exercise a wise caution as we travel through life, and not play the part of the 'simple who believeth every word' (*Prov.* 14:15). We must not lightly put confidence in every new religious volunteer, nor hastily take it for granted that all people are good who talk like good men. Such caution at first sight may appear narrow-minded and uncharitable. But the longer we live the more shall we find that it is needful. We shall discover by experience that all is not gold that glitters, and all are not true Christians who make a loud profession of Christianity. The *language* of Christianity is precisely that part of religion which a false Christian finds it most easy to attain. The walk of a man's daily life, and not the talk of his lips, is the only safe test of his character.

Let us mark, for another thing, in these verses, *the consummate wisdom of our Lord's answer to his enemies.* We read that a most difficult and subtle question was proposed to him for solution. 'Is it lawful to give tribute to Cæsar, or no?' It was a question eminently calculated to entangle anyone who attempted to answer it. If our Lord had replied that it was not lawful to pay tribute to Cæsar, he would have been accused to Pilate as a rebel against the Roman power. If our Lord had replied that it was lawful to pay tribute to Cæsar, he would have been denounced to the people as regardless of the rights and privileges of the Jewish nation. An answer which would not involve our Lord in difficulties, seemed at first sight impossible to be found. But he who is truly called 'the wisdom of God,' found an answer which silenced his adversaries. He bade them show him a penny. He asked them whose image and superscription was on that penny? 'They answered and said, Cæsar's.' At once our Lord made that penny the groundwork of a reply, at which even his enemies were obliged to marvel. 'Render,' he said, 'unto Cæsar the things which be Cæsar's, and unto God the things which be God's.'

They were to 'render to Cæsar the things which were Cæsar's.' Their own lips had just confessed that Cæsar had a certain temporal authority over them. They used the money which Cæsar had coined. It was a lawful tender between man and man. They probably had no objection to receive gifts and payments in Roman coin. They must not therefore pretend to say that all payments to Cæsar were unlawful. By their own admission he exercised some dominion over them. Let them obey that dominion in all temporal things. If they did not refuse to use Cæsar's coin, let them not refuse to pay Cæsar's temporal dues.

They were to 'render to God the things which were God's.' There were many dues which God required at their hands which they might easily pay, if they were inclined. Honour, love, obedience, faith, fear, prayer, spiritual worship, were payments to God which they might daily make, and payments with which the Roman government did not interfere. They could not say that Cæsar made such payments impossible. Let them see to it that they gave to God his dues in spiritual things, as well as to Cæsar his dues in temporal things. There was no necessity for collision between the demands of their temporal and their heavenly sovereign. In temporal things, let them obey the powers, under whose authority they allowed themselves to be. In spiritual things let them do as their forefathers had done, and obey God.

The principles laid down by our Lord in this well-known sentence are deeply instructive. Well would it have been for the peace of the world, if they had been more carefully weighed and more wisely applied!

The attempts of the civil power in some countries to control men's conscience by intolerant interference, and the attempts of the church in other countries to interfere with the action of the civil power, have repeatedly led to strifes, wars, rebellions, and social disorder. The injuries which the cause of true religion has received from morbid scrupulosity on one side, and servile obsequiousness to state demands on the other, have been neither few nor small. Happy is he who has attained to a sound mind on the whole subject! To distinguish rightly between the things of Cæsar, and the things of God,—and to pay to each their real dues regularly, habitually, and cheerfully, is a great help towards a quiet and peaceable life.

Let us often pray that we may have wisdom from above, in order to answer rightly, when perplexing questions are put to us. The servant of Christ must expect a portion like his Master. He must count it no strange thing, if the wicked and worldly-minded endeavour to 'entangle him in his talk,' and to provoke him to speak unadvisedly with his lips. In order to be prepared for such occasions let him often ask the Lord Jesus for the gift of sound wisdom and a discreet tongue. In the presence of those who watch for our halting, it is a great thing to know what to say and how to say it, when to be silent, and when to speak. Blessed be God, he who silenced the chief priest and scribes by his wise answers, still lives to help his people and has all power to help them. But he loves to be entreated.

Notes—Luke 20:20-26

20.—[*Spies.*] The Greek word so rendered is only found here. Parkhurst defines it as meaning 'Liers in wait.'

22.—[*Lawful to give tribute to Cæsar, etc.*] Let it be remembered, that a large party among the Jews bore the yoke of the Roman government most uneasily, and were disposed to regard with the greatest enmity any Jew who conceded that the Jewish nation was altogether in a tributary position under the Roman emperor, or 'Cæsar.' The question of our Lord's enemies was so artfully framed, that it seemed to place him in a dilemma. Whatever answer he gave, it seemed that he must offend one of two parties.—He must either give offence to the friends of the Romish supremacy or to the zealots among the Jews.

23.—[*Craftiness.*] The Greek word so translated is only found five times in the New Testament. It is the same word that is used in describing Satan's 'subtlety' in tempting Eve (2 *Cor.* 11:3).

24.—[*Whose image and superscription?*] Lightfoot tells us that the Jews have a tradition among them, that to admit the title of any prince on their current coin was an acknowledgment of subjection to him.

25.—[*Things which be Cæsar's …things which be God's.*] Few principles contain more deep wisdom than the famous one in this verse. Few however have been found to admit of such difference as to practical application.

The grand difficulty in applying the principle arises from this, that men do not agree what are the 'things of Cæsar,' and what are the 'things of God,'—where the claims of Cæsar end, and where the claims of God begin. A meeting place there must be. A boundary to the respective claims of each party must be laid down. The definition of this boundary has been in every age a fertile cause of strifes, divisions, and controversies.

On the one hand the English government under the Stuarts used to push the claims of 'Cæsar' to a fearful extreme. Men were persecuted, and punished, and fined, and imprisoned, like felons, because they would not worship God in a particular way. In this case 'Cæsar,' beyond all doubt, was stepping out of his province.

On the other hand, the Roman Catholic Church, in modern times, is continually interfering with the civil power of every nation where Roman Catholics live, and claiming for her members immunities and privileges which threaten to interfere with the existence of civil government altogether. In this case we have an extravagant and unreasonable assertion of the claim on behalf of the 'things that are God's.'

There are few subjects on which Christians have such need to pray for a sound mind and a clear judgment, and to ask for deliverance from a morbidly scrupulous conscience, and especially on the question of the dues of 'Cæsar.'

A conscience which is very tender and sensitive about a money payment which the state demands, but very careless in all matters of faith, and hope, and charity, and humility, and private holiness, is a conscience which, to say the least, is very suspicious.

So long as we have liberty to worship God in Christ, according to our conscience, and to serve him in the way of his commandments, we may safely submit to many requirements of the state, which in our own private opinion we do not thoroughly approve.

It is evident to every reflecting person, that all government must be the result of compromise, and that every member of the commonwealth must be willing to give up something of his private opinions for the sake of the general good. If every subject is to be excused paying the tax to which he feels an objection, common sense tells us that all government must soon come to a standstill. One will object to one tax, and another to another, until the whole state is thrown into confusion.

Gualter has a very useful note on this passage, in which he maintains the principle just laid down by the example of the Jews under the rule of their Babylonian conquerors, and also bears his protest against the excesses committed by Anabaptists in Germany, in the days of the Reformation, under the colour of conscientious scruples.

Our Lord had probably in view two parties among his hearers. One party was that of the Jewish zealots. To them he said 'render to Cæsar the things that are Cæsar's.' The other was that of the worldly Herodians. To them he said, 'Render to God the things that are God's.'

LUKE 20:27-40

27 Then came to *him* certain of the Sadducees, which deny that there is any resurrection; and they asked him,

28 Saying, Master, Moses wrote unto us, If any man's brother die, having a wife, and he die without children, that his brother should take his wife, and raise up seed unto his brother.

29 There were therefore seven brethren: and the first took a wife, and died without children.

30 And the second took her to wife, and he died childless.

31 And the third took her; and in like manner the seven also: and they left no children, and died.

32 Last of all the woman died also.

33 Therefore in the resurrection whose wife of them is she? for seven had her to wife.

34 And Jesus answering said unto them, The children of this world marry, and are given in marriage:

35 But they which shall be accounted worthy to obtain that world and the resurrection from the dead, neither marry, nor are given in marriage:

36 Neither can they die any more: for they are equal unto the angels; and are the children of God, being the children of the resurrection.

37 Now that the dead are raised, even Moses shewed at the bush, when he calleth the Lord the God of Abraham, and the God of Isaac, and the God of Jacob.

38 For he is not a God of the dead, but of the living: for all live unto him.

39 Then certain of the scribes answering said, Master, thou hast well said.

40 And after that they durst not ask him any *questions at all.*

WE see in these verses *what an old thing unbelief is.* We are told that 'there came to our Lord certain of the Sadducees, which deny that there is any resurrection.' Even in the Jewish church, the church of Abraham, and Isaac, and Jacob,—the church of Moses, and Samuel, and David, and the prophets,—we find that there were bold, avowed, unblushing sceptics. If infidelity like this existed among God's peculiar people, the Jews, what must the state of heathenism have been? If these things existed in a green tree, what must have been the condition of the dry?

We must never be surprised when we hear of infidels, deists, heretics, and free-thinkers rising up in the church, and drawing away disciples after them. We must not count it a rare and a strange thing. It is only one among many proofs that man is a fallen and corrupt being. Since the day when the devil said to Eve 'ye shall not surely die,' and Eve believed him, there never has been wanting a constant succession of forms of unbelief.—There is nothing new about any of the modern theories of infidelity. There is not one of them that is

251

not an old disease under a new name. They are all mushrooms which spring up spontaneously in the hot-bed of human nature. It is not in reality a wonderful thing that there should rise up so many who call in question the truths of the Bible. The marvel is rather, that in a fallen world the sect of the Sadducees should be so small.

Let us take comfort in the thought that in the long run of years the truth will always prevail. Its advocates may often be feeble, and their arguments very weak. But there is an inherent strength in the cause itself which keeps it alive. Bold infidels like Porphyry, and Julian, and Hobbes, and Hume, and Voltaire, and Payne arise from time to time and make a stir in the world. But they produce no lasting impression. They pass away like the Sadducees and go to their own place. The great evidences of Christianity remain like the Pyramids, unshaken and unmoved. The 'gates of hell' shall never prevail against Christ's truth (*Matt.* 16:18).

We see, secondly, in these verses, *what a favourite weapon of sceptics is a supposed case*. We are told that the Sadducees brought to our Lord a difficulty arising out of the case of a woman who had married seven brothers in succession. They professed a desire to know 'whose wife of the seven' the woman would be in the resurrection. The intention of the inquiry is clear and plain. They wished to pour contempt on the whole doctrine of a life to come. The case itself is one which we cannot suppose had really arisen. It seems the highest probability that it was a story invented for the occasion, in order to raise a difficulty and found an argument.

Reasoning of this kind will often meet us, if we are thrown into company with persons of a sceptical turn of mind. Some imaginary difficulty or complication, and that connected probably with some fancied state of things in the world to come, will often prove the stronghold of an unbeliever.—'He cannot understand it! He cannot reconcile it! It seems to him revolting and absurd! It offends his common sense!'—Such is the language which is often used.

Reasoning of this kind should never shake us for a moment. For one thing, we have nothing to do with supposed and imaginary cases.

It will be time enough to discuss them when they really arise. Enough for us to talk and argue about facts as they are. For another thing, it is a mere waste of time to speculate about difficulties connected with the state of existence in a world to come. We know so little of anything beyond the visible world around us, that we are very poor judges of what is possible or not possible in the unseen world. A thousand things beyond the grave must necessarily be unintelligible to us at present. In the meantime it is our wisdom to wait patiently. What we know not now, we shall know hereafter.

We see, thirdly, in these verses, *something of the true character of the saints' existence in the world to come*. We read that our Lord said to the Pharisees, 'They which shall be accounted worthy to obtain that world, and the resurrection from the dead, neither marry nor are given in marriage: neither can they die any more: for they are equal unto the angels.'

Two things are abundantly clear from this description, respecting the saints in glory. For one thing, their happiness is not a carnal happiness, but a spiritual one. 'They neither marry nor are given in marriage.' The glorified body shall be very unlike what it is now. It shall no longer be a clog and a hindrance to the believer's better nature. It shall be a meet habitation for a glorified soul. For another thing, their happiness shall be eternal. 'They can die no more.' No births shall be needed, to supply the constant waste caused by death. Weakness, and sickness, and disease, and infirmity, shall be no more at all. The curse shall be clean removed. Death himself shall die.

The nature of what we call 'heaven' is a subject which should often engage our thoughts. Few subjects in religion are so calculated to show the utter folly of unconverted men, and the awful danger in which they stand. A heaven where all the joy is spiritual, would surely be no heaven to an unconverted soul!—Few subjects are so likely to cheer and animate the mind of a true Christian. The holiness and spiritual-mindedness which he follows after in this life will be the very atmosphere of his eternal abode. The cares of family relationship shall no longer distract his mind. The fear of death shall no longer bring him into bondage. Then let him press on and bear his cross patiently. Heaven will make amends for all.

We see, lastly, in these verses, *the antiquity of belief in a resurrection.* Our Lord shows that it was the belief of Moses. 'That the dead are raised, even Moses shewed at the bush.'

Faith in a resurrection and a life to come has been the universal belief of all God's people from the beginning of the world. Abel, and Enoch, and Noah, and Abraham, and all the patriarchs, were men who looked forward to a better inheritance than they had here below. 'They looked for a city which had foundations.' 'They desired a better country, that is, an heavenly' (*Heb.* 11:10, 16). The words of our own seventh Article are clear and unmistakeable: 'They are not to be heard which feign that the old Fathers did look only for transitory promises.' This witness is true.

Let us anchor our own souls firmly on this great foundation truth, 'that we shall all rise again.' Whatever ancient or modern Sadducees may say, let us believe firmly that we are not made like the beasts that perish, and that there shall be 'a resurrection of the dead, both of the just and unjust' (*Acts* 24:15). The recollection of this truth will cheer us in the day of trial, and comfort us in the hour of death. We shall feel that though earthly prosperity fail us, there is a life to come where there is no change. We shall feel that though worms destroy our body, yet in the flesh we shall see God (*Job* 19:26). We shall not lie always in the grave. Our God is 'not a God of the dead, but of the living.'

Notes—Luke 20:27-40

27.—[*Certain of the Sadducees.*] The only certain thing which we know about the sect of the Sadducees is this, that they denied that there was any resurrection, or angel, or spirit (*Acts* 23:8). The common opinion that they rejected all the books of the Old Testament, excepting the five books of Moses, appears to be a vulgar error. There is no foundation for it. Josephus, the historian, was a Pharisee, and not likely to spare the errors of Sadducees in describing them. But though he charges them with rejecting traditions, he nowhere charges them with rejecting any of the sacred books.

[*Any resurrection.*] Campbell has a long note to prove that by this term 'resurrection' we are not to understand the reunion of soul and body, but simply a renewal of life, in whatever manner this may happen.

He holds that the fundamental error of the Sadducees was not barely the denial of the resurrection of the body, but the denial of the immortality of the soul, and that our Lord's argument in this passage tends to prove no more than that the soul survives the body and subsists after the body is dissolved.

The opinion must be received with caution. It solves some difficulties undoubtedly, but involves us in others.

28.—[*His brother should take his wife.*] The law of Moses here referred to (*Deut.* 25:5), ought to be carefully studied, and compared with Leviticus 18:16. It is clear that marriage with a deceased husband's brother was only allowed under certain peculiar circumstances, and as a general rule was unlawful. How any Bible reader can advocate a man's marriage with a deceased wife's sister, in the face of such texts as Leviticus 18:16 and 20:21, is, to my mind, quite incomprehensible. If it is wrong for a woman to marry two brothers, it must be wrong for a man to marry two sisters. The exceptional permission to a woman to marry two brothers was only granted when the first brother had died without leaving any children. To argue from this permission that a man may marry two sisters in succession, on the ground that the first wife left *children*, who need an aunt's care, seems very singular logic!

29.—[*First took a wife, and died without children.*] Let it be noted that Ambrose and Jerome attach allegorical meanings to this story, and regard the woman as an emblem of the Jewish synagogue. The idea seems utterly improbable.

31.—[*The seven also ... left no children.*] The possibility of such a thing happening as that which is here described, of course cannot be denied. The gross improbability of it, however, must be evident to all reflecting minds. The most probable view is that the story was a supposed case invented to supply a foundation for a difficulty.

34.—[*Children of this world marry.*] We must beware that we do not allow these words to give any sanction to Roman Catholic notions of the superior holiness of the state of virginity to the state of matrimony. The distinction our Lord draws implies no reflection on matrimony. It is simply a declaration that the condition of men and women in a world to come is utterly unlike their condition in this world.

'The children of this world,' we must remember, do not in this place signify unconverted people, but simply people who are living on earth.

35.—[*The resurrection from the dead.*] The Greek words here are remarkable. They would be rendered more literally, 'the resurrection out from the dead.' They seem strongly to favour the opinion that there is a first resurrection peculiar to the righteous (*Rev.* 20:5 etc.). The expression, 'children of the resurrection,' in the following verse, seems to point the same way.

36.—[*Equal unto the angels.*] We must not conclude from these words that the glorified saints are exactly like the angels. Angels have not bodies like ours, but are spiritual beings. The meaning appears to be, that in freedom from death and disease, and in complete deliverance from a condition of being in which marriage and birth are needful to supply the continual waste occasioned by death, the saints shall be like the angels.

[*The children of God.*] This means evidently, that the saints are introduced into a state of peculiar privilege as members of God's family, and residents in God's house, after a fashion that they know nothing of here on earth.

37.—[*That dead raised ... Moses shewed, etc.*] The quotation contained in this verse has caused much controversy. At first sight it does not appear to be any proof of a resurrection, but only of a life to come.

Some have thought that stress ought to be laid on the expression in the original quotation, 'I *am*,' not 'I *was*' the God of Abraham, etc.

Some think, with Mede and others, that our Lord refers to the promise of the land of Canaan to Abraham and his seed, and to the fact, that this promise, yet unfulfilled, will literally be fulfilled one day by Abraham rising again, and possessing the land.

Some think, with Campbell, that our Lord's object all through is not so much to prove a resurrection as a life to come.

One thing, however, is very clear. The argument which our Lord used completely silenced the Sadducees, and called forth the approbation of the scribes. Now if the Sadducees had not felt the argument convincing and silencing, they would not have submitted to it so quietly as they did. If we do not see the full force of the argument, the fault is evidently in ourselves. We do not see the fulness of Scripture as we ought to do. There is depth of meaning in many texts which we have not fathomed.

38.—[*All live unto him.*] This expression is remarkable, and peculiar to St Luke's Gospel. It probably means, 'In his sight all are living,' though long dead, buried, and removed from this world. There is no such thing as annihilation.

LUKE 20:41-47

41 And he said unto them, How say they that Christ is David's son?

42 And David himself saith in the book of Psalms, The Lord said unto my Lord, Sit thou on my right hand,

43 Till I make thine enemies thy footstool.

44 David therefore calleth him Lord, how is he then his son?

45 Then in the audience of all the people he said unto his disciples,

46 Beware of the scribes, which desire to walk in long robes, and love greetings in the markets, and the highest seats in the synagogues, and the chief rooms at feasts;

47 Which devour widows' houses, and for a shew make long prayers: the same shall receive greater damnation.

LET us observe in this passage, *what striking testimony to Christ's divinity the book of Psalms contains.* We read that after patiently replying to the attacks of his enemies, our Lord in turn propounds a question to them. He asks them to explain an expression in the hundred and tenth Psalm, where David speaks of the Messiah as his Lord. To this question the scribes could find no answer. They did not see the mighty truth, that Messiah was to be God as well as man, and that while as man he was to be David's son, as God he was to be David's Lord. Their ignorance of Scripture was thus exposed before all the people. Professing themselves to be instructors of others and possessors of the key of knowledge, they were proved unable to explain what their own Scriptures contained. We may well believe that of all the defeats which our Lord's malicious enemies met with, none galled them more than this. Nothing so mortifies the pride of man, as to be publicly proved ignorant of that which he fancies is his own peculiar department of knowledge.

We have probably little idea how much deep truth is contained in the book of Psalms. No part of the Bible perhaps is better known in the letter, and none so little understood in the spirit. We err greatly if we suppose that it is nothing but a record of David's feelings, of David's experience, David's praises, and David's prayers. The hand that held the pen was generally David's. But the subject matter was often something far deeper and higher than the history of the son of Jesse. The book of Psalms, in a word, is a book full of Christ,—Christ suffering,—Christ in humiliation,—Christ dying,—Christ rising again,—Christ coming the second time,—Christ reigning over all. Both the advents are here,—the advent in suffering to bear the cross,—the advent in power to wear the crown. Both the kingdoms are here,—the kingdom of grace, during which the elect are gathered,—the kingdom of glory, when every tongue shall confess that Jesus is Lord. Let us always read the Psalms with a peculiar reverence. Let us say to ourselves as we read, 'A greater than David is here.'

The remark now made, applies more or less to all the Bible. There is a fulness about the whole Book, which is a strong proof of its inspiration. The more we read it, the more it will seem to contain. All other books become threadbare, if they are constantly read. Their weak points, and their shallowness become every year more apparent. The Bible alone seems broader, and deeper, and fuller, the oftener it is studied. We have no need to look for allegorical and mystical meanings. The fresh truths that will constantly spring up before our eyes, are simple, plain, and clear. Of such truths the Bible is an inexhaustible mine. Nothing can account for this, but the great fact, that the Bible is the Word, not of man, but of God.

Let us observe, secondly, in this passage, *how abominable is hypocrisy in the eyes of Christ*. We are told that 'in the audience of all the people he said unto his disciples, beware of the scribes, which desire to walk in long robes, and love greetings in the markets, and the highest seats in the synagogues, and the chief rooms at feasts; which devour widows' houses, and for a shew make long prayers.' This was a bold and remarkable warning. It was a public denunciation, we must remember, of men who 'sat in Moses' seat,' and were the recognized teachers of the Jewish people. It teaches us clearly that there may be times when the sins of people in high places make it a positive duty to protest publicly against them. It shows us that it is possible to speak out, and yet not to 'speak evil of dignities.'

No sin seems to be regarded by Christ as more sinful than hypocrisy. None certainly drew forth from his lips such frequent, strong, and withering condemnation, during the whole course of his ministry. He was ever full of mercy and compassion for the chief of sinners. 'Fury was not in him' when he saw Zacchæus, the penitent thief, Matthew the publican, Saul the persecutor, and the woman in Simon's house. But when he saw scribes and Pharisees wearing a mere cloak of religion, and pretending to great outward sanctity, while their hearts were full of wickedness, his righteous soul seems to have been full of indignation. Eight times in one chapter (*Matt.* 23) we find him saying, 'Woe unto you, scribes and Pharisees, hypocrites.'

Let us not forget that the Lord Jesus never changes. He is the same yesterday, and today, and for ever. Whatever else we are in religion let us be *true*. However feeble our faith, and hope, and love, and obedience may be, let us see to it that they are real, genuine, and sincere. Let us abhor the very idea of part-acting and mask-wearing in our Christianity. At any rate let us be *thorough*. It is a striking fact that the very first piece of armour which St Paul recommends to the Christian soldier is 'truth.' 'Stand therefore,' he says, 'having your loins girt about with truth' (*Eph.* 6:14).

Let us observe, lastly, in this passage, that *there will be degrees of condemnation and misery in hell*. The words of our Lord are distinct and express. He says of those who live and die hypocrites, 'the same shall receive greater damnation.'

The subject opened up in these words is a deeply painful one. The reality and eternity of future punishment are among the great foundation truths of revealed religion, which it is hard to think upon without a shudder. But it is well to have all that the Bible teaches about heaven and hell firmly fixed on our minds. The Bible teaches distinctly that there will be degrees of glory in heaven. It teaches with no less distinctness both here and elsewhere, that there will be degrees of misery in hell.

Who, after all, are those who will finally receive condemnation? This is the practical point that concerns us most. All who will not come to Christ,—all who know not God and obey not the gospel,— all who refuse to repent and go on still in wickedness, all such will be finally condemned. They will reap according as they have sown. God willeth not their eternal ruin. But if they will not hear his voice, they must die in their sins.

But who among those who are condemned will receive the heaviest condemnation? It will not fall on heathens who never heard the truth. It will not fall on ignorant and neglected Englishmen, for whose souls, however sunk in profligacy, no man cared. It will fall on those who had great light and knowledge, but made no proper use of it. It will fall on those who professed great sanctity and religiousness, but in reality clung to their sins. In one word, the hypocrite will have the lowest place in hell. These are awful things. But they are true.

Notes—Luke 20:41-47

41.—[He said unto them.] The connection between this verse and the two preceding ones should not be overlooked. It seems clear that it is 'the scribes' to whom our Lord now addresses himself. They were ready enough to approve of his answer to the Sadducees. But did they themselves understand the Scriptures? Our Lord shows them that they did not.

[How say they.] This expression implies that it was a common saying among Jewish theologians,—an acknowledged and received opinion.

[Christ is David's son.] Let it be noted, that this expression shows us, that when sick persons and others who applied to our Lord called him, 'Thou son of David,' they meant more than at first sight perhaps appears. The expression was tantamount to a confession that our Lord was the Messiah.

42.—[David himself saith, etc.] Let it be noted, that the very Psalm which our Lord here brings forward is the one which the Apostle Peter presses on the Jews, in the first public sermon he addresses to them on the day of Pentecost (Acts 2:34). It is interesting to reflect, that on that day Peter probably remembered his Master's use of the Psalm, and wisely walked in his steps by quoting it to the Jews.

44.—[*How is he then his son?*] This was a question concerning Messiah's person, which could only be answered by admitting that he was God as well as man, and man as well as God. This the scribes and Pharisees did not understand.

Our Lord had probably a double object in view in the question which he put to the scribes.

For one thing, he desired to convince them of their own ignorance of the Scriptures, which they proudly supposed they understood.

For another thing, he desired to teach them higher and more exalted views of the true nature of the Messiah. One grand error of the scribes and Pharisees, and indeed of most Jews, during our Lord's earthly ministry, was the low, carnal view which they held of Messiah's nature and person. They expected one who would be a prophet and a king, one greater than Moses and David, undoubtedly, but still not one who would be at the same time very God. To correct this error, and show the inconsistency of it with Scripture, appears to have been one part of our Lord's intention in this last public conversation which he held with his enemies.

Those who secretly wonder that our Lord did not fulfil prophecies, and apply them publicly to himself, in such a plain way that there could be no room left for anyone to doubt, would do well to remember that this is not God's way of dealing with man. God never forces conviction on man's mind. If men are not willing to believe, there is always room left for unbelief. This is a most important principle and one which we shall do well to remember in the interpretation of unfulfilled prophecy. To expect the book of Revelation, for instance, to be fulfilled so clearly that there shall be no possibility of dispute or doubt as to its fulfilment, is expecting that which is entirely contrary to the analogy of all God's dealings with man.

46.—[*Walk in long robes.*] This expression either refers to garments of an extravagantly large size on which the scribes prided themselves, or else to the fringes and borders to their garments which they put on, in obedience to the law (*Num.* 15:38). These fringes they made excessively large in order to impress on the minds of the common people an opinion of their own holiness, and their great reverence for the law.

[*Love greetings.*] This expression is explained in the Gospel of St Matthew (*Matt.* 23:7-10). They loved appellations of honour and respect, such as 'Rabbi, Father, Master, Teacher,' to be given to them in public places. Men often profess a desire to magnify their office, when in truth they want to magnify themselves.

[*Highest seats ... chief rooms.*] The grand characteristic of hypocritical and formal religion, is love of man's praise, and the honour that comes from man. True grace can wait for honour, and cares little what it has upon earth.

The Greek word which we have rendered 'chief rooms,' means literally, 'the chief or uppermost reclining places 'round a table at a feast. It does not mean the principal apartment out of several chambers.

47.—[*Devour widows' houses.*] The most probable explanation of this phrase is, that the scribes, under pretence of charity, took charge of the property of widows, and pretended to manage it for them. But instead of managing it honestly and faithfully, they embezzled it, and privately used it for their own interests.

LUKE 21:1-4

1 And he looked up, and saw the rich men casting their gifts into the treasury.

2 And he saw also a certain poor widow casting in thither two mites.

3 And he said, Of a truth I say unto you, that this poor widow hath cast in more than they all:

4 For all these have of their abundance cast in unto the offerings of God: but she of her penury hath cast in all the living that she had.

WE learn, for one thing, from these verses, *how keenly our Lord Jesus Christ observes the things that are done upon earth*. We read that 'he looked up, and saw the rich men casting their gifts into the treasury. And he saw also a certain poor widow casting in thither two mites.' We might well suppose that our Lord's mind at this season would have been wholly occupied with the things immediately before him. His betrayal, his unjust judgment, his cross, his passion, his death, were all close at hand; and he knew it.—The approaching destruction of the temple, the scattering of the Jews, the long period of time before his second advent, were all things which were spread before his mind like a picture. It was but a few moments and he spoke of them.—And yet at a time like this we find him taking note of all that is going on around him! He thinks it not beneath him to observe the conduct of a 'certain poor widow.'

Let us remember, that the Lord Jesus never changes. The thing that we read of in the passage before us is the thing that is going on all over the world. 'The eyes of the Lord are in every place' (*Prov.* 15:3). Nothing is too little to escape his observation. No act is too trifling to be noted down in the book of his remembrance. The same hand that formed the sun, moon, and stars, was the hand that formed the tongue of the gnat and the wing of the fly with perfect wisdom. The same eye that sees the council-chambers of kings and emperors, is the eye that notices all that goes on in the labourer's cottage. 'All things are naked and opened to the eyes of him with whom we have to do' (*Heb.* 4:13). He measures littleness and greatness by a very different measure from the measure of man. Events in our own daily life to which we attach no importance, are often very grave and serious matters in Christ's sight. Actions and deeds in the weekly history of a poor man, which the great of this world think trivial and contemptible, are often registered as weighty and important in Christ's books. He lives who marked the gift of one 'poor widow' as attentively as the gifts of many 'rich men.'

Let the believer of low degree take comfort in this mighty truth. Let him remember daily that his Master in heaven takes account of everything that is done on earth, and that the lives of cottagers are noticed by him as much as the lives of kings. The acts of a poor believer have as much dignity about them as the acts of a prince. The little contributions to religious objects which the labourer makes out of his scanty earnings, are as much valued in God's sight as a ten thousand pound note from a peer. To know this thoroughly is one great secret of contentment. To feel that Christ looks at what a man *is*, and not at what a man *has*, will help to preserve us from envious and murmuring thoughts. Happy is he who has learned to say with David, 'I am poor and needy; yet the Lord thinketh upon me' (*Psa.* 40:17).

We learn, for another thing, from these verses, *who they are whom Christ reckons most liberal in giving money to religious purposes.* We read that he said of her who cast in two mites into the treasury, 'She hath cast in more than they all. All these of their abundance have cast in unto the offerings of God: but she of her penury hath cast in all the living that she had.' These words teach us that Christ looks at something more than the mere amount of men's gifts in measuring their liberality. He looks at the proportion which their gifts bear to their property. He looks at the degree of self-denial which their giving entails upon them. He would have us know that some persons appear to give much to religious purposes who in God's sight give very little, and that some appear to give very little who in God's sight give very much.

The subject before us is peculiarly heart-searching. On no point perhaps do professing Christians come short so much as in the matter of giving money to God's cause. Thousands, it may be feared, know nothing whatever of 'giving' as a Christian duty. The little giving that there is, is confined entirely to a select few in the churches. Even among those who give, it may be boldly asserted, that the poor generally give far more in proportion to their means than the rich. These are plain facts which cannot be denied. The experience of all who collect for religious societies and Christian charities, will testify that they are correct and true.

Let us judge ourselves in this matter of giving, that we may not be judged and condemned at the great day. Let it be a settled principle with us to watch against stinginess, and whatever else we do with our money, to give regularly and habitually to the cause of God.—Let us remember, that although Christ's work does not depend on our money, yet Christ is pleased to test the reality of our grace by allowing us to help him. If we cannot find it in our hearts to give anything to Christ's cause, we may well doubt the reality of our faith and charity.—Let us recollect that our use of the money God has given us, will have to be accounted for at the last day. The 'Judge of all' will be he who noticed the widow's mite. Our incomes and expenditures will be brought to light before an assembled world. If we prove in that day to have been rich towards ourselves, but poor towards God, it would be good if we had never been born.—Not least, let us look round the world and ask where are the men that were ever ruined by liberal giving to godly purposes, and whoever found himself really poorer by lending to the Lord? We shall find that the words of Solomon are strictly true: 'There is that scattereth and yet increaseth; and there is that withholdeth more than is meet, but it tendeth to poverty' (*Prov.* 11:24).

Finally, let us pray for rich men, who as yet know nothing of the luxury of 'giving,' that their riches may not be their ruin. Hundreds of charitable and religious movements are standing still continually for want of funds. Great and effectual doors are open to the church of Christ for doing good all over the world, but for want of money few can be sent to enter in by them. Let us pray for the Holy Ghost to come down on all our congregations, and to teach all our worshippers what to do with their money. Of all people on earth, none ought to be such liberal givers as Christians. All that they have they owe to the free gift of God. Christ, the Holy Ghost, the gospel, the Bible, the means of grace, the hope of glory, all are undeserved, incomparable *gifts*, which millions of heathen never heard of. The possessors of such gifts, ought surely to be 'ready to distribute' and 'willing to communicate.' A giving Saviour ought to have giving disciples. Freely we have received: freely we ought to give (*1 Tim.* 6:18; *Matt.* 10:8).

Notes—Luke 21:1-4

1.—[*Casting ... gifts ... treasury.*] Major says, 'In the second court of the temple, in the court of the women, were fixed thirteen chests, with inscriptions, directing to what use the offerings in each were allotted. Into one of these the widow cast her two mites. This court was hence called occasionally "the treasury" (*John* 8:20). These offerings were made at the three great feasts, to compound for tithes and dues, and to fulfil the precept, "Thou shalt not appear empty before the Lord" (*Exod.* 23:15; *Deut.* 16:16).' See 2 Kings 12:9.

2.—[*Poor widow.*] Here, as in other places in the Bible, we must remember the exceedingly depressed and dependent condition of a poor man's widow in the countries where our Lord was. The expression is almost proverbial for one very badly off, and most unlikely to contribute anything to a charitable purpose.

[*Two mites.*] A mite was the smallest coin in use among the Jews in our Saviour's time. Major says that it was equal to about three-eighths of a farthing of our money.

3.—[*Hath cast in more.*] 'More,' in this expression, does not of course mean a larger sum in reality, but more in God's sight, a gift which God values more than one of far more value in man's eyes;—more in the judgment of him who looks at the motives of givers, and at the money they keep for themselves as well as the money they give;—more in proportion to her means.

4.—[*They have of their abundance cast in.*] This means that what the rich gave, they gave out of a large and abundant store, and hardly felt what they gave, because much was left behind.

[*She of her penury hath cast in.*] This means that what the widow gave, she gave out of a store so small that, after giving, nothing seemed to be left.

[*All her living.*] The meaning of this expression is disputed. Some think that it means that the widow gave the whole of her property. Others think that it means that she gave the whole amount of her daily income. The latter view seems the more probable one. A person so poor as the widow would necessarily live from hand to mouth, and possess no capital or property, except what she received from one source or another day after day.

Let it be noted in leaving this passage, that our Lord says not a word here against the lawfulness and propriety of giving money to these treasuries in the temple, though he doubtless knew that the money was often ill-applied, and the temple dispensation soon passing away. An excessive censoriousness about the failings and infirmities of religious societies which are sound in principle, is not to be praised. All institutions worked by man must needs be imperfect.

Finally, let us beware of lightly using the expression 'giving our mite,' in reference to giving money to religious or charitable causes. The phrase is often employed without thought or consideration. If people would 'give their mite' really and literally as the widow gave hers, many would have to give far more money than they ever give now. Her 'mite' meant something that she gave with immense self-denial, and at great sacrifice. Most men's 'mite,' nowadays, means something that is not felt, not missed, and makes no difference to their comfort. If all people gave their 'mite,' as the widow gave hers, the world and the church would soon be in a very different state.

LUKE **21**:5-9

5 And as some spake of the temple, how it was adorned with goodly stones and gifts, he said,

6 *As for* these things which ye behold, the days will come, in the which there shall not be left one stone upon another, that shall not be thrown down.

7 And they asked him, saying, Master, but when shall these things be? and what sign *will* *there be* when these things shall come to pass?

8 And he said, Take heed that ye be not deceived: for many shall come in my name, saying, I am *Christ*; and the time draweth near: go ye not therefore after them.

9 But when ye shall hear of wars and commotions, be not terrified: for these things must first come to pass; but the end *is* not by and by.

L ET us notice in this passage, *our Lord Jesus Christ's words about the temple at Jerusalem.* We read that some spake of it, 'how it was adorned with goodly stones and gifts.' They praised it for its outward beauty. They admired its size, its architectural grandeur, and its costly decorations. But they met with no response from our Lord. We read that he said, 'As for these things which ye behold, the days will come in the which there shall not be left one stone upon another, that shall not be thrown down.'

These words were a striking prophecy. How strange and startling they must have sounded to Jewish ears, an English mind can hardly conceive. They were spoken of a building which every Israelite regarded with almost idolatrous veneration. They were spoken of a building which contained the ark, the holy of holies, and the symbolical furniture formed on a pattern given by God himself. They were spoken of a building associated with most of the principal names in Jewish history; with David, Solomon, Hezekiah, Josiah, Isaiah, Jeremiah, Ezra, and Nehemiah. They were spoken of a building towards which every devout Jew turned his face in every quarter of the world, when he offered up his daily prayers (1 Kings 8:44; Jon. 2:4; Dan. 6:10). But they were words spoken advisedly. They were spoken in order to teach us the mighty truth that the true glory of a place of worship does not consist in outward ornaments. 'The Lord seeth not as man seeth' (1 Sam. 16:7). Man looketh at the outward appearance of a building. The Lord looks for spiritual worship, and the presence of the Holy Ghost. In the temple at Jerusalem these things were utterly wanting, and therefore Jesus Christ could take no pleasure in it.

Professing Christians will do well to remember our Lord's words in the present day. It is meet and right beyond doubt that buildings set apart for Christian worship, should be worthy of the purpose for which they are used. Whatever is done for Christ ought to be well done. The house in which the gospel is preached, and the Word of God read, and prayer offered up, ought to lack nothing that can make it comely and substantial. But let it never be forgotten that the material part of a Christian church is by far the least important part of it. The fairest combinations of marble, and stone, and wood, and painted glass, are worthless in God's sight, unless there is truth in the pulpit, and grace in the congregation. The dens and caves in which the early Christians used to meet, were probably far more beautiful in the eyes of Christ, than the noblest cathedral that was ever reared by man. The temple in which the Lord Jesus delights most, is a broken and contrite heart, renewed by the Holy Ghost.

Let us notice, for another thing in this passage, *our Lord Jesus Christ's solemn warning against deception.* His striking words about the temple drew from his disciples an important question: 'Master, but when shall these things be? and what sign will there be, when these things shall come to pass?' Our Lord's reply to that question was long and full. And it began with a pointed caution, 'Take heed that ye be not deceived.'

The position which this caution occupies is very remarkable. It stands in the forefront of a prophecy of vast extent and universal importance to all Christians,—a prophecy reaching from the day in which it was delivered, to the day of the second advent,—a prophecy revealing matters of the most tremendous interest both to Jews and Gentiles,—and a prophecy of which a large portion remains yet to be fulfilled. And the very first sentence of this wondrous prophecy is a caution against deception, 'Take heed that ye be not deceived.'

The necessity of this caution has been continually proved in the history of the church of Christ. On no subject perhaps have divines made so many mistakes as in the interpretation of unfulfilled prophecy. On no subject have they shown so completely the weakness of man's intellect, and confirmed so thoroughly the words of St Paul, 'We see through a glass darkly:—we know in part' (1 Cor. 13:12). Dogmatism, positiveness, controversial bitterness, obstinacy in maintaining untenable positions, rash assertions and speculations, have too often brought discredit on the whole subject of the prophetical Scriptures, and caused the enemies of Christianity to blaspheme. There are only too many books on prophetical interpretation, on the title-pages of which might be justly written, 'Who is this that darkeneth counsel by words without knowledge?' (Job 38:2).

Let us learn from our Lord's warning words to pray for a humble teachable spirit, whenever we open the pages of unfulfilled prophecy. Here, if anywhere, we need the heart of a little child, and the prayer 'open thou mine eyes' (Psa. 119:18). Let us beware, on the one side, of that lazy indifference which turns away from all prophetical Scripture, on account of its difficulties. Let us beware, on the other side, of that dogmatical and arrogant spirit, which makes men forget that they are students, and talk as confidently as if they were prophets themselves. Above all, let us read prophetical Scripture with a thorough conviction that the study carries with it a blessing, and that more light may be expected on it every year. The promise remains in full force, 'Blessed is he that readeth.' At the time of the end, the vision shall be unsealed (Rev. 1:3; Dan. 12:9).

Notes—Luke 21:5-9

5.—[*Some spake ... temple.*] The feeling with which all Jews, in our Lord's time, regarded the temple, was something far beyond what we can imagine in the present day. This should be borne in mind, in order to estimate rightly the effect which our Lord's words, in this place, must have produced on those who heard them.

[*Goodly stones.*] The enormous size of the stones with which the temple was built by Herod at its last restoration, is specially mentioned by Josephus. He says that 'many of them were about twenty-five cubits in length, eight in height, and twelve in breadth.' A cubit was about twenty-two inches of our measure.

[*Gifts.*] Tacitus, the Roman historian, and Josephus, the Jewish writer, both mention the enormous riches contained in the temple, consisting chiefly of offerings given by pious persons, or by rulers who wished to testify respect for the building. In particular there was a golden vine given by Herod, with clusters of grapes as tall as a man. Many of these offerings were suspended in the portico of the temple, so that all could see them.

6.—[*Not be left one stone upon another.*] These words were literally fulfilled when Titus took Jerusalem, and Turrus Rufus, one of his officers, ploughed up the foundations of the temple.

It may be well to remember, that these words do not necessarily apply to the substructure on the side of the hill on which the temple stood. There are remains of a wall built of enormous stones still seen at Jerusalem, which the best-informed travellers agree in thinking must have been standing when our Lord spoke this prophecy.

Burkitt remarks, 'Sin will undermine and blow up the most magnificent and famous structure. Sin brings cities and kingdoms, as well as particular persons, to their end.'

8.—[*Take heed ... be not deceived.*] The caution given by our Lord is very significant. The mistakes that theologians have made about the fulfilment of prophecy, in every age of the church, have been many and great. In our own day we see some putting a literal meaning on figurative prophecy, and others putting a figurative meaning on literal prophecy.—Some can see nothing but 'the church' in passages where Israel is mentioned. Others can see nothing but Israel in every prophecy in the Bible.—Some say that nearly all prophecy is fulfilled. Others say that it is nearly all unfulfilled.—Some see the Church of Rome everywhere in prophecy. Others cannot see Rome in prophecy at all.—Some can see no Antichrist except the Pope. Others can see no Antichrist except a future general Antichrist yet to be revealed.—Some think that events around us are fulfilling the book of Revelation. Others think that every word of Revelation remains yet to be fulfilled.—Amidst this tangled maze of discordant opinions, we need greatly the solemn warning of our Lord. 'Take heed that ye be not deceived.'

[*Many shall come ... saying, I am Christ.*] There were many impostors who appeared in the latter days of Jewish history, who pretended to be the Messiah. It must not surprise us if some in like manner shall arise and make similar claims about the time of the second advent of Christ.

9.—[*By and by.*] The Greek word so rendered is almost always translated in the New Testament, 'immediately,' 'forthwith,' or 'straightway.' This is clearly the meaning in this place.

LUKE 21:10-19

10 Then said he unto them, Nation shall rise against nation, and kingdom against kingdom:

11 And great earthquakes shall be in divers places, and famines, and pestilences; and fearful sights and great signs shall there be from heaven.

12 But before all these, they shall lay their hands on you, and persecute *you*, delivering *you* up to the synagogues, and into prisons, being brought before kings and rulers for my name's sake.

13 And it shall turn to you for a testimony.

14 Settle *it* therefore in your hearts, not to meditate before what ye shall answer:

15 For I will give you a mouth and wisdom, which all your adversaries shall not be able to gainsay nor resist.

16 And ye shall be betrayed both by parents, and brethren, and kinsfolks, and friends; and *some* of you shall they cause to be put to death.

17 And ye shall be hated of all *men* for my name's sake.

18 But there shall not an hair of your head perish.

19 In your patience possess ye your souls.

WE should notice, for one thing, in this passage, *Christ's prediction concerning the nations of the world.* He says, 'Nation shall rise against nation, and kingdom against kingdom: and great earthquakes shall be in divers places, and famines and pestilences; and fearful sights and great signs shall there be from heaven.'

These words no doubt received a partial fulfilment, in the days when Jerusalem was taken by the Romans, and the Jews were led into captivity. It was a season of unparalleled desolation to Judæa, and the countries round about Judæa. The last days of the Jewish dispensation were wound up by a struggle which for bloodshed, misery, and tribulation, has never been equalled since the world began.

But the words before us have yet to receive a more complete accomplishment. They describe the time which shall immediately precede the second advent of Jesus Christ. The 'time of the end' shall be a time of war, and not of universal peace. The Christian dispensation shall pass away like the Jewish one, amidst wars, tumults, and desolation, amidst a general crash of empires and kingdoms, such as the eyes of man have never yet seen.

A thorough understanding of these things is of great importance to our souls. Nothing is so calculated to chill the heart and damp the faith of a Christian as indulgence in unscriptural expectations.—Let us dismiss from our minds the vain idea that nations will ever give up wars entirely, before Jesus Christ comes again. So long as the devil is the prince of this world, and the hearts of the many are unconverted, so long there must be strife and fighting. There will be no universal peace before the second advent of the Prince of peace. Then, and then only, men shall 'learn war no more' (*Isa.* 2:4). Let us cease to expect that missionaries and ministers will ever convert the world, and teach all mankind to love one another. They will do nothing of the kind. They were never intended to do it. They will call out a witnessing people who shall serve Christ in every land, but they will do no more. The bulk of mankind will always refuse to obey the gospel. The nations will always go on quarrelling, wrangling, and fighting. The last days of the earth shall be its worst days. The last war shall be the most fearful and terrible war that ever desolated the earth.

The duty of the true Christian is clear and plain. Whatever others do, he must give all diligence to make his own calling and election sure. While others are occupied in national conflicts and political speculations, he must steadily seek first the kingdom of God. So doing he shall feel his feet upon a rock, when the foundations of the earth are out of course, and the kingdoms of this world are going to ruin. He shall be like Noah, safe within the ark. He shall be 'hid in the day of the Lord's anger' (*Zeph.* 2:3).

We should notice, for another thing, in this passage, *Christ's prediction concerning his own disciples.* He does not prophesy smooth things, and promise them an uninterrupted course of temporal comfort. He says that they shall be 'persecuted,' put in 'prison,' 'brought before kings and rulers,' 'betrayed,' 'put to death,' and 'hated of all men for his name's sake.'

The words of this prophecy were doubtless intended to apply to every age of the church of Christ. They began to be fulfilled in the days of the apostles. The book of Acts supplies us with many an instance of their fulfilment.—They have been repeatedly fulfilled during the last eighteen hundred years. Wherever there have been disciples of

Christ, there has always been more or less persecution.—They will yet receive a more full accomplishment before the end comes. The last tribulation will probably be marked by special violence and bitterness. It will be a 'great tribulation' (*Rev.* 7:14).

Let it be a settled principle in our minds that the true Christian must always enter the kingdom of God 'through much tribulation' (*Acts* 14:22). His best things are yet to come. This world is not our home. If we are faithful and decided servants of Christ, the world will certainly hate us, as it hated our Master. In one way or another grace will always be persecuted. No consistency of conduct, however faultless, no kindness and amiability of character, however striking, will exempt a believer from the world's dislike, so long as he lives. It is foolish to be surprised at this. It is mere waste of time to murmur at it. It is a part of the cross, and we must bear it patiently. The children of Cain will hate the children of Abel as long as the earth continues. 'Marvel not, my brethren,' says St John, 'if the world hate you.' 'If ye were of the world,' says our Lord, 'the world would love his own: but because ye are not of the world, but I have chosen you out of the world, therefore the world hateth you' (*1 John* 3:13; *John* 15:18, 19).

We should notice, lastly, in this passage, *Christ's gracious promise to his disciples.* He says 'there shall not an hair of your head perish.' Our blessed Lord knew well the hearts of his disciples. He saw that the prophecy he had just spoken might well make them faint. He supplies them with a cheering word of encouragement,—'Not a hair of your head shall perish.'

The promise before us is wide and comprehensive, and one which is the property of all believers in every age. A literal interpretation of it is clearly impossible. It cannot apply to the bodies of disciples. To say that would be contradictory to the notorious fact that James and other of the apostles died violent deaths. A figurative interpretation must evidently be placed upon the words. They form a great proverbial saying. They teach us that whatever sufferings a disciple of Christ may go through, his best things can never be injured. His life is hid with Christ in God. His treasure in heaven can never be touched. His soul is beyond the reach of harm. Even his vile body shall be raised again, and made like his Saviour's glorious body at the last day.

If we know anything of true religion let us lean back on the words of the glorious promises in every time of need. If we believe in Christ, let us rest in the comfortable thought that Christ has pledged his word that we shall not perish. We may lose much by serving Christ, but we shall never lose our souls. The world may deprive a believer of property, friends, country, home, liberty, health, and life. It has done so in innumerable cases from the days of Stephen to the present time. The roll of the noble army of martyrs is a very long one. But one thing the world cannot do to any believer. It cannot deprive him of his interest in Christ's love. It cannot break the union between Christ and his soul. Surely it is worthwhile to be a thorough-going believer! 'I am persuaded,' says St Paul, 'that neither death, nor life, nor angels, nor principalities, nor powers, nor things present, nor things to come, nor height, nor depth, nor any other creature shall be able to separate us from the love of God, which is in Christ Jesus our Lord' (*Rom.* 8:38, 39).

Notes—Luke 21:10-19

10.—[*Then said he unto them.*] The part of the prophecy commencing here, and extending to the nineteenth verse, appears to admit of a double interpretation. Primarily it applies to the wars connected with the taking of Jerusalem, and the afflictions of Christians after our Lord's death until the end of the Jewish dispensation. Secondarily it applies to the times immediately preceding the second advent of Christ and the end of the world.

[*Nation shall rise, etc.*] The times preceding the last Jewish war and destruction of Jerusalem were remarkable for repeated insurrections, and a most disturbed state of things in Judæa, and the countries immediately around Judæa. The 'time of the end' just preceding our Lord's second advent,

will in like manner, be a time of war, confusion, and disorder among the nations of Christendom.

11.—[*Earthquakes ... famines ... pestilences.*] These visitations of God were remarked to be specially frequent and severe in the last days of the Jewish dispensation. In particular, myriads died from famine and pestilence at Jerusalem during the siege, before the city was taken.

[*Fearful sights and great signs.*] The following note of Bishop Pearce, deserves reading. 'Josephus has given us a very particular account of the prodigies of this kind which preceded the destruction of Jerusalem. He speaks of a flaming sword seen over the city, and of a comet which appeared there for a twelve-month. He mentions a light, which for the space of half an hour, shone so bright in the night between the temple and the altar, that it seemed as if it was noonday. He takes notice also, of what eye-witnesses had related to him, that chariots and armed troops were seen fighting in the sky upon a certain day. He adds, that on the day of Pentecost, when the priests entered into the inner temple, they heard a great noise and voice as of a multitude, crying out "let us depart hence." The substance of this account is also given by Tacitus the Roman historian.'

There seems no reason to doubt the correctness of this report of Josephus. At any rate, being an unconverted Jew, he had no intention of confirming the statements contained in the Gospels.

It is in the highest degree probable that the second advent of Jesus Christ will be preceded by similar signs and unusual appearances in the framework of nature.

12.—[Lay hands ... persecute ... etc.] This verse appears to have a special reference to the persecutions undergone by the early Christians, between the time of Christ's ascension and the destruction of Jerusalem. The Acts of the Apostles describe the fulfilment of the verse.

13.—[It shall turn ... for a testimony.] The meaning of this verse seems to be, that the 'sufferings of the Christians shall prove an evidence of the truth of Christianity.'

It may be well to remark here, that if the first professors of Christianity had always received riches, and honour, and temporal rewards, as soon as they became Christians, the heathen world might fairly have doubted their sincerity, and the truth of their cause. But when the world saw thousands of them patiently enduring tremendous sufferings rather than give up their religion, the sight must have supplied a very strong proof that it was a religion which was true. A man here and there might be found who, in a fit of enthusiasm or fanaticism, might endure suffering and death for a false religion, which he foolishly believed to be true, or for a religion which he knew to be false. But when myriads suffered and died for Christianity, in the early days of the church of Christ, an argument

was supplied for the truth of Christianity, which infidels have never been able to overthrow.

14.—[Settle it ... not to meditate.] Here, as in other places, the right application of this precept must not be overlooked. It was not intended to encourage ministers in neglecting preparation for the pulpit. It does not apply to their case at all. It was spoken for the comfort of persecuted Christians. The promises connected with it were marvellously fulfilled in the case of the apostles in the Acts, as well as in the trials of many martyrs in modern times.

15.—[I will give you a mouth and wisdom.] Scott remarks on this promise that it is an incidental proof of the divinity of Christ. None but One who was very God could have made such a promise as this.

16.—[Ye shall be betrayed.] We have no particular instances of such betrayal given to us in the Acts. But that they were far from uncommon in the persecutions of the early church, is well known to all readers of ecclesiastical history.

17.—[Ye shall be hated of all men.] These words should be carefully noticed. They show that universal popularity is not a thing that Christians should covet, nor yet value much if it should fall to their lot. The Christian of whom everybody speaks well, can hardly be a faithful man.

It is no reply to this to point to the honours paid to eminent Christians after their deaths, and the respect with which worldly men have attended their funerals and spoken of their memories. The world has always liked dead saints better than living ones. The Pharisees could build the tombs of the prophets, when they were dead.

19.—[In patience ... possess ...souls.] We must not suppose that these words mean, 'Keep your souls in a state of patience.' This is a common interpretation, but not a correct one. The meaning appears rather to be, 'Win, or procure, or keep in possession the salvation of your souls, through or by patience.' Alford paraphrases it, 'This endurance is God's appointed way in and by which your salvation is to be put in your possession.' The expression 'Work out your own salvation' (Phil. 2:12), will naturally occur to a Bible reader as some-what similar.

Pearce takes the word 'souls' to mean nothing more than 'your lives,' and thinks the verse may be paraphrased, 'Your perseverance shall be rewarded with the preservation of your lives in the general ruin.' Yet the expression of the verse preceding is so clearly a spiritual promise, that the verse before us seems to mean something more than the saving of mere bodily life.

LUKE 21:20-24

20 And when ye shall see Jerusalem compassed with armies, then know that the desolation thereof is nigh.

21 Then let them which are in Judæa flee to the mountains; and let them which are in the midst of it depart out; and let not them that are in the countries enter thereinto.

22 For these be the days of vengeance, that all things which are written may be fulfilled.

23 But woe unto them that are with child, and to them that give suck, in those days! for there shall be great distress in the land, and wrath upon this people.

24 And they shall fall by the edge of the sword, and shall be led away captive into all nations: and Jerusalem shall be trodden down of the Gentiles, until the times of the Gentiles be fulfilled.

THE subject of the verses before us is the taking of Jerusalem by the Romans. It was meet and right that this great event, which wound up the Old Testament dispensation, should be specially described by our Lord's mouth. It was fitting that the last days of that holy city, which had been the seat of God's presence for so many centuries, should receive a special notice in the greatest prophecy which was ever delivered to the church.

We should mark in this passage, *our Lord Jesus Christ's perfect knowledge.* He gives us a fearful picture of the miseries which were coming on Jerusalem. Forty years before the armies of Titus encompassed the city, the dreadful circumstances which would attend the siege are minutely described. The distress of weak and helpless women,—the slaughter of myriads of Jews,—the final scattering of Israel in captivity among all nations,—the treading down of the holy city by the Gentiles for eighteen hundred years, are things which our Lord narrates with as much particularity as if he saw them with his own eyes.

Foreknowledge like this is a special attribute of God. Of ourselves we 'know not what a day may bring forth' (*Prov.* 27:1). To say what will happen to any city or kingdom in forty years from the present time, is far beyond the power of man. The words in Isaiah are very solemn: 'I am God, and there is none like me, declaring the end from the beginning, and from ancient times the things that are not yet done' (*Isa.* 46:9–10). He who could speak with authority of things to come, as our Lord did in this place, must have been very God as well as very man.

The true Christian should continually keep in mind this perfect knowledge of Christ. Past things, present things, and things to come, are all naked and open to the eyes of him with whom we have to do. The recollection of the sins of youth may well make us humble. The sense of present weakness may make us anxious. The fear of trials yet to come may make our hearts faint. But it is a strong consolation to think that Christ knows all. For past, present, and future things we may safely trust him. Nothing can ever happen to us that Christ has not known long ago.

We should mark, secondly, in this passage, *our Lord's words about flight in time of danger.* He says respecting the days preceding the siege of Jerusalem, 'Then let them which are in Judæa flee to the mountains; and let them which are in the midst of it depart out; and let not them that are in the countries enter thereinto.'

The lesson of these words is very instructive. They teach us plainly that there is nothing cowardly or unworthy of a Christian in endeavouring to escape from danger. There is nothing unbecoming our high vocation in a diligent use of means in order to secure our safety. To meet death patiently and courageously, if it comes on us in the path of God's providence, is a duty incumbent on every believer. But to court death and suffering, and rush needlessly into danger, is the part of the fanatic and enthusiast, not of the wise disciple of Christ. It is those who use all means which God has placed within their reach, who may confidently expect God's protection. There is a wide difference between presumption and faith.

We should mark, thirdly, in this passage, *our Lord's words about vengeance.* He says, with reference to the siege of Jerusalem, 'These be the days of vengeance, that all things which are written may be fulfilled.'

There is something peculiarly awful in this expression. It shows us that the sins of the Jewish nation had been long noted down in the book of God's remembrance. The Jews, by their unbelief and impenitence, had been treasuring up wrath against themselves for many hundred years. The anger of God, like a pent-up river, had been silently accumulating for ages. The fearful tribulation which attended the siege of Jerusalem, would only be the outburst of a thunderstorm which had been gradually gathering since the days of the kings. It would only be the fall of a sword which had been long hanging over Israel's head.

The lesson of the expression is one which we shall do well to lay to heart. We must never allow ourselves to suppose that the conduct of wicked men or nations is not observed by God. All is seen, and all is known; and a reckoning-day will certainly arrive at last. It is a mighty truth of Scripture, that 'God requireth that which is past' (*Eccles.* 3:15). In the days of Abraham 'the iniquity of the Amorites was not yet full,' and four hundred years passed away before they were punished. Yet punishment came at last, when Joshua and the twelve tribes of Israel took possession of Canaan.—God's 'sentence against an evil work' is not always executed speedily, but it does not follow that it will not be executed at all. The wicked may flourish for many years 'like a green bay tree,' but his latter end will be that his sin will find him out (*Gen.* 15:16; *Eccles.* 8:11; *Psa.* 37:35).

We should mark, lastly, in this passage, *our Lord's words about the times of the Gentiles.* We read that he said, 'Jerusalem shall be trodden down of the Gentiles, until the times of the Gentiles be fulfilled.'

A fixed period is here foretold, during which Jerusalem was to be given over into the hands of Gentile rulers, and the Jews were to have no dominion over their ancient city. A fixed period is likewise foretold which was to be the time of the Gentiles' visitation, the time during which they were to enjoy privileges, and occupy a position something like that of Israel in ancient days.—Both periods are one day to end. Jerusalem is to be once more restored to its ancient inhabitants. The Gentiles, because of their hardness and unbelief, are to be stripped of their privileges, and endure the just judgments of God. But the times of the Gentiles are not yet run out. We ourselves are living within them at the present day.

The subject before us is a very affecting one, and ought to raise within us great searchings of heart. While the nations of Europe are absorbed in political conflicts and worldly business, the sands in their hour-glass are ebbing away. While governments are disputing about secular things, and parliaments can hardly condescend to find a place for religion in their discussions, their days are numbered in the sight of God. Yet a few years, and the 'times of the Gentiles will be fulfilled.' Their day of visitation will be past and gone. Their misused privileges will be taken away. The judgments of God shall fall on them. They shall be cast aside as vessels in which God has no pleasure. Their dominion shall crumble away, and their vaunted institutions shall fall to pieces. The Jews shall be restored. The Lord Jesus shall come again in power and great glory. The kingdoms of this world shall become the kingdoms of our God and of his Christ, and the 'times of the Gentiles' shall come to an end.

Happy is he who knows these things, and lives the life of faith in the Son of God! He is the man, and he only, who is ready for the great things coming on the earth, and the appearing of the Lord Jesus Christ. The kingdom to which he belongs, is the only kingdom which shall never be destroyed. The King whom he serves, is the only King whose dominion shall never be taken away (*Dan.* 2:44; 7:14).

Notes—Luke 21:20-24

20.—[*When ye shall see, etc.*] From this verse down to the end of the twenty-fourth, our Lord's prophecy is entirely confined to the last days of Jerusalem, and the duties of his disciples during that eventful period. Here at all events there is no reference to his second advent, and the last siege of Jerusalem, after its future restoration.

The siege by Titus and destruction by the Romans are exclusively the subject under our eyes.

[*Jerusalem compassed with armies, then know.*] The following historical facts are well worthy of notice. They show in a remarkable manner how the words of our Lord in this verse were accomplished. It appears that three years before the siege of Jerusalem by Titus, the Roman army under Cestius Gallus made a sudden attack upon Jerusalem, but most unaccountably and without any apparent reason, withdrew again, although the city might have been taken with ease. The consequence of this attack was that a large number of the inhabitants of Jerusalem took alarm, and withdrew from the city as soon as the Roman army had retired. To use the words of Josephus, they 'swam away, as from a ship about to sink.' Among those who escaped were the Christians, some of them retiring to Pella, and some to Mount Libanus. The result of this was, that when the last great war, under Vespasian and Titus, broke out shortly afterwards, the Christians almost entirely escaped its desolation.

It seems a high probability that the Christians remembered the very words of our Lord which we are now considering, and that the remembrance of them was the preservation of their lives. They saw in the advance of the Roman army under Cestius Gallus the predicted sign of 'desolation drawing nigh.' They at once acted on the advice of their Master, and so escaped the miseries of the final siege.

21.—[*Flee to the mountains, etc.*] Major remarks, 'These were the mountains to the north-east of Jerusalem, towards the source of the Jordan, which was in the territories of Agrippa. He continued faithful to the Romans; and hence the Christians avoided the destruction which overspread Judæa.'

22.—[*Days of vengeance ... things written fulfilled.*] The 'vengeance' spoken of here appears to me to be the righteous retribution of God on the Jewish nation, for all their sins against him, from the time when they first entered Canaan. I cannot confine it to 'vengeance' for the sins of the nation during the last few hundred years

of their existence after the Babylonish captivity. The words of our Lord in Matthew 23:35, 36, appear to confirm this view.

The 'things written' appear to me to include all the heavy judgments foretold in the Old Testament as coming on the Jews, and to begin with the twenty-sixth chapter of Leviticus.

23.—[*Woe unto them ... with child ... give suck, etc.*] The miseries of women in the siege of Jerusalem are specially foretold in Deuteronomy 28:56.

[*In the land.*] Here, as in many other places in the Gospels, 'the land' seems specially to mean the land of Palestine.

24.—[*Fall by edge of sword, etc.*] Josephus records that there perished in the siege of Jerusalem, by sword and by famine, no less than eleven hundred thousand Jews.

[*Led away captive, etc.*] Josephus records that in the course of the war ninety-seven thousand Jews were made captives. Most of them were sent as slaves into Egypt, or dispersed over the provinces of the Roman empire, to be cast to the wild beasts in the amphitheatres.

[*Jerusalem trodden down of the Gentiles.*] This expression means that the city of Jerusalem shall be possessed by Gentile nations, and cruelly oppressed as a captive city, until the Jews shall be restored to their own land. How literally and exactly these words have been fulfilled all readers of history know. In spite of all the efforts of the Crusaders, Jerusalem has almost always been a city trampled under foot and cruelly oppressed, by Romans, Greeks, Saracens, and Turks, from the time of Titus down to the present day.

[*Until ... times of ... Gentiles be fulfilled.*] This expression is variously interpreted.

1. Some, with Bishop Pearce, put a vague general meaning on it, and say it signifies 'till the Gentiles have done all which God intended them to do.'

2. Some think, with Hammond, that it refers entirely to something already past, and that it was accomplished after the days of Adrian, when a church composed of Gentiles, Christians, and converted Jews was set up at Jerusalem, and flourished for a short time.

3. Some think, with Whitby and Newcome, that it refers entirely to things to come, and that the time of the Gentiles will be fulfilled when they are all fully converted to Christianity.

4. The true view I believe to be this. The 'times of the Gentiles' I regard as the period between the first and second advents of Christ, during which the Gentile nations have a day of visitation and enjoy the privileges of the gospel.—These times will come to an end at last, as the old Jewish dispensation did, because of the hardness and unbelief of the Gentile churches. They too, because they continue not in God's goodness, will be cut off.—And when their time of visitation comes to an end, and they have been found as faithless and hardened as the Jews, then at last will the Jews be converted, and Jerusalem restored to its rightful possessors.

Our own times, be it remembered, are the 'times of the Gentiles.' They are times which seem rapidly drawing to an end. When they do end, the conversion of the Jews and the restoration of Jerusalem will take place.

LUKE 21:25-33

25 And there shall be signs in the sun, and in the moon, and in the stars; and upon the earth distress of nations, with perplexity; the sea and the waves roaring;

26 Men's hearts failing them for fear, and for looking after those things which are coming on the earth: for the powers of heaven shall be shaken.

27 And then shall they see the Son of man coming in a cloud with power and great glory.

28 And when these things begin to come to pass, then look up, and lift up your heads; for your redemption draweth nigh.

29 And he spake to them a parable; Behold the fig-tree, and all the trees;

30 When they now shoot forth, ye see and know of your own selves that summer is now nigh at hand.

31 So likewise ye, when ye see these things come to pass, know ye that the kingdom of God is nigh at hand.

32 Verily I say unto you, This generation shall not pass away, till all be fulfilled.

33 Heaven and earth shall pass away: but my words shall not pass away.

THE subject of this portion of our Lord's great prophecy is his own second coming to judge the world. The strong expressions of the passage appear inapplicable to any event less important than this. To confine the words before us, to the taking of Jerusalem by the Romans, is an unnatural straining of Scripture language.

We see, firstly, in this passage, *how terrible will be the circumstances accompanying the second advent of Christ.* Our Lord tells us that 'there shall be signs in the sun, and in the moon, and in the stars; and upon the earth distress of nations, with perplexity; the sea and the waves roaring; men's hearts failing them for fear, and for looking after those things which are coming on the earth: for the powers of heaven shall be shaken. And then shall they see the Son of man coming in a cloud.'

This is a singularly awful picture. It may not be easy perhaps to attach a precise meaning to every part of it. One thing, however, is abundantly plain. The second coming of Christ will be attended by everything which can make it alarming to the senses and heart of man. If the giving of the law at Sinai was so terrible that even Moses said, 'I exceedingly fear and quake,' the return of Christ when he comes to earth in power and great glory shall be much more terrible.—If the hardy Roman soldiers 'became as dead men,' when an angel rolled the stone away and Christ rose again, how much greater will the terror be when Christ shall return to judge the world. No wonder that St Paul said, 'Knowing the terror of the Lord, we persuade men' (*Heb.* 12:21; *Matt.* 28:4; *2 Cor.* 5:11).

The thoughtless and impenitent man may well tremble when he hears of this second advent of Christ. What will he do when worldly business is suddenly stopped and the precious things of the world are made worthless?—What will he do when the graves on every side are opening, and the trumpet is summoning men to judgment?—What will he do when that same Jesus whose gospel he has so shamefully neglected shall appear in the clouds of heaven, and put down every enemy under his feet?—Surely he will call on the rocks to fall on him and on the hills to cover him (*Hos.* 10:8). But he will call in vain for help, if he has never called on Christ before. Happy will they be in that day who have fled betimes from the wrath to come, and been washed in the blood of the Lamb!

We see, secondly, in this passage, *how complete will be the security of true Christians at the second advent of Christ*. We read that our Lord said to his disciples, 'When these things begin to come to pass, then look up, and lift up your heads; for your redemption draweth nigh.'

However terrible the signs of Christ's second coming may be to the impenitent, they need not strike terror into the heart of the true believer. They ought rather to fill him with joy. They ought to remind him that his complete deliverance from sin, the world, and the devil, is close at hand, and that he shall soon bid an eternal farewell to sickness, sorrow, death, and temptation. The very day when the unconverted man shall lose everything, shall be the day when the believer shall enter on his eternal reward. The very hour when the worldly man's hopes shall perish, shall be the hour when the believer's hopes shall be exchanged for joyful certainty and full possession.

The servant of God should often look forward to Christ's second advent. He will find the thought of that day a cordial to sustain him under all the trials and persecutions of this present life. 'Yet a little while,' let him remember, 'and he that shall come will come and will not tarry.' The words of Isaiah shall be fulfilled, 'The Lord God shall wipe away tears from off all faces; and the rebuke of his people shall he take away from off all the earth.' One sure receipt for a patient spirit is to expect little from this world, and to be ever 'waiting for the coming of our Lord Jesus Christ' (*Heb.* 10:37; *Isa.* 25:8; *1 Cor.* 1:7).

We see, thirdly, in this passage, *how needful it is to watch the signs of the times in the prospect of the second advent of Christ.* Our Lord teaches this lesson by a parable: 'Behold the fig tree, and all the trees; when they now shoot forth, ye see and know of your own selves that summer is now nigh at hand. So likewise ye, when ye see these things come to pass, know ye that the kingdom of God is nigh at hand.' The disciples ignorantly supposed that Messiah's kingdom would be ushered in by universal peace. Our Lord, on the contrary, tells them that the signs which shall immediately precede it shall be wars, confusions, perplexity, and distress.

The general duty which these words should teach us is very plain. We are to observe carefully the public events of the times in which we live. We are not to be absorbed in politics, but we are to mark political events. We are not to turn prophets ourselves, but we are to study diligently the signs of our times. So doing, the day of Christ will not come upon us entirely unawares.

Are there any signs in our own day? Are there any circumstances in the world around us which specially demand the believer's attention? Beyond doubt there are very many. The drying up of the Turkish empire,—the revival of the Romish church,—the awakened desire of the Protestant churches to preach the gospel to the heathen,—the general interest in the state of the Jews,—the universal shaking of governments and established institutions,—the rise and progress of the subtlest forms of infidelity,—all, all are signs peculiar to our day. All should make us remember our Lord's words about the fig-tree. All should make us think of the text, 'Behold, I come quickly' (*Rev.* 22:7).

We see, lastly, in this passage, *how certain it is that all our Lord's predictions about the second advent will be fulfilled.* Our Lord speaks as if he foresaw the unbelief and incredulity of man on this mighty subject. He knew how ready people would be to say 'Improbable! impossible! The world will always go on as it has done.' He arms his disciples against the infection of this sceptical spirit by a very solemn saying. 'Heaven and earth shall pass away: but my words shall not pass away.'

We shall do well to remember this saying, whenever we are thrown into the company of those who sneer at unfulfilled prophecy. The sneers of unbelievers must not be allowed to shake our faith. If God has said a thing he will certainly bring it to pass, and the probability or possibility of it are matters which need not trouble us for a moment. That Christ should come again in power to judge the world and reign, is not half so improbable as it was that Christ should come to suffer and die. If he came the first time, much more may we expect that he will come the second time. If he came to be nailed to the cross, much more may we expect that he will come in glory and wear the crown. He has said it, and he will do it. 'His words shall not pass away.'

Let us turn from the study of these verses with a deep conviction, that the second advent of Christ is one of the leading truths of Christianity. Let the Christ in whom we believe, be not only the

Christ who suffered on Calvary, but the Christ who is coming again in person to judge the earth.

Notes—Luke 21:25-33

25.—[*And there shall be signs, etc.*] The prophecy, from this verse down to the end, takes a very wide range. It describes the last days of the world, the second personal advent of Jesus Christ, the circumstances which will attend that advent, and the duties which the prospect of that advent entail on all Christians.

[*Sun ... moon ... stars ... earth ... sea ... waves.*] It is not agreed among commentators whether these expressions are to be interpreted literally or figuratively. It is undeniable that in symbolical prophecy the sea is an emblem of nations, and the heavenly bodies an emblem of the rulers of nations (see *Gen.* 37:9; *Ezek.* 32:8; *Joel* 2:10, 30; *Rev.* 17:15). But it must be remembered, that the prophecy before us is not a symbolical one. Its predictions are plain, simple facts, and not clothed in figurative language. It seems, therefore, a high probability, that the language before us will receive a literal fulfilment in the events preceding and accompanying the second advent of Christ. The frame of nature was convulsed when the law of God was given at Sinai, and when Christ died on the cross. It is surely not too much to expect that it will be convulsed when Christ returns to judge the world.

26.—[*Failing them.*] The Greek word so translated is only found here in the New Testament. It means literally 'fainting.' Schleusner says that it signifies, 'to faint from fear, to become next to dead, but as if dead.'

[*Looking after.*] The Greek word so rendered means literally 'expectation' (*Acts* 12:11). It seems to signify that state of anxious suspense in which the world will be when it sees the first symptoms of the approaching advent of Christ, and yet knows not, and is unwilling to know, what they mean.

[*On the earth.*] Let it be noted, that the Greek word so translated, in all the other fourteen places in the New Testament where it is used, is rendered, 'the world.'

[*The powers of heaven.*] The remarks made on verse 25 apply to this expression. It seems safest to take it literally.

27.—[*See the Son of man coming, etc.*] These words appear to me to admit of only one signification. They describe a literal, personal coming of that same Jesus Christ, who ascended up in a cloud before the eyes of the disciples from Mount Olivet (*Acts* 1:9-12).

28.—[*When these things begin to come to pass.*] This expression deserves notice. It shows that although the advent of Christ will be a sudden advent at last, it will have been preceded by signs and symptoms which all intelligent and lively Christians may observe, however hidden they may be to the world.

[*Your redemption.*] The word 'redemption' is here used in the same sense as in the following passages.—Romans 8:23; Ephesians 1:14; 4:30. It signifies that full and complete redemption of the believer, which will be accomplished when his body is raised again, and soul and body once more united. From the guilt and power of sin believers are redeemed already. But from all the humbling consequences of sin they will not be completely redeemed until Jesus comes again, and calls them from their graves at the last day.

29.—[*Fig-tree and all the trees.*] It admits of a question, whether our Lord, by this expression, did not mean the Jewish and Gentile churches. The fig-tree, barren, and cursed for its barrenness, was undoubtedly a figure of the Jewish church. It seems not impossible that this was in our Lord's mind, when we remember that his curse on the fruitless fig-tree had been pronounced the very week when he spoke this prophecy before us. See also Song of Solomon 2:11-13.

31.—[*The kingdom of God ... nigh at hand.*] There is probably a reference in these words to the mistaken ideas of our

Lord's disciples about the kingdom of God. They looked for it to be set up at once, and expected their Master to be its King without delay. Our Lord here teaches them that his kingdom will not be nigh at hand until after a period of fearful wars and tribulations.

32.—[*This generation shall not pass away till all be fulfilled.*] The meaning of this sentence is a point on which commentators differ widely. An excellent summary of various opinions will be found in Gerhard's Commentary.

1. Some think that 'this generation,' means simply 'the present generation of men who were living when our Lord was speaking.' This view is a favourite one with many modern Protestants, but it is very unsatisfactory. For one thing, nearly forty years passed away before the prophecy before us was even partially fulfilled by the destruction of Jerusalem. For another thing, it seems a most violent straining of the meaning of words to say, that the destruction of Jerusalem at all fulfilled a very large part of the prophecy before us. The coming of the Son of man is surely a totally different thing from the taking of a city.

2. Some think that 'this generation,' means, 'the heaven and earth' (as in the following verses), and the whole frame of creation. This is the view of Maldonatus.

3. Some think that 'this generation,' means, 'the whole race of mankind.' This is the view of Jerome and Barradius.

4. Some think that 'this generation,' means, 'this order of things,' or dispensation, and that our Lord meant to teach us that the present dispensation was the last one, the 'last time' of which St John speaks (1 *John* 2:18).

5. Some think that 'this generation,' should have been rendered, 'the same generation,' and that it signifies, 'the same generation which sees the beginning of the signs of my second advent, will also see the end of them and my personal appearing.' I venture the remark that this rendering would not be the natural sense of the Greek words.

6. Some think that 'this generation,' means 'the faithful, the believers, the company of Christ's disciples,' and that the general sense is that Christ shall always have a believing people even at the awful tribulations of the time of the end. The elect shall never be destroyed. This is a favourite opinion of the Fathers. Origen, Chrysostom, Hilary, Euthymius, and Theophylact all hold it.

7. The soundest and most satisfactory opinion to my mind, is that which makes 'this generation' mean the Jewish nation. They had been spoken of by our Lord in this prophecy. Their captivity and scattering had been plainly predicted. The disciples might naturally wonder how such a prediction could be reconciled with the many promises of glory to Israel in the Old Testament prophets. Our Lord answers their thoughts by declaring that this nation, the 'Jewish people,' as a separate people, shall not pass away. Though cast down, they were not to be destroyed. Though scattered, they were yet to be gathered again before all things were fulfilled.

Of course the correctness of this view turns entirely on the question, whether the Greek word translated 'generation,' will honestly bear the sense of 'nation,' or 'people.' My own belief is, that it will bear the sense, and that it does really bear it in many places of the New Testament. I mention as instances, Matthew 11:16; 12:39; 23:36; Luke 11:50, 51; Acts 2:40; Philippians 2:15. In this last text our translators have actually translated the word 'nation.'

I will only add that the view I maintain is held by Mede, Flacius, Ravanellus, Aretius, and Bullinger. Mede's argument in defence of the view will be found in his works, page 752 fol. 1672.

To point out how strikingly this view of the text is confirmed by the fact that the Jews are still a distinct and separate people all over the world, is of course needless.

33.—[*Heaven and earth ... pass away.*] This expression is a peculiarly strong and solemn mode of declaring the certainty of the whole prophecy being fulfilled. The heavens were to pass away like a scroll, at our Lord's second coming. But his word was to stand for ever. Nothing could prevent its being accomplished.

LUKE 21:34-38

34 And take heed to yourselves, lest at any time your hearts be overcharged with surfeiting, and drunkenness, and cares of this life, and so that day come upon you unawares.

35 For as a snare shall it come on all them that dwell on the face of the whole earth.

36 Watch ye therefore, and pray always, that ye may be accounted worthy to escape all these things that shall come to pass, and to stand before the Son of man.

37 And in the day time he was teaching in the temple; and at night he went out, and abode in the mount that is called *the mount of Olives.*

38 And all the people came early in the morning to him in the temple, for to hear him.

THESE verses form the practical conclusion of our Lord Jesus Christ's great prophetical discourse. They supply a striking answer to those who condemn the study of unfulfilled prophecy as speculative and unprofitable. It would be difficult to find a passage more practical, direct, plain, and heart-searching than that which is now before our eyes.

Let us learn from these verses, *the spiritual danger to which even the holiest believers are exposed in this world.* Our Lord says to his disciples, 'Take heed to yourselves, lest at any time your hearts be overcharged with surfeiting, and drunkenness, and cares of this life, and so that day come upon you unawares.'

These words are exceedingly startling. They were not addressed to carnal-minded Pharisees, or sceptical Sadducees, or worldly Herodians. They were addressed to Peter, James, and John, and the whole company of the apostles. They were addressed to men who had given up everything for Christ's sake, and had proved the reality of their faith by loving obedience and steady adhesion to their Master. Yet even to them our Lord holds out the peril of surfeiting, and drunkenness, and worldliness! Even to them he says, 'Take heed to yourselves.'

The exhortation before us should teach us the immense importance of humility. There is no sin so great but a great saint may fall into it. There is no saint so great but he may fall into a great sin. Noah escaped the pollutions of the world before the flood; and yet he was afterwards overtaken by drunkenness.—Abraham was the father of the faithful; and yet through unbelief he said falsely that Sarah was his sister.—Lot did not take part in the horrible wickedness of Sodom; and yet he afterwards fell into foul sin in the cave.—Moses was the meekest man on earth; and yet he so lost self-command that he spoke angrily and unadvisedly.—David was a man after God's own heart; and yet he plunged into most heinous adultery.—These examples are all deeply instructive. They all show the wisdom of our Lord's warning in the passage before us. They teach us to be 'clothed with humility.' 'Let him that thinketh he standeth take heed lest he fall' (*1 Pet.* 5:5; *1 Cor.* 10:12).

The exhortation before us should teach us furthermore the great importance of an unworldly spirit. The 'cares of this life' are placed side by side with surfeiting and drunkenness. Excess in eating and drinking is not the only excess which injures the soul. There is an excessive anxiety about the innocent things of this life, which is just as ruinous to our spiritual prosperity, and just as poisonous to the inner man. Never, never let us forget that we may make spiritual shipwreck on lawful things, as really and as truly as on open vices. Happy is he who has learned to hold the things of this world with a loose hand, and to believe that seeking first the kingdom of God, 'all other things shall be added to him!' (*Matt.* 6:33).

Let us learn, secondly, from these verses, *the exceeding suddenness of our Lord's second coming.* We read that 'as a snare shall it come on all them that dwell on the face of the whole earth.' As a trap falling suddenly on an animal, and catching it in a moment,—as the lightning flash shining suddenly in heaven, before the thunder is heard,—as a thief coming suddenly in the night, and not giving notice that he will come,—so sudden, so instantaneous will the second advent of the Son of Man be.

The precise date of our Lord Jesus Christ's return to this world has been purposely withheld from us by God. 'Of that day and hour knoweth no man.' On one point however all the teaching of Scripture about it is clear and unmistakable. Whenever it shall take place, it shall be a most sudden and unexpected event. The business of the world shall be going on as usual. As in the days of Sodom, and the days before the flood, men shall be 'eating and drinking, marrying and given in marriage.' Few, even among true believers, shall be found completely alive to the great fact, and living in a state of thorough expectation. In a moment, in the twinkling of an eye, the whole course of the world shall be stopped. The King of kings shall appear. The dead shall be raised. The living shall be changed. Unbelief shall wither away. Truth shall be known by myriads too late. The world with all its trifles and shadows shall be thrust aside. Eternity with all its awful realities shall begin. All this shall begin at once, without notice, without warning, without note of preparation. 'As a snare shall it come on the face of the whole earth.'

The servant of God must surely see that there is only one state of mind which becomes the man who believes these things. That state is one of perpetual preparedness to meet Christ. The gospel does not call on us to retire from earthly callings, or neglect the duties of our stations. It does not bid us retire into hermitages, or live the life of a monk or a nun. But it does bid us live like men who expect their Lord to return. Repentance toward God, faith toward our Lord Jesus Christ, and holiness of conversation, are the only true habitual preparedness required. The Christian who knows these things by experience, is the man who is always ready to meet his Lord.

Let us learn, lastly, from these verses, *the special duties of believers in the prospect of the second advent of Christ.* Our Lord sums up these duties under two great heads. One of these two is watchfulness. The other is prayer. 'Watch ye therefore,' he says, 'and pray always.'

We are to 'watch.' We are to live on our guard like men in an enemy's country. We are to remember that evil is about us, and near us, and in us,—that we have to contend daily with a treacherous heart, an ensnaring world, and a busy devil. Remembering this, we must put on the whole armour of God, and beware of spiritual drowsiness. 'Let us not sleep, as do others;' says St Paul, 'but let us watch and be sober' (*1 Thess.* 5:6).

We are to 'pray always.' We are to keep up a constant habit of real, businesslike prayer. We are to speak with God daily, and hold daily communion with him about our souls. We are to pray specially for grace to lay aside every weight, and to cast away everything which may interfere with readiness to meet our Lord. Above all we are to watch our habits of devotion with a godly jealousy, and to beware of hurrying over or shortening our prayers.

Let us leave the whole passage with a hearty determination, by God's help, to act on what we have been reading. If we believe that Christ is coming again, let us get ready to meet him. 'If we know these things, happy are we if we do them' (*John* 13:17).

Notes—Luke 21:34-38

34.—[*Overcharged with surfeiting.*] Let it be noticed that both the Greek words so translated, are only found here in the New Testament.

The whole verse is full of singularly searching expressions. The 'heart' is the part which the Christian must guard, if he would live ready to meet Christ.—The heart is in constant danger of being 'weighed down,' or 'pressed down.'—Intemperance in eating and drinking is a fault against which even the best of men must watch. The most eat and drink far too much. It does not follow because Roman Catholics fast superstitiously that Protestants are never to fast at all. The 'cares of this life' may inflict great injury on the soul, as well as open sins.—All these things require diligent attention and unceasing watchfulness. The words of Matthew Henry are most true on this verse, 'We cannot be safe, if we are secure.'

[*Unawares.*] The Greek word so rendered is only found in one other place in the New Testament, and in the same connection. It is there translated, 'sudden.' Parkhurst defines it as 'sudden, unexpected, unforeseen.'

36.—[*Watch … pray always.*] The Greek words so rendered are even more striking when translated literally. They would then be, 'watch therefore, in every season praying.'

[*Accounted worthy to escape, etc., … and to stand.*] It admits of some question whether these words do not point to the possibility of some believers being allowed to pass through great tribulation in the last days, because of their sloth and inconsistency. There certainly are expressions in the New Testament which seem to indicate that all Christ's people will not 'stand' before him with equal boldness in the day of his appearing. St Peter speaks of an 'abundant entrance.' St Paul speaks of some 'saved so as by fire' (2 *Pet.* 1:11; 1 *Cor.* 3:15).

37.—[*Day time … teaching in the temple.*] Let it be noted, that from the time of our Lord's public entry into Jerusalem up to his death, he never withdrew from his enemies, but did all openly, and before their eyes. He knew that his time was come.

[*Abode.*] The Greek word so rendered is only found in one other place, and there is translated 'lodged.' Matthew 21:17. Major says, that the expression, 'abode in the Mount of Olives,' means, 'at Bethany, because it was a town on the Mount of Olives.' Comparison with the text just quoted in Matthew, makes this highly probable. It is not necessary to suppose that our Lord lodged in the open air.

LUKE 22:1-13

1 Now the feast of unleavened bread drew nigh, which is called the Passover.

2 And the chief priests and scribes sought how they might kill him; for they feared the people.

3 Then entered Satan into Judas surnamed Iscariot, being of the number of the twelve.

4 And he went his way, and communed with the chief priests and captains, how he might betray him unto them.

5 And they were glad, and covenanted to give him money.

6 And he promised, and sought opportunity to betray him unto them in the absence of the multitude.

7 Then came the day of unleavened bread, when the passover must be killed.

8 And he sent Peter and John, saying, Go and prepare us the passover, that we may eat.

9 And they said unto him, Where wilt thou that we prepare?

10 And he said unto them, Behold, when ye are entered into the city, there shall a man meet you, bearing a pitcher of water; follow him into the house where he entereth in.

11 And ye shall say unto the goodman of the house, The Master saith unto thee, Where is the guestchamber, where I shall eat the passover with my disciples?

12 And he shall shew you a large upper room furnished: there make ready.

13 And they went, and found as he had said unto them: and they made ready the passover.

THE chapter which opens with these verses, begins St Luke's account of our Lord's sufferings and death. No part of the Gospels is so important as this. The death of Christ was the life of the world.—No part of our Lord's history is so fully given by all the Gospel writers as this. Only two of them describe the circumstances of Christ's birth. All four dwell minutely on Christ's death. And of all the four, no one supplies us with such full and interesting details as St Luke.

We see, firstly, in these verses, that *high offices in the church do not preserve the holders of them from great blindness and sin*. We read that 'the chief priests and scribes sought how they might kill' Jesus.

The first step in putting Christ to death, was taken by the religious teachers of the Jewish nation. The very men who ought to have welcomed the Messiah, were the men who conspired to kill him. The very pastors who ought to have rejoiced at the appearing of the Lamb of God, had the chief hand in slaying him. They sat in Moses' seat. They claimed to be 'guides of the blind,' and 'lights of them which were in darkness' (*Rom.* 2:19). They belonged to the tribe of Levi. They were, most of them, in direct succession and descent from

Aaron. Yet they were the very men who crucified the Lord of glory! With all their boasted knowledge, they were far more ignorant than the few Galilean fishermen who followed Christ.

Let us beware of attaching an excessive importance to ministers of religion because of their office. Orders and rank confer no exemption from error. The greatest heresies have been sown, and the greatest practical abuses introduced into the church by ordained men. Respect is undoubtedly due to high official position. Order and discipline ought not to be forgotten. The teaching and counsel of regularly appointed teachers ought not to be lightly refused.—But there are limits beyond which we must not go. We must never suffer the blind to lead us into the ditch. We must never allow modern chief priests and scribes to make us crucify Christ afresh. We must try all teachers by the unerring rule of the Word of God. It matters little *who* says a thing in religion;—but it matters greatly *what* it is that is said. Is it scriptural? Is it true? This is the only question.—'To the law and to the testimony: if they speak not according to this word, it is because there is no light in them' (*Isa.* 8:20).

We see, secondly, in these verses, *how far men may fall after making a high profession.* We read that the second step towards our Lord's crucifixion, was the treachery of one of the twelve apostles: 'Then entered Satan into Judas Iscariot, being of the number of the twelve.' These words are peculiarly awful. To be tempted by Satan is bad enough. To be sifted, buffeted, led captive by him is truly terrible. But when Satan 'enters into a man,' and dwells in him, the man becomes indeed a child of hell.

Judas Iscariot ought to be a standing beacon to the church of Christ. This man, be it remembered, was one of our Lord's chosen apostles. He followed our Lord during the whole course of his ministry. He forsook all for Christ's sake. He heard Christ preach and saw Christ's miracles. He preached himself. He spoke like the other apostles. There was nothing about him to distinguish him from Peter, James, and John. He was never suspected of being unsound at heart. And yet this man turns out at length a hypocrite, betrays his Master, helps his enemies to deliver him up to death, and dies himself a 'son of perdition' (*John* 17:12). These are fearful things. But they are true.

Let the recollection of Judas Iscariot constrain every professing Christian to pray much for humility. Let us often say, 'Search me, O God, and know my heart: try me, and know my thoughts' (*Psa.* 139:23). At best we have but a faint conception of the deceitfulness of our hearts. The lengths to which men may go in religion, and yet be without grace, is far greater than we suppose.

We see, thirdly, in these verses, *the enormous power of the love of money.* We are told that when Judas went to the chief priests and offered to betray his Master, they 'covenanted to give him money.' That little sentence reveals the secret of this wretched man's fall. He was fond of money. He had doubtless heard our Lord's solemn warning, 'Take heed, and beware of covetousness' (*Luke* 12:15). But he had either forgotten it, or given it no heed. Covetousness was the rock on which he made shipwreck. Covetousness was the ruin of his soul.

We need not wonder that St Paul called the love of money 'the root of all evil' (*1 Tim.* 6:10). The history of the church is full of mournful proofs, that it is one of the choicest weapons of Satan for corrupting and spoiling professors of religion. Gehazi, Ananias and Sapphira are names which naturally occur to our minds. But of all proofs, there is none so melancholy as the one before us. For money a chosen apostle sold the best and most loving of Masters! For money Judas Iscariot betrayed Christ!

Let us watch and pray against the love of money. It is a subtle disease, and often far nearer to us than we suppose. A poor man is just as liable to it as a rich man. It is possible to love money without having it, and it is possible to have it without loving it. Let us be 'content with such things as we have' (*Heb.* 13:5). We never know what we might do if we became suddenly rich. It is a striking fact, that there is only one prayer in all the book of Proverbs, and that one of the three petitions in that prayer, is the wise request,—'Give me neither poverty nor riches' (*Prov.* 30:8).

We see, lastly, in these verses, *the close connection between our Lord Jesus Christ's death and the feast of the passover.* Four times we are reminded here that the evening before his crucifixion was the time of the great Jewish feast. It was 'the day when the passover must be killed.'

We cannot doubt that the time of our Lord's crucifixion was over-ruled by God. His perfect wisdom and controlling power arranged that the Lamb of God should die, at the very time when the passover lamb was being slain. The death of Christ was the fulfilment of the passover. He was the true sacrifice to which every passover lamb had been pointing for fifteen hundred years. What the death of the lamb had been to Israel in Egypt, his death was to be to sinners all over the world. The safety which the blood of the passover lamb had provided for Israel, his blood was to provide far more abundantly for all that believed in him.

Let us never forget the sacrificial character of Christ's death. Let us reject with abhorrence the modern notion that it was nothing more than a mighty instance of self-sacrifice and self-denial. It was this no doubt;—but it was something far higher, deeper, and more important than this. It was a propitiation for the sins of the world. It was an atonement for man's transgression. It was the killing of the true passover, through whose death destruction is warded off from sinners believing on him. 'Christ our passover,' says St Paul, 'is sacrificed for us' (*1 Cor.* 5:7). Let us grasp that truth firmly and never let it go.

Notes—Luke 22:1-13

1.—[*Which is called the passover.*] Let it be noted that this expression shows that St Luke wrote his Gospel specially for the benefit of the Gentiles. Such an explanatory phrase as this would not have been used, if it had been written for the Jews.

2.—[*Chief priests and scribes sought how, etc.*] Burkitt remarks on this verse, 'As general councils have erred, and may err fundamentally, both in matter of doctrine and practice, so did this general council at Jerusalem, consisting of chief priests, doctors and elders, with the high priest for their president.'

[*Feared the people.*] The dread of public opinion is curiously shown here, as well as in the famous case of Herod desiring to kill John the Baptist, and yet afraid. Well-directed public opinion is one of God's most powerful instruments for controlling tyrants and oppressors, and keeping the world in order.

3.—[*Then entered Satan into Judas.*] Calvin remarks on this expression, 'Though Satan drives us every day to crime, and reigns in us, when he hurries us into a course of extraordinary wickedness; yet he is said to enter into the reprobate when he takes possession of all their senses, over-throws the fear of God, extinguishes the light of reason, and destroys every feeling of shame.'

4.—[*Captains.*] These were not Roman officers. They were commanders of the Jewish guard of the temple.

5.—[*To give him money.*] Quesnel remarks, 'It is avarice and the desire of earthly riches, which generally lays open the hearts of ecclesiastical persons to the devil, as it did that of the apostle. They deliver up the key of their hearts when they deliver up themselves to this passion.'

6.—[*He promised.*] The Greek word so rendered, is translated in every other place where it is used in the New Testament, 'thank,' or 'confess.' Hammond thinks that it indicates 'promising with great profes-sions of thankfulness and gratitude.'

7.—[*The day ... when the passover must be killed.*] There is a difficulty here which has occasioned much speculation among commentators.

The difficulty is this. Our Lord appears to have eaten the passover one day in the week, and the Jews his enemies to have eaten it on another. He ate the passover on Thursday evening, while we are distinctly told that the next morning early 'they went not into the judgment hall, lest they should be defiled, but that they might eat the passover' (*John* 18:28). The law was distinct that the passover was to be killed the evening of the fourteenth day, and eaten that night. Why then did our Lord and the chief priests and scribes not eat the passover at the same time? How is this to be explained?

1. Some think that our Lord kept the passover on the right and lawful day, but the Jews on the wrong one. They think that the Jews kept it on the wrong day, because of some tradition they had adopted, or because their time, on the lawful night, was

entirely occupied with taking Christ pris-oner, and preparing for his trial. This last view is that of Chrysostom and Eusebius.

2. Pearce says, that 'in the days of Jesus, the number of Jews assembled to eat the passover was exceedingly great, and that from necessity they took the liberty of eating the passover on any hour before the second evening, or fifteenth day.'

I offer no opinion on the difficulty beyond the two following remarks.

For one thing, I think it noteworthy that at the original appointment of the passover, the command is distinct to *kill* the lamb in the evening, but not equally distinct to *eat* it immediately. On the contrary, it is only said 'they shall eat the flesh in that night' (*Exod.* 12:8). May it not therefore be pos-sible, that when the chief priests would not go into the judgment hall at the 'early hour,' mentioned by St John, they seized the opportunity to eat the passover, before the day broke, and so kept within the letter of the law?—Our Lord would then, in that case, have eaten the passover at the begin-ning of the night, and his enemies at the end of it.

For another thing, I venture to suggest, that in the passover, as well as in other things, it is highly probable that great irregularities had crept in among the Jews, and that the letter of the law was not strictly observed, but infringed in many things, on the authority of rabbinical traditions. That our Lord kept the passover at the right day and hour, I feel no doubt. I see much force in the Greek word, 'when the passover *must* be killed.' But that his enemies may have been less strict in their time of keeping it, I think highly probable.

10.—[*There shall a man meet you, etc.*] There is difference of opinion among com-mentators about this man. Some think that he was a friend and disciple of our Lord, and that he knew well what Peter and John meant, when they spoke of the 'Master.' Others think that he was an entire stranger, and that the ease with which he received the disciples and made all the arrangements, may be accounted for by the fact, that the inhabitants of Jerusalem were accustomed to receive strange Jews, and accommodate them at the time of the passover feast. The latter view seems perhaps the more probable of the two.

Here, as in other places, we ought to note our Lord's perfect knowledge. He mentions a number of circumstances in this and the following verses, with as much minuteness and precision as if the whole transaction had been previously arranged. And yet the disciples found things exactly as he had said to them.

[*Bearing a pitcher of water.*] Some writers see much significance in this pitcher of water, and remind us of the many occasions where mercies are described in Scripture as having befallen some in connection with water, and hint that there is here an allusion to the water of baptism introducing us to the Lord's supper! I cannot see anything in the circumstance beyond a simple fact designating the man and marking him out to the disciples.

13.—[*They made ready the passover.*] We may suppose that the following things were required, in order to make ready,—the lamb, the wine, the bitter herbs and the unleavened bread. These things being procured and placed in order, the upper room was ready.

LUKE 22:14-23

14 And when the hour was come, he sat down, and the twelve apostles with him.

15 And he said unto them, With desire I have desired to eat this passover with you before I suffer.

16 For I say unto you, I will not any more eat thereof, until it be fulfilled in the kingdom of God.

17 And he took the cup, and gave thanks, and said, Take this, and divide *it* among yourselves:

18 For I say unto you, I will not drink of the fruit of the vine, until the kingdom of God shall come.

19 And he took bread, and gave thanks, and brake *it*, and gave unto them, saying, This is my body, which is given for you: this do in remembrance of me.

20 Likewise also the cup after supper, saying, This cup *is* the new testament in my blood, which is shed for you.

21 But, behold, the hand of him that betrayeth me *is* with me on the table.

22 And truly the Son of man goeth, as it was determined: but woe unto that man by whom he is betrayed!

23 And they began to enquire among themselves, which of them it was that should do this thing.

T HESE verses contain St Luke's account of the institution of the Lord's supper. It is a passage which every true Christian will always read with deep interest. How wonderful it seems that an ordinance, so beautifully simple at its first appointment, should have been obscured and mystified by man's inventions! What a painful proof it is of human corruption, that some of the bitterest controversies which have disturbed the church, have been concerning the table of the Lord! Great indeed is the ingenuity of man, in perverting God's gifts! The ordinance that should have been for his wealth is too often made an occasion of falling.

We should notice, for one thing, in these verses, that *the principal object of the Lord's supper was to remind Christians of Christ's death for sinners*. In appointing the Lord's supper, Jesus distinctly tells his disciples that they were to do what they did, 'in remembrance of him.' In one word the Lord's supper is not a sacrifice. It is eminently a commemorative ordinance.

The bread that the believer eats, at the Lord's table, is intended to remind him of Christ's body given to death on the cross for his sins. The wine that he drinks is intended to remind him of Christ's blood shed to make atonement for his transgressions. The whole ordinance was meant to keep fresh in his memory the sacrifice of Christ on the cross, and the satisfaction which that sacrifice made for the sin of the world. The two elements of bread and wine were intended to preach Christ crucified as our substitute under lively emblems. They were to be a visible sermon, appealing to the believer's senses, and teaching the old foundation truth of the gospel, that Christ's death on the cross is the life of man's soul.

We shall do well to keep steadily in view this simple view of the Lord's supper. That a special blessing is attached to a worthy use of it, as well to the worthy use of every ordinance appointed by Christ, there is of course no doubt. But that there is any other means by which Christians can eat Christ's body, and drink Christ's blood excepting faith, we must always steadily deny. He that comes to the Lord's table with faith in Christ, may confidently expect to have his faith increased by receiving the bread and wine. But he that comes without faith has no right to expect a blessing. Empty he comes to the ordinance and empty he will go away.

The less mystery and obscurity we attach to the Lord's supper, the better will it be for our souls. We should reject with abhorrence the unscriptural notion that there is any oblation or sacrifice in it,—that the substance of the bread and wine is at all changed,—or that the mere formal act of receiving the sacrament can do any good to the soul. We should cling firmly to the great principle laid down at its institution, that it is eminently a *commemorative* ordinance, and that reception of it without faith and a thankful remembrance of Christ's death can do us no good. The words of the Church Catechism are wise and true: 'It was ordained for the continual remembrance of the sacrifice of the death of Christ.'—The declaration of the Articles is clear and distinct: 'The means whereby the body of Christ is received and taken in the supper is faith.'—The exhortation of the Prayer Book points out the only way in which we can feed on Christ: 'Feed on him in your hearts by faith with thanksgiving.'—Last, but not least, the caution of the Homily is most instructive: 'Let us take heed lest of the memory it be made a sacrifice.'

We should notice, for another thing, in these verses, that *the observance of the Lord's supper is a duty binding on all true Christians.* The words of our Lord on this point are direct and emphatic:—'Do this in remembrance of me.' To suppose, as some do, that these words are only an injunction to the apostles and all ministers to administer the Lord's supper to others, is a thoroughly unsatisfactory interpretation. The obvious sense of the words is a general precept to all disciples.

The command before us is overlooked to a fearful extent. Myriads of members of Christian churches never go to the Lord's table. They would be ashamed perhaps to be known as open breakers of the Ten Commandments. Yet they are not ashamed of breaking a plain command of Christ! They appear to think there is no great sin in not being communicants. They seem utterly unconscious that if they had lived in the days of the apostles they would not have been reckoned Christians at all.

The subject no doubt is one on which we must beware of mistakes. It is not, of course, to be desired that every baptized person should receive the Lord's supper as a mere matter of form. It is an ordinance which was intended for the living and not for the dead in sins. But when we see vast numbers of church-goers never going to the Lord's table, and no-wise ashamed of their neglect of the sacrament, it is clear that there is something very wrong in the state of the churches. It is a sign either of widespread ignorance, or of callous indifference to a divine precept. When such multitudes of baptized persons habitually break a command of Christ, we cannot doubt that Christ is displeased.

What are we doing ourselves? This, after all, is the point that concerns us. Do we stay away from the Lord's supper under a vague notion that there is no great necessity for receiving it? If we hold such an opinion, the sooner we give it up the better. A plain precept of God's own Son, is not to be trifled with in this way.—Do we stay away from the Lord's supper because we are not fit to be communicants? If we do, let us thoroughly understand that we are not fit to die. Unfit for the Lord's table, we are unfit for heaven, unprepared for the judgment day, and not ready to meet God! Surely this is a most serious state of things. But the words before us are clear and explicit. Christ gives us a plain command. If we wilfully disobey it, we are in danger of ruining our souls. If we are not fit to obey it, we ought to repent without delay.

Let us notice, lastly, *who were the communicants at the first appointment of the Lord's supper.* They were not all holy. They were not all believers. St Luke informs us that the traitor, Judas Iscariot, was one of them. The words of our Lord admit of no other fair interpretation. 'Behold,' he says, 'the hand of him that betrayeth me is with me on the table.'

The lesson of these words is deeply important. They show us that we must not regard all communicants as true believers and sincere servants of Christ. The evil and good will be found side by side even at the Lord's supper. No discipline can possibly prevent it.—They show us furthermore that it is foolish to stay away from the Lord's supper because some communicants are unconverted, or to leave a church because some of its members are unsound. The wheat and the tares will grow together until the harvest. Our Lord himself tolerated a Judas at the first communion that ever took place.

The servant of God must not pretend to be more exclusive than his Master. Let him see to his own heart, and leave others to answer for themselves to God.

And now, if we are not communicants, let us ask ourselves, as we leave this passage, 'Why are we not? What satisfactory reason can we possibly give for neglecting a plain command of Christ?' May we never rest, till we have looked this inquiry in the face! If we are communicants, let us take heed that we receive the sacrament worthily. 'The sacraments have a wholesome effect and operation in those only who worthily receive them.' Let us often enquire whether we repent, and believe, and strive to live holy lives. So living, we need not be afraid to eat of that bread and drink of that cup, which the Lord has commanded to be received.

Notes—Luke 22:14-23

14.—[*The twelve apostles with him.*] It is clear from this expression that at this time Judas Iscariot was one of the company.

15.—[*With desire I have desired, etc.*] This is a Hebrew form of speech signifying 'I have desired exceedingly.' The reason of our Lord's great desire is not distinctly stated, and we are left to conjecture it. Some refer it to the whole work of redemption which he was about to accomplish that week, and the strong desire which he felt to accomplish it.—Others refer it to the institution of the Lord's supper, and the affectionate desire which our Lord felt to leave this parting memorial of himself among his disciples, before he died.

[*Before I suffer.*] Alford remarks that this is the only place in the Gospels where this absolute use of the word 'suffered' is found. It is like the expression in the Apostles' Creed, 'he suffered.' The word is elsewhere found in some such active form as 'he suffered these things, etc.'

16.—[*Until it be fulfilled, etc.*] The meaning of this expression is that our Lord 'would never eat of the passover again.' Macknight observes, 'The particle "until," both here and in the eighteenth verse, does not imply that after the accomplishment of

the salvation of men our Lord was to eat the passover. It is a Hebrew form of expression, signifying that the thing mentioned was no more to be done for ever. So it is said in Samuel (1 Sam. 15:35), "Samuel came no more to see Saul until the day of his death." That is he saw him no more at all.'

17.—[*He took the cup, etc.*] Let it be noted that the action described in this and the following verse took place in the passover feast, and that the appointment of the Lord's supper does not begin till the nineteenth verse. The meaning, as before said, appears to be 'that our Lord's days of eating and drinking with his disciples were coming to an end.' He was about to be taken from them, and to drink the cup of thanksgiving with them for the last time.

19.—[*This is my body.*] It is almost needless to remark that the Protestant view of these words is the only satisfactory one: 'This *represents* and is an emblem of my body.' To a Jewish ear the expression would be simple and intelligible. There is no word in the Syriac or Hebrew which expresses, to 'signify,' or 'represent.' See Genesis 40:12; Daniel 7:24; Revelation 1:20; John 15:1-5.

[*Given for you.*] It may be asked by whom and to what was our Lord's body given? It was given by his own free will and choice, as well as by God the Father's love, to suffering, to death, and to the grave, on behalf of a world of sinners, to procure eternal life for as many as would believe on him.

[*This do.*] The Roman Catholics struggle hard to make out that these words mean 'Offer up this sacrifice,' and that the words were specially intended to be confined to priests consecrating the bread and wine, and offering it up as a sacrifice in the mass. The idea will not bear calm examination. The natural meaning of the words is a command addressed to all disciples. 'Practise this,'—'Do what I have just showed you,'—'Keep up the ordinance I have just appointed,'—'Break, take, eat this bread in all ages, in remembrance of me.'

20.—[*This cup is the new testament.*] Here, as well as in the former verse, the meaning is, 'This cup represents the new covenant, which is to be sealed and ratified with my blood,—which blood is shed, or going to be shed for you.' There is a peculiarity in the Greek words, which can only be conveyed to an English reader by a paraphrase.

It is clear that a 'cup' is not literally a 'testament' or covenant. The Roman Catholic who contends that in the former verse, where our Lord says, 'this is my body,' he meant 'this is my literal body, really and truly,' will find it hard to explain our Lord's meaning here.—The Protestant view that in both cases our Lord meant 'this bread *represents* my body,' and 'this cup *represents* the new covenant which is ratified by my blood,' is the only rational and satisfactory view.

If our Lord had really meant that what he gave his disciples was literally his 'blood,' it seems impossible to understand the calmness with which they received the announcement. They were all Jews, and as Jews had all been taught from their infancy that to eat blood was a great sin. They evidently understood the words as Protestants do now (*Lev.* 3:17; 7:26).

21.—[*The hand ... is with me on the table.*] These words make it clear and plain that Judas Iscariot was one of those who received the Lord's supper. No other honest conclusion seems possible. If so, according to Roman Catholics, Judas must actually have eaten Christ's body, and drank Christ's blood! And yet he was a son of perdition!

To keep away from the Lord's table at some particular church, because some of the communicants live inconsistent lives, is a proceeding which cannot be reconciled with the Scripture before us. The expression in Corinthians, which is often quoted on the subject, 'with such an one no not to eat' (*1 Cor.* 5:11), has no reference to the Lord's supper at all.

Burkitt remarks, 'Nothing is more ordinary than for unholy persons to press into the holy ordinances of God, which they have no right to. Yet their presence pollutes the ordinance only to themselves.'

22.—[*Goeth, as it was determined; but woe, etc.*] Let us note in this verse that though the wickedness of Judas was foreknown, and foreseen, and permitted by God in his infinite wisdom,—yet Judas was not the less guilty in God's sight. God's foreknowledge does not destroy man's responsibility, or justify man in going on still in wickedness, under the excuse that he cannot help sinning. Nothing can happen, in heaven or in earth, without God's knowledge and permission. But sinners are always addressed by God as responsible, and as free agents.

Augustine, quoted by Ford, remarks, that 'God is said to will things, in the way of permission, which he does not will in the way of approbation.'

Bishop Hall says, 'It is the greatest praise of God's wisdom that he can turn the sins of man to his own glory.'

LUKE 22:24-30

24 And there was also a strife among them, which of them should be accounted the greatest.

25 And he said unto them, The kings of the Gentiles exercise lordship over them; and they that exercise authority upon them are called benefactors.

26 But ye *shall* not *be* so: but he that is greatest among you, let him be as the younger; and he that is chief, as he that doth serve.

27 For whether *is* greater, he that sitteth at meat, or he that serveth? *is* not he that sitteth at meat? but I am among you as he that serveth.

28 Ye are they which have continued with me in my temptations.

29 And I appoint unto you a kingdom, as my Father hath appointed unto me;

30 That ye may eat and drink at my table in my kingdom, and sit on thrones judging the twelve tribes of Israel.

LET us observe, in this passage, *how firmly pride and love of pre-eminence can stick to the hearts of good men.* We are told, that 'There was a strife among the disciples, which of them should be accounted the greatest.' The strife was one which had been rebuked by our Lord on a former occasion. The ordinance which the disciples had just been receiving, and the circumstances under which they were assembled, made the strife peculiarly unseemly. And yet at this very season, the last quiet time they could spend with their Master before his death, this little flock begins a contention who should be the greatest! Such is the heart of man, ever weak, ever deceitful, ever ready, even at its best times, to turn aside to what is evil.

The sin before us is a very old one. Ambition, self-esteem, and self-conceit lie deep at the bottom of all men's hearts, and often in the hearts where they are least suspected. Thousands fancy that they are humble, who cannot bear to see an equal more honoured and favoured than themselves. Few indeed can be found who rejoice heartily in a neighbour's promotion over their own heads. The quantity of envy and jealousy in the world is a glaring proof of the prevalence of pride. Men would not envy a brother's advancement, if they had not a secret thought that their own merit was greater than his.

Let us live on our guard against this sore disease, if we make any profession of serving Christ. The harm that it has done to the church of Christ is far beyond calculation. Let us learn to take pleasure in the prosperity of others, and to be content with the lowest place for ourselves. The rule given to the Philippians should be often before our eyes;—'In lowliness of mind let each esteem other better than themselves.' The example of John the Baptist is a bright instance of the spirit at which we should aim. He said of our Lord, 'he must increase, but I must decrease' (*Phil.* 2:3; *John* 3:30).

Let us observe, secondly, in this passage, *the striking account which our Lord gives of true Christian greatness.* He tells his disciples that the worldly standard of greatness was the exercise of lordship and authority. 'But ye,' he says, 'shall not be so. He that is greatest among you, let him be as the younger; and he that is chief, as he that doth serve.' And then he enforces this principle by the mighty fact of his own example. 'I am among you as he that serveth.'

Usefulness in the world and church,—a humble readiness to do anything, and put our hands to any good work,—a cheerful willingness to fill any post, however lowly, and discharge any office, however unpleasant, if we can only promote happiness and holiness on earth,—these are the true tests of Christian greatness. The hero in Christ's army is not the man who has rank, and title, and dignity, and chariots, and horsemen, and fifty men to run before him. It is the man who looks not on his own things, but the things of others. It is the man who is kind to all, tender to all, thoughtful for all, with a hand to help all, and a heart to feel for all. It is the man who spends and is spent to make the vice and misery of the world less, to bind up the broken-hearted, to befriend the friendless, to cheer the sorrowful, to enlighten the ignorant, and to raise the poor. This is the truly great man in the eyes of God. The world may ridicule his labours and deny the sincerity of his motives. But while the world is sneering, God is pleased. This is the man who is walking most closely in the steps of Christ.

Let us follow after greatness of this sort, if we desire to prove ourselves Christ's servants. Let us not be content with clear head-knowledge, and loud lip-profession, and keen insight into controversy, and fervent zeal for the interests of our own party. Let us see that we minister to the wants of a sin-burdened world, and do good to bodies and souls. Blessed be God! the greatness which Christ commended is within the reach of all. All have not learning, or gifts, or money. But all can minister to the happiness of those around them, by passive or by active graces. All can be useful, and all can be kind. There is a grand reality in constant kindness. It makes the men of the world think.

Let us observe, thirdly, in this passage, *our Lord's gracious commendation of his disciples*. He said to them, 'Ye are they which have continued with me in my temptations.'

There is something very striking in these words of praise. We know the weakness and infirmity of our Lord's disciples during the whole period of his earthly ministry. We find him frequently reproving their ignorance and want of faith. He knew full well that within a few hours they were all going to forsake him. But here we find him graciously dwelling on one good point in their conduct, and holding it up to the perpetual notice of his church. They had been faithful to their Master, notwithstanding all their faults. Their hearts had been right, whatever had been their mistakes. They had clung to him in the day of his humiliation, when the great and noble were against him. They had 'continued with him in his temptations.'

Let us rest our souls on the comfortable thought that the mind of Christ is always the same. If we are true believers, let us know that he looks at our graces more than at our faults, that he pities our infirmities, and that he will not deal with us according to our sins. Never had master such poor, weak servants as believers are to Christ, but never had servants such a compassionate and tender master as Christ is to believers! Surely we cannot love him too well. We may come short in many things. We may fail in knowledge, and courage, and faith, and patience. We may stumble many times. But one thing let us always do. Let us love the Lord Jesus with heart, and soul, and mind, and strength. Whatever others do, let us 'continue with him,' and cleave to him with purpose of heart. Happy is he who can say with Peter, however humbled and ashamed, 'Lord, thou knowest that I love thee' (*John* 21:15).

Let us observe, lastly, *what a glorious promise our Lord holds out to his faithful disciples.* He says, 'I appoint unto you a kingdom, as my Father hath appointed unto me; that ye may eat and drink at my table in my kingdom, and sit on thrones judging the twelve tribes of Israel.'

These words were our Lord's parting legacy to his little flock. He knew that in a few hours his ministry among them would be ended. He winds it up by a wonderful declaration of good things laid up in store for them. We may not perhaps see the full meaning of every part of the promise. Enough for us to know that our Lord promised his eleven faithful ones, glory, honour, and rewards, far exceeding anything they had done for him. They had gone a little way with him, like Barzillai with David, and done a little for him. He assures them that they shall have in another world a recompense worthy of a king.

Let us leave the whole passage with the cheering thought that the wages which Christ will give to his believing people will be far out of proportion to anything they have done for him. Their tears will be found in his bottle. Their least desires to do good will be found recorded. Their weakest efforts to glorify him will be found written in his book of remembrance. Not a cup of cold water shall miss its reward.

Notes—Luke 22:24-30

24.—[*There was a strife among them, etc.*] Let it be noted that this is the second instance of contention for pre-eminence among the apostles, recorded by St Luke. On the first occasion it was a 'reasoning' (*Luke* 9:46); here it was a 'strife.'

It is impossible to reconcile this twice-recorded contention with the Roman Catholic theory, that Peter was the recognized head of the apostles. Neither here nor elsewhere is there any intimation of such primacy being known in our Lord's times!

If our Lord had really appointed Peter the chief of the apostles, the strife before us in this passage could not have taken place.

25.—[*Benefactors.*] The Greek word so translated ('euergetes'), was a title often assumed by heathen monarchs, who prided themselves on being special benefactors of their subjects.—One of the Ptolemies, king of Egypt, was so called.

26.—[*He that is greatest.*] This expression here may perhaps mean 'greatest in age,' the oldest. It is so translated in Romans

9:12. In the following verse it clearly means 'greater in dignity.'

27.—[*As he that serveth.*] There is an evident reference here to the act of washing the disciples' feet, recorded by St John, which had taken place a very short time before the conversation we are now considering. At the same time the expression describes the whole tenor of our Lord's course on earth. 'He took on him the form of a servant.' 'He came not to be ministered to, but to minister.'

In making a practical use of our Lord's words in this place, we must carefully draw a distinction between a genuine, and a self-imposed, voluntary, ostentatious humility. It would be absurd and profane to compare the Pope's annual practice of publicly washing the feet of a certain number of poor people with the 'serving' to which our Lord refers. Cornelius à Lapide, in his commentary on the passage before us, gives a melancholy list of instances of self-imposed humility.

28.—[*In my temptations.*] This expression probably includes the whole course of our Lord's earthly ministry. It was a period of almost uninterrupted trial and suffering. It would be manifestly impossible to confine the word to the special temptations of Satan to which our Lord was subjected.

29.—[*I appoint.*] The Greek word so rendered seems to bear a stronger sense than our translators have put upon it. It might be translated, 'I appoint unto you by covenant.' It is the root of the words used in the well-known passage in Hebrews: 'Where a *testament* is, there must be the death of the *testator*' (*Heb.* 9:16).

[*A kingdom.*] The meaning of this phrase must probably not be pressed too closely. It signifies honour, dignity, reward, majesty, of which a king's position in this world furnishes the only emblem. Christ will have a real kingdom, covenanted to him from all eternity. In that kingdom of Christ, the apostles will have a principal place. They will be like kings within a kingdom.

30.—[*Eat and drink at my table.*] This expression admits of two interpretations. We must either interpret it literally, as referring to the marriage supper of the Lamb, when the Lamb's wife shall have made herself ready (*Rev.* 19:7-9), to which our Lord seems to refer in Matthew 26:29. Or else we must interpret it figuratively, as signifying that complete satisfaction of every want, which the saints in glory shall enjoy, when they shall 'awake up after Christ's likeness and be satisfied.'

[*Sit on thrones judging ... Israel.*] This remarkable expression is differently interpreted by commentators.

1. Some think, with Brentius, that our Lord only meant that the doctrine of the gospel preached by the apostles, should be the rule by which not only Israel, but all the church should be judged at the last day.

2. Some think, with Gualter, that the words mean that the apostles shall rise in the judgment and condemn the Jews at the last day, because they believed the gospel, while Israel remained unbelieving. Like the Ninevites and the Queen of Sheba, they shall deprive the Jews of all excuse.

3. Some think that the word 'judging,' means that the apostles shall literally be assessors with Christ in the judgment day, just as St Paul says to the Corinthians, 'we shall judge angels' (*1 Cor.* 6:3).

4. Some think that the word 'judging,' means that the apostles shall have a pre-eminent place in the government of Israel, after Christ has come again and the Jews have been restored to their own land. It is clear that the word 'judge' in many places in the Bible, means nothing more than 'ruling or governing,' and has no reference to passing a judicial sentence.

I cannot pretend to speak decidedly on a question so mysterious as this. I am however inclined to think, that the last view of the four is the most probable one. The following quotations given by Ford, throw light on this view, and are worth reading.

Bishop Smalridge says, 'However difficult it may be to determine wisely the full meaning of these expressions, yet certainly we may rationally infer from them, that there are some particular marks of glory, with which the apostles of our Lord will be honoured above other Christians.'

Mede says, 'Whatsoever is meant by the reward, it is plain there is some peculiar and eminent degree of glory promised here to the apostles, which shall not be common to others with them;—firstly, because it is the reward of their proper and peculiar service of Christ;—secondly, because these twelve thrones, in regard of their number, can befit no more but these twelve;—thirdly, because supposing the twelve tribes of Israel to be in a condition of bliss, it must needs be that those who sit on twelve thrones to judge or govern them, must be in a higher degree of dignity than those over whom they are set.'

Let us add to this, that we are told that on the twelve foundations of the mystical city described in Revelation, there were the names of the 'twelve apostles of the Lamb' (*Rev.* 21:14).

[*Twelve tribes of Israel.*] Let it be noted, that the 'twelve tribes' are four times mentioned in the New Testament, here, and in Matthew 19:28; Acts 26:7; and James 1:1. It is clear that although the ten tribes never came back from captivity, they were regarded in the New Testament time as still existing, distinct and separate, and not lost and mingled among other nations. We need not therefore doubt that the ten tribes exist now somewhere on the face of the globe, and in due time will be brought forth and shown to the world.

LUKE 22:31-38

31 And the Lord said, Simon, Simon, behold, Satan hath desired *to have* you, that he may sift *you* as wheat:

32 But I have prayed for thee, that thy faith fail not: and when thou art converted, strengthen thy brethren.

33 And he said unto him, Lord, I am ready to go with thee, both into prison, and to death.

34 And he said, I tell thee, Peter, the cock shall not crow this day, before that thou shalt thrice deny that thou knowest me.

35 And he said unto them, When I sent you without purse, and scrip, and shoes, lacked ye any thing? And they said, Nothing.

36 Then said he unto them, But now, he that hath a purse, let him take *it*, and likewise *his* scrip: and he that hath no sword, let him sell his garment, and buy one.

37 For I say unto you, that this that is written must yet be accomplished in me, And he was reckoned among the transgressors: for the things concerning me have an end.

38 And they said, Lord, behold, here *are* two swords. And he said unto them, It is enough.

WE learn, from these verses, *what a fearful enemy the devil is to believers.* We read that 'the Lord said, Simon, Simon, Satan hath desired to have you, that he may sift you as wheat.' He was near Christ's flock, though they saw him not. He was longing to compass their ruin, though they knew it not. The wolf does not crave the blood of the lamb more than the devil desires the destruction of souls.

The personality, activity, and power of the devil are not sufficiently thought of by Christians. This is he who brought sin into the world at the beginning, by tempting Eve. This is he who is described in the book of Job as 'going to and fro in the earth, and walking up and down in it.' This is he whom our Lord calls 'the prince of this world,' a 'murderer' and a 'liar.' This is he whom Peter compares to a 'roaring lion, seeking whom he may devour.' This is he whom John speaks of as 'the accuser of the brethren.' This is he who is ever working evil in the churches of Christ, catching away good seed from the hearts of hearers, sowing tares amidst the wheat, stirring up persecutions, suggesting false doctrines, and fomenting divisions. The world is a snare to the believer. The flesh is a burden and a clog. But there is no enemy so dangerous as that restless, invisible, experienced enemy, the devil.

If we believe the Bible, let us not be ashamed to believe that there is a devil. It is an awful proof of the hardness and blindness of unconverted men, that they can jest and speak lightly of Satan.

If we profess to have any real religion, let us be on our guard against the devil's devices. The enemy who overthrew David and Peter, and assaulted Christ himself, is not an enemy to be despised. He is very subtle. He has studied the heart of man for six thousand years. He can approach us under the garb of an 'angel of light.' We have need to watch and pray, and put on the whole armour of God. It is a blessed promise, that if we resist him he will flee from us. It is a still more blessed thought, that when the Lord comes, he will bruise Satan under our feet, and bind him in chains (*James* 4:7; *Rom.* 16:20).

We learn, secondly, in these verses, *one great secret of a believer's perseverance in the faith*. We read that our Lord said to Peter, 'I have prayed for thee, that thy faith fail not.' It was owing to Christ's intercession that Peter did not entirely fall away.

The continued existence of grace in a believer's heart is a great standing miracle. His enemies are so mighty, and his strength is so small, the world is so full of snares, and his heart is so weak, that it seems at first sight impossible for him to reach heaven. The passage before us explains his safety. He has a mighty Friend at the right hand of God, who ever lives to make intercession for him. There is a watchful Advocate, who is daily pleading for him, seeing all his daily necessities, and obtaining daily supplies of mercy and grace for his soul. His grace never altogether dies, because Christ always lives to intercede (*Heb.* 7:25).

If we are true Christians, we shall find it essential to our comfort in religion to have clear views of Christ's priestly office and intercession. Christ lives, and therefore our faith shall not fail. Let us beware of regarding Jesus only as one who died for us. Let us never forget that he is alive for evermore. St Paul bids us specially remember that he is risen again, and is at the right hand of God, and also maketh intercession for us (*Rom.* 8:34). The work that he does for his people is not yet over. He is still appearing in the presence of God for them and doing for their souls what he did for Peter. His present life for them is just as important as his death on the cross eighteen hundred years ago. Christ lives, and therefore true Christians 'shall live also.'

We learn, thirdly, from these verses, *the duty incumbent on all believers who receive special mercies from Christ*. We read that our Lord said to Peter, 'When thou art converted, strengthen thy brethren.'

It is one of God's peculiar attributes, that he can bring good out of evil. He can cause the weaknesses and infirmities of some members of his church to work together for the benefit of the whole body of his people. He can make the fall of a disciple the means of fitting him to be the strengthener and upholder of others.—Have we ever fallen, and by Christ's mercy been raised to newness of life? Then surely we are just the men who ought to deal gently with our brethren. We should tell them from our own experience what an evil and bitter thing is sin. We should caution them against trifling with temptation. We should warn them against pride, and presumption, and neglect of prayer. We should tell them of Christ's grace and compassion, if they have fallen. Above all, we should deal with them humbly and meekly, remembering what we ourselves have gone through.

Well would it be for the church of Christ, if Christians were more ready to good works of this kind! There are only too many believers who in conference add nothing to their brethren. They seem to have no Saviour to tell of, and no story of grace to report. They chill the hearts of those they meet, rather than warm them. They weaken rather than strengthen. These things ought not so to be. The words of the apostle ought to sink down into our minds, 'Having received mercy we faint not. We believe, and therefore we speak' (*2 Cor.* 4:1, 13).

We learn, lastly, from these verses, that *the servant of Christ ought to use all reasonable means in doing his Master's work.* We read that our Lord said to his disciples, 'He that hath a purse, let him take it, and likewise his scrip: and he that hath no sword, let him sell his garment, and buy one.'

It is safest to take these remarkable words in a proverbial sense. They apply to the whole period of time between our Lord's first and second advents. Until our Lord comes again, believers are to make a diligent use of all the faculties which God has implanted in them. They are not to expect miracles to be worked, in order to save them trouble. They are not to expect bread to fall into their mouths, if they will not work for it. They are not to expect difficulties to be surmounted, and enemies to be overcome, if they will not wrestle, and struggle, and take pains. They are to remember that it is 'the hand of the diligent which maketh rich' (*Prov.* 10:4).

We shall do well to lay to heart our Lord's words in this place, and to act habitually on the principle which they contain. Let us labour, and toil, and give, and speak, and act, and write for Christ, as if all depended on our exertions. And yet let us never forget that success depends entirely on God's blessing! To expect success by our own 'purse' and 'sword' is pride and self-righteousness. But to expect success without the 'purse and sword' is presumption and fanaticism. Let us do as Jacob did when he met his brother Esau. He used all innocent means to conciliate and appease him. But when he had done all, he spent all night in prayer (*Gen.* 32:1-24).

Notes—Luke 22:31-38

31.—[*Simon, Simon.*] The repetition of Simon's name implies solemnity and importance in the statement about to be made, and deep concern on behalf of Simon's soul. It is like the address to Martha, when she was 'careful about many things,' and to Saul, when he was persecuting disciples (*Luke* 10:41; *Acts* 9:4).

Our Lord's addressing Peter in this place, seems to make it probable that Peter was one of those who were most forward in contending for the pre-eminence in the verses preceding those we are now considering. Our Lord tells him that while he is seeking greatness, he is on the very point of making a grievous fall.

[*Satan hath desired to have you.*] There is something very awful in this expression. It shows us that the devil is often 'desiring' to accomplish our ruin, and striving to accomplish it, while we know nothing of his doings, because he is invisible. On the other hand, there is some comfort in the expression. It teaches us that Satan can do nothing without God's permission. However great his 'desire' to do mischief, he works in chains.

The distinction should be marked between 'you' in the verse before us and 'thee' in the verse following. Satan desired to have all the apostles. Christ's intercessory prayer was specially on behalf of Peter.

[*Sift you as wheat.*] This expression signifies that Satan desired to shake, toss to and fro, and harass the apostle, just as corn is shaken to and fro when it is dressed and winnowed, to separate the grain from the chaff. It aptly describes the effect of temptation on a believer. Whatever Satan's intention may be, the result of temptation is to bring out the chaff, or infirmity of a believer, and generally in the long run to purify his soul. It was strikingly so with Peter and the other apostles in the present instance.

32.—[*I have prayed for thee.*] We need not hesitate to regard this as an example of our Lord's exercise of his office as an intercessor for his people. What he did for Peter, when Peter knew nothing of his danger, he is daily and hourly doing for all who believe on his name.

[*That thy faith fail not.*] The Greek word translated 'fail' is the root of our English word 'eclipse.' The object of our Lord's intercession was that Peter's faith might not altogether die, though for a time it might be very weak.

Let it be noted that 'faith' is the root of the whole Christian character, and the part which Satan specially labours to overthrow. In the temptation of Eve, of Peter, and of our Lord himself, the assault was in each case directed against the same point, and the object sought was to produce unbelief.

The Roman Catholic commentators, Cornelius à Lapide, Maldonatus, and Stella, endeavour to prove from the words before us, that the Roman Catholic Church, of which, they say, Peter was the head, was never to depart from the faith, and that our Lord gave a prophetical intimation of its perpetuity and fidelity. It is because of the words before us, we are told, that the Church of Rome has never fallen, while the churches of Alexandria, Constantinople, and Antioch, have gone to decay!

A more gratuitous and baseless application of Scripture it is difficult to conceive. For one thing, there is not the slightest proof that Peter was the founder or head of the Roman Church; or indeed that he was bishop of Rome at all. For another thing, the words before us apply most clearly to Peter only as an individual, and have no reference whatever to any church. Above all, the words were not spoken as indicating any special honour put upon Peter. They were meant on the contrary to teach, that Peter was about to fall more shamefully than any of the apostles, and that nothing but Christ's special intercession would save him from total ruin. The faith of all the apostles was about to prove very weak, but no one would be so near a complete eclipse of faith as Peter!

Lightfoot says, 'Certainly it was Peter's advantage, that Christ prayed for him; but it was not so much for Peter's honour, that he, beyond all others, should stand in need of such a prayer.'

Wordsworth says, 'The Roman divines say that the prayer and precept of our Lord extends to all the bishops of Rome, as St Peter's successors, and that in speaking to St Peter, our Lord spoke to them. Will they complete the parallel, and say that the bishops of Rome specially need prayer, because they deny Christ? Let them not take a part and leave the rest.'

[*When thou art converted.*] This expression is somewhat remarkable, and has occasioned difference of opinion among commentators. For one thing, the word translated 'art converted,' would be rendered more literally 'hast converted.' For another thing, to speak of an apostle like Peter being 'converted,' seems a strange saying to some. The following explanations of the expression have been given.

1. Some think that the word rendered 'converted' was not intended to bear so strong a meaning. They regard it as a Hebrew form of speech, and a kind of expletive word. They compare it to such phrases as this in the New Testament, 'Then God *turned*, and gave them up to worship the host of heaven' (*Acts* 7:42). They would then render it as Bengel does, like an adverb, 'do thou in thy turn strengthen thy brethren.'

2. Some think, with Sir Norten Knatchbull, that the word translated 'art converted,' should have been rendered in an active sense, and that it means, 'When thou hast converted thy brethren, strengthen them.'

3. Some think that the conversion here spoken of, means simply 'recovery from a fall,' and that it does not necessarily mean that first conversion to God which takes place when an unconverted person becomes a Christian. This is by far the most satisfactory interpretation of the expression. For the Greek word being rendered, 'art converted,' though an active verb, there is authority in Acts 3:19.

Burkitt remarks, 'This conversion was not from a state of sin: Peter was so converted before: but it was from an act of sin into which he should lapse and relapse.'

[*Strengthen thy brethren.*] There seems a tacit reference here to the dispute about pre-eminence, which had just taken place among the apostles. 'Instead of wasting time in wrangling about primacy, give thyself to the better work of raising up, confirming, and doing good to thy brethren. Warn the unruly. Comfort the feeble-minded. Teach all the beauty of humility. Show them by thine own sad experience the danger of pride and high thoughts.'

Most commentators think that the general tone of the Epistles of St Peter shows special marks of the effect of this command. They are pre-eminently hortatory, direct, and instructive to believers.

Alford calls attention to the fact that the Greek word for 'strengthen' in this place, is twice used by Peter in his two epistles, and the word 'steadfastness,' which is also used, is directly derived from it (*1 Pet.* 5:10; *2 Pet.* 1:12; *2 Pet.* 3:17).

I would add to this the interesting fact that it is Peter who describes the devil under the vivid figure of a 'roaring lion, walking about, and seeking whom he may devour' (*1 Pet.* 5:8).

[*Thy brethren.*] This expression probably contains a tacit reference to the dispute for pre-eminence. Peter is reminded that he must regard the other disciples, not as his inferiors, but as his 'brethren.'

33.—[*I am ready to go, etc.*] This profession was the language of a self-confident, inexperienced disciple who had not yet found out the weakness of his own faith, and the deceitfulness of his own heart. Men little know what they will do, till the time of temptation actually comes. 'Is thy servant a dog,' said Hazael, 'that he should do this great thing?' (*2 Kings* 8:13).

34.—[*Peter.*] Burgon remarks that this is the only place in which our Lord addresses Peter by this name, the name which signified 'stone.' It was surely meant to remind him how weak even the strongest disciples are.

[*Thrice deny ... knowest me.*] This, be it remembered, was a very remarkable prediction, and a striking evidence of our Lord's foreknowledge. That Peter should deny his Master at all,—that he should actually deny him that very night after receiving the Lord's supper,—that he should deny him after plain warnings, and after strong protestations that he would rather die,—and that he should deny his Master three times,—were all most improbable events. Yet they all took place!

35.—[*When I sent you, etc.*] This verse refers to the occasion when our Lord sent out the apostles two and two to preach the kingdom of God. It is evident from the expression before us, that in these first excursions our Lord exercised a miraculous superintendence over the disciples, and so ordered things that friends were raised up for them wherever they went, and they 'lacked nothing.' This was doubtless done in condescension to their inexperience and infirmity, and to enable them to attend on their work without distraction.

36.—[*But now, etc.*] The general drift of this verse is to teach that from the time of Christ's ascension into heaven, the disciples must not expect such a constant miraculous interposition of God on their behalf, as would make them independent of the use of means. On the contrary they must diligently employ all lawful and reasonable means for their support and protection. They were to 'work with their own hands,' as St Paul did at tent making. They were to have regular gatherings of money for the support of those that wanted, as the Corinthians had. They were not to despise their rights as subjects and citizens, but to use them in their own defence, as St Paul did before Lysias, and Festus, and at Philippi.

The general purport of the verse appears to be a caution against the indolent and fanatical notion that diligence in the use of means is 'carnal,' and an unlawful dependence on an arm of flesh. To my own mind the whole verse supplies an unanswerable argument against the strange notions maintained by some in the present day, who tell us that making provision for our families is wrong,—and insuring our lives is wrong,—and collecting money for religious societies is wrong,—and studying for the work of the ministry is wrong,—and taking part in civil government is wrong,—and supporting

police, standing armies, and courts of law is wrong. I respect the conscientiousness of those who maintain these opinions. But I am utterly unable to reconcile them with our Lord's language in this place.

[*A purse ... scrip ... sword.*] I regard all these three expressions as proverbial and symbolical. They contain a general lesson for the guidance of the church of Christ, until the Lord comes again. We are not to neglect human instrumentality, in doing Christ's work, or to expect Christ's blessing if we do not diligently use all lawful means within our reach.

[*He that hath no sword ... buy one.*] This expression is undoubtedly a difficult one.

1. Some think that our Lord meant literally that the disciples were to get a sword in order that the scene in the garden when Peter struck Malchus, and the miraculous healing of Malchus's ear, might take place. This explanation is eminently bald, tame, and unsatisfactory.

2. Some think, with Olshausen, that the sword which our Lord means is the 'sword of the Spirit,' the Word of God. This explanation seems far-fetched. Moreover we surely cannot suppose that the disciples had never used this 'sword of the Spirit,' before this time.

3. The most satisfactory interpretation is that which regards the whole verse as proverbial and symbolical. The words 'purse, scrip, and sword,' are not to be pressed too closely. They are parabolic expressions, indicating that a time was drawing near when all human means, of which the 'purse,' the 'scrip,' and the 'sword' are emblems, must be diligently used by the apostles. In Romans 13:4, Suicer shows that 'the sword' is evidently an emblematic expression.

This view is ably stated by Theophylact in his commentary on the passage.

Stella calls attention to the remarkable parallel between the condition of the apostles, before and after our Lord's ascension, and the condition of Israel before and after they entered Canaan. Before the Jews entered Canaan, they were miraculously fed with manna daily, and miraculously guided by the pillar of cloud and fire. From the time they entered Canaan, they were thrown upon their own exertions. It was much the same with the apostles. They were not to expect constant miracles to be worked on their behalf, from the time that Christ left the world.

37.—[*This … written … accomplished, etc.*] Let it be noted here, that when our Lord speaks of his approaching crucifixion, he does not speak of it as his 'death' merely. He specially describes it as his being 'reckoned among the transgressors.' The expression was evidently meant to remind us, that the chief end of his death was not to be an example of self-denial, but to be a substitute for us,—a sacrifice for us,—to become sin for us, and be made a curse for us.

[*The things concerning me have an end.*] This expression means, 'The work I came to do is well-nigh finished. The great sacrifice is going to be offered. I am going to leave the world, and go to my Father.' It is like the saying on the cross, 'It is finished.'

38.—[*Here are two swords … It is enough.*] The general opinion of all the best commentators on this verse appears to be correct, that the disciples did not understand aright our Lord's meaning, and that our Lord seeing their dullness of understanding, dismissed the subject he had been speaking of, and said no more about it. The disciples took his words about the sword literally. He meant them to be taken figuratively. If they could not see his meaning now, they would hereafter. At present he had said 'enough,' and for wise reasons would say no more. 'Speak no more unto me of this matter' (*Deut.* 3:26).

The idea maintained by some, that our Lord used the word 'it is enough,' ironically, is not satisfactory. It may be doubted whether our Lord ever used irony. Those who hold this view maintain that our Lord meant, 'Truly two swords are enough! This is a sufficient defence indeed!'

The Roman Catholic writers, Maldonatus and Cornelius à Lapide, interpret the two swords mentioned in this verse of the temporal and spiritual power which they claim for the Church of Rome. It is almost needless to say that the passage does not afford the least ground for the doctrine which they try to support from it. Even Stella, the Spanish Roman Catholic, is ashamed of such an interpretation, and denounces it as 'wrested and discordant with the passage.'

Chrysostom thinks, that the expression 'here are two swords,' may refer to the two sacrificial knives or swords, which the disciples had got because of the passover lamb. The explanation seems needless. In the days when our Lord was upon earth, it was common for men to carry weapons of offence and defence.

LUKE 22:39-46

39 And he came out, and went, as he was wont, to the mount of Olives; and his disciples also followed him.

40 And when he was at the place, he said unto them, Pray that ye enter not into temptation.

41 And he was withdrawn from them about a stone's cast, and kneeled down, and prayed,

42 Saying, Father, if thou be willing, remove this cup from me: nevertheless not my will, but thine, be done.

43 And there appeared an angel unto him from heaven, strengthening him.

44 And being in an agony he prayed more earnestly: and his sweat was as it were great drops of blood falling down to the ground.

45 And when he rose up from prayer, and was come to his disciples, he found them sleeping for sorrow.

46 And said unto them, Why sleep ye? rise and pray, lest ye enter into temptation.

THE verses before us contain St Luke's account of our Lord's agony in the garden. It is a passage of Scripture which we should always approach with peculiar reverence. The history which it records is one of the 'deep things of God.' While we read it, the words of Exodus should come across our minds, 'Put off thy shoes from off thy feet, for the place whereon thou standest is holy ground' (*Exod.* 3:5).

We see, firstly, in this passage, *an example of what believers ought to do in time of trouble.* The great Head of the church himself supplies the pattern. We are told that when he came to the Mount of Olives, the night before he was crucified, 'he kneeled down and prayed.'

It is a striking fact, that both the Old and New Testaments give one and the same receipt for bearing trouble. What says the book of Psalms? 'Call upon me in the day of trouble: I will deliver thee' (*Psa.* 50:15). What says the Apostle James? 'Is any afflicted? let him pray' (*James* 5:13). Prayer is the receipt which Jacob used, when he feared his brother Esau.—Prayer is the receipt which Job used when property and children were suddenly taken from him.—Prayer is the receipt which Hezekiah used when Sennacherib's threatening letter arrived. And prayer is the receipt which the Son of God himself was not ashamed to use in the days of his flesh. In the hour of his mysterious agony he 'prayed.'

Let us take care that we use our Master's remedy, if we want comfort in affliction. Whatever other means of relief we use, let us pray. The first Friend we should turn to ought to be God. The first message we should send ought to be to the throne of grace. No depression of spirits must prevent us. No crushing weight of sorrow must make us dumb. It is a prime device of Satan, to supply the afflicted man with false reasons for keeping silence before God. Let us beware of the temptation to brood sullenly over our wounds. If we can say nothing else, we can say, 'I am oppressed; undertake for me' (*Isa.* 38:14).

We see, secondly, in these verses, *what kind of prayers a believer ought to make to God in time of trouble.* Once more the Lord Jesus himself affords a model to his people. We are told that he said, 'Father, if thou be willing, remove this cup from me: nevertheless not my will, but thine, be done.' He who spake these words, we must remember, had two distinct natures in one person. He had a human will as well as a divine. When he said, 'Not my will be done,' he meant that will which he had as man, with a body, flesh and blood, like our own.

The language used by our blessed Master in this place shows exactly what should be the spirit of a believer's prayer in his distress. Like Jesus, he should tell his desires openly to his heavenly Father, and spread his wishes unreservedly before him. But like Jesus, he should do it all with an entire submission of will to the will of God. He should never forget that there may be wise and good reasons for his affliction. He should carefully qualify every petition for the removal of crosses with the saving clause, 'If thou be willing.' He should wind up all with the meek confession, 'Not my will, but thine be done.'

Submission of will like this is one of the brightest graces which can adorn the Christian character. It is one which a child of God ought to aim at in everything, if he desires to be like Christ. But at no time is such submission of will so needful as in the day of sorrow, and in nothing does it shine so brightly as in a believer's prayers for relief. He who can say from his heart, when a bitter cup is before him, 'Not my will, but thine be done,' has reached a high position in the school of God.

We see, thirdly, in these verses, *an example of the exceeding guilt and sinfulness of sin.* We are meant to learn this in Christ's agony and bloody sweat, and all the mysterious distress of body and mind, which the passage describes. The lesson at first sight may not be clear to a careless reader of the Bible. But the lesson is there.

How can we account for the deep agony which our Lord underwent in the garden? What reason can we assign for the intense suffering, both mental and bodily, which he manifestly endured? There is only one satisfactory answer. It was caused by the burden

314

of a world's imputed sin, which then began to press upon him in a peculiar manner. He had undertaken to be 'sin for us,'—to be 'made a curse for us,'—and to allow our iniquities to be laid on himself (2 *Cor.* 5:21; *Gal.* 3:13; *Isa.* 53:6). It was the enormous weight of these iniquities which made him suffer agony. It was the sense of a world's guilt pressing him down which made even the eternal Son of God sweat great drops of blood, and called from him 'strong crying and tears.' The cause of Christ's agony was man's sin (*Heb.* 5:7).

We must beware jealously of the modern notion that our blessed Lord's life and death were nothing more than a great example of self-sacrifice. Such a notion throws darkness and confusion over the whole gospel. It dishonours the Lord Jesus, and represents him as less resigned in the day of death than many a modern martyr. We must cling firmly to the old doctrine that Christ was 'bearing our sins,' both in the garden and on the cross. No other doctrine can ever explain the passage before us, or satisfy the conscience of guilty man.

Would we see the sinfulness of sin in its true colours? Would we learn to hate sin with a godly hatred? Would we know something of the intense misery of souls in hell? Would we understand something of the unspeakable love of Christ? Would we comprehend Christ's ability to sympathize with those that are in trouble? Then let the agony in the garden come often into our minds. The depth of that agony may give us some idea of our debt to Christ.

We see, lastly, in these verses, *an example of the feebleness of the best of saints.* We are told that while our Lord was in agony, his disciples fell asleep. In spite of a plain injunction to pray, and a plain warning against temptation, the flesh overcame the spirit. While Christ was sweating great drops of blood, his apostles slept!

Passages like these are very instructive. We ought to thank God that they have been written for our learning. They are meant to teach us humility. When apostles can behave in this way, the Christian who thinks he stands should take heed lest he fall. They are meant to reconcile believers to death, and make them long for that glorious body which they will have when Christ returns. Then, and not till then, we shall be able to wait upon God without bodily weariness, and to serve him day and night in his temple.

Notes—Luke 22:39-46

39.—[*Went, as he was wont.*] Christ's habit of going in the evening to the Mount of Olives has been already mentioned in a former passage (*Luke* 21:37). At the feast of the passover, it must be remembered, multitudes of Jews came to Jerusalem from all parts of the world. It was no doubt impossible to find lodgings for all of them within the walls of the city. Many of them probably passed the night in the villages round Jerusalem, or in the gardens lying near the city. This circumstance explains what we read in this verse. There was one particular place on the Mount of Olives, to which our Lord was in the habit of going, which was well known to all the disciples, and to Judas Iscariot among the rest. Hence it was that Judas was able, though it was night, to lead our Lord's enemies to the very spot where his Master was. To take anyone prisoner by night of course requires an intimate knowledge of his habits, and of the place where he is. If Judas therefore had not guided the party which took Jesus, they might have spent the night in searching for him in vain.

40.—[*Pray ... enter not into temptation.*] Let it be carefully noted, that to be assaulted by temptation is one thing, but to enter into it quite another. We cannot avoid the assault, but we are not obliged to give way to it. We cannot prevent temptation coming to us, but it is our own fault if we 'enter into temptation.' To be tempted is a painful thing, and a heavy trial; but to 'enter into temptation' is a sin. It is vain to expect that we shall not be tempted, so long as there is a devil, and so long as we are in the body. But it must be our prayer and endeavour not to 'enter into' the temptation. This is what our Lord sets before his disciples.

42.—[*This cup.*] Doddridge says, of this expression, 'It was customary among the ancients to assign to each guest at a feast a particular cup, as well as a dish, and by the kind and quantity of the liquor contained in it, the respect of the entertained was expressed. Hence the word "cup" came in general to signify a portion assigned, whether of pleasure or sorrow.' See Psalm 11:6; 73:10; 75:8; Isaiah 51:17; Jeremiah 25:15; Matthew 20:23.

[*Not my will, but thine, be done.*] In this expression, and indeed throughout the verse, the great and mysterious truth that our Lord had two wills, a human and a divine will, is distinctly taught. In his person the human nature and the divine were marvellously united. To use the words of the Article, 'Two whole and perfect natures, the Godhead and manhood, were joined together in one Person, never to be divided.' But still we must carefully remember that while the two natures were united, the two wills were not confounded. Our Lord had a will as perfect man, and he had also a will as perfect God. As God he had a will in entire harmony with the will of the Father, a will to suffer, to die, to bear our sins, and to provide redemption on the cross. But as man he had a will which naturally shrank from death and pain, as everything which has the breath of life instinctively does. This is the will which we hear speaking in the verse before us. 'Man,' says Theophylact, 'naturally loves life.' Our Lord was a man exactly like ourselves in all things, sin only excepted. His bodily constitution, his nervous system, his capability of suffering, were all precisely like our own. Therefore it is that he says, 'Remove this cup from me,' and yet adds, 'not my will, but thine, be done.'

The subject is undoubtedly a very mysterious one. The mystery, be it remembered, arises necessarily from our utter inability to understand the union of two natures in one person. It is a depth which we have no line to fathom. How the Lord Jesus could be at the same time God and man, as man weak but as God almighty,—for what reasons we see him sometimes in the Gospels speaking as God, and sometimes as man,—why we see him sometimes veiling his divinity, and sometimes exhibiting it most clearly,—all these are questions which it is more easy to ask than to answer. Enough for us to know that it is so, and to believe and admire what we cannot explain.

One thing, however, we may safely remark, that at no period of our Lord's earthly ministry does the reality of his manhood come out so clearly as in his agony in the garden, and his death on the cross. As man, he endured temptation for us, and overcame Satan. As man he showed the intensity of his sufferings by bloody sweat, strong crying, and tears. As man he thirsted on the cross, and said, 'My God, why hast thou forsaken me?' The infinite merit of his passion unquestionably arose from the inseparable union of his Godhead and his manhood. But the nature which is most prominently brought before us in his passion, is his nature as man.

43.—[*There appeared an angel.*] This circumstance in our Lord's agony in the garden is only mentioned by St Luke. It has given rise to many strange comments, and has even stumbled some Christians. It is a curious fact, that in the early ages of Christianity, this verse and the following one were entirely omitted in some copies of St Luke's Gospel. It was ignorantly supposed that they were so derogatory to our Lord's dignity, and so favourable to the Arian heresy, that they were not genuine. The omission was entirely unjustifiable. There is an immense preponderance of evidence to show, that the two verses were as much inspired as any other part of the Gospel, and were really written by St Luke. The omission, moreover, was entirely needless, and the fears which gave rise to it, were fears without cause.

The object of the verse appears to be to supply additional proof that our Lord was really and truly man. As man, he was for a little time 'lower than the angels' (*Heb.* 2:9). As man, he condescended to receive comfort from angelic ministry. As man,

he was willing to receive an expression of sympathy from angels, which the weakness of his disciples prevented them from giving. The reality of weakness is never so shown as when a person becomes the object of sympathy and help. As very God of very God, and Lord of angels and men, Jesus of course needed no angel to strengthen him. But as very man, in the hour of his greatest weakness, he allowed an angel to minister to him.

The German notion that no real angel appeared to our Lord and that this whole transaction took place in a trance or vision is utterly untenable. At this rate we might explain away every fact in the Bible.

Lightfoot and others have a theory that the devil appeared to our Lord in the garden, in a visible horrible form, and that this angel appeared specially to strengthen our Lord against him. There seems nothing to justify the theory, and nothing to be gained if we admit it.

44.—[*In an agony, etc.*] There can be little doubt, that at this mysterious moment, our Lord's distress of body and mind was most intense and bitter. It is plain, that Satan was permitted to harass and assail him with peculiar and special temptations. The prince of this world had indeed come. It is perfectly reasonable to suppose that as man, our Lord felt that shrinking from death and sufferings, of which he foreknew every particular, to which all flesh and blood, even sinless, must needs be liable.

But it is clear, that we want some further explanation still. It will doubtless strike every well-informed person that hundreds of martyrs have been known to suffer the most painful deaths, without any such demonstrations of mental and bodily agony, as are here recorded in the case of our Lord. How are we to account for this? How are we to explain the remarkable circumstance that our Lord appears to have felt more distressed, than many a martyr has done in the prospect of being burned alive, or even when at the stake?

I believe that these questions can never be satisfactorily answered by any Socinian, or by any upholder of the modern strange opinions about Christ's death. I believe that the favourite new theory, that both in death and life, we are meant to see in Jesus only a great *example* of self-sacrifice and self-denial, utterly breaks down here. It makes our blessed Lord show less calmness in his last hours, than many of his poor weak servants have shown, when they were martyred.

The only satisfactory explanation of Christ's intense agony is the old doctrine of imputed sin. He had engaged to die for our sins. His death was a vicarious death. As our substitute, he was about to bear our iniquities, to suffer for us, and to pay our debts to God with his own blood. He was about to be counted a sinner, and be punished, that we might be counted righteous, and be delivered from punishment. The sin of the world began to be laid upon him in a special manner in the garden. He was being 'made a curse' for us, by bearing our sins. This was the principal cause of his agony and bloody sweat. The words of Isaiah were being fulfilled:—'It pleased the Lord to bruise him; he hath put him to grief.'—'The Lord made the iniquity of us all to meet on him' (Isa. 53:10, 6).

The following quotations on this most important subject are worth reading.

Baxter says, 'This agony was not from the fear of death, but from the deep sense of God's wrath against sin; which he as our sacrifice was to bear; in greater pain than mere dying, which his servants often bear with peace.'

Sir Matthew Hale, quoted by Ford, says, 'Christ stood under the imputation of all our sins; and though he was personally innocent, yet judicially and by way of imputation, he was the greatest offender that ever was. As our Lord was pleased to be our representative in bearing our sins, and to stand in our stead, so all these affections and motions of his soul did bear the same conformity as if acted by us. As he put on the person of the sinner, so he put on the same sorrow, the same shame, the same trembling, under the apprehension of the wrath of his Father, that we must have done. And as an imputed sin drew with it the obligation to punishment, so it did by necessary consequences, raise all those storms and compassions in the soul of

Christ, as it would have done in the person of a sinner, sin only excepted.'

[*His sweat ... great drops of blood.*] It is observed by all the best commentators, that there is good medical evidence that such a mixture of blood and sweat as that here recorded, can take place, and has taken place, in cases of great mental and bodily distress.

It is worthy of remark, that St Luke is the only one of the four Evangelists who mentions the circumstance now before us, and that he was himself a physician.

Theophylact observes, that this bloody sweat is one among many strong evidences that our Lord's body was a real body, like ours, with flesh, blood, and all other things pertaining to man's constitution. He observes also, that it supplies an unanswerable argument against the heresy of those who maintained that our Lord's body was only a seeming, or 'phantastic' body, but not a real one.

An unworthy question has been started by some as to the manner in which St Luke knew of this bloody sweat, when our Lord was manifestly alone at the time of its occurrence. And we are gravely told, as a solution of the supposed difficulty, that probably 'the marks of such drops would be visible after the termination of the agony!' Questions like this are calculated to strike a blow at the root of all inspiration. If we are not to suppose the Gospel writers recorded anything except what they obtained from eye-witnesses, or saw with their own eyes, we shall take a miserably low view of the real nature of the inspiration of Scripture. We need not doubt that in this, and many other instances, St Luke simply wrote down what was revealed to him by the Holy Ghost, and that in supplying or withholding facts in our Lord's history, he was not dependent on mere human information, but was entirely guided by God.

The whole subject of this verse and the preceding one will be found very fully and ably discussed in the Commentary of Calovius, the Lutheran commentator.

45.—[*Sleeping for sorrow.*] Let it be noted here, that St Luke is the only Evangelist who mentions the cause of the disciples' being asleep. Flesh and blood cannot endure much either of sorrow or joy, without giving way. The same three who slept in Gethsemane were the three who slept at the transfiguration.

46.—[*Rise and pray.*] Bengel remarks here with much shrewdness, that a standing posture of the body is best suited for overcoming drowsiness in prayer.

LUKE 22:47-53

47 And while he yet spake, behold a multitude, and he that was called Judas, one of the twelve, went before them, and drew near unto Jesus to kiss him.

48 But Jesus said unto him, Judas, betrayest thou the Son of man with a kiss?

49 When they which were about him saw what would follow, they said unto him, Lord, shall we smite with the sword?

50 And one of them smote the servant of the high priest, and cut off his right ear.

51 And Jesus answered and said, Suffer ye thus far. And he touched his ear, and healed him.

52 Then Jesus said unto the chief priests, and captains of the temple, and the elders, which were come to him, Be ye come out, as against a thief, with swords and staves?

53 When I was daily with you in the temple, ye stretched forth no hands against me: but this is your hour, and the power of darkness.

WE should learn, for one thing, from these verses, *that the worst and most wicked acts may be done under a show of love to Christ.* We read that when the traitor Judas brought the enemies of Christ to take him, he betrayed him 'with a kiss.' He made a pretence of affection and respect, at the very moment when he was about to deliver his Master into the hands of his deadliest enemies.

Conduct like this, unhappily, is not without its parallels. The pages of history record many an instance of enormous wickedness wrought out and perfected under the garb of religion. The name of God has too often been pressed into the service of persecution, treachery, and crime. When Jezebel would have Naboth killed, she ordered a 'fast to be proclaimed,' and false witnesses to accuse him of 'blaspheming God and the king' (*1 Kings* 21:9, 10).—When Count de Montfort led a crusade against the Albigenses, he ordered them to be murdered and pillaged as an act of service to Christ's church. When the Spanish Inquisition tortured and burned suspected heretics, they justified their abominable dealings by a profession of zeal for God's truth.—The false apostle Judas Iscariot has never wanted successors and imitators. There have always been men ready to betray Christ with a kiss, and willing to deliver the gospel to its enemies under a show of respect.

Conduct like this, we need not doubt, is utterly abominable in the sight of God. To injure the cause of religion under any circumstances is a great sin, but to injure it while we pretend to show kindness is the blackest of crimes. To betray Christ at any time is the very height of wickedness, but to betray him with a kiss, proves a man to have become a very child of hell.

We should learn, for another thing, from these verses, that *it is much easier to fight a little for Christ, than to endure hardness and go to prison and death for his sake.* We read that when our Lord's enemies drew near to take him, one of his disciples 'smote the servant of the high priest, and cut off his right ear.' Yet the zeal of that disciple was very short-lived. His courage soon died away. The fear of man overcame him. By and by when our Lord was led away prisoner, he was led away alone. The disciple who was so ready to fight and smite with the sword, had actually forsaken his Master and fled!

The lesson before us is deeply instructive. To suffer patiently for Christ is far more difficult than to work actively. To sit still and endure calmly, is far more hard than to stir about and take part in the battle. Crusaders will always be found more numerous than martyrs. The passive graces of religion are far more rare and precious than the active graces. *Work* for Christ may be done from many spurious motives, from excitement, from emulation, from party-spirit, or from love of praise. *Suffering* for Christ will seldom be endured from any but one motive. That motive is the grace of God.

We shall do well to remember these things in forming our estimate of the comparative grace of professing Christians. We err greatly if we suppose that those who do public work, and preach, and speak, and write, and fill the eyes of the church, are those who are most honourable in God's sight. Such men are often far less esteemed by him than some poor unknown believer, who has been lying for years on his back, enduring pain without a murmur. Their public efforts perhaps will prove at last to have brought less glory to Christ than his patience, and to have done less good than his prayers. The grand test of grace is patient suffering. 'I will shew Saul,' said the Lord Jesus, 'what great things he shall suffer for my name' (*Acts* 9:16). Peter, we may be sure, did far less good when he drew his sword and cut off a man's ear, than he did when he stood calmly before the council as a prisoner, and said, 'We cannot but speak the things which we have seen and heard' (*Acts* 4:20).

We should learn, lastly, from these verses, that *the time during which evil is permitted to triumph is fixed and limited by God.* We read that our Lord said to his enemies when they took him, 'This is your hour and the power of darkness.'

The sovereignty of God over everything done upon earth is absolute and complete. The hands of the wicked are bound until he allows them to work. They can do nothing without his permission.—But this is not all. The hands of the wicked cannot stir one moment before God allows them to begin, and cannot stir one moment after God commands them to stop. The very worst of Satan's instruments are working in chains. He could not touch Job's property or person until God allowed him. He could not prevent Job's prosperity returning, when God's designs on Job were accomplished. Our Lord's enemies could not take and slay him, until the appointed 'hour' of his weakness arrived. Nor yet could they prevent his rising again, when the hour came in which he was declared the Son of God with power, by his resurrection from the dead (*Rom.* 1:4). When he was led forth to Calvary, it was 'their hour.' When he rose victorious from the grave, it was his.

The verses before us throw light on the history of believers in ages gone by, from the time of the apostles down to the present day. They have often been sorely oppressed and persecuted, but the hand of their enemies has never been allowed entirely to prevail. The 'hour' of their trials has generally been succeeded by a season of light. The triumph of their enemies has never been entire and complete. They have had their 'hour,' but they have had no more. After the persecution about Stephen, came the conversion of St Paul. After the martyrdom of John Huss, came the German Reformation. After the Marian persecution, came the establishment of English Protestantism. The longest night has had its morning. The sharpest winters have been followed by spring. The heaviest storms have been changed for blue sky.

Let us take comfort in these words of our Lord, in looking forward to our own future lives. If we are followers of Christ, we shall have an 'hour' of trial, and it may be a long hour too. But we may rest assured that the darkness shall not last one moment longer than God sees fit for us. In his good time it shall vanish away. 'At evening time there shall be light.'

Finally, let us take comfort in these words of our Lord, in looking forward to the future history of the church and the world. Clouds and darkness may gather round the ark of God. Persecutions and tribulations may assail the people of God. The last days of the church and world will probably be their worst days. But the 'hour' of trial, however grievous, will have an end. Even at the worst we may boldly say, 'The night is far spent and the day is at hand' (*Rom.* 13:12).

Notes—Luke 22:47-53

49.—[*What would follow.*] The Greek expression so translated is literally 'the thing about to be, or about to take place.'

50.—[*One of them smote the servant.*] We know from St John's Gospel, that the servant's name was Malchus, and the disciple who smote him was St Peter. The two names are not given by Matthew, Mark, or Luke, though all three mention the fact. This cautious silence of the three first Gospel writers is easily accounted for. St John's Gospel was probably not written till many years had passed away after the crucifixion. There was then no necessity for keeping back names from motives of prudence.

[*Cut off his right ear.*] Theophylact sees an allegorical meaning in this incident. He regards the high priest's servant as a type of the whole Jewish priesthood, who from that time were to become slaves and lose their right ear (*Deut.* 15:17).

Barradius takes another allegorical view, and regards the servant as an emblem of the whole Jewish nation, which had no ear to hear Christ and the prophets, and was deservedly punished by judicial deafness. But as Malchus was mercifully healed and had his ear restored, so was it to be with many of the Jews.

Strange as these views may seem, it is

fair to say that Major quotes a passage from a modern writer, containing an elaborate attempt to maintain much the same theory, the main point of it being that the cutting off of the ear typified the abolition of the Levitical priesthood.

For my own part I am unable to see that these allegorical views are sound, and according to the mind of the Spirit.

51.—[*Suffer ye thus far.*] The meaning of these words is a point on which commentators are not agreed. The following are the three principal interpretations.

1. Some think that the words were addressed to our Lord's enemies, and had special reference to his disciples. 'Bear with them. Suffer them to go away quietly. Let them go away.' This is the view of Whitby, Scott, and Henry.

2. Some think that the words were addressed to our Lord's disciples, and were intended to calm them, and restrain them from fighting. 'Suffer them to take me. Permit them to lay hands on me. Do not attempt resistance. Let them carry out the will of God, by taking me.' This is the view of Calvin, Brentius, Gerhard, Bengel, Major, Olshausen, Burgon.

3. Some think that the words were addressed to our Lord's enemies, but with special reference to the case of Malchus. 'Suffer me to heal this wounded man. Before binding me, let me do an act of kindness, to repair the wrong done by my hasty disciple.' This is the view of Bullinger, Barradius, Doddridge, Clarke, Alford.

The first and second views are certainly in harmony with the account given by the other Evangelists. The last is perhaps the one most in accordance with the simple view of the Greek words.

[*He touched ... ear ... healed him.*] There are several remarkable things about this miracle.

It is the only instance in the Gospels of our Lord healing a fresh wound caused by external violence.

It is a striking instance of a miracle worked on an enemy, unasked for, without faith in the person healed, and without any apparent thankfulness for the cure.

It is an extraordinary proof of the wickedness and hardness of our Lord's enemies, that so wonderful a miracle as this could be wrought without any effect being produced on them. Some think that in the darkness the miracle was not seen by anyone except those immediately round Malchus.

52.—[*The chief priests.*] Let it be noted, that so much importance was attached to making our Lord a prisoner, that men of the rank and dignity of high priests were not ashamed to go out at night to accompany the soldiers who went to arrest him.

53.—[*Your hour ... power of darkness.*] Two parties seem to be brought in here,—the wicked Jews, who were about to deliver our Lord to Pilate, and the devil, under whose instigation they were acting. It was the brief 'hour' of triumph which the unbelieving Jews, by the determinate counsel and foreknowledge of God, were to enjoy. It was the little season, during which the prince of the darkness of this world was to have 'power,' and to all appearance to prevail over the second Adam, as he had prevailed over the first. And yet neither wicked men nor a malicious devil could go a hair's breadth beyond the limit appointed by God, or triumph over the Son of God a minute beyond the time decreed by the eternal counsels. They knew it not, but so it was. Even now, our Lord would have them know they were only able to take him prisoner because God permitted them a little season of 'power.'

LUKE 22:54-62

54 Then took they him, and led *him*, and brought him into the high priest's house. And Peter followed afar off.

55 And when they had kindled a fire in the midst of the hall, and were set down together, Peter sat down among them.

56 But a certain maid beheld him as he sat by the fire, and earnestly looked upon him, and said, This man was also with him.

57 And he denied him, saying, Woman, I know him not.

58 And after a little while another saw him, and said, Thou art also of them. And Peter said, Man, I am not.

59 And about the space of one hour after another confidently affirmed, saying, Of a truth this *fellow* also was with him: for he is a Galilæan.

60 And Peter said, Man, I know not what thou sayest. And immediately, while he yet spake, the cock crew.

61 And the Lord turned, and looked upon Peter. And Peter remembered the word of the Lord, how he had said unto him, Before the cock crow, thou shalt deny me thrice.

62 And Peter went out, and wept bitterly.

THE verses we have now read describe the fall of the Apostle Peter.—It is a passage which is deeply humbling to the pride of man, but singularly instructive to true Christians. The fall of Peter has been a beacon to the church, and has probably preserved myriads of souls from destruction.—It is a passage which supplies strong proof that the Bible is inspired and Christianity is from God. If the Christian religion had been the invention of uninspired men, its first historians would never have told us that one of the chiefest apostles denied his Master three times.

The story of Peter's fall teaches us, firstly, *how small and gradual are the steps by which men may go down into great sins.*

The various steps in Peter's fall are clearly marked out by the Gospel writers. They ought always to be observed in reading this part of the apostle's history. The first step was proud self-confidence. Though all men denied Christ, yet he never would! He was ready to go with him both to prison and to death!—The second step was indolent neglect of prayer. When his Master told him to pray, lest he should enter into temptation, he gave way to drowsiness, and was found asleep.—The third step was vacillating indecision. When the enemies of Christ came upon him, Peter first fought, then ran away, then turned again, and finally 'followed afar off.'—The fourth step was mingling with bad company. He went into the high priest's house and sat among the servants by the fire, trying to conceal his religion, and hearing and seeing all manner of evil.—The fifth and last step was the natural consequence of the preceding four. He was overwhelmed with fear when suddenly charged with being a disciple. The snare was round his neck. He could not escape. He plunged deeper into error than ever. He denied his blessed Master three times. The mischief, be it remembered, had been done before. The denial was only the disease coming to a head.

Let us beware of the beginnings of backsliding, however small. We never know what we may come to, if we once leave the king's highway. The professing Christian who begins to say of any sin or evil habit, 'it is but a little one,' is in imminent danger. He is sowing seeds in his heart, which will one day spring up and bear bitter fruit. It is a homely saying, that 'if men take care of the pence the pounds will take care of themselves.' We may borrow a good spiritual lesson from the saying. The Christian who keeps his heart diligently in little things shall be kept from great falls.

The story of Peter's fall teaches us, secondly, *how very far a believer may backslide.*

In order to see this lesson clearly, the whole circumstances of Peter's case ought to be fully weighed. He was a chosen apostle of Christ. He had enjoyed greater spiritual privileges than most men in the world. He had just received the Lord's supper. He had just heard that wonderful discourse recorded in the fourteenth, fifteenth, and sixteenth chapters of St John. He had been most plainly warned of his own danger. He had protested most loudly that he was ready for anything that might come upon him. And yet this very man denies his gracious Master, and that repeatedly and after intervals giving him space for reflection. He denies him once, twice, and three times!

The best and highest saint is a poor weak creature, even at his best times. Whether he knows it or not, he carries within him an almost boundless capacity of wickedness, however fair and decent his outward conduct may seem. There is no enormity of sin into which he may not run, if he does not watch and pray, and if the grace of God does not hold him up. When we read the falls of Noah, Lot, and Peter, we only read what might possibly befall any of ourselves. Let us never presume. Let us never indulge in high thoughts about our own strength, or look down upon others. Whatever else we pray for, let us daily pray that we may 'walk humbly with God' (Mic. 6:8).

The story of Peter's fall teaches us, thirdly, *the infinite mercy of our Lord Jesus Christ.*

This is a lesson which is brought out most forcibly by a fact which is only recorded in St Luke's Gospel. We are told that when Peter denied Christ the third time, and the cock crew, 'the Lord turned and looked upon Peter.' Those words are deeply touching! Surrounded by bloodthirsty and insulting enemies, in the full prospect of horrible outrages, an unjust trial, and a painful death, the Lord Jesus yet found time to think kindly of his poor erring disciple. Even then he would have Peter know, he did not forget him. Sorrowfully no doubt, but not angrily,—he 'turned and looked upon Peter.' There was deep meaning in that look. It was a sermon which Peter never forgot.

The love of Christ towards his people, is a deep well which has no bottom. Let us never measure it by comparison with any kind of love of man or woman. It exceeds all other love, as far as the sun exceeds the rushlight. There is about it a mine of compassion, and patience, and readiness to forgive sin, of whose riches we have but a faint conception. Let us not be afraid to trust that love, when we first feel our sins. Let us never be afraid to go on trusting it after we have once believed. No man need despair, however far he may have fallen, if he will only repent and turn to Christ. If the heart of Jesus was so gracious when he was a prisoner in the judgment hall, we surely need not think it is less gracious, when he sits in glory at the right hand of God.

The story of Peter's fall teaches us, lastly, *how bitter sin is to believers, when they have fallen into it and discovered their fall.*

This is a lesson which stands out plainly on the face of the verses before us. We are told that when Peter remembered the warning he had received, and saw how far he had fallen, 'he went out and wept bitterly.' He found out by experience the truth of Jeremiah's words, 'It is an evil thing and bitter, that thou hast forsaken the Lord' (*Jer.* 2:19). He felt keenly the truth of Solomon's saying, 'The backslider in heart shall be filled with his own ways' (*Prov.* 14:14). No doubt he could have said with Job, 'I abhor myself, and repent in dust and ashes' (*Job* 42:6).

Sorrow like this, let us always remember, is an inseparable companion of true repentance. Here lies the grand distinction between 'repentance unto salvation,' and unavailing remorse. Remorse can make a man miserable, like Judas Iscariot, but it can do no more. It does not lead him to God.—Repentance makes a man's heart soft and his conscience tender, and shows itself in real turning to a Father in heaven. The falls of a graceless professor are falls from which there is no rising again. But the fall of a true saint always ends in deep contrition, self-abasement, and amendment of life.

Let us take heed, ere we leave this passage, that we always make a right use of Peter's fall. Let us never make it an excuse for sin. Let us learn from his sad experience, to watch and pray, lest we fall into temptation. If we do fall, let us believe that there is hope for us as there was for him. But above all, let us remember, that if we fall as Peter fell, we must repent as Peter repented, or else we shall never be saved.

Notes—Luke 22:54-62

55.—[*Kindled a fire.*] It must be remembered, that although the climate of Palestine is generally very warm, the nights about the passover season, according to the testimony of all travellers, are intensely cold.

[*The hall.*] The Greek word so rendered is more frequently translated 'palace.' Parkhurst thinks that here it means, 'an open court enclosed by buildings,—a courtyard exposed to the open air.' In Revelation 11:2, it is translated 'court,' and can there bear no other sense.

[*Sat down among them.*] Let it be noted, that the Greek expression rendered 'among' them, is the very same that in the former part of the verse is translated, 'in the midst.'

56.—[*Sat by the fire.*] It is a curious fact, that the Greek word here rendered, 'fire,' is a totally different word from the one rendered, 'fire,' in the preceding verse. Here it means literally, 'the light.' The word is found sixty-nine times in the New Testament, and in sixty-seven places is translated 'light.' The two exceptions when it is rendered 'fire,' are the passage before us, and the parallel passage in St Mark, describing the same transaction (*Mark* 14:54).

It is evident that the word was used intentionally by St Luke, in order to show us, that it was 'by the light of the fire' that Peter was recognized and charged with being a disciple. Had he kept in the background, and been content with a darker position, he might have escaped notice.

59.—[*He is a Galilæan.*] It is clear from this expression that Peter had been talking and conversing with those among whom he was sitting. Had he been content to say nothing, and await silently the result of his Master's trial, he might even now have escaped detection.

61.—[*Looked upon Peter.*] Parkhurst says, that the Greek word rendered 'looked,' signifies, 'to look with steadfastness and attention.'

Some have thought it strange that our Lord Jesus Christ should have been in a position where he could see Peter, and Peter could see him, and also that he could hear Peter denying him.

It is not at all necessary to reply to this, that our Lord had a miraculous knowledge of what Peter was saying, or that he was passing through the courtyard, or hall, where Peter was, at the time of the third denial and the cock-crowing.

It is most probable that our Lord was either in the same hall with Peter, or in a room opening out of it. There is no improbability in supposing that he was within sight and hearing of the apostle. Above all it must be remembered that the vehemence of Peter's third denial, when he even cursed and swore, would most likely make him speak so loud that he might be easily heard at some distance. The crowing of the cock of course would be heard much further even than Peter's voice.

Augustine, Stella, and others, go so far as to regard the whole transaction as an inward and spiritual one,—a turning of the Lord's heart towards Peter, and a gracious looking of the Lord's mind towards him. They consider that our Lord was not in the same room with Peter, and could not literally look at him. But this view seems most unsatisfactory. It is not the natural meaning of the words before us, and there is really no necessity for it in the nature of the event described.

LUKE 22:63-71

63 And the men that held Jesus mocked him, and smote *him*.

64 And when they had blindfolded him, they struck him on the face, and asked him, saying, Prophesy, who is it that smote thee?

65 And many other things blasphemously spake they against him.

66 And as soon as it was day, the elders of the people and the chief priests and the scribes came together, and led him into their council, saying,

67 Art thou the Christ? tell us. And he said unto them, If I tell you, ye will not believe:

68 And if I also ask *you*, ye will not answer me, nor let *me* go.

69 Hereafter shall the Son of man sit on the right hand of the power of God.

70 Then said they all, Art thou then the Son of God? And he said unto them, Ye say that I am.

71 And they said, What need we any further witness? for we ourselves have heard of his own mouth.

W E should notice, firstly, in these verses, *the shameful treatment that our Lord Jesus Christ underwent at the hands of his enemies.* We read that the men who held him, 'mocked' him, 'smote' him, 'blindfolded' him, and 'struck him on the face.' It was not enough to have taken prisoner a person of most blameless and charitable life. They must needs add insult to injury.

Conduct like this shows the desperate corruption of human nature. The excesses of savage malice to which unconverted men will sometimes go, and the fierce delight with which they will sometimes trample on the most holy and the most pure, almost justify the strong saying of an old divine, that 'man left to himself is half-beast and half-devil.' He hates God and all who bear anything of God's image about them. 'The carnal mind is enmity against God' (*Rom.* 8:7). We have probably a very faint idea of what the world would become, if it were not for the constant restraint that God mercifully puts upon evil. It is not too much to say that if unconverted men had their own way entirely, the earth would soon be little better than a hell.

Our Lord's calm submission to insults like those here described, shows the depth of his love towards sinners. Had he so willed, he could have stopped the insolence of his enemies in a moment. He who could cast out devils with a word, could have summoned legions of angels to his side, and scattered these wretched tools of Satan to the winds. But our Lord's heart was set on the great work he had come on earth to do. He had undertaken to purchase our redemption by his own humiliation, and he did not flinch from paying the uttermost farthing of the price. He had undertaken to drink the bitter cup of vicarious suffering to save sinners, and 'for the joy set before him he despised the shame,' and drank the cup to the very dregs (*Heb.* 12:2).

Patience like that which our blessed Lord exhibited on this occasion should teach his professing people a mighty lesson. We should forbear all murmuring and complaining, and irritation of spirit, when we are ill-treated by the world. What are the occasional insults to which we have to submit compared to the insults which were heaped on our Master? Yet 'when he was reviled he reviled not again. When he suffered he threatened not.' He left us an example that we should walk in his steps. Let us go and do likewise (1 Pet. 2:21-23).

We should notice, secondly, in these verses, *the striking prophecy which our Lord delivers about his own coming glory*. He says to his insulting enemies, 'Hereafter shall the Son of man sit on the right hand of the power of God.' Did they find fault with his lowly appearance and want a glorious Messiah? They would see him in glory one day.—Did they think he was weak, powerless, and contemptible, because at present there was no outward majesty about him? They would behold him one day in the most honourable position in heaven, fulfilling the well-known prophecy of Daniel, with all judgment committed to his hands (*Dan.* 7:9, 10).

Let us take heed that the future glory of Christ forms a part of our creed, as much as Christ's cross and passion. Let it be a first principle in our religion, that the same Jesus who was mocked, despised, and crucified, is he who has now 'all power in heaven and earth,' and will one day come again in his Father's glory with all his angels. We see but half the truth if we see nothing but the cross and the first advent. It is essential to our own comfort to see also the second advent, and the crown. That same Jesus who stood before the bar of the high priest and of Pilate, will one day sit upon a throne of glory and summon all his enemies to appear before him. Happy is that Christian who keeps steadily before his mind that word 'hereafter!' Now in this present time believers must be content to take part in their Master's sufferings and with him to be weak. 'Hereafter' they shall share in his glory, and with him be strong.—Now like their Lord they must not be surprised if they are mocked, despised, and disbelieved. 'Hereafter' they shall sit with him on the right hand of God.

We should notice, lastly, in these verses, *what a full and bold confession our Lord makes of his own Messiahship and divinity*. We read that in reply to this question of his enemies, 'Art thou the Son of God?'—'he said unto them, Ye say that I am.' The meaning of this short sentence may not be clear at first sight to an English reader. It signifies in other words, 'Ye speak the truth. I am, as ye say, the Son of God.'

Our Lord's confession deprived his enemies of all excuse for unbelief. The Jews can never plead that our Lord left their forefathers in ignorance of his mission, and kept them in doubt and suspense. Here we see our Lord telling them plainly who he was, and telling them in words, which would convey even more to a Jewish mind than they do to ours. And yet the confession had not the least good effect upon the Jews! Their hearts were hardened by prejudice. Their minds were darkened by judicial blindness. The veil was over the eyes of their inward man. They heard our Lord's confession unmoved, and only plunged deeper into the most awful sin.

The bold confession of our Master upon this occasion, is intended to be an example to all his believing people. Like him, we must not shrink from speaking out when occasion requires our testimony. The fear of man, and the presence of a multitude, must not make us hold our peace (*Job* 31:34). We need not blow a trumpet before us, and go out of our way, to proclaim our own religion. Opportunities are sure to occur in the daily path of duty, when, like St Paul on board ship, we may show 'whose we are and whom we serve' (*Acts* 27:23). At such opportunities, if we have the mind of Christ, let us not be afraid to show our colours. A confessing Master loves bold, uncompromising, and confessing disciples. Them that honour him by an outspoken, courageous testimony, he will honour, because they are walking in his steps. 'Whosoever,' he says, 'shall confess me before men, him will I confess before my Father which is in heaven' (*Matt.* 10:32).

Notes—Luke 22:63-71

63.—[*Mocked him, etc.*] We must understand that this took place after our Lord's first examination before the priests, of which St Luke gives no account. That there were two separate examinations, will be seen in the next note.

66.—[*As soon as it was day.*] Some little explanation is necessary at this point in St Luke's history of our Lord's passion. It is clear, from the account of the Evangelists Matthew and Mark, that as soon as our Lord was taken prisoner, he was brought *at once* before Caiaphas, the high priest, and examined.—It is also clear from the same Evangelists, that Peter's thrice-repeated denial of his Master took place *after* this examination.—How then are we to explain the fact that St Luke speaks of St Peter's denial, as having taken place *before* any examination of our Lord at the high priest's bar?

The most satisfactory reply to this inquiry, is the explanation given by Gerhard, Scott, Burgon, and Stier. They maintain that after the council had condemned Jesus the first time, they separated, and met again early in the morning, and that the words used by St Luke, 'as soon as it was day,' refer to this second meeting of the council.—'Nor is it improbable,' says Scott, 'that the high priest should again put the same questions to our Lord, as he had done the night before; both to see, whether he would stand to what he had said, and also that such members of the council as had been absent, might hear his answers.'

Two arguments may be mentioned in support of the above explanation.—One is the great improbability that our Lord's enemies, having taken him prisoner, would wait until it was morning before they examined him. On the contrary it is plain, from Matthew and Mark, that Jesus was taken before Caiaphas as soon as he was apprehended.—The other argument is the great improbability, that the men who held Jesus would have mocked and insulted him as they did, if he had not been already examined, and condemned.

We must understand then, that our Lord was twice examined before the chief priests and elders, and that the examination mentioned by St Luke, is the second of the two, and answers to the morning 'consultation,' mentioned by St Mark (*Mark* 15:1).—I am aware that Poole, Doddridge, and Alford, maintain that there was only one examination before the priests. But their reasoning does not satisfy me.

Horne remarks, in his Introduction to Scripture, 'According to the Talmud, capital causes were prohibited from being heard in the night, as also was the institution of an examination, pronouncing a sentence, and carrying it into execution on one and the same day. It was enjoined that at least the execution of a sentence should be deferred to the following day. How flagrantly these injunctions were disregarded in the case of Jesus Christ, it is scarcely necessary to mention.'

67.—[*Ye will not believe.*] Assuming the correctness of the view put forth in the last note, there is much point in these words. When our Lord had told them who he was at the first examination, they would not believe. To this unbelief he here seems to refer.

68.—[*If I ask you.*] This expression has occasioned some surprise and called forth many remarks. It seems strange at first sight, that a prisoner should talk of putting questions to his judges.

Major paraphrases the expression, 'If I advance any arguments to prove that I am the Messiah.' He adds, 'to interrogate was a usual mode of argumentation among the Hebrews' (see *Luke* 20:2; 7:44).

Pellican paraphrases the passage, 'If I enquire of you what kind of Messiah is promised in Scripture, and ask you whether the signs of Messiah appear sufficiently in me, you will not give me an honest answer.'

Gill renders it, 'If I require an answer to the arguments proving me to be the Messiah, or desire to know what objection can be made to them, you will not answer me, or dismiss me though I should appear to be the Messiah. You are resolved, right or wrong, to detain me in bonds and take away my life.'

Heinsius mentions an opinion of some, that the Greek word rendered 'ask' might also be rendered 'petition or supplicate.' This, however, would be a most undignified sense to put on the words, and is utterly improbable.

69.—[*Hereafter ... Son of man ... right hand ... God.*] There is a plain reference in these words to the famous prophecy of Daniel (*Dan.* 7:9-14). Our Lord evidently implies that he was the person to whom that prophecy pointed, and that, although condemned by the Jews, he would shortly be exalted to the highest position of dignity in heaven. The Jews saw this at once, and proceeded to put the question of the next verse.

This, be it noted, is the last occasion on which our Lord ever called himself the 'Son of man.'

70.—[*Art thou ... Son of God?*] It is very worthy of note here, that our Lord in the preceding verse had called himself the 'Son of man.' His enemies in this question, ask him if he is the 'Son of God.' They did so, because his solemn saying about sitting at God's right hand, showed them that he claimed to be the Messiah and very God.

[*Ye say that I am.*] It is almost needless to remark, that this expression means, 'Ye say rightly that I am.' Major gives instances of a similar form of speech both in Greek and Latin writers.

LUKE 23:1-12

1 And the whole multitude of them arose, and led him unto Pilate.

2 And they began to accuse him, saying, We found this *fellow* perverting the nation, and forbidding to give tribute to Cæsar, saying, that he himself is Christ a King.

3 And Pilate asked him, saying, Art thou the King of the Jews? And he answered him and said, Thou sayest *it*.

4 Then said Pilate to the chief priests and *to* the people, I find no fault in this man.

5 And they were the more fierce, saying, He stirreth up the people, teaching throughout all Jewry, beginning from Galilee to this place.

6 When Pilate heard of Galilee, he asked whether the man were a Galilæan.

7 And as soon as he knew that he belonged unto Herod's jurisdiction, he sent him to Herod, who himself also was at Jerusalem at that time.

8 And when Herod saw Jesus, he was exceeding glad: for he was desirous to see him of a long *season*, because he had heard many things of him; and he hoped to have seen some miracle done by him.

9 Then he questioned with him in many words; but he answered him nothing.

10 And the chief priests and scribes stood and vehemently accused him.

11 And Herod with his men of war set him at nought, and mocked *him*, and arrayed him in a gorgeous robe, and sent him again to Pilate.

12 And the same day Pilate and Herod were made friends together: for before they were at enmity between themselves.

L ET us observe, for one thing, in this passage, *what false accusations were laid to our Lord Jesus Christ's charge.* We are told that the Jews accused him of 'perverting the nation,—forbidding to give tribute to Cæsar,—and stirring up the people.' In all this indictment, we know, there was not a word of truth. It was nothing but an ingenious attempt to enlist the feelings of a Roman governor against our Lord.

False witness and slander are two favourite weapons of the devil. He was a liar from the beginning, and is still the father of lies (*John* 8:44). When he finds that he cannot stop God's work, his next device is to blacken the character of God's servants, and to destroy the value of their testimony. With this weapon he assaulted David: 'False witnesses,' he says, 'did rise up: they laid to my charge things that I knew not.' With this weapon he assaulted the prophets. Elijah was a 'troubler of Israel!' Jeremiah was a man who 'sought not the welfare of this people, but the hurt!' (*Psa.* 35:11; *1 Kings* 18:17; *Jer.* 38:4). With this weapon he assaulted the apostles. They were 'pestilent fellows,' and men who 'turned the world upside down' (*Acts* 24:5; 17:6). With this weapon he assaulted our Lord all through his ministry. He stirred up his agents to call him a gluttonous man and a winebibber, a Samaritan and a devil (*Luke* 7:34; *John* 8:48). And here, in the verses before us, we find him plying his old weapon to the very last. Jesus is arraigned before Pilate upon charges which were utterly untrue.

The servant of Christ must never be surprised if he has to drink of the same cup with his Lord. When he who was holy, harmless, and undefiled, was foully slandered, who can expect to escape? 'If they have called the master of the house Beelzebub, how much more shall they call them of his household?' (*Matt.* 10:25). Nothing is too bad to be reported against a saint. Perfect innocence is no fence against enormous lying, calumny, and misrepresentation. The most blameless character will not secure us against false tongues. We must bear the trial patiently. It is part of the cross of Christ. We must sit still, lean back on God's promises, and believe that in the long run truth will prevail. 'Rest in the Lord,' says David, 'and wait patiently for him.'—'He shall bring forth thy righteousness as the light, and thy judgment as the noonday' (*Psa.* 37:6, 7).

Let us observe, for another thing, in this passage, *the strange and mingled motives which influence the hearts of unconverted great men.* We are told that when our Lord was sent by Pilate to Herod, king of Galilee, 'Herod was exceeding glad: for he was desirous to see him of a long season, because he had heard many things of him; and he hoped to have seen some miracle done by him.'

These words are remarkable. Herod was a sensual, worldly man,—the murderer of John the Baptist,—a man living in foul adultery with his brother's wife. Such a man, we might have supposed, would have had no desire to see Christ. But Herod had an uneasy conscience. The blood of God's murdered saint no doubt, rose often before his eyes, and destroyed his peace. The fame of our Lord's preaching and miracles had penetrated even into his court. It was said that another witness against sin had risen up, who was even more faithful and bold than John the Baptist, and who confirmed his teaching by works which even the power of kings could not perform. These rumours made Herod restless and uncomfortable. No wonder that his curiosity was stirred, and he 'desired to see Christ.'

It may be feared that there are many great and rich men like Herod in every age of the church, men without God, without faith, and living only for themselves. They generally live in an atmosphere of their own, flattered, fawned upon, and never told the truth about their souls,—haughty, tyrannical, and knowing no will but their own. Yet even these men are sometimes conscience-stricken and afraid. God raises up some bold witness against their sins, whose testimony reaches their ears. At once their curiosity is stirred. They feel 'found out,' and are ill at ease. They flutter round his ministry, like the moth round the candle, and seem unable to keep away from it, even while they do not obey it. They praise his talents and openly profess their admiration of his power. But they never get any further. Like Herod, their conscience produces within them a morbid curiosity to see and hear God's witnesses. But, like Herod, their heart is linked to the world by chains of iron. Tossed to and fro by storms of lust or ungovernable passions, they are never at rest while they live, and after all their fitful struggles of conscience, they die at length in their sins.—This is a painful history. But it is the history of many rich men's souls.

Let us learn from Herod's case to pity great men. With all their greatness and apparent splendour, they are often thoroughly miserable within. Silks and satins and official robes often cover hearts which are utter strangers to peace. That man knows not what he is wishing, who wishes to be a rich man.—Let us pray for rich men, as well as pity them. They carry weight in the race for eternal life. If they are saved, it can only be by the greatest miracles of God's grace. Our Lord's words are very solemn, 'It is easier for a camel to go through the eye of a needle, than for a rich man to enter into the kingdom of God' (*Matt.* 19:24).

Let us observe, finally, in this passage, *how easily and readily unconverted men can agree in disliking Christ.* We are told that when Pilate sent our Lord a prisoner to Herod, 'the same day Pilate and Herod were made friends together: for before they were at enmity between themselves.' We know not the cause of their enmity. It was probably some petty quarrel, such as will arise among great as well as small. But whatever the cause of enmity, it was laid aside when a common object of contempt, fear, or hatred was brought before them. Whatever else they disagreed about, Pilate and Herod could agree to despise and persecute Christ.

The incident before us is a striking emblem of a state of things, which may always be seen in the world. Men of the most discordant opinions can unite in opposing truth. Teachers of the most opposite doctrines can make common cause in fighting against the gospel. In the days of our Lord, the Pharisees and the Sadducees, might be seen combining their forces to entrap Jesus of Nazareth and put him to death. In our own times we sometimes see Romanists and Socinians,—infidels and idolaters,—worldly pleasure-lovers and bigoted ascetics,—the friends of so-called liberal views and the most determined opponents of all changes,—all ranked together against evangelical religion. One common hatred binds them together. They hate the cross of Christ. To use the words of the apostles in the Acts: 'Against thy holy child Jesus, whom thou hast anointed, both Herod, and Pontius Pilate, with the Gentiles, and the people of Israel, were gathered together' (*Acts* 4:27). All hate each other very much, but all hate Christ much more.

The true Christian must not count the enmity of the world a strange thing. He must not marvel, if like St Paul at Rome, he finds the way of life, a 'way everywhere spoken against,' and if all around him agree in disliking his religion (*Acts* 28:22). If he expects that by any concession he can win the favour of man, he will be greatly deceived. Let not his heart be troubled. He must wait for the praise of God. The saying of his Master should often come across his mind: 'If ye were of the world, the world would love his own: but because ye are not of the world, but I have chosen you out of the world, therefore the world hateth you' (*John* 15:19).

Notes—Luke 23:1-12

1.—[*Unto Pilate.*] Pilate was the Roman governor of Judæa. Without him the Jews had no power to put our Lord to death. The mere fact that they were obliged to apply publicly to a foreign ruler for the carrying out of their murderous plan, was a striking proof that the 'sceptre had departed from Judah,' and the time of Messiah had come (*Gen.* 49:10).

2.—[*Perverting ... forbidding to give tribute.*] The duplicity and dishonesty of this charge are evident. When the enemies of our Lord wanted to bring him into disfavour with the Jews, they had asked him 'if it was lawful to pay tribute unto Cæsar' (*Luke* 20:22). But now when they want to make him out an offender at the bar of the Roman governor, they charge him with forbidding to give tribute to Cæsar the Roman emperor. The falseness of the charge is as striking as its dishonesty.

3.—[*Thou sayest it.*] This is the remarkable saying which St Paul refers to, when he tells Timothy that our Lord 'before Pontius Pilate witnessed a good confession' (*1 Tim.* 6:13). But we must remember that St Luke only reports a portion of what our Lord said. The Gospel of St John contains other particulars which are not reported here (*John* 18:28-38).

4.—[*I find no fault in this man.*] It is clear that Pilate said this after the conversation with our Lord, reported by St John, and after satisfying himself that he claimed no temporal kingdom, and was not such a king as would interfere with the Roman authority. He had in particular heard our Lord's words, 'My kingdom is not of this world' (*John* 18:36).

5.—[*They were the more fierce.*] The Greek word so translated, means literally, 'they grew more strong, more violent, more urgent,—they persisted in their accusation.'

7.—[*He sent him to Herod.*] This Herod was Herod Antipas, the same Herod who put to death John the Baptist. He was son of Herod the Great, who caused all the children under two years of age to be murdered at Bethlehem, and uncle of Herod Agrippa, who slew James the apostle with the sword, and would have slain Peter if he had not been miraculously delivered from prison.

The family of the Herods was Idumæan. They were all descended from Esau, the father of Edom. This circumstance is noteworthy, when we see their unceasing enmity against Christ and his people. The seed of Esau seems to carry on the old enmity against the seed of Jacob.

8.—[*Exceeding glad ... desirous to see ... heard many things, etc.*] The expressions in this verse are very remarkable. They bring before us the fearful history of Herod's sins, and throw light on the power of conscience. Herod had not forgotten John the

Baptist and his testimony. Moreover he had probably heard much about our Lord from his steward Chuza, whose wife Joanna was one of our Lord's disciples (*Luke* 8:3).

9.—[*He answered him nothing.*] It is probable that it would have been useless to answer Herod's questions. Herod had heard the truth often from John the Baptist's mouth. What he wanted was not more knowledge, but a heart and a will to act upon what he knew.

10.—[*The chief priests and scribes stood.*] It is clear that these bitter enemies of our Lord followed him from place to place, and from court to court with their accusations. The great additional fatigue which this going backwards and forwards from one ruler to another must have entailed on our Lord, should be remembered in estimating the whole amount of his sufferings.

11.—[*With his men of war.*] The Greek word so rendered, means literally, 'his armed force,' or 'guards.' Of course we cannot suppose that Herod had a large army with him. The soldiers around him were only his bodyguard or escort.

[*Set him at nought ... mocked ... gorgeous robe.*] It is evident that Herod regarded our Lord as little better than a foolish, fanatical, and contemptible person,—a person to be mocked and ridiculed, but not to be feared. The gorgeous, or shining robe put on him, was probably such as candidates for high office used to wear. It was intended to ridicule his supposed claim to be a king, and to show that Herod thought it absurd. Thus was our Lord made 'a scorn of men, and the outcast of the people' (*Psa.* 22:6).

[*Sent him again to Pilate.*] It is worthy of remark that we are specially told that neither the ruler of Galilee, nor the ruler of Judæa, could find any fault in our Lord. In Galilee most of his miracles had been wrought, and much of his time spent. Yet the ruler of Galilee had nothing to lay to his charge. He was to be crucified as 'a lamb without blemish or spot.'

12.—[*Pilate and Herod were made friends.*] It is doubtless true that neither Pilate nor Herod were afraid of Christ, or were animated by any special feeling of hatred towards him personally. But it is no less true that they agreed in despising him, and insulting him, and were utterly unbelieving as to his claim to faith and respect. Their reconciliation therefore on the occasion of his trial, is a fact that is very significant and instructive.

It is certain that the circumstance struck the apostles very much. They regarded it as a fulfilment of part of the second Psalm. They mentioned in prayer to God the union of Pilate, Herod, and the Jews against their Master. See Acts 4:23-30.

I mention this, because there is a disposition in some quarters, nowadays, to deny the significance of the reconciliation of Pilate and Herod, and the correctness of the lesson commonly drawn from it. The comment of the Holy Ghost on the transaction outweighs all the reasonings of man.

Theophylact remarks on this verse, that 'It is matter of shame to Christians, that while the devil can persuade wicked men to lay aside their enmities, in order to do harm, Christians cannot even keep up friendship in order to do good.'

LUKE 23:13-25

13 And Pilate, when he had called together the chief priests and the rulers and the people,

14 Said unto them, Ye have brought this man unto me, as one that perverteth the people: and, behold, I, having examined *him* before you, have found no fault in this man touching those things whereof ye accuse him:

15 No, nor yet Herod: for I sent you to him; and, lo, nothing worthy of death is done unto him.

16 I will therefore chastise him, and release *him*.

17 (For of necessity he must release one unto them at the feast.)

18 And they cried out all at once, saying, Away with this *man*, and release unto us Barabbas:

19 (Who for a certain sedition made in the city, and for murder, was cast into prison.)

20 Pilate therefore, willing to release Jesus, spake again to them.

21 But they cried, saying, Crucify *him*, crucify him.

22 And he said unto them the third time, Why, what evil hath he done? I have found no cause of death in him: I will therefore chastise him, and let *him* go.

23 And they were instant with loud voices, requiring that he might be crucified. And the voices of them and of the chief priests prevailed.

24 And Pilate gave sentence that it should be as they required.

25 And he released unto them him that for sedition and murder was cast into prison, whom they had desired; but he delivered Jesus to their will.

W E should observe, for one thing, in this passage, *what striking testimony was borne to our Lord Jesus Christ's perfect innocence by his judges.*

We are told that Pilate said to the Jews, 'Ye have brought this man unto me, as one that perverteth the people: and behold, I, having examined him before you, have found no fault in this man touching those things whereof ye accuse him: no, nor yet Herod.' The Roman and the Galilean governors were both of one mind. Both agreed in pronouncing our Lord not guilty of the things laid to his charge.

There was a peculiar fitness in this public declaration of Christ's innocence. Our Lord, we must remember, was about to be offered up as a sacrifice for our sins. It was meet and right that those who examined him should formally pronounce him a guiltless and blameless person. It was meet and right that the Lamb of God should be found by those who slew him 'a Lamb without blemish and without spot' (*1 Pet.* 1:19). The overruling hand of God so ordered the events of his trial, that even when his enemies were judges, they could find no fault and prove nothing against him.

The circumstance before us may seem of trifling moment to a care-less Bible reader. It ought however to commend itself to the heart of every well-instructed Christian. We ought to be daily thankful that our great Substitute was in all respects perfect, and that our Surety was a complete and faultless Surety.—What child of man can count the number of his sins? We leave undone things we should do and do things we ought not to do, every day we live. But this must be our comfort, that Christ the Righteous has undertaken to stand in our place, to pay the debt we all owe, and to fulfil the law we have all broken. He did fulfil that law completely. He satisfied all its demands. He accomplished all its requirements. He was the second Adam, who had 'clean hands and a pure heart,' and could therefore enter with boldness into God's holy hill (*Psa.* 24:4). He is the righteousness of all sinners who believe in him (*Rom.* 10:4). In him all believers are counted perfect fulfillers of the law. The eyes of a holy God behold them in Christ, clothed with Christ's perfect righteousness. For Christ's sake God can now say of the believer, 'I find in him no fault at all.'

Let us learn, for another thing, in this passage, *how thoroughly the Jews took on themselves the whole responsibility of our Lord Jesus Christ's death.* We are told that when Pilate was 'willing to release Jesus,' the Jews 'cried, saying, crucify him, crucify him!' Again, we are told that 'they were instant with loud voices, requiring that he might be crucified.'

This fact in the history of our Lord's passion deserves particular notice. It shows the strict accuracy of the words of the apostles in after times, when speaking of Christ's death. They speak of it as the act of the Jewish nation, and not of the Romans. 'Ye killed the Prince of life,' says Peter to the Jews at Jerusalem. 'Ye slew and hanged him on a tree' (*Acts* 3:15; 5:30). 'The Jews have both killed the Lord Jesus and their own prophets,' says Paul to the Thessalonians (1 *Thess.* 2:15). So long as the world stands, the fact before us is a memorial of man's natural hatred against God. When the Son of God came down to earth and dwelt among his own chosen people, they despised him, rejected him, and slew him.

The fearful responsibility which the Jews took on themselves in the matter of our Lord's death was not forgotten by God. The righteous blood which they shed has been crying against them as a people for eighteen hundred years. Scattered all over the earth, wanderers among the nations, without a land, without a government, without a home, the Jews show to this day that their own words have been terribly fulfilled. The blood of their slain Messiah 'is upon them and upon their children.' They are a standing warning to the world that it is a fearful thing to reject the Lord Christ, and that the nation which speaks stoutly against God, must not be surprised if God deals with it according to its words. Marvellous indeed is the thought that there is mercy in store for Israel, notwithstanding all its sins and unbelief! The nation which pierced and slew him, shall yet look to him by faith and be restored to favour (*Zech.* 12:10).

We should observe, lastly, in this passage, *the remarkable circumstances connected with the release of Barabbas.* We are told that Pilate 'released him that for sedition and murder was cast into prison, whom the Jews had desired; but delivered Jesus to their will.' Two persons were before him, and he must needs release one of the two. The one was a sinner against God and man, a malefactor stained with many crimes. The other was the holy, harmless, and undefiled Son of God, in whom there was no fault at all. And yet Pilate condemns the innocent prisoner and acquits the guilty! He orders Barabbas to be set free, and delivers Jesus to be crucified.

The circumstance before us is very instructive. It shows the bitter malice of the Jews against our Lord. To use the words of St Peter, 'They denied the Holy One and the Just, and desired a murderer to be granted to them' (*Acts* 3:14). It shows the deep humiliation to which our Lord submitted, in order to procure our redemption. He allowed himself to be reckoned lighter in the balance than a murderer, and to be counted more guilty than the chief of sinners!

But there is a deeper meaning yet beneath the circumstance before us, which we must not fail to observe. The whole transaction is a lively emblem of that wondrous exchange that takes place between

Christ and the sinner, when a sinner is justified in the sight of God. Christ has been made 'sin for us who knew no sin, that we might be made the righteousness of God in him' (2 Cor. 5:21). Christ the innocent has been reckoned guilty before God, that we the guilty might be reckoned innocent, and be set free from condemnation.

If we are true Christians, let us daily lean our souls on the comfortable thought that Christ has really been our Substitute, and has been punished in our stead. Let us freely confess, that, like Barabbas, we deserve death, judgment, and hell. But let us cling firmly to the glorious truth that a sinless Saviour has suffered in our stead, and that believing in him the guilty may go free.

Notes—Luke 23:13-25

13.—[*He had called together.*] This expression seems to denote a general gathering of the leading persons among the Jews, in order that the declaration of our Lord's innocence might be as public and unmistakable as possible. It made it impossible for the Jews afterwards to deny that the Roman governor found our Lord 'not guilty.'

14.—[*Have found no fault.*] Burgon remarks here, that we ought to notice, 'how many and what various persons bear testimony to the innocence of the Holy One,—Pilate, Herod, Pilate's wife, Judas Iscariot, the thief on the cross, and the centurion,' who superintended the crucifixion. We cannot doubt that this was specially overruled and ordered by the providence of God.

15.—[*Nothing worthy of death is done unto him.*] There seems no doubt that these words would have been better rendered, 'nothing worthy of death has been done by him.' This is the opinion of Scholefield, Major, and Alford. Compare Acts 25:11, 25; 26:31.

16.—[*Chastise.*] This means 'chastise by scourging.' Doddridge paraphrases the verse, 'When I have chastised him by scourging, which will be an admonition to him for the future not to use those wild and enthusiastical expressions, which have

given so much umbrage and suspicion, I will let him go.' Pilate appears to have hoped that by this comparatively slight punishment of one whom he regarded as a harmless fanatic, he should satisfy the Jews.

17.—[*Of necessity he must release one.*] Major remarks, 'By whom or at what time this practice originated, is not determined. The most probable opinion is that it was introduced by the Romans, and perhaps by Pilate, at the beginning of his government, in order to gratify the Jewish people.'

18.—[*Barabbas.*] I am quite unable to receive the opinion held by some, that the scapegoat in the Jewish law was a type of Barabbas. I believe that the scapegoat was a type of Christ rising again, and not of Christ crucified. Barabbas was a type of the sinner deserving judgment, and yet set free.

20.—[*Willing to release Jesus.*] Pilate's desire to acquit our Lord and set him free, coupled with his great desire to please the Jews and get the praise of man, is a striking picture of the slavery to which a great man without principle may be reduced.

21.—[*Crucify him.*] Crucifixion was not only the most painful, but the most ignominious and disgraceful death, to which a person could be sentenced. Bishop Pearson remarks, 'By the ignominy of this punishment, we are taught how far our Saviour descended for us, that while we were slaves,

342

and in bondage unto sin, he might redeem us by a servile death.'

22.—[*The third time*.] Pilate's thrice-repeated declaration of our Lord's innocence is deserving of notice. Bishop Pearson remarks, 'It was thought necessary to include the name of Pilate in the creed, as of one who gave a most powerful external testimony to the certainty of our Saviour's death, and the innocency of his life. He did not only profess, to the condemnation of the Jews, that he found nothing worthy of death in Christ; but left the same written to the Gentiles of the Roman empire. Two ways he is related to have given most ample testimony to the truth, first by an express written to Tiberius and by him presented to the senate, and secondly by records written in tables of all things of moment which were acted in his government.' For this last statement Pearson gives the authority of Tertullian, Eusebius, and Justin Martyr.

23.—[*They were instant*.] This is the same Greek word that is translated 'pressed upon him' in Luke 5:1, and 'lay upon us' in Acts 27:20.

24.—[*That it should be as they required*.] These words would have been rendered more literally 'that their request should be.'

25.—[*To their will*.] This means 'the will of the Jews.' Let it be noted here, and throughout St Luke's account of our Lord's passion, how much less he says of the things done by the Roman soldiers, than either Matthew, Mark, or John. The reason is simple. St Luke wrote specially for the use of the Gentile Christians. He desired to keep before their minds prominently, that though our Lord was crucified under Pontius Pilate, the persons most to blame for his death were not Gentiles but Jews.

LUKE 23:26-38

26 And as they led him away, they laid hold upon one Simon, a Cyrenian, coming out of the country, and on him they laid the cross, that he might bear *it* after Jesus.

27 And there followed him a great company of people, and of women, which also bewailed and lamented him.

28 But Jesus turning unto them said, Daughters of Jerusalem, weep not for me, but weep for yourselves, and for your children.

29 For, behold, the days are coming, in the which they shall say, Blessed *are* the barren, and the wombs that never bare, and the paps which never gave suck.

30 Then shall they begin to say to the mountains, Fall on us; and to the hills, Cover us.

31 For if they do these things in a green tree, what shall be done in the dry?

32 And there were also two other, malefactors, led with him to be put to death.

33 And when they were come to the place, which is called Calvary, there they crucified him, and the malefactors, one on the right hand, and the other on the left.

34 Then said Jesus, Father, forgive them; for they know not what they do. And they parted his raiment, and cast lots.

35 And the people stood beholding. And the rulers also with them derided *him*, saying, He saved others; let him save himself, if he be Christ, the chosen of God.

36 And the soldiers also mocked him, coming to him, and offering him vinegar,

37 And saying, If thou be the king of the Jews, save thyself.

38 And a superscription also was written over him in letters of Greek, and Latin, and Hebrew, THIS IS THE KING OF THE JEWS.

W E ought to notice, in this passage, *our Lord's words of prophetical warning.* We read that he said to the women who followed him, as he was being led away to Calvary, 'Weep not for me, but for yourselves. For, behold, the days are coming, in the which they shall say, Blessed are the barren, and the wombs that never bare, and the paps which never gave suck.'

These words must have sounded peculiarly terrible to the ears of a Jewish woman. To her it was always a disgrace to be childless. The idea of a time coming when it would be a blessing to have no children must have been a new and tremendous thought to her mind. And yet within fifty years this prediction of Christ was literally fulfilled! The siege of Jerusalem by the Roman army, under Titus, brought down on all the inhabitants of the city the most horrible sufferings from famine and pestilence that can be conceived. Women are reported to have actually eaten their own children during the siege for want of food. Upon none did the last judgments sent upon the Jewish nation fall so heavily as upon the wives, the mothers, and the little children.

Let us beware of supposing that the Lord Jesus holds out to man nothing but mercy, pardon, love, and forgiveness. Beyond all doubt he is plenteous in mercy. There is mercy with him like a mighty stream. He 'delighteth in mercy' (*Mic.* 7:18). But we must never forget that there is justice with him as well as mercy. There are judgments preparing for the impenitent and the unbelieving. There is wrath revealed in the gospel for those who harden themselves in wickedness. The same cloud which was bright to Israel was dark to the Egyptians. The same Lord Jesus who invites the labouring and heavy-laden to come to him and rest, declares most plainly that unless a man repents he will perish, and that he who believeth not shall be damned (*Luke* 13:3; *Mark* 16:16). The same Saviour who now holds out his hands to the disobedient and gainsaying, will come one day in flaming fire, taking vengeance on those that know not God and obey not the gospel (2 *Thess.* 1:8). Let these things sink down into our hearts. Christ is indeed most gracious. But the day of grace must come to an end at last. An unbelieving world will find at length, as Jerusalem did, that there is judgment with God as well as mercy. No wrath will fall so heavily as that which has been long accumulating and heaping up.

We ought to notice, for another thing, in this passage, *our Lord's words of gracious intercession*. We read that when he was crucified, his first words were, 'Father forgive them, for they know not what they do.' His own racking agony of body did not make him forget others. The first of his seven sayings on the cross was a prayer for the souls of his murderers. His prophetical office he had just exhibited by a remarkable prediction. His kingly office he was about to exhibit soon by opening the door of paradise to the penitent thief. His priestly office he now exhibited by interceding for those who crucified him. 'Father,' he said, 'forgive them.'

The fruits of this wonderful prayer will never be fully seen until the day when the books are opened, and the secrets of all hearts are revealed. We have probably not the least idea how many of the conversions to God at Jerusalem which took place during the first six months after the crucifixion, were the direct reply to this marvellous prayer. Perhaps this prayer was the first step towards the penitent thief's repentance. Perhaps it was one means of affecting the centurion, who declared our Lord 'a righteous man,' and the people who 'smote their breasts and returned.' Perhaps the three thousand converted on the day of Pentecost, foremost, it may be at one time among our Lord's murderers, owed their conversion to this very prayer.—The day will declare it. There is nothing secret that shall not be revealed. This only we know, that 'the Father heareth the Son always' (*John* 11:42). We may be sure that this wondrous prayer was heard.

Let us see in our Lord's intercession for those who crucified him, one more proof of Christ's infinite love to sinners. The Lord Jesus is indeed most pitiful, most compassionate, most gracious. None are too wicked for him to care for. None are too far gone in sin for his almighty heart to take interest about their souls. He wept over unbelieving Jerusalem. He heard the prayer of the dying thief. He stopped under the tree to call the publican Zacchæus. He came down from heaven to turn the heart of the persecutor Saul. He found time to pray for his murderers even on the cross. Love like this is a love that passeth knowledge. The vilest of sinners have no cause to be afraid of applying to a Saviour like this. If we want warrant and encouragement to repent and believe, the passage before us surely supplies enough.

Finally, let us see in our Lord's intercession, a striking example of the spirit which should reign in the hearts of all his people. Like him, let us return good for evil, and blessing for cursing. Like him, let us pray for those who evil entreat us and persecute us. The pride of our hearts may often rebel against the idea. The fashion of this world may call it mean-spirited to behave in such a way. But let us never be ashamed to imitate our divine Master. The man who prays for his enemies, shows the mind that was in Christ, and will have his reward.

Notes—Luke 23:26-38

26.—[*As they led him away, etc.*] Let it be noted, that St Luke says nothing about the cruel treatment which our Lord received from the Roman soldiers, after Pilate had condemned him. His Gospel was specially written for the Gentiles, and he purposely passes over the conduct of the Gentiles at this particular stage of our Lord's passion.

I cannot admit the justice of Alford's remark on this verse. He says, 'The break between the twenty-fifth and twenty-sixth verses is harsh in the extreme, and if Luke had any materials wherewith to fill it up, I have no doubt he would have done so.' I deeply regret the tendency of this remark. I believe that St Luke was entirely guided by the Holy Ghost, both in the details which he omits and the details which he inserts. And I believe that the omission of any details of Christ's passion between the condemnation and the going forth to Calvary, was advisedly and wisely ordered, in order to meet the prejudices of Gentile readers.

[*They laid hold upon one Simon, etc.*] It would appear that our Lord carried the cross himself until he was exhausted, and that after this Simon was pressed into the service of carrying it by the soldiers.

Nothing certain is known about this Simon, although the mention of his sons, Alexander and Rufus, by St Mark (*Mark* 15:21), would lead us to suppose that he was a disciple of Christ when the Gospels were written, whatever he was at the time of the crucifixion. Cornelius à Lapide mentions several traditions concerning Simon and his sons, which are not worth repeating.

27.—[*A great company of people and of women.*] Who these were we are not told. Some commentators think they were disciples and friends of Christ. Most think that they were persons who were moved to pity by the sight of an innocent person suffering, but had no sense of their own sins, and no faith in Christ. 'Melting affections,' says Burkitt, 'are not infallible marks of grace, even when they proceed from a sense of Christ's sufferings.' This last opinion seems most probable, when we consider the tenor of the next two verses.

Burgon quotes a remark, 'That no woman is mentioned as speaking against our Lord in his life, or having a share in his death. On the contrary, he was anointed by a woman for his burial;—women were the last at his grave and the first at his resurrection;—to a woman he first appeared when he rose again;—women ministered to his wants;—women bewailed and lamented him;—a heathen woman interceded for his life with her husband, Pilate;—and, above all, of a woman he was born.'

28.—[*Daughters of Jerusalem.*] This expression helps the theory that the people who accompanied our Lord to Calvary were not disciples. We have no account in the Gospels of any women of Jerusalem who believed.

[*Yourselves and your children.*] Let it be noted, that many of the women to whom our Lord here spoke, might easily have been living forty years after, when Titus took Jerusalem.

29.—[*The days are coming, etc.*] These 'days' mean the period of the last wars between the Jews and the Romans, and in particular the siege of Jerusalem.

30.—[*To say to the mountains ... to the hills, etc.*] The expressions of this verse are figurative and parabolical. They signify the intense misery and distress, and the desperate helplessness of all who would be found inside Jerusalem during its siege. See Isaiah 2:19; Hosea 10:8; Revelation 6:16.

Some have seen a reference in the words to the caverns and excavations in the rocks under Jerusalem, in which many of the Jews took refuge when the city was taken.

31.—[*A green tree ... the dry.*] The common opinion of all the best commentators is, that our Lord here contrasts himself and the Jewish nation. 'If the Romans practise such cruelties on me, who am a green tree, and the very source of life, what will they

do one day to your nation, which is like a barren, withered trunk, dead in trespasses and sins?'

Bengel maintains that the 'green tree' here represents the young, strong, and healthy,—and the 'dry tree,' the old, feeble, and barren. In support of this view he quotes a passage from Josephus, describing how the Romans, after Jerusalem was taken, slew the old and feeble Jews, but shut up in confinement those who were vigorous and serviceable. In this opinion, however, Bengel stands almost alone.

32.—[*Malefactors led with him.*] This, let it be noted, was a literal fulfilment of Isaiah's prophecy, that Messiah was to be 'numbered with the transgressors' (*Isa.* 53:12).

33.—[*The place which is called Calvary.*] The reason why this place was so called is not known with certainty, and has given rise to many conjectures.

Origen, Tertullian, Athanasius, Epiphanius, Augustine, Cyril, and others, according to Cornelius à Lapide, hold the absurd opinion, that Calvary was the place where Adam was buried.

Jerome, Beda, Jansenius, and others, hold that Calvary was a place where criminals were executed, and sometimes beheaded, and where skulls and bones of dead men were consequently lying about.

Some have thought that Calvary was a bare, rocky hill, not unlike a skull in shape and appearance, and that hence arose its name.

Let it be noted, that at the time when our Lord was crucified, Calvary was outside the walls of Jerusalem. It was meet and right that our Lord, as the great sacrifice for sin, should suffer without the gate (*Heb.* 13:12). At the present day, the place commonly supposed to have been Calvary is within the walls of Jerusalem.

The common opinion that Calvary was a mount or hill is, at any rate, destitute of any foundation in Scripture. All the four Gospel writers speak of it as 'a place.' Not one of them calls it a 'mount.'

34.—[*Father, forgive them.*] These words were probably spoken while our Lord was being nailed to the cross, or as soon as the cross was reared up on end. It is worthy of remark that as soon as the blood of the great Sacrifice began to flow, the great High Priest began to intercede.

Let it be noted, that during the six hours in which our Lord was on the cross, he showed that he possessed full power as the Son of God, and that though he suffered, his sufferings were voluntarily undertaken. As King and Prophet he opened the gates of life to the penitent thief, and foretold his entrance into paradise. As Priest, he intercedes, in the words before us, for those who crucified him.

[*They know not what they do.*] The principle involved in this saying deserves notice, and requires fencing with two preliminary remarks.

On the one hand, we must beware of supposing that ignorance is not blameworthy, and that ignorant persons *deserve* to be forgiven their sins. At this rate ignorance would be a desirable thing. All spiritual ignorance is more or less culpable. It is part of man's sin, that he does not know better than he does. His not knowing God is only part of his guilt.

On the other hand, we cannot fail to observe in Scripture that sins of ignorance are less sinful before God than sins of knowledge, and that no case is apparently so hopeless as that of the man who sins wilfully against light.

Our Lord's meaning in the words before us appears to be that those who crucified him did not at the time know the full amount of the wickedness they were committing. They knew that they were crucifying one whom they regarded as an impostor. They did not know that they were actually crucifying their own Messiah, the Son of God.—This is what St Peter distinctly asserts, 'I wot that through ignorance ye did it' (*Acts* 3:17). So also St Paul says, 'Had they known it, they would not have crucified the Lord of glory' (*1 Cor.* 2:8). To use the words of Gill on this place, our Lord 'does not mention the ignorance of those he prays for as a plea for pardon, but as a description of their state.' As Clarke observes, 'If ignorance does not excuse a crime, at least it diminishes the intensity of it.'

The question naturally arises, 'Who were those for whom our Lord prayed?'—I cannot, as some do, confine his prayer to the Roman soldiers who nailed him to the cross. I rather regard it as applying also to the great bulk of the Jewish people who were standing by, and aiding and abetting his crucifixion. They were mere tools in the hands of the leading scribes and Pharisees. They were blindly led by blind teachers. They did not really know what they were doing.

Whether our Lord included the chief priests and scribes, Annas and Caiaphas and their companions, who had heard his declaration that he was the Christ, and yet formally rejected and condemned him, I think more than doubtful. I believe they were given over to judicial blindness, and most of them probably perished in their sins. We never read of any of them being converted. The priests who were 'obedient to the faith' (*Acts* 6:7), were probably of a different party from those who condemned Christ.

Let it be noted, that the union of clear head-knowledge of Christ with wilful heart-rejection of him, is the nearest approach that can be made to a definition of the unpardonable sin. St Paul seems to teach this in the sixth chapter of Hebrews. Above all, he seems to point to this when he says of himself, 'I obtained mercy, because I did it ignorantly in unbelief' (*1 Tim.* 1:13).

[*Parted his raiment and cast lots.*] Let it be noted here, that our Lord was evidently crucified naked. The shame and unseemliness of such a posture in death, must doubtless have added much to the misery of the punishment of crucifixion.

The literal fulfilment of the twenty-second Psalm in this verse and in the following one, ought to be carefully observed (*Psa.* 22:17, 18). The prophecies about Christ's first advent to suffer were fulfilled and accomplished in every word. In like manner, and by analogy, we are justified in expecting a literal fulfilment of every word in the prophecies of Christ's second advent to reign in glory.

35.—[*He saved others; let him save himself, if he be Christ.*] The utter blindness of the Jewish nation on the subject of Messiah's sufferings is a very remarkable

348

fact. To us those sufferings appear most plainly foretold by David, Daniel, and Isaiah (*Psa.* 22; *Dan.* 9; *Isa.* 53), and most plainly prefigured and typified by all the sacrifices of the Mosaic law. Yet the Jewish teachers of our Lord's time could not see them. The idea of Messiah 'saving others' by his own death seems never to have entered into their minds. The words before us are a striking proof of the blindness of the rulers. They might have been told most truly, 'Because this person before you is Christ, he does not save himself; and he does not save himself in order that he may save others.'

37.—[*If thou be the king of the Jews, save thyself.*] The difference between the mockery of the Jewish rulers and of the soldiers ought to be noticed. The Jews mocked our Lord as a helpless 'Christ,' or Messiah unable to save himself, and therefore unfit to be a Saviour of Israel.—The ignorant Gentile soldiers, on the contrary, mocked him as a helpless 'King of the Jews,' without a crown, a kingdom, or an army, and therefore only fit to be ridiculed.—The Jew scoffed at his claim to be called the Messiah. The Gentile scoffed at his claim to be regarded as a king. The cross and the apparent weakness were, as usual, the stumbling-stone in both cases.

38.—[*A superscription ... Greek ... Latin ... Hebrew.*] All careful readers of the Bible must have observed that the superscription placed over our Lord's head on the cross is variously given by the Gospel writers. Each one reports it in a manner slightly different from the other three. This apparent discrepancy has given rise to various explanations.

In order to solve the difficulty, we must remember that the superscription was written in three different languages. Greek was the language best known in the world at the time when our Lord was crucified, and there was a Greek superscription for the benefit of strangers from foreign parts.—Latin was the language of the Romans, and there was a Latin superscription, because the sentence on our Lord was passed by a Latin judge, and executed by Latin soldiers.—Hebrew was the language of the Jews, and there was a superscription in the Hebrew tongue, or in some dialect of the Hebrew, because Jesus was crucified as a Jew, that all Jews might see it.—But for anything we know, the superscription in each language may have slightly varied from the superscription in other languages. Matthew may have recorded it as it was in Hebrew,—Mark as it was in Latin,—Luke as it was in Greek;—and John, writing many years after the others, may have given the general substance of the other three.

This solution of the difficulty appears reasonable, and preferable to any other.

[*The King of the Jews.*] Let it be observed, that our Lord was crucified at last as a King. He came to set up a spiritual kingdom, and as a King he died.

LUKE **23**:39-43

39 And one of the malefactors which were hanged railed on him, saying, If thou be Christ, save thyself and us.

40 But the other answering rebuked him, saying, Dost not thou fear God, seeing thou art in the same condemnation?

41 And we indeed justly; for we receive the due reward of our deeds: but this man hath done nothing amiss.

42 And he said unto Jesus, Lord, remember me when thou comest into thy kingdom.

43 And Jesus said unto him, Verily I say unto thee, To day shalt thou be with me in paradise.

T HE verses we have now read deserve to be printed in letters of gold. They have probably been the salvation of myriads of souls. Multitudes will thank God to all eternity that the Bible contains this story of the penitent thief.

We see, firstly, in the history before us, *the sovereignty of God in saving sinners.* We are told that two malefactors were crucified together with our Lord, one on his right hand and the other on his left. Both were equally near to Christ. Both saw and heard all that happened, during the six hours that he hung on the cross. Both were dying men, and suffering acute pain. Both were alike wicked sinners, and needed forgiveness. Yet one died in his sins, as he had lived, hardened, impenitent, and unbelieving. The other repented, believed, cried to Jesus for mercy, and was saved.

A fact like this should teach us humility. We cannot account for it. We can only say, 'Even so, Father; for so it seemed good in thy sight' (*Matt.* 11:26). How it is that under precisely the same circumstances one man is converted and another remains dead in sins,—why the very same sermon is heard by one man with perfect indifference and sends another home to pray and seek Christ,—why the same gospel is hid to one and revealed to another, all these are questions which we cannot possibly answer. We only know that it is so, and that it is useless to deny it.

Our own duty is clear and plain. We are to make a diligent use of all the means which God has appointed for the good of souls. There is no necessity that anyone should be lost. There is no such thing as decreed damnation in the Bible. The offers of the gospel are wide, free, and general. 'In all our doings,' says the 17th Article, 'that will of God is to be followed, which we have expressly declared to us in the Word of God.' God's sovereignty was never meant to destroy man's responsibility. One thief was saved that no sinner might despair, but only one, that no sinner might presume.

We see, secondly, in this history, *the unvarying character of repentance unto salvation.* This is a point in the penitent thief's story which is fearfully overlooked. Thousands look at the broad fact that he was saved in the hour of death, and look no further. They do not look at the distinct and well-defined evidences of repentance which fell from his lips before he died. Those evidences deserve our closest attention.

The first notable step in the thief's repentance was his concern about his companion's wickedness in reviling Christ. 'Dost thou not fear God,' he said, 'seeing thou art in the same condemnation?'—The second step was a full acknowledgment of his own sin. 'We indeed are justly in condemnation. We receive the due reward of our deeds.'—The third step was an open confession of Christ's innocence. 'This man hath done nothing amiss.'—The fourth step was faith in Jesus Christ's power and will to save him. He turned to a crucified sufferer, and called him 'Lord,' and declared his belief that he had a kingdom.—The fifth step was prayer. He cried to Jesus when he was hanging on the cross, and asked him even then to think upon his soul.—The sixth and last step was humility. He begged to be 'remembered' by our Lord. He mentions no great thing. Enough for him if he is remembered by Christ. These six points should always be remembered in connection with the penitent thief. His time was very short for giving proof of his conversion. But it was time well used. Few dying people have ever left behind them such good evidences as were left by this man.

Let us beware of a repentance without evidences. Thousands, it may be feared, are every year going out of the world with a lie in their right hand. They fancy they will be saved because the thief was saved in the hour of death. They forget that if they would be saved as he was, they must repent as he repented. The shorter a man's time is, the better must be the use he makes of it. The nearer he is to death, when he first begins to think, the clearer must be the evidence he leaves behind. Nothing, it may safely be laid down as a general rule, nothing is so thoroughly unsatisfactory as a death-bed repentance.

We see, thirdly, in this history, *the amazing power and willingness of Christ to save sinners.* It is written that he is 'able to save to the uttermost' (*Heb.* 7:25). If we search the Bible through, from Genesis to Revelation, we shall never find a more striking proof of Christ's power and mercy than the salvation of the penitent thief.

The time when the thief was saved was the hour of our Lord's greatest weakness. He was hanging in agony on the cross. Yet even then he heard and granted a sinner's petition, and opened to him the gate of life. Surely this was 'power!'

The man whom our Lord saved was a wicked sinner at the point of death, with nothing in his past life to recommend him, and nothing notable in his present position but a humble prayer. Yet even he was plucked like a brand from the burning. Surely this was 'mercy.'

Do we want proof that salvation is of grace and not of works? We have it in the case before us. The dying thief was nailed hand and foot to the cross. He could do literally nothing for his own soul. Yet even he through Christ's infinite grace was saved. No one ever received such a strong assurance of his own forgiveness as this man.

Do we want proof that sacraments and ordinances are not *absolutely* needful to salvation, and that men may be saved without them when they cannot be had? We have it in the case before us. The dying thief was never baptized, belonged to no visible church, and never received the Lord's supper. But he repented and believed, and therefore he was saved.

Let these things sink down into our hearts. Christ never changes. The way of salvation is always one and the same. He lives who saved the penitent thief. There is hope for the vilest sinner, if he will only repent and believe.

We see, lastly, in the history before us, *how near a dying believer is to rest and glory.* We read that our Lord said to the malefactor in reply to his prayer, 'Today shalt thou be with me in paradise.'

That word 'today' contains a body of divinity. It tells us that the very moment a believer dies, his soul is in happiness and in safe keeping. His full redemption is not yet come. His perfect bliss will not begin before the resurrection morning. But there is no mysterious delay, no season of suspense, no purgatory, between his death and a state of reward. In the day that he breathes his last he goes to paradise. In the hour that he departs he is with Christ (*Phil.* 1:23).

Let us remember these things, when our believing friends fall asleep in Christ. We must not sorrow for them as those who have no hope. While we are sorrowing they are rejoicing. While we are putting on our mourning, and weeping at their funerals, they are safe and happy with their Lord.—Above all, let us remember these things, if we are true Christians, in looking forward to our own deaths. To die is a solemn thing. But if we die in the Lord, we need not doubt that our death will be gain.

Notes—Luke 23:39-43

39.—[*One of the malefactors ... railed ... etc.*] The question naturally arises, How are we to reconcile St Luke's account of the conduct of the thieves with the account given by Matthew and Mark? They distinctly say that both the thieves railed. St Luke says, 'one of them.'

1. Some think that only one thief railed, and that Matthew and Mark use the plural number, in the general way that people sometimes use it, when describing a transaction. They adduce as instances Psalm 2:2; Hebrews 11:33, 34, 37. This, according to Maldonatus, is the opinion of Cyprian, Cyril of Jerusalem, Augustine, Ambrose, Jerome, Gregory, and Leo. It is also held by Scott and Doddridge.

2. Some think that both the thieves railed at first, but that one of them afterwards repented, ceased to rail, and began to pray. This is the opinion of Athanasius, Origen, Hilary, Chrysostom, Theophylact, and Euthymius. If seems far the most probable opinion.

Let it be noted that the impenitent thief is a striking proof that pain, suffering, and the approach of death, are not sufficient, without grace, to convert a soul. The followers of the impenitent thief are unhappily far more numerous than those of the penitent thief.

40.—[*The other answering rebuked him.*] Who this malefactor was, and what

first struck his conscience and moved him to repent, we are not told. Some say, as Bengel, that he was a Gentile; and some, as Scott, that he was a Jew.—Some think, as Suarez, that he had heard our Lord preach, and seen him work miracles at some former period.—Some think, as Euthymius, that he had heard our Lord's answers to Pilate, and been struck by them, and so learned to believe in our Lord's kingdom.—Some think, as Stier, that he was struck by the title put over our Lord's head on the cross.—Some think, as Theophylact, that he was pricked to the heart by hearing our Lord's prayer for his enemies, and by seeing our Lord's patience under sufferings. All these are purely conjectural ideas.

Cornelius à Lapide surpasses all other writers in his remarks on the thief. He mentions with much gravity an opinion of Fererius, that the shadow of Christ on the cross, as the day wore on, fell on the thief, and was the cause of his conversion, as the shadow of Peter healed the sick! He adds another opinion, that the Virgin Mary stood between the thief and Christ and obtained grace for him! He also tells us that the name of the thief was Dismas, that his day in the calendar of saints is March the 25th, and that chapels are erected in honour of his name! It is well that people should know how much rubbish can be found in the pages of an accredited Roman Catholic commentator.

As to the nation of the thief, it is probable that he was a Jew. Our Lord's words to him seem to imply that. He would hardly have spoken of 'paradise' to a Gentile. As to the cause of his conversion, it is safest to rest in the belief that it arose from the free, sovereign grace of Christ, and was intended to be a proof of Christ's power to save even at his time of greatest weakness, and a pattern of Christ's willingness to save the chief of sinners.

[*Dost not thou fear God?*] Our English version has hardly given the full sense of the Greek words. Scholefield would render it, 'Dost not even thou fear God? Even thou, in thy circumstances of desperate wretchedness,—whatever others may do in the unthinking levity of present security.'

41.—[*This man hath done nothing amiss.*] The Greek word here translated, 'amiss,' is only found in two other places (*Acts* 28:6; 2 *Thess.* 3:2). In one it is rendered, 'harm;'—in the other 'unreasonable.'

The sentence rather favours the idea that the thief had either heard or seen something of our Lord before, though he had not been a disciple. We must either suppose this, or else we must suppose that he knew generally that he was being crucified in company with a man whom Pilate and Herod thought innocent.

42.—[*Lord remember me, etc.*] The remarks of Ness on this wonderful prayer are worth reading. 'This short prayer contained a very large and long creed, the articles whereof are these. 1. He believed that the soul died not with the body of man;—2. that there is a world to come for rewarding the pious and penitent, and for punishing the impious and impenitent;—3. that Christ though now under crucifying and killing tortures, yet had right to a kingdom;—4. that this kingdom was in a better world than the present evil world;—5. that Christ would not keep this kingdom all to himself;—6. that he would bestow a part and portion hereof on those that be truly penitent;—7. that the key of this kingdom did hang at Christ's girdle, though he now hung dying on the cross;—8. that he does roll his whole

soul for eternal salvation upon a dying Saviour.'

Ness remarks, also, that the two malefactors, one penitent and the other impenitent, one on the right hand and the other on the left, are 'a clear emblem of the sheep and goats' in the day of judgment.

[*Into thy kingdom.*] Scholefield remarks, that these words would have been better translated, 'in thy kingdom.'

It is observed, justly, by Lightfoot, Bengel, and other writers, that not one of the twelve apostles had such a clear and correct view of the real nature of Christ's 'kingdom' as this penitent thief had.

43.—[*Verily I say unto thee.*] The use of the word 'amen,' or 'verily' here, shows the authority and power with which our Lord even on the cross could save souls, and the certainty with which the grant of paradise was made to the thief. His great faith received a great reward. No child of Adam ever received such an assurance as this.

[*Today shalt thou be with me.*] This sentence deserves close attention.

It is a distinct answer to the Romish doctrine of purgatory. It shows clearly that no purification of any kind after death is needed for the person that dies a penitent believer. If the thief needed no purgatory, the whole doctrine of purgatory falls to the ground.

It is an instructive intimation as to the state of believers after death. The moment they die they are 'with Christ.' Their condition of course is one we cannot pretend to explain. We cannot comprehend the state of a soul separate from the body. Enough for us to know that a dead believer is immediately with Christ.

It is a clear proof of the separate existence of the soul when the body is dead. We shall live and have a being, even when our earthly tabernacle is mouldering in the grave. The thief's body was that day to be broken and mangled by Roman soldiers. But the thief himself was to be with Christ.

Maldonatus, the Roman Catholic commentator, struggles in vain to show that the passage before us does not disprove purgatory. He maintains that the thief must have believed in purgatory, from the fact of his praying to be remembered when Christ came in his kingdom, and not before! Such arguing shows the straits to which a man is reduced by an unscriptural theory.

[*In paradise.*] The word so translated is only found in two other places in the New Testament (2 *Cor.* 12:4 and *Rev.* 2:7). Parkhurst says, 'This is without controversy an oriental word. The Greeks borrowed it from the Persians, among whom it signified a garden, park, or enclosure, full of all the valuable products of the earth. In this sense the word is found in Herodotus, Xenophon, and Diodorus. In the New Testament the word is applied to the state of faithful souls between death and the resurrection, when like Adam in Eden, they are admitted to immediate communion with God in Christ, and to a participation of the true tree of life.'

Brentius maintains that the passion of Christ opened paradise, which had been closed since Adam fell, and that these words proclaimed the opening.

It is clear from the whole narrative that the penitent thief died unbaptized. To avoid this difficulty some writers of Romish tendency have actually caught at the idea, suggested by Augustine, that he was baptized with the blood and water which came from our Lord's side, when it was pierced with a spear! This baseless and gratuitous assertion shows the absurdities into which men may be driven to maintain their theory of baptismal regeneration. It is clear that the thief was born again. It is equally clear that he was never baptized. It follows therefore that a man may be born again without baptism.

The general remarks made by all the best commentators on the case of the penitent thief are very striking. It would be impossible to give them all. Cornelius à Lapide collects many good things from the Fathers, and Gerhard is peculiarly full of good matter in considering the whole narrative.

Heinsius remarks that Christ never wrought a greater or more illustrious miracle than he did in saving the penitent thief.

The Church of England *Homily of Good Works*, quotes Chrysostom, saying, 'I can show a man that by faith without works lived and came to heaven: but without faith never man had life. The thief, that was hanged when Christ suffered, did believe only, and the most merciful God justified him. And because no man shall say, that he lacked time to do good works, for else he would have done them, truth it is, I will not contend therein: but this I will surely affirm that faith only saved him.'

Luther, quoted by Stier, says, 'This is a comfortable symbol and example for all Christians, how that God will never let faith in Christ and a confession of his name go down. If the disciples as a body, and those otherwise related to Christ, confess not and lose their faith, deny him in fear, are offended, and forsake him, this malefactor and murderer must come forward to confess him, to preach him to others, and teach all men who he is and what consolation all may find in him.'

Rollock, on the Passion, says, 'I say of this man, to the glory of God, that he shamed all that stood by. He shamed the apostles and made them cast down their faces. He shamed all men who will not believe, when they see Christ not crucified as he saw, but glorified in the heavens, and sitting at the right hand of Majesty.'—'The Lord raised him up on the gallows to be a teacher of faith and repentance, of hope, of patience, of love, and of all graces. Think no shame to learn of him.'

Baxter says, 'The thief's example showeth us what election freely doeth in calling one, while another is passed by. Christ would give this present proof of the virtue of his sacrifice to call and justify sinners. True conversion is never too late to the obtaining of mercy and salvation. True repentance and faith, however late, will have its fruits. This man was not saved without good works.'

LUKE 23:44-49

44 And it was about the sixth hour, and there was a darkness over all the earth until the ninth hour.

45 And the sun was darkened, and the veil of the temple was rent in the midst.

46 And when Jesus had cried with a loud voice, he said, Father, into thy hands I commend my spirit: and having said thus, he gave up the ghost.

47 Now when the centurion saw what was done, he glorified God, saying, Certainly this was a righteous man.

48 And all the people that came together to that sight, beholding the things which were done, smote their breasts, and returned.

49 And all his acquaintance, and the women that followed him from Galilee, stood afar off, beholding these things.

LET us observe in these verses, *the miraculous signs which accompanied our Lord's death on the cross*. We are told that there was 'a darkness over all the earth' for three hours. 'The sun was darkened, and the veil of the temple was rent in the midst.'

It was meet and right that the attention of all around Jerusalem should be arrested in a marked way, when the great sacrifice for sin was being offered and the Son of God was dying. There were signs and wonders wrought in the sight of all Israel, when the law was given on Sinai. There were signs and wonders in like manner when the atoning blood of Christ was shed on Calvary. There was a sign for an unbelieving world. The darkness at midday was a miracle which would compel men to think.—There was a sign for the professing church and the ministers of the temple. The rending of the veil which hung between the holy place and the holy of holies, was a miracle which would strike awe into the heart of every priest and Levite in Jewry.

Signs like these, on special occasions, let us remember, are a part of God's ways in dealing with man. He knows the desperate stupidity and unbelief of human nature. He sees it necessary to arouse our attention by miraculous works, when he brings in a new dispensation. He thus compels men to open their eyes whether they will or no, and to hear his voice for a little season. He has done so frequently in the days that are past. He did so when he gave the law. He did so in the passage before us when he brought in the gospel. He will do so once more when Christ comes again the second time. He will

356

show a sneering, unbelieving world that he can suspend the laws of nature at his pleasure, and alter the framework of creation as easily as he called the earth into being. He will yet fulfil his words, 'Yet once more, I shake not the earth only, but also heaven.' 'The moon shall be confounded, and the sun ashamed, when the Lord of hosts shall reign in mount Zion' (*Heb.* 12:26; *Isa.* 24:23).

Let us observe, secondly, in these verses, *the remarkable words which our Lord spoke when he died.* We read that 'When he had cried with a loud voice, he said, Father, into thy hands I commend my spirit: and having said thus, he gave up the ghost.'

There is a depth of meaning, no doubt, in these words, which we have no line to fathom. There was something mysterious about our Lord's death, which made it unlike the death of any mere man. He who spoke the words before us, we must carefully remember, was God as well as man. His divine and human nature were inseparably united. His divine nature of course could not die. He says himself, 'I lay down my life, that I might take it again. No man taketh it from me, but I lay it down of myself. I have power to lay it down, and I have power to take it again' (*John* 10:17, 18). Christ died, not as we die when our hour is come,—not because he was compelled and could not help dying,—but voluntarily, and of his own free will.

There is a sense, however, in which our Lord's words supply a lesson to all true Christians. They show us the manner in which death should be met by all God's children. They afford an example which every believer should strive to follow. Like our Master, we should not be afraid to confront the king of terrors. We should regard him as a vanquished enemy, whose sting has been taken away by Christ's death. We should think of him as a foe who can hurt the body for a little season, but after that has no more that he can do. We should await his approaches with calmness and patience, and believe that when flesh fails our soul will be in good keeping. This was the mind of dying Stephen; 'Lord Jesus,' he said, 'receive my spirit.' This was the mind of Paul the aged, when the time of his departure was at hand. He says, 'I know whom I have believed, and am persuaded that he is able to keep that which I have committed to him against that day' (*Acts* 7:59; *2 Tim.* 1:12). Happy indeed are those who have a last end like this!

Let us observe, lastly, in these verses, *the power of conscience in the case of the centurion and the people who saw Christ die.* We are told that the centurion 'glorified God, saying, Certainly this was a righteous man.' We are told that the people who had come together to the sight, 'Smote their breasts, and returned.'

We know not exactly the nature of the feelings here described. We know not the extent to which they went, or the after-fruit which they brought forth. One thing, at all events, is clear. The Roman officer felt convinced that he had been superintending an unrighteous action, and crucifying an innocent person. The gazing crowd were pricked to the heart by a sense of having aided, countenanced, and abetted a grievous wrong. Both Jew and Gentile left Calvary that evening heavy-hearted, self-condemned, and ill at ease.

Great indeed is the power of conscience! Mighty is the influence which it is able to exercise on the hearts of men! It can strike terror into the minds of monarchs on their thrones. It can make multitudes tremble and shake before a few bold friends of truth, like a flock of sheep. Blind and mistaken as conscience often is, unable to convert man or lead him to Christ, it is still a most blessed part of man's constitution, and the best friend in the congregation that the preacher of the gospel has. No wonder that Paul says, 'By manifestation of the truth we commend ourselves to every man's conscience' (*2 Cor.* 4:2).

He that desires inward peace must beware of quarrelling with his conscience. Let him rather use it well, guard it jealously, hear what it has to say, and reckon it his friend. Above all, let him pray daily that his conscience may be enlightened by the Holy Ghost, and cleansed by the blood of Christ. The words of St John are very significant: 'If our heart condemn us not, then have we confidence toward God' (*1 John* 3:21). That man is doing well who can say, 'I exercise myself to have a conscience void of offence toward God and toward man' (*Acts* 24:16).

Notes—Luke 23:44-49

44.—[*About the sixth hour.*] According to the Jewish mode of reckoning, the day began at what we should call six o'clock in the evening. Our Lord was crucified at the third hour, answering to our nine o'clock. The darkness began at the sixth hour, answering to our twelve o'clock in the day. It should be observed, therefore, that the supernatural darkness mentioned here took place precisely at the brightest part of the day, between twelve o'clock and three. Six hours was the whole length of time during which Jesus hung on the cross before he gave up the ghost.

[*There was a darkness.*] This was a miraculous darkness. It could not have been an eclipse of the sun, because our Lord's crucifixion took place at the passover, and the passover was always kept at the full moon, when an eclipse of the sun is impossible.

[*Over all the earth.*] The marginal reading of this expression seems preferable,—'over all the land.' There seems no necessity for supposing that the darkness extended beyond Palestine. Our Lord's ministry was specially directed to Israel, and the land of Israel was the land to which all miracles connected with his life and death were confined. See the same expression in Luke 21:23.

It is difficult to imagine any miraculous sign better calculated to arrest the attention of all people, and to strike awe into all minds than this sudden and unexpected darkness. It necessarily stopped all business and obliged all men to be still, and think what could be its cause.

45.—[*The sun was darkened.*] We are not meant to regard this as a sign, or miracle, distinct from the darkness spoken of in the preceding verse. It is simply an amplification of the same fact, and intended to show how deep and intense the darkness was.

[*The veil of the temple was rent.*] This miracle must have been as striking and terrible to the priests who ministered in the temple, as the darkness was to the inhabitants of Palestine. It signified the opening of the way into the holiest by Christ's death,—the passing away of the Jewish dispensation,—and the revelation of the gospel way of salvation to all mankind.

Doddridge remarks, 'This being a high day, it is probable that Caiaphas the high priest might now be performing the solemn act of burning incense before the veil, which, if he did, it is astonishing that his obstinate heart should not be impressed with so awful and significant a phenomenon. There is no room to doubt that many of the other priests who had a hand in Christ's death saw the pieces of the veil, which considering its texture and other circumstances, must as fully have convinced them of this extraordinary fact, as if they had been present.'

46.—[*Cried with a loud voice.*] This expression, as well as all the verse, deserves particular notice. It shows that there was something peculiar and uncommon about our Lord's death. A dying man's voice is generally not 'loud,' but feeble.

To this circumstance, as well as to the expression 'he gave up the ghost,' all the best commentators from Ambrose downwards, very properly direct our attention. It is evident, they tell us, that the Lord Jesus did not die because he was obliged, but because he chose voluntarily and of his own free will to submit to death. His death was 'his own act.' He '*offered himself* without spot to God.'

Alford, after Stier, remarks that 'none of the Evangelists say that Jesus *died*, although that expression is ever after used of his death, when stated as one great fact.' Matthew says that he 'yielded up the ghost.' Mark, Luke, and John, though in different Greek words, say much the same, 'he gave up the ghost.'

I add to this remark that in all the five Old Testament passages which our translators have rendered, 'giving up the ghost,' the Septuagint Greek translators have not used the expressions applied in the Gospels to our Lord's death, nor anything like them. Genesis 49:33; Job 10:18; 11:20; 14:10; Jeremiah 15:9. I also remark that the Greek expression about Sapphira, which is rendered, 'yielded up the ghost' (*Acts* 5:10), is totally different from those used about our Lord's death.

The remarks of Brentius on the whole verse are peculiarly valuable.

47.—[*This was a righteous man.*] It may be doubted whether these words exactly convey the literal sense of the Greek expression. Alford would render it, 'truly this man was innocent or just.'

48.—[*Beholding the things which were done.*] This expression seems to point to the darkness, and the earthquake which immediately followed our Lord's death. These signs struck awe into the minds of the gazing mob, which had mocked our Lord a few hours before. There was no raillery or mocking after this.

Poole maintains that there is no proof that 'the people' took part in mocking our Lord on the cross, but that it was confined to the scribes and priests. Yet the expression of St Matthew and St Mark about 'those who passed by railing,' besides the priests, seems to make his theory doubtful.

49.—[*The women.*] These would appear to be different from the women to whom our Lord spoke as he was carrying the cross. These came from Galilee. Those were 'daughters of Jerusalem.'

LUKE 23:50-56

50 And, behold, *there was* a man named Joseph, a counseller; *and he was* a good man, and a just:

51 (The same had not consented to the counsel and deed of them;) *he was* of Arimathæa, a city of the Jews: who also himself waited for the kingdom of God.

52 This *man* went unto Pilate, and begged the body of Jesus.

53 And he took it down, and wrapped it in linen, and laid it in a sepulchre that was hewn in stone, wherein never man before was laid.

54 And that day was the preparation, and the sabbath drew on.

55 And the women also, which came with him from Galilee, followed after, and beheld the sepulchre, and how his body was laid.

56 And they returned, and prepared spices and ointments; and rested the sabbath day according to the commandment.

WE see from these verses that *Christ has some disciples of whom little is known.* We are told of one Joseph, 'a good man, and a just,'—a man who 'had not consented to the counsel' of those who condemned our Lord,—a man who 'himself waited for the kingdom of God.' This man went boldly to Pilate after the crucifixion, begged the body of Jesus, 'took it down,' from the cross, and 'laid it in a sepulchre.'

We know nothing of Joseph excepting what is here told us. In no part of the Acts or Epistles do we find any mention of his name. At no former period of our Lord's ministry does he ever come forward. His reason for not openly joining the disciples before, we cannot explain. But here, at the eleventh hour, this man is not afraid to show himself one of our Lord's friends. At the very time when the apostles had forsaken Jesus, Joseph is not ashamed to show his love and respect. Others had confessed him while he was living and doing miracles. It was reserved for Joseph to confess him when he was dead.

The history of Joseph is full of instruction and encouragement. It shows us that Christ has friends of whom the church knows little or nothing, friends who profess less than some do, but friends who in real love and affection are second to none. It shows us, above all, that events may bring out grace in quarters where at present we do not expect it; and that the cause of Christ may prove one day to have many supporters, of whose existence we are at present not aware. These are they whom David calls 'hidden ones,' and Solomon compares to a 'lily among thorns' (*Psa.* 83:3; *Song of Sol.* 2:2).

Let us learn from the case of Joseph of Arimathæa to be charitable and hopeful in our judgments. All is not barren in this world, when our eyes perhaps see nothing. There may be some latent sparks of light when all appear dark. Little plants of spiritual life may be existing in some remote Romish, or Greek, or Armenian congregations, which the Father himself has planted. Grains of true faith may be lying hid in some neglected English parish, which have been placed there by God. There were seven thousand true worshippers in Israel of whom Elijah knew nothing. The day of judgment will bring forward men who seemed last, and place them among the first (*1 Kings* 19:18).

We see, secondly, from these verses, *the reality of Christ's death*. This is a fact which is placed beyond dispute, by the circumstances related about his burial. Those who took his body from the cross, and wrapped it in linen, could not have been deceived. Their own senses must have been witnesses to the fact, that he whom they handled was a corpse. Their own hands and eyes must have told them, that he whom they laid in Joseph's sepulchre was not alive but dead.

The importance of the fact before us, is far greater than a careless reader supposes. If Christ did not really die, there would be an end of all the comfort of the gospel. Nothing short of his death could have paid man's debt to God. His incarnation, and sermons, and parables, and miracles, and sinless obedience to the law, would have availed nothing, if he had not died. The penalty threatened to the first Adam, was death eternal in hell. If the second Adam had not really and actually died in our stead, as well as taught us truth, the original penalty would have continued in full force against Adam and all his children. It was the life-blood of Christ which was to save our souls.

For ever let us bless God that our great Redeemer's death is a fact beyond all dispute. The centurion who stood by the cross, the friends who took out the nails, and laid the body in the grave, the women who stood by and beheld, the priests who sealed up the grave, the soldiers who guarded the sepulchre, all, all are witnesses that Jesus actually was dead. The great sacrifice was really offered. The life of the Lamb was actually taken away. The penalty due to sin, has actually been discharged by our divine Substitute. Sinners believing in Jesus may hope and not be afraid. In themselves they are guilty. But Christ hath died for the ungodly; and their debt is now completely paid.

We see, lastly, in these verses, *the respect paid by Christ's disciples to the fourth commandment.* We are told that the women who had prepared spices and ointment to anoint our Lord's body, 'rested the sabbath day, according to the commandment.'

This little fact is a strong indirect argument in reply to those who tell us that Christ abolished the fourth commandment. Neither here nor elsewhere do we find anything to warrant any such conclusion. We see our Lord frequently denouncing the man-made traditions of the Jews about sabbath observance. We see him purifying the blessed day from superstitious and unscriptural opinions. We see him maintaining firmly that works of necessity and works of mercy were not breaches of the fourth commandment. But nowhere do we find him teaching that the sabbath was not to be kept at all. And here, in the verse before us, we find his disciples as scrupulous as any about the duty of keeping holy a sabbath day. Surely they could never have been taught by their Master that the fourth commandment was not intended to be binding on Christians.

Let us cling firmly to the old doctrine that the sabbath is not a mere Jewish institution, but a day which was meant for man from the beginning, and which was intended to be honoured by Christians quite as much as by Jews. Let us not doubt that the apostles were taught by our Lord to change the day from the last day of the week to the first, although mercifully checked from publicly proclaiming the change in order to avoid giving offence to Israel. Above all, let us regard the sabbath as an institution of primary importance to man's soul, and contend earnestly for its preservation among us in all its integrity. It is good for body, mind, and soul. It is good for the nation which observes it, and for the church which gives it honour. It is but a few steps from 'no sabbath' to 'no God.' The man who would make the sabbath a day for business and pleasure, is an enemy to the best interests of his fellow-creatures. The man who supposes that a believer ought to be so spiritual as not to need the separation of one day in the week from the rest, can know but little of the human heart, or the requirements of our position in an ensnaring and evil world.

Notes—Luke 23:50-56

50.—[*Joseph, a counsellor.*] The meaning of this probably is that Joseph belonged to the great council or Sanhedrim of the Jewish nation. The beginning of the following verse appears to prove that he was present when it was determined to seize Jesus and put him to death, and had voted, or protested, against the decision of the majority.

51.—[*Waited for the kingdom of God.*]

This expression reminds us of the expressions used about Simeon and Anna. Joseph expected the Messiah's spiritual kingdom to be set up, and believed that Jesus was the Messiah.

52.—[*Begged the body.*] This expression deserves notice. It shows that Joseph believed our Lord to be dead. We are also distinctly told by St Mark (*Mark* 15:44) that Pilate only granted the request of Joseph on the express assurance of the centurion that Jesus was dead.

53.—[*Took it down ... wrapped in linen.*] This expression again deserves notice. It is absurd to suppose that the nails could have been drawn from our Lord's hands and feet, and the body prepared for burial by wrapping it in linen, without some signs of life being perceived, if life had remained in him. To see the vastness of the miracle of Christ's resurrection, it is essential to be thoroughly persuaded that Christ really died.

[*A sepulchre that was hewn in stone.*] These sepulchres were generally caves hewn out of the side of a rock, and not graves sunk perpendicularly in the ground. The common pictures of Christ's resurrection give a most incorrect notion of his sepulchre.

The fact that the sepulchre was hewn out of a *rock* deserves notice. It shows that there could not possibly have been any clandestine withdrawal of the body by a subterranean passage dug through earth.

[*Wherein never man before was laid.*] This circumstance is specially mentioned in order to show that no other body but that of our Lord was in the sepulchre, and that the person who rose was Jesus Christ, and no one else.

54.—[*The preparation.*] The day on which our Lord was crucified was the day before the passover sabbath, an occasion of peculiar solemnity. Gill says, 'It was the preparation both for the sabbath and for the Chagigah,—a grand festival which they kept on the fifteenth day of the month in a very pompous manner.'

[*The sabbath drew on.*] This expression is remarkable, and requires explanation. The literal meaning of the Greek would be, 'The sabbath was dawning.' But the Jewish sabbath we know began in the evening at sunset. How then can we explain St Luke's saying, 'The sabbath was dawning?'

Gill says, 'This is so said, though it was evening, on account of the lights which were lighted up in every house at this time.'

Lightfoot says, 'The sabbatical candles which were lighted in honour of the sabbath were now set up.' He also gives a quotation from a rabbinical writer, which says, 'By the light of the fourteenth day they made a search for leaven by the light of a candle.'

Poole says that some refer the expression to the evening star which was beginning to rise. Cocceius thinks it must mean the next morning.

Campbell says, 'In all other nations but the Jewish, it was customary to reckon the morning the first part of the day, and the evening the second. Luke, who according to Eusebius had lived much among the Gentiles and those who used this style of speaking, would insensibly acquire a habit of using it.'

Alford considers that St Luke employed 'a natural word, used of the conventional day beginning at sunset.'

I believe this last explanation to be the right one. We use several expressions ourselves, such as the sun 'rising' and 'setting,' which are not strictly accurate and scientifically correct. But they are the only expressions that the most would understand. If Luke had said, 'The sabbath began to grow dusky or gloomy,' no Gentile reader would have understood him.

55.—[*The women which, etc.*] This verse is meant to show us, that friends of our Lord who could not possibly be mistaken as to his identity, were witnesses to the fact of his burial, and actually saw his body laid in the grave. They saw the linen in which he was wrapped, and could therefore testify two days after, that the very same linen was found wrapped together in the empty tomb.

56.—[*They prepared spices and ointments.*] This shows that the women were fully satisfied that our Lord was dead and had also no expectation that he would rise again.

[*Rested the sabbath day.*] Burgon remarks, 'These pious women, eager as they were to perform the last offices of love to their Lord, yet would not transgress the commandment. How blessed was the result! How unblessed would have been the impatient yielding to their own inclination! Had they presented themselves sooner at the grave, they would have been grieved by the presence or molested by the rudeness of the Roman soldiers; while their purpose could not possibly have been effected. By waiting till the sabbath was past, they found the guard dispersed, and their Lord already risen. They unbound those limbs alive, which they had come to weep over and anoint in death.'

LUKE 24:1-12

1 Now upon the first *day* of the week, very early in the morning, they came unto the sepulchre, bringing the spices which they had prepared, and certain *others* with them.

2 And they found the stone rolled away from the sepulchre.

3 And they entered in, and found not the body of the Lord Jesus.

4 And it came to pass, as they were much perplexed thereabout, behold, two men stood by them in shining garments:

5 And as they were afraid, and bowed down *their* faces to the earth, they said unto them, Why seek ye the living among the dead?

6 He is not here, but is risen: remember how he spake unto you when he was yet in Galilee,

7 Saying, The Son of man must be delivered into the hands of sinful men, and be crucified, and the third day rise again.

8 And they remembered his words,

9 And returned from the sepulchre, and told all these things unto the eleven, and to all the rest.

10 It was Mary Magdalene, and Joanna, and Mary *the mother* of James, and other *women that were* with them, which told these things unto the apostles.

11 And their words seemed to them as idle tales, and they believed them not.

12 Then arose Peter, and ran unto the sepulchre; and stooping down, he beheld the linen clothes laid by themselves, and departed, wondering in himself at that which was come to pass.

THE resurrection of Christ is one of the great foundation stones of the Christian religion. In practical importance it is second only to the crucifixion. The chapter we have now begun directs our mind to the evidence of the resurrection. It contains unanswerable proof that Jesus not only died, but rose again.

We see, in the verses before us, *the reality of Christ's resurrection.* We read, that 'upon the first day of the week' certain women came to the sepulchre in which the body of Jesus had been laid, in order to anoint him. But when they came to the place, 'they found the stone rolled away. And they entered in, and found not the body of the Lord Jesus.'

This simple fact is the starting point in the history of the resurrection of Christ. On Friday evening his body was safe in the tomb. On Sunday morning his body was gone. By whose hands had it been taken away? Who had removed it? Not surely the priests and scribes and other enemies of Christ! If they had had Christ's body to show in disproof of his resurrection, they would gladly have shown it.—Not the apostles and other disciples of our Lord! They were far too much frightened and dispirited to attempt such an action, and the more so when they had nothing to gain by it. One explanation, and one only, can meet the circumstance of the case. That explanation is the one supplied by the angels in the verse before us. Christ 'had risen' from the grave. To seek him in the sepulchre was seeking 'the living among the dead.' He had risen again, and was soon seen alive and conversing in the body by many credible witnesses.

The fact of our Lord's resurrection rests on evidence which no infidel can ever explain away. It is confirmed by testimony of every kind, sort, and description. The plain unvarnished story which the Gospel writers tell about it, is one that cannot be overthrown. The more the account they give is examined, the more inexplicable will the event appear, unless we accept it as true. If we choose to deny the truth of their account we may deny everything in the world. It is not so certain that Julius Cæsar once lived, as it is that Christ rose again.

Let us cling firmly to the resurrection of Christ, as one of the pillars of the gospel. It ought to produce in our minds a settled conviction of the truth of Christianity. Our faith does not depend merely on a set of texts and doctrines. It is founded on a mighty fact which the sceptic has never been able to overturn.—It ought to assure us of the certainty of the resurrection of our own bodies after death. If our Master has risen from the grave, we need not doubt that his disciples shall rise again at the last day.—Above all it ought to fill our hearts with a joyful sense of the fulness of gospel salvation. Who is he that shall condemn us? Our great Surety has not only died for us but risen again (*Rom.* 8:34). He has gone to prison for us, and come forth triumphantly after atoning for our sins. The payment he made for us has been accepted. The work of satisfaction has been perfectly accomplished. No wonder that St Peter exclaims, 'Blessed be the God and Father of our Lord Jesus Christ, which according to his abundant mercy, has begotten us again unto a lively hope by the resurrection of Jesus Christ from the dead' (*1 Pet.* 1:3).

We see, secondly, in the verses before us, *how dull the memory of the disciples was about some of our Lord's sayings.* We are told that the angels who appeared to the women, reminded them of their Master's words in Galilee, foretelling his own crucifixion and resurrection. And then we read, 'They remembered his words.' They had heard them but made no use of them. Now after many days they call them to mind.

This dullness of memory is a common spiritual disease among believers. It prevails as widely now as it did in the days of the first disciples. It is one among many proofs of our fallen and corrupt condition. Even after men have been renewed by the Holy Ghost, their readiness to forget the promises and precepts of the gospel is continually bringing them into trouble. They hear many things which they ought to store up in their hearts, but seem to forget as fast as they hear. And then, perhaps after many days, affliction brings them up before their recollection, and at once it flashes across their minds that they heard them long ago! They find that they had heard, but heard in vain.

The true cure for a dull memory in religion, is to get deeper love toward Christ, and affections more thoroughly set on things above. We do not readily forget the things we love, and the objects which we keep continually under our eyes. The names of our parents and children are always remembered. The face of the husband or wife we love is graven on the tablets of our hearts. The more our affections are engaged in Christ's service, the more easy shall we find it to remember Christ's words. The words of the apostle ought to be carefully pondered: 'We ought to give the more earnest heed to the things which we have heard, lest at any time we should let them slip' (*Heb.* 2:1).

We see, lastly, *how slow of belief the first disciples were on the subject of Christ's resurrection.* We read that when the women returned from the sepulchre and told the things they had heard from the angels to the eleven apostles, 'their words seemed to them as idle tales, and they believed them not.' In spite of the plainest declarations from their Master's own lips that he would rise again the third day,—in spite of the distinct testimony of five or six credible witnesses that the sepulchre was empty, and that angels had told them he was risen,—in spite of the manifest impossibility of accounting for the empty tomb on any other supposition than that of a miraculous resurrection,—in spite of all this, these eleven faithless ones would not believe!

Perhaps we marvel at their unbelief. No doubt it seems at first sight most senseless, most unreasonable, most provoking, most unaccountable. But shall we not do well to look at home? Do we not see around us in the Christian churches a mass of unbelief far more unreasonable and far more blameworthy than that of the apostles? Do we not see, after eighteen centuries of additional proofs that Christ has risen from the dead, a general want of faith, which is truly deplorable? Do we not see myriads of professing Christians who seem not to believe that Jesus died and rose again, and is coming to judge the world? These are painful questions. Strong faith is indeed a rare thing. No wonder that our Lord said, 'When the Son of man cometh, shall he find faith on the earth?' (*Luke* 18:8).

Finally, let us admire the wisdom of God, which can bring great good out of seeming evil. The unbelief of the apostles is one of the strongest indirect evidences that Jesus rose from the dead. If the disciples were at first so backward to believe our Lord's resurrection, and were at last so thoroughly persuaded of its truth that they preached it everywhere, Christ must have risen indeed. The first preachers were men who were convinced in spite of themselves, and in spite of determined, obstinate unwillingness to believe. If the apostles at last believed, the resurrection must be true.

Notes—Luke 24:1-12

1.—[*The first day of the week.*] This, we must remember, was our Sunday. The Jewish sabbath was our Saturday.

[*Very early in the morning.*] Let it be noted that this early visit to the sepulchre is a strong proof of the love and affection of these holy women. For women to go to a place of burial near a crowded city, before the sun was risen, faith and courage were needed.

[*The spices.*] We are told by John that Joseph and Nicodemus had already used 'a hundred pounds weight' of myrrh and aloes, when they buried our Lord (*John* 19:39). But it is probable that for want of time these spices were used hurriedly and imperfectly. Some commentators say, that the process of embalming and applying spices to dead bodies, was usually repeated for several days together, in order that the aromatic and antiseptic compounds might have their full effect.

2.—[*The stone rolled away.*] This, according to St Matthew (*Matt.* 28:2), had been the first great sign attending the resurrection. At the sight of the angels who rolled away the stone, the Roman guard was first terrified and then fled. After this the women came, and found the grave empty.

3.—[*The Lord Jesus.*] Bishop Brownrig remarks that this is the first time in the New Testament that our Saviour is so termed. The Lord,—Christ,—Jesus, are names he frequently has had. Here, after his resurrection as a conqueror, St Luke calls him 'the Lord Jesus.'

4.—[*Much perplexed.*] They could not tell what to make of the facts before them,—the empty sepulchre,—the linen clothes lying by themselves,—the body gone.

[*Two men.*] Here, as in another place (*Acts* 1:10), we are, of course, to understand angels in the appearance of men. The frequency with which St Luke mentions angels is a peculiar feature in his Gospel. An angel appears to Zacharias, an angel appears to the Virgin Mary, angels appear to the shepherds when our Lord is born, all mentioned only in St Luke.

5.—[*The living.*] It admits of doubt whether the Greek expression here would not have been more literally rendered, 'the living One,'—the great source of life, the life of the world.

6.—[*In Galilee.*] This expression shows, no less than many other similar ones, that the greater part of our Lord's discourses and sermons were delivered in Galilee.

Some have indulged in unprofitable speculations on this verse, as to the remembrance of the things spoken in Galilee, which the angels exhibit in this verse. It ought to content us to remember that these angels were executing a commission and delivering a message entrusted to them by God. There is no warrant for the assertion that angels know everything spoken to God's people, and can afterwards repeat it.

7.—[*Must be delivered.*] The Greek words here mean, 'It is necessary that he should be delivered,'—necessary for the fulfilment of prophecies and types, necessary for the redemption of sinners.

8.—[*They remembered.*] Ford quotes a good remark of Cecil's on this expression: 'It is not sufficiently considered how much more we need recollection than information.'

9.—[*Told all these things, etc.*] Augustine remarks that these women were 'the first preachers of the resurrection of Christ.'

[*To all the rest.*] Who these were we do not know. It is evident that our Lord had other disciples in Jerusalem beside the eleven. On the day of his ascension the number of names was a 'hundred and twenty.'

10.—[*Other women.*] Who these were we do not know. They were probably the same spoken of in a former place, who ministered to our Lord (*Luke* 8:2).

11.—[*Idle tales.*] The Greek word so rendered is only found here. According to Parkhurst it means, 'Words of no value; idle nonsense.'

12.—[*Peter.*] We can well understand that Peter would be in a peculiarly sensitive and anxious state of conscience. On the very chance of the report being true he goes to see for himself.

[*The linen clothes laid by themselves.*] All writers on the resurrection of Christ, call attention with much justice to this fact. If the body of our Lord had been stolen from the grave by his friends, it is most improbable that those who stole it would have taken the trouble to remove the linen clothes and wrap them together in an orderly manner.

[*Departed ... wondering in himself.*] It is the opinion of those who are best judges, that these words would be better rendered, 'departed to his own house wondering' (see *John* 20:10).

LUKE 24:13-35

13 And, behold, two of them went that same day to a village called Emmaus, which was from Jerusalem *about* threescore furlongs.

14 And they talked together of all these things which had happened.

15 And it came to pass, that, while they communed *together* and reasoned, Jesus himself drew near, and went with them.

16 But their eyes were holden that they should not know him.

17 And he said unto them, What manner of communications *are* these that ye have one to another, as ye walk, and are sad?

18 And the one of them, whose name was Cleopas, answering said unto him, Art thou only a stranger in Jerusalem, and hast not known the things which are come to pass there in these days?

19 And he said unto them, What things? And they said unto him, Concerning Jesus of Nazareth, which was a prophet mighty in deed and word before God and all the people:

20 And how the chief priests and our rulers delivered him to be condemned to death, and have crucified him.

21 But we trusted that it had been he which should have redeemed Israel: and beside all this, to day is the third day since these things were done.

22 Yea, and certain women also of our company made us astonished, which were early at the sepulchre;

23 And when they found not his body, they came, saying, that they had also seen a vision of angels, which said that he was alive.

24 And certain of them which were with us went to the sepulchre, and found *it* even so as the women had said: but him they saw not.

25 Then he said unto them, O fools, and slow of heart to believe all that the prophets have spoken:

26 Ought not Christ to have suffered these things, and to enter into his glory?

27 And beginning at Moses and all the prophets, he expounded unto them in all the scriptures the things concerning himself.

28 And they drew nigh unto the village, whither they went: and he made as though he would have gone further.

29 But they constrained him, saying, Abide with us: for it is toward evening, and the day is far spent. And he went in to tarry with them.

30 And it came to pass, as he sat at meat with them, he took bread, and blessed *it*, and brake, and gave to them.

31 And their eyes were opened, and they knew him; and he vanished out of their sight.

32 And they said one to another, Did not our heart burn within us, while he talked with us by the way, and while he opened to us the scriptures?

33 And they rose up the same hour, and returned to Jerusalem, and found the eleven gathered together, and them that were with them,

34 Saying, The Lord is risen indeed, and hath appeared to Simon.

35 And they told what things *were done* in the way, and how he was known of them in breaking of bread.

T HE history contained in these verses is not found in any other Gospel but that of St Luke. Of all the eleven appearances of Christ after his resurrection, none perhaps is so interesting as the one described in this passage.

Let us mark, in these verses, *what encouragement there is to believers to speak to one another about Christ.* We are told of two disciples walking together to Emmaus, and talking of their Master's crucifixion. And then come the remarkable words, 'While they communed together and reasoned, Jesus himself drew near, and went with them.'

Conference on spiritual subjects is a most important means of grace. As iron sharpeneth iron, so does exchange of thoughts with brethren sharpen a believer's soul. It brings down a special blessing on all who make a practice of it. The striking words of Malachi were meant for the church in every age;—'Then they that feared the Lord spake often one to another: and the Lord hearkened, and heard it, and a book of remembrance was written before him for them that feared the Lord, and that thought upon his name. And they shall be mine, saith the Lord of hosts, in that day when I make up my jewels' (*Mal.* 3:16, 17).

What do we know ourselves of spiritual conversation with other Christians? Perhaps we read our Bibles, and pray in private, and use public means of grace. It is all well, very well. But if we stop short here we neglect a great privilege and have yet much to learn. We ought to 'consider one another to provoke unto love and good works.' We ought to 'exhort' and 'edify one another' (*Heb.* 10:24; *1 Thess.* 5:11). Have we no time for spiritual conversation? Let us think again. The quantity of time wasted on frivolous, trifling, and unprofitable talk, is fearfully great.—Do we find nothing to say on spiritual subjects? Do we feel tongue-tied and dumb on the things of Christ? Surely if this is the case, there must be something wrong within. A heart right in the sight of God will generally find words. 'Out of the abundance of the heart the mouth speaketh' (*Matt.* 12:34).

Let us learn a lesson from the two travellers to Emmaus. Let us speak of Jesus, when we are sitting in our houses and when we are walking by the way, whenever we can find a disciple to speak to (*Deut.* 6:7). If we believe we are journeying to a heaven where Christ will be the central object of every mind, let us begin to learn the manners of heaven, while we are yet upon earth. So doing we shall often have One with us whom our eyes will not see, but One who will make our hearts 'burn within us' by blessing the conversation.

Let us mark, secondly, in these verses, *how weak and imperfect was the knowledge of some of our Lord's disciples.* We are told that the two disciples confessed frankly that their expectations had been disappointed by the crucifixion of Christ. 'We trusted,' said they, 'that it had been he which should have redeemed Israel.' A temporal redemption of the Jews by a conqueror appears to have been the redemption which they looked for. A spiritual redemption by a sacrificial death was an idea which their minds could not thoroughly take in.

Ignorance like this, at first sight, is truly astounding. We cannot be surprised at the sharp rebuke which fell from our Lord's lips, 'O fools, and slow of heart to believe.' Yet ignorance like this is deeply instructive. It shows us how little cause we have to wonder at the spiritual darkness which obscures the minds of careless Christians. Myriads around us are just as ignorant of the meaning of Christ's suffering as these travellers to Emmaus. As long as the world stands the cross will seem foolishness to natural man.

Let us bless God that there may be true grace hidden under much intellectual ignorance. Clear and accurate knowledge is a most useful thing, but it is not absolutely needful to salvation, and may even be possessed without grace. A deep sense of sin, a humble willingness to be saved in God's way, a teachable readiness to give up our own prejudices when a more excellent way is shown, these are the principal things. These things the two disciples possessed, and therefore our Lord 'went with them' and guided them into all truth.

Let us mark, thirdly, in these verses, *how full the Old Testament is of Christ.* We are told that our Lord began 'at Moses and all the prophets, and expounded in all the scriptures the things concerning himself.'

How shall we explain these words? In what way did our Lord show 'things concerning himself,' in every part of the Old Testament field? The answer to these questions is short and simple. Christ was the substance of every Old Testament sacrifice, ordained in the law of Moses. Christ was the true Deliverer and King, of whom all the judges and deliverers in Jewish history were types. Christ was the coming Prophet greater than Moses, whose glorious advent filled the pages of prophets. Christ was the true seed of the woman who was to bruise the serpent's head,—the true seed in whom all nations were to be blessed,—the true Shiloh to whom the people were to be gathered,—the true scapegoat,—the true brazen serpent,—the true Lamb to which every daily offering pointed,—the true High Priest of whom every descendant of Aaron was a figure. These things, or something like them, we need not doubt, were some of the things which our Lord expounded in the way to Emmaus.

Let it be a settled principle in our minds, in reading the Bible, that Christ is the central sun of the whole book. So long as we keep him in view, we shall never greatly err, in our search for spiritual knowledge. Once losing sight of Christ, we shall find the whole Bible dark and full of difficulty. The key of Bible knowledge is Jesus Christ.

Let us mark, finally, in these verses, *how much Christ loves to be entreated by his people*. We are told, that when the disciples drew nigh to Emmaus, our Lord 'made as though he would have gone further.' He desired to see if they were weary of his conversation. But it was not so. 'They constrained him, saying, Abide with us: for it is toward evening, and the day is far spent. And he went in to tarry with them.'

Cases like this are not uncommon in Scripture. Our Lord sees it good for us to prove our love, by withholding mercies till we ask for them. He does not always force his gifts upon us, unsought and unsolicited. He loves to draw out our desires, and to compel us to exercise our spiritual affections, by waiting for our prayers. He dealt so with Jacob at Peniel. 'Let me go,' he said, 'for the day breaketh.' And then came the noble declaration from Jacob's lips, 'I will not let thee go, except thou bless me' (*Gen.* 32:26). The story of the Canaanitish mother, the story of the healing of two blind men at Jericho, the story of the nobleman at Capernaum, the parables of the unjust judge and friend at midnight, are all meant to teach the same lesson. All show that our Lord loves to be entreated, and likes importunity.

Let us act on this principle in all our prayers, if we know anything of praying. Let us ask much, and ask often, and lose nothing for want of asking. Let us not be like the Jewish king who smote three times on the ground, and then stayed his hand (*2 Kings* 13:18). Let us rather remember the words of David's Psalm, 'Open thy mouth wide, and I will fill it' (*Psa.* 81:10). It is the man who puts a holy constraint on Christ in prayer, who enjoys much of Christ's manifested presence.

Notes—Luke 24:13-35

13.—[*Two of them.*] We are not told who these two disciples were, except that one of them was named Cleopas. Several conjectures have been made about the other one. Epiphanius supposes he was Nathanael. Origen calls him Simeon. Ambrose calls him Amaon. Theophylact suggests that it was Luke himself. All this is guesswork. We know nothing certain about it, excepting this, that it could not have been one of the apostles. We are distinctly told that when these two disciples returned to Jerusalem 'they found the eleven gathered together.'—This point ought to be carefully noticed.

Lightfoot says, 'It seems to me beyond question, that one of the disciples going to Emmaus was Peter, who hearing from the women that the Lord had risen, and sent him a message, and spoken of going to Galilee, took Cleopas and made off towards Galilee.'—This opinion seems very improbable.

[*Went that same day.*] Henry says on this expression, 'I suspect that they were going homeward to Galilee, with an intention not to inquire more about this Jesus;

that they were meditating a retreat, and went away from their company without asking or taking leave.'—This is, no doubt, an ingenious conjecture. But I see nothing to warrant it.

16.—[*Should not know him.*] Let it be noted here, that St Mark mentions that he 'appeared in another form' (*Mark* 16:12). This circumstance would account for their not recognizing him. At the same time it is clear that in some miraculous way the eyes of the disciples were holden or restrained from seeing aright (see *2 Kings* 6:17-20).

17.—[*He said.*] Bengel remarks here, that 'it is the part of wisdom to pass with ease into profitable conversation.'

[*What manner of communications ... ye have.*] The literal rendering of the Greek words here would be, 'What sayings or words are these which ye cast against one another, or bandy about?'

The parallel between Joseph and our Lord Jesus Christ ought to be noticed at this part of our Lord's history. The conduct of Joseph in not discovering himself to his brethren, and in trying them by delay, was a type of our Lord's dealings with his two disciples before manifesting himself to them. The whole history of Joseph is probably much more typical than we suppose.

18.—[*Art thou only a stranger, etc.*] The Greek words so rendered are somewhat peculiar. Alford translates them, 'Dost thou lodge alone at Jerusalem?'—Major renders them, 'Art thou that one individual who sojournest at Jerusalem, and hast not known,' etc.,—meaning, 'There surely cannot be another, whether stranger or resident, who has not heard of these events.'

The whole verse is an important evidence of the publicity and notoriety of our Lord Jesus Christ's crucifixion.

19.—[*What things?*] Our Lord, both here and at a latter part of his history draws out from the disciples their opinions, feelings, and wishes. By asking a question he elicits a declaration of the exact state of their minds about himself.

[*A prophet, etc.*] The exceeding dimness of the disciples' apprehension of our Lord's divinity and atonement, is strikingly brought out in this description.

[*Before God and the people.*] This must mean 'By the testimony both of God and the Jewish nation.'—We read elsewhere that 'God bare him witness by signs and wonders' (*Acts* 2:22). The people also 'bare record' (*John* 12:17).

21.—[*He which should have redeemed Israel.*] The exact kind of redemption expected by the disciples we are left to conjecture. But it is clear that like most Jews, they looked much more for a temporal Redeemer than a spiritual one. They looked for a redemption like that of their forefathers out of Egypt. Hence their excessive perplexity and amazement, when he who they thought would prove the Redeemer was crucified.

[*Today is the third day.*] There certainly seems a reference in the mind of Cleopas to something which was to happen on the 'third day,' according to promise. He speaks like one who had an indistinct recollection of our Lord's sayings about rising again upon the third day, but had never understood their meaning.

Lightfoot remarks on this verse, what notice the rabbins take of the third day, and conjectures that the Jewish idea about the third day may be traced in the saying of Cleopas, as well as a reference to our Lord's predictions. He points out the frequency with which the third day is referred to in the Old Testament (*Gen.* 22:4; *Hos.* 6:2; *Gen.* 42:18; *Josh.* 2:16; *Exod.* 19:16; *Jon.* 1:17; *Ezra* 8:15; *Esther* 5:1.)

24.—[*Certain of them, etc.*] St Luke has only told us of Peter having gone to the grave. From St John we learn that John accompanied him.

25.—[*Fools.*] The Greek word so rendered is not the same word which is so translated in the Sermon on the Mount (*Matt.* 5:22). Here it only means 'wanting in thought, understanding, and consideration,' and does not imply any contempt.

[*Slow of heart to believe all ... prophets have spoken.*] This expression should be carefully noted. The disciples believed *many* things which the prophets had spoken. But they did not believe *all*. They believed the predictions of Messiah's glory, but not of Messiah's sufferings. Christians in modern times too often err in like manner, though in a totally different direction. They believe *all* that the prophets say about Christ's sufferings, but *not all* that they say about Christ coming the second time in glory.

26.—[*Ought not.*] This means, 'was it not fitting, meet, and needful;'—'did it not behove,' in order to the fulfilment of prophecies and types, that Christ should suffer? It is the same Greek word translated 'behoved,' at the forty-sixth verse.

[*Suffered ... enter ... glory.*] Here our Lord briefly states the whole truth concerning the expected Messiah. He was one who was to suffer first and afterwards to reign,—to be cut off first and afterwards have a kingdom,—to be led as a lamb to the slaughter first, and afterwards to divide the spoil as a conqueror.

27.—[*Beginning at Moses, etc.*] Many a commentator has remarked on this verse, that it would have been a blessing to the church if it had possessed the exposition which our Lord here gave. For wise reasons it has been withheld from us. Several have attempted to supply conjecturally the general substance of this exposition, and specially Gerhard, Bullinger, and Stella. But it is probable that we have, at best, very

375

inadequate ideas of the fulness of our Lord's exposition. Judging from the use he made of Scripture during his ministry, he saw probably many 'things concerning himself' which modern commentators utterly fail to discover.

Alford remarks, 'Observe the testimony which this verse gives to the divine authority, and Christian interpretation of the Old Testament Scriptures. The denial of reference to Christ's death and glory in the Old Testament, is a denial of Christ's own teaching.'

28.—[*He made as though ... gone further.*] Many very unprofitable remarks have been made on this expression. Some have gone so far as to assert that it justifies dissimulation and a certain degree of untruthfulness on some occasions. Such assertions are too monstrous and absurd to deserve serious refutation.

Alford remarks, 'It is not implied that our Lord said anything to indicate that he would go further, but simply that he was passing on.' He quotes also a passage from Jeremy Taylor's *Sermon on Christian Simplicity*, explanatory of this expression:—'Our blessed Saviour pretended that he would pass forth from Emmaus; but if he intended not to do it, he did no injury to the two disciples, for whose good he intended to make this offer. Neither did he prevaricate the strictness of simplicity and sincerity, because they were persons with whom he had made no contracts, to whom he had passed no obligations. In the nature of the thing it is proper and natural by an offer to give an occasion to another to do good actions; and in case it succeeds not then, to do what was intended not. And so the offer was conditional.'

I have quoted this passage from a desire to meet the possible objections of scrupulous consciences. To my own mind it seems surprising that anyone can stumble at the expression before us, or can find ground for supposing that our Lord meant to deceive. Our Lord used the readiest and most natural means to draw out the feelings of his disciples, by walking on as if he intended to go further. But it seems to me as unreasonable to see in this an intention to deceive, as it would be to see dishonesty in his first

question, 'What manner of communications are these that ye have?' He knew all things, and had no real occasion to ask. But he asked in order to draw out the minds of his disciples.

29.—[*They constrained him.*] Let it be noted that we have several instances of expressions like this in Scripture used upon similar occasions. Abraham said, 'Pass not away, I pray thee, from thy servant' (*Gen.* 18:3). Gideon said, 'Depart not hence, I pray thee, until I come unto thee' (*Judg.* 6:18). Manoah and his wife said, 'I pray thee, let us detain thee' (*Judg.* 13:15). All show that God loves to be entreated of his people, and that those who would have much must ask much, and even use a holy violence.

30.—[*He took bread, and blessed ... brake ... gave, etc.*] The action mentioned here has occasioned much difference of opinion.

1. Some think that no particular sense is to be attached to the expression, and that it means that Jesus was recognized at the time when he brake bread.

2. Some think that there was something peculiar in our Lord's manner and demeanour at breaking of bread, which was well known to the disciples. Lyranus and Stella even go so far as to say that he broke bread in a miraculous manner, like one cutting with a knife. According to Schoettgen, Jewish teachers used to be known and recognized by their disciples by their peculiar gestures.

3. Some think that the whole passage refers to the Lord's supper. This opinion is stoutly defended by Maldonatus and Cornelius à Lapide, the Romish commentators, and maintained even by Wordsworth among modern English Protestants.—The two Romish writers go so far as to maintain that the passage shows the propriety of the bread only and not the cup being given to the laity in the Lord's supper. It is only fair to say that not all Romish writers maintain this opinion respecting the Lord's supper being meant. Jansenius and Stella deny it entirely. Barradius and Bellarmine allow that it is just as probable that the Lord's supper is not meant, as that it is meant!

I have little doubt that the expression

refers to some well-known and peculiar gesture of our Lord in the act of breaking bread, with which all his disciples were familiar. I think it even possible that there is a reference to our Lord's demeanour at the miracle of feeding the multitude with a few loaves and fishes.

Alford suggests that the marks of the nails in our Lord's hands may have been first noticed as he was breaking bread.

That it could not be the Lord's supper appears clear to my own mind for the following reasons.—Firstly, it was impossible that the two disciples could recognize anything in our Lord's manner of breaking the bread to remind them of the Lord's supper, because they were not present at the institution, and the two disciples were evidently not apostles.—Secondly, it is mere gratuitous assumption to say that the Lord's supper is meant, when we find no words of consecration used, and no mention of wine. Even the Roman Catholics must allow that without consecration and the presence of wine, there is no sacrament. They will hardly dare to say that the two disciples at Emmaus were *laymen*.—Thirdly, the words of our Lord at the time of the first institution of the Lord's supper, that he would no more 'drink the fruit of the vine' with his disciples, make it highly improbable that the sacrament can be here referred to.

The quotations of the Fathers given by the Romish writers in defence of this opinion about the Lord's supper are most meagre and unsatisfactory. At best they only prove, as Jansenius remarks, that some of the Fathers thought the transaction at Emmaus figurative of the Lord's supper.

The plain truth is that both here and elsewhere the carnal mind of man catches at the least pretext for making everything in religion material and sensual, and strains every possible expression into a material sense. All texts about eating, and drinking, and a cup, and bread, must needs signify the Lord's supper! All texts about washing, and water, and purifying, and the like, must needs mean baptism! Against such interpretations of Scripture we must always be on our guard.

Lightfoot remarks, 'It is strange that any should interpret this breaking of bread of the holy eucharist, when Christ himself had determined to disappear in the very distribution of the bread, and so interrupt the supper. And where indeed doth it appear that any of them tasted a bit? The supper was ended before it began.'—'The rabbins say, if three eat together, they are bound to say grace.'

31.—[*Their eyes were opened ... knew him.*] The manner of this sudden revelation of Christ we cannot explain. The whole transaction is so miraculous that we can only take the words as we find them, and must not waste time in attempting to define what is beyond our comprehension.

[*Vanished out of their sight.*] This and other expressions concerning our Lord's risen body, show plainly that it was a body in some wonderful way different from the common body of man. It was a real material body and true flesh and blood. But it was a body capable of moving, appearing, and disappearing after a manner that we cannot explain. We may fairly suppose that it was a pattern of what our own bodies will be after they are raised again. They will be true bodies, material and real, but bodies endued with capacities of which now we know nothing.

32.—[*Did not our heart burn.*] These words would be more literally rendered, 'was not our heart burning within us.' It is a strong expression to indicate the warmth and delight of their feelings while they listened to our Lord's exposition of Scripture. See Psalm 39:3; Jeremiah 20:9.

33.—[*Found the eleven gathered together.*] This expression deserves notice. Was Thomas with them or not? If he was, he must have gone out immediately after the two disciples came in. Otherwise it would be difficult to reconcile the verses which immediately follow, describing our Lord's appearing, with the account given in St John, of Christ's appearing when Thomas was not present.—If Thomas was not present on this occasion, how can we explain St Luke, speaking of 'the eleven?' Doddridge must supply the answer;—'As Paul calls the company of apostles *the twelve* (1 Cor. 15:5), though Judas the twelfth person was dead; so Luke here calls them *the eleven*, though Thomas the eleventh person was absent, as appears from John 20:24.'

Let us add to this, that St Mark distinctly tells us, also, that the Lord 'appeared to *the eleven*, as they sat at meat' (*Mark* 16:14).

34.—[*Saying, The Lord is risen indeed.*] Major remarks here, 'These words which Luke attributes to the eleven apostles are not altogether consistent with what we read in Mark (*Mark* 16:13), that when the two disciples returning acquainted the rest, 'they did not believe them.'—Campbell thus solves the difficulty: 'This does not imply that none of them believed, but that several, perhaps the greater part, did not believe. When Luke tells us that they said "the Lord is risen indeed," we are not to conclude that everyone said this, or even believed it, but only that some believed, and that one of them expressly affirmed it. Such latitude in using pronouns is common in every language. So, according to Matthew and Mark, both malefactors reproached Jesus on the cross. But from Luke we learn that it was only one of them who acted thus.'

[*Appeared to Simon.*] This appearance to Simon Peter alone is only mentioned in this place, and in the Epistle to the Corinthians (*1 Cor.* 15:5). The circumstances of the appearance we do not know.

It may be well to mention here the eleven distinct appearances of our Lord after his resurrection. He appeared,

1. To Mary Magdalene alone. Mark 16:9; John 20:14.

2. To the women returning from the sepulchre. Matthew 28:9, 10.

3. To Simon Peter alone. Luke 24:34.

4. To the two disciples going to Emmaus. Luke 24:13, etc.

5. To the apostles at Jerusalem, excepting Thomas who was absent. John 20:19.

6. To the apostles at Jerusalem, a second time, when Thomas was present. John 20:26, 29.

7. At the Sea of Tiberias, when seven disciples were fishing. John 21:1.

8. To the eleven disciples, on a mountain in Galilee. Matthew 28:16.

9. To above five hundred brethren at once. 1 Corinthians 15:6.

10. To James only. 1 Corinthians 15:7.

11. To all the apostles on Mount Olivet at his ascension. Luke 24:51.

Three times we are told that his disciples 'touched' him after he rose. Matthew 28:9; Luke 24:39; John 20:27. Twice we are told that he ate with them. Luke 24:42; John 21:12, 13.

35.—[*Things ... done in the way.*] This must necessarily mean the wonderful exposition of Scripture which had made their 'hearts burn.'

[*Known of them in breaking of bread.*] It is only necessary to remark here that to apply this expression to the Lord's supper is mere accommodation of Scripture words, and not justified by the context.

LUKE 24:36-43

36 And as they thus spake, Jesus himself stood in the midst of them, and saith unto them, Peace *be* unto you.

37 But they were terrified and affrighted, and supposed that they had seen a spirit.

38 And he said unto them, Why are ye troubled? and why do thoughts arise in your hearts?

39 Behold my hands and my feet, that it is I myself: handle me, and see; for a spirit hath not flesh and bones, as ye see me have.

40 And when he had thus spoken, he shewed them *his* hands and *his* feet.

41 And while they yet believed not for joy, and wondered, he said unto them, Have ye here any meat?

42 And they gave him a piece of a broiled fish, and of an honeycomb.

43 And he took *it*, and did eat before them.

W E should observe, in this passage, *the singularly gracious words with which our Lord introduced himself to his disciples after his resurrection.* We read that he suddenly stood in the midst of them and said, 'Peace be unto you.'

This was a wonderful saying, when we consider the men to whom it was addressed. It was addressed to eleven disciples, who three days before had shamefully forsaken their Master and fled. They had broken their promises. They had forgotten their professions of readiness to die for their faith. They had been scattered, 'every man to his own,' and left their Master to die alone. One of them had even denied him three times. All of them had proved backsliders and cowards. And yet behold the return which their Master makes to his disciples! Not a word of rebuke is spoken. Not a single sharp saying falls from his lips. Calmly and quietly he appears in the midst of them, and begins by speaking of peace. 'Peace be unto you!'

We see, in this touching saying, one more proof that the love of Christ 'passeth knowledge.' It is his glory to pass over a transgression. He 'delighteth in mercy.' He is far more willing to forgive than men are to be forgiven, and far more ready to pardon than men are to be pardoned. There is in his almighty heart an infinite willingness to put away man's transgressions. Though our sins have been as scarlet he is ever ready to make them white as snow, to blot them out, to cast them behind his back, to bury them in the depths of the sea, to remember them no more. All these are scriptural phrases intended to convey the same great truth. The natural man is continually stumbling at them, and refusing to understand them. At this we need not wonder. Free, full, and undeserved forgiveness to the very uttermost is not the manner of man. But it is the manner of Christ.

Where is the sinner, however great his sins, who need be afraid of beginning to apply to such a Saviour as this? In the hand of Jesus there is mercy enough and to spare.—Where is the backslider, however far he may have fallen, who need be afraid of returning? 'Fury is not in Christ' (*Isa.* 27:4). He is willing to raise and restore the very worst.—Where is the saint who ought not to love such a Saviour, and to pay him willingly a holy obedience? There is forgiveness with him, that he may be feared (*Psa.* 130:4).—Where is the professing Christian who ought not to be forgiving towards his brethren? The disciples of a Saviour whose words were so full of peace, ought to be peaceable, gentle, and easy to be entreated (*Col.* 3:13).

We should observe, for another thing, in this passage, *our Lord's marvellous condescension to the infirmity of his disciples.* We read that when his disciples were terrified at his appearance, and could not believe that it was himself, he said, 'behold my hands and feet: handle me and see.'

Our Lord might fairly have commanded his disciples to believe that he had risen. He might justly have said, 'Where is your faith? Why do ye not believe my resurrection, when ye see me with your own eyes?' But he does not do so. He stoops even lower than this. He appeals to the bodily senses of the eleven. He bids them touch him with their own hands, and satisfy themselves that he was a material being, and not a spirit or ghost.

A mighty principle is contained in this circumstance, which we shall do well to store up in our hearts. Our Lord permits us to use our *senses* in testing a fact or an assertion in religion. Things above our reason we must expect to find in Christianity. But things contrary to reason, and contrary to our own senses, our Lord would have us know, we are not meant to believe. A doctrine, so called, which contradicts our senses, is not a doctrine which came from him who bade the eleven touch his hands and his feet.

Let us remember this principle in dealing with the Romish doctrine of a change in the bread and wine at the Lord's supper. There is no such change at all. Our own eyes and our own tongues tell us that the bread is bread and the wine is wine, after consecration as well as before. Our Lord never requires us to believe that which is contrary to our senses. The doctrine of transubstantiation is therefore false and unscriptural.

Let us remember this principle in dealing with the Romish doctrine of baptismal regeneration. There is no inseparable connection between baptism and the new birth of man's heart. Our own eyes and senses tell us that myriads of baptized people have not the Spirit of God, are utterly without grace, and are servants of the devil and the world. Our Lord never requires us to believe that which is contrary to our senses. The doctrine that regeneration invariably accompanies baptism is therefore undeserving of credit. It is mere antinomianism to say that there is grace where no grace is to be seen.

A mighty practical lesson is involved in our Lord's dealing with the disciples, which we shall do well to remember. That lesson is the duty of dealing gently with weak disciples, and teaching them as they are able to bear. Like our Lord, we must be patient and longsuffering. Like our Lord, we must condescend to the feebleness of some men's faith, and treat them as tenderly as little children, in order to bring them into the right way. We must not cast off men because they do not see everything at once. We must not despise the humblest and most childish means, if we can only persuade men to believe. Such dealing may require much patience. But he who cannot condescend to deal thus with the young, the ignorant, and the uneducated, has not the mind of Christ. Well would it be for all believers, if they would remember St Paul's words more frequently, 'To the weak became I as weak, that I might gain the weak' (*1 Cor.* 9:22).

Notes—Luke 24:36-43

36.—[*Stood in the midst of them.*] We are not told in what manner our Lord entered the room where the disciples were. We know from John's words that the doors were shut (*John* 20:19), 'for fear of the Jews.' Whether our Lord passed through the doors miraculously without opening them, or whether he opened them miraculously, as the angel did when he brought Peter out of prison, we cannot tell (*Acts* 12:10). In either case there was a miracle. In any case the appearance was sudden and instantaneous.

[*Peace be unto you.*] I am quite unable to regard this expression as being nothing more than the ordinary salutation of courtesy. It seems to me to be full of deep and comfortable truth. It implied that the great battle was fought and the great victory won over the prince of this world, and peace with God obtained for man according to the old promise. It implied that our Lord came to his disciples with peaceful, gracious, and forgiving feelings, and with no resentment for their having forsaken him.

Let it be noted, that 'peace' was the last word in the prophetical hymn of Zacharias,—'peace on earth,' part of the good news proclaimed by angels when Christ was born,—'peace' the proclamation which the seventy disciples were ordered to

make in every house which they visited,—
'peace' the legacy which our Lord left and
gave to the apostles on the night before he
was crucified,—and 'peace' was the first
word which he spoke when he appeared
among them again after his resurrection
(*Luke* 1:79; 2:14; 10:5; *John* 14:27).

Peace, in short, is one main ingredient of
the gospel. Every one of St Paul's epistles,
excepting the one to the Hebrews, begins
with a gracious wish of 'peace' to those to
whom it is addressed.

Stella has a long and excellent passage
on this expression.

37.—[*Terrified and affrighted.*] It is
striking to remark, both here and elsewhere
in Scripture, how invariably the appearance
of any supernatural being, or any inhabitant of another world appears to strike
terror into the heart of man. It seems an
instinct of human nature to be afraid on
such occasions, and is a strong indirect
proof of man's utter inability to meet God in
peace without a mediator. If man is afraid of
spirits and ghosts, what would man feel if
he saw God himself?

38.—[*Thoughts arise in your hearts.*]
Here, as elsewhere, our Lord shows his
knowledge of the inward man. The reasonings and questionings of the apostles were
all known to him.

39.—[*Behold my hands and my feet.*]
Some writers cannot see anything in this
mention of 'hands and feet,' but a reference
to the uncovered parts of our Lord's body, to
which our Lord directs his disciples' attention, as a palpable proof that he had a real
material body. I cannot, however, think that
this was all that our Lord meant. I believe
that he called attention to the nail-prints in
his hands and feet, and thus showed that
he was that very Saviour who had been
crucified.

[*It is I myself.*] The Greek words here
mean literally 'I am I myself.'

[*Handle me and see.*] Here is a direct
appeal to two senses, touch and sight.

[*A spirit hath not flesh and bones.*] Stier
and Alford both observe the absence of the
word 'blood' in this expression, and attach
significance to it. I am unable to do so.
Our Lord had just referred to the senses of
touch and sight. Flesh and bones could be

touched, looked at, scrutinized, felt, without difficulty. Blood of course could not.
Our Lord therefore purposely mentions
only 'flesh and bones.' But to infer that his
resurrection body had no blood, as Alford
suggests, appears to me to be going further
than we have any warrant to go.

Let it be noted that our Lord spoke here
of 'a spirit,' and the qualities of 'a spirit,'
in such a manner that it is impossible to
deny the existence of incorporeal beings.
To believe every idle story about ghosts and
apparitions is foolish and unreasonable.
But we must take care that we do not go
into the other extreme, and deny the existence of spirits altogether. Our Lord's words
about them are clear and unmistakable.

41.—[*Believed not for joy.*] Poole
remarks, 'If they had not believed now, they
would doubtless not have rejoiced, for faith
was the cause of their joy. Yet the excess of
their joy was the hindrance of their faith.
So dangerous are the excessive motions of
our affections!'

[*Any meat.*] The Greek word so rendered, means literally 'anything eatable,
any food.' The English word 'meat,' at the
time when our version of the Bible was last
revised, did not mean 'flesh' exclusively, as
it does now.

43.—[*Did eat before them.*] The speculative questions raised on this circumstance,
about the capacity of our Lord's resurrection body really to eat and really to drink,
are most unprofitable and vain. Let it suffice
us to believe that it was a real eating and
drinking, and not a mere optical delusion,
or apparent eating and drinking, as some
have ventured to insinuate. We need not
inquire further. That it was so, Peter's words
in another place appear to prove plainly
(*Acts* 10:41). The same remarks apply to
the eating of the angels who appeared to
Abraham (*Gen.* 18:8).

Our Lord's manner of dealing with the
disciples in this passage ought to be carefully remembered. He appeals to their
senses, and allows them to satisfy their
senses of the reality of his risen body. He
even implies that if their senses had not
been satisfied they might fairly and justly
doubt whether his body had risen. This
mode of arguing strikes a blow at the

Romish doctrine of transubstantiation, and the Lutheran doctrine of consubstantiation, in the Lord's supper. When our senses detect no change in the substance of the bread and wine, it is monstrous and unreasonable to require us to believe that any change has taken place in them after the act of consecration.

LUKE 24:44-49

44 And he said unto them, These *are* the words which I spake unto you, while I was yet with you, that all things must be fulfilled, which were written in the law of Moses, and *in* the prophets, and *in* the psalms, concerning me.

45 Then opened he their understanding, that they might understand the scriptures,

46 And said unto them, Thus it is written, and thus it behoved Christ to suffer, and to rise from the dead the third day:

47 And that repentance and remission of sins should be preached in his name among all nations, beginning at Jerusalem.

48 And ye are witnesses of these things.

49 And, behold, I send the promise of my Father upon you: but tarry ye in the city of Jerusalem, until ye be endued with power from on high.

LET us observe, firstly, in these verses, *the gift which our Lord bestowed on his disciples immediately before he left the world.* We read that he 'opened their understanding, that they might understand the Scriptures.'

We must not misapprehend these words. We are not to suppose that the disciples knew nothing about the Old Testament up to this time, and that the Bible is a book which no ordinary person can expect to comprehend. We are simply to understand that Jesus showed his disciples the full meaning of many passages, which had hitherto been hid from their eyes. Above all, he showed the true interpretation of many prophetical passages concerning the Messiah.

We all need a like enlightenment of our understandings. 'The natural man receiveth not the things of the Spirit of God: for they are foolishness unto him: neither can he know them, because they are spiritually discerned' (*1 Cor.* 2:14). Pride, and prejudice, and love of the world blind our intellects, and throw a veil over the eyes of our minds in the reading of the Scriptures. We see the words, but do not thoroughly understand them until we are taught from above.

He that desires to read his Bible with profit, must first ask the Lord Jesus to open the eyes of his understanding by the Holy Ghost. Human commentaries are useful in their way. The help of good and learned men is not to be despised. But there is no commentary to be compared with the teaching of Christ. A humble and prayerful spirit will find a thousand things in the Bible, which the proud, self-conceited student will utterly fail to discern.

Let us observe, secondly, in these verses, *the remarkable manner in which the Lord Jesus speaks of his own death on the cross.* He does not speak of it as a misfortune, or as a thing to be lamented, but as a necessity. He says, 'It behoved Christ to suffer, and to rise again the third day.'

The death of Christ was necessary to our salvation. His flesh and blood offered in sacrifice on the cross were 'the life of the world' (*John* 6:51). Without the death of Christ, so far as we can see, God's law could never have been satisfied,—sin could never have been pardoned,—man could never have been justified before God,—and God could never have shown mercy to man. The cross of Christ was the solution of a mighty difficulty. It untied a vast knot. It enabled God to be 'just, and yet the justifier' of the ungodly (*Rom.* 3:26). It enabled man to draw near to God with boldness, and to feel that though a sinner he might have hope. Christ by suffering as a Substitute in our stead, the just for the unjust, has made a way by which we can draw near to God. We may freely acknowledge that in ourselves we are guilty and deserve death. But we may boldly plead, that One has died for us, and that for his sake, believing on him, we claim life and acquittal.

Let us ever glory in the cross of Christ. Let us regard it as the source of all our hopes, and the foundation of all our peace. Ignorance and unbelief may see nothing in the sufferings of Calvary but the cruel martyrdom of an innocent person. Faith will look far deeper. Faith will see in the death of Jesus the payment of man's enormous debt to God, and the complete salvation of all who believe.

Let us observe, thirdly, in these verses, *what were the first truths which the Lord Jesus bade his disciples preach after he left the world.* We read that 'repentance and remission of sins' were to be preached in his name among all nations.

'Repentance and remission of sins' are the first things which ought to be pressed on the attention of every man, woman, and child throughout the world.—All ought to be told the necessity of repentance. All are by nature desperately wicked. Without repentance and conversion, none can enter the kingdom of God.—All ought to be told God's readiness to forgive everyone who believes on Christ. All are by nature guilty and condemned. But anyone may obtain by faith in Jesus, free, full, and immediate pardon.—All, not least, ought to be continually reminded, that repentance and remission of sins are inseparably linked together. Not that our repentance can purchase our pardon. Pardon is the free gift of God to the believer in Christ. But still it remains true, that a man impenitent is a man unforgiven.

He that desires to be a true Christian, must be experimentally acquainted with repentance and remission of sins. These are the principal things in saving religion. To belong to a pure church, and hear the gospel, and receive the sacraments, are great privileges. But are we converted? Are we justified? If not, we are dead before God. Happy is that Christian who keeps these two points continually before his eyes! Repentance and remission are not mere elementary truths, and milk for babes. The highest standard of sanctity is nothing more than continual growth in practical knowledge of these two points. The brightest saint is the man who has the most heart-searching sense of his own sinfulness, and the liveliest sense of his own complete acceptance in Christ.

Let us observe, fourthly, *what was the first place at which the disciples were to begin preaching.* They were to begin 'at Jerusalem.'

This is a striking fact, and one full of instruction. It teaches us that none are to be reckoned too wicked for salvation to be offered to them, and that no degree of spiritual disease is beyond the reach of the gospel remedy. Jerusalem was the wickedest city on earth when our Lord left the world. It was a city which had stoned the prophets and killed those whom God sent to call it to repentance. It was a city full of pride, unbelief, self-righteousness, and desperate hardness of heart. It was a city which had just crowned all its transgressions by crucifying the Lord of glory. And yet Jerusalem was the place at which the first proclamation of repentance and pardon was to be made.—The command of Christ was plain;—'Begin at Jerusalem.'

We see in these wondrous words, the length, and breadth, and depth, and height of Christ's compassion towards sinners. We must never despair of anyone being saved, however bad and profligate he may have been. We must open the door of repentance to the chief of sinners. We must not be afraid to invite the worst of men to repent, believe, and live. It is the glory of our great Physician, that he can heal incurable cases. The things that seem impossible to men are possible with Christ.

Let us observe, lastly, *the peculiar position which believers, and especially ministers, are meant to occupy in this world.* Our Lord defines it in one expressive word. He says, 'Ye are witnesses.'

If we are true disciples of Christ, we must bear a continual testimony in the midst of an evil world. We must testify to the truth of our Master's gospel,—the graciousness of our Master's heart,—the happiness of our Master's service,—the excellence of our Master's rules of life,—and the enormous danger and wickedness of the ways of the world. Such testimony will doubtless bring down upon us the displeasure of man. The world will hate us, as it did our Master, because we 'testify of it, that its works are evil' (*John* 7:7). Such testimony will doubtless be believed by few comparatively, and will be thought by many offensive and extreme. But the duty of a witness is to bear his testimony, whether he is believed or not. If we bear a faithful testimony, we have done our duty, although, like Noah, and Elijah, and Jeremiah, we stand almost alone.

What do we know of this witnessing character? What kind of testimony do we bear? What evidence do we give that we are disciples of a crucified Saviour, and, like him, are 'not of the world?' (*John* 17:14). What marks do we show of belonging to him who said, 'I came that I should bear witness unto the truth?' (*John* 18:37). Happy is he who can give a satisfactory answer to these questions, and whose life declares plainly that he 'seeks a country' (*Heb.* 11:14).

Notes—Luke 24:44-49

44.—[*These are the words, etc.*] This expression must be paraphrased, in order to give the full meaning of it. Alford renders it, 'Behold the realization of the words.'—It signifies, 'You now see actually fulfilled, the words which I so often spake to you, saying that the predictions about my sufferings must be accomplished. You could not then believe that I was really going to suffer and afterwards rise again. You see now that it was true.'

[**Must be fulfilled.**] The Greek word here translated 'must,' is the same that is rendered 'ought' in the twenty-sixth verse and 'behoved' in the forty-sixth.

[*Law of Moses ... prophets ... psalms.*] It should be remembered that this three-fold division was the Jewish division of the Old Testament. They classed all its contents under these three heads.

When our Lord speaks of the things in the 'law of Moses' concerning himself, there can be little doubt that he points to all the types and figures which were emblems of himself, and specially to the sacrifices.

45.—[*Opened he their understanding, etc.*] We are taught here that the minds of the disciples had been closed by prejudice and traditional interpretations. Our Lord opened the doors and windows of their minds, and let in the light.

Poole remarks, 'He did not open their understanding without the Scripture; he sends them thither. He knows that Scripture would not give them a sufficient knowledge of the things of God, without the influence and illumination of his Spirit. They are truly taught by God who are taught by his Spirit to understand the Scriptures. Christ gives great honour to the Scriptures. The devil cheats those whom he persuades to cast away the Scriptures in expectation of a teaching by the Spirit. The Spirit teacheth by, not without, not contrary to, the Holy Scriptures.'

Cornelius à Lapide tries in vain to argue from this verse that the laity cannot understand the Bible without the teaching of the church, that the Bible is not suited for the laity, and that the apostles had the knowledge of the Scriptures specially entrusted to them.—There is not the slightest proof that the apostles alone had their 'understandings opened' on the present occasion. On the contrary, the context distinctly tells us that those who were here assembled were the apostles and 'they that were with them.'—Moreover, the fact that our Lord opened the understandings of all, is a plain proof that all, whether apostles or not, require teaching from above, and that Christ is able, ready, and willing to give it to all, whether apostles or not, as long as the world stands.

46.—[*Thus it is written.*] This is a general expression, signifying 'It was written in Scripture that things concerning me should take place in the way in which they have taken place.' It was 'written' that it should be so, and it was necessary, or 'behoved' therefore that so it should be. If Christ had not suffered and risen again, Scripture would not have been fulfilled. The chief reference here, no doubt, is to Isaiah 53, Psalm 22, and Daniel 9:26.

[*Rise from the dead the third day.*] The question has been raised here, 'Where does the Old Testament say that Christ should rise again the *third day*?' Pearce remarks that it does not appear, unless in Hosea 6:2, and Jonah 1:17.—I am not however convinced that either here or in 1 Corinthians 15:4, it was intended that we should lay stress on the *third day*, in understanding the sentence. The meaning of the verse seems to me to be simply, 'that it was written, and was therefore necessary, that Christ should suffer and rise again.' I cannot see that the sense obliges us to find an Old Testament prediction about the *third day*. Even if it did, I feel no doubt that there are more passages to prove it than anyone has yet discovered. There is a depth of meaning in the Old Testament, I suspect, with reference to Christ, which no one has yet fully fathomed.

47.—[*And that.*] The governing words here, we must remember, are still, 'it is written, and was therefore necessary that,' etc.

[*Repentance and remission of sins.*] These words are a brief summary of the main doctrines of the gospel. The necessity of repentance, and the possibility of remission,—the willingness of God to grant repentance unto life, and the full provision made by Christ for the pardon of man's sins, were to be proclaimed and published like a notice given publicly by a herald. And all was to be done 'in Christ's name.' That expression is the leading one in the whole sentence. It signifies, 'By the authority of Christ,' and 'Through the merit and mediation of Christ.' Both ideas are included.

No Christian teaching, be it remembered, is scriptural and sound, which does not give the principal place to these two great doctrines.

[*Among all nations.*] The Greek words here would be equally well translated, 'Among all Gentiles.' And considering that 'Jerusalem' is brought in at the end of the verse, it is highly probable that this was the idea intended to be conveyed. The gospel was to be preached to Gentiles as well as Jews.

[*Beginning at Jerusalem.*] This expression taught two things. One was, that the apostles and first preachers of the gospel should not shrink from offering salvation to the worst and greatest sinners. They were not to regard even the city where their Master was crucified as hopelessly wicked, and too bad to be benefited by the gospel. The result showed that this command was not given without cause. The greatest triumph ever won by the gospel, perhaps, was the conversion of three thousand Jerusalem hearers on the day of Pentecost.—The other lesson was that the first offer of salvation should always be made to the Jews. Hardened, unbelieving as they were, they were still 'beloved for the fathers' sakes,' and were not to be despised (*Rom.* 11:28).

The Acts of the Apostles, in instances too many to be quoted, as well as St Paul's words in the Epistle to the Romans (*Rom.* 1:16), show how faithfully the apostles discharged the duty of preaching to the Jews.

The duty of Christians to care specially for the souls of Jews seems plainly pointed out in the expression before us.

Let it be noted, that the conclusions of Peter's two first sermons at Jerusalem, in Acts 2 and 3, exactly carried out the command of the verse before us. He preached 'repentance and remission in Christ's name.'

48.—[*Ye are witnesses of these things.*] The 'things' here spoken of must be the 'things concerning himself,' which our Lord had just been expounding.

The office which the first disciples, and, after them, all ministers and believers were to fill, is stated in the word 'witnesses.'

Stier remarks, 'It is not the Lord's will to appoint and send forth orators, or enthusiasts, or even simple teachers, but before all, and in all, *witnesses*. The idea contained in Luke 1:2 "which from the beginning were eyewitnesses and ministers of the word," is here found once more.'

49.—[*I send the promise of my Father.*] This expression means the Holy Ghost, whom the Father had promised in the Old Testament prophecies to send, and who came down on the day of Pentecost (see *Isa.* 44:3; *Joel* 2:28; *Jer.* 31:33; *Ezek.* 36:27).

Let it be noted, that our Lord here speaks of 'sending the Holy Ghost.' We see in this his equality and unity with God the Father. We also see that the Holy Ghost *proceeds* from the Son, no less than from the Father.

Let it be noted, that the Holy Ghost is evidently a person, and not an influence. The words 'I send' can only be used of a 'person.'

Let it be noted, that our Lord says, 'I send,'—not 'I will send.' This shows the certainty of the coming of the Holy Ghost, and the speedy approach of his coming. May it not also show that even from the very time at which our Lord spoke, the disciples would begin to receive grace and power from the Holy Ghost?

[*Tarry ye in the city ... until, etc.*] This expression is remarkable. It seems to denote that our Lord would have his disciples go forth into all nations immediately after the day of Pentecost, and wait at Jerusalem no longer. Their backwardness to do this, when compared with the expression before us, is noteworthy.

[*Endued.*] This word means literally, 'Be clothed upon, or invested with.' It is frequently used in the New Testament, and implies a putting on something which we do not naturally possess (see *Rom.* 13:14; *1 Cor.* 15:53; *Gal.* 3:27; *Col.* 3:9, 10).

[*Power from on high.*] Some have thought that this expression is only a form of speech for the Holy Ghost himself. It seems more likely that it signifies the energy and influence imparted by the Holy Ghost. It is very like the expression used about the Virgin Mary, 'The Holy Ghost shall come upon thee, and the power of the Highest shall overshadow thee' (*Luke* 1:35). It would then mean in this place, 'Tarry till ye be endued with that heavenly power which the Holy Ghost, whom the Father has promised, and I also send, shall impart to you.'

Alford quotes a remark of Stier, that this 'enduing with the Holy Ghost, was the true and complete clothing of the nakedness of the fall.' This appears to me only partially correct. I believe the 'imputed righteousness of Christ, unto all and upon all them that believe,' is the true garment which remedies the nakedness of the fall (*Rom.* 3:22). The indwelling grace of the Spirit is doubtless never separate from that righteousness. But it is in itself a distinct and separate thing, and should be kept distinct in our minds.

LUKE 24:50-53

50 And he led them out as far as to Bethany, and he lifted up his hands, and blessed them.

51 And it came to pass, while he blessed them, he was parted from them, and carried up into heaven.

52 And they worshipped him, and returned to Jerusalem with great joy:

53 And were continually in the temple, praising and blessing God. Amen.

THESE verses are the winding up of St Luke's history of our Lord's ministry. They form a suitable conclusion to a Gospel, which in touching tenderness and full exhibition of Christ's grace, stands first among the four records of the things which Jesus did and taught (*Acts* 1:1).

Let us notice, firstly, in this passage, *the remarkable manner in which our Lord left his disciples.* We read that 'he lifted up his hands, and blessed them. And it came to pass, while he blessed them, he was parted from them.' In one word, he left them when in the very act of blessing.

We cannot for a moment doubt that there was a meaning in this circumstance. It was intended to remind the disciples of all that Jesus had brought with him when he came into the world. It was intended to assure them of what he would yet do, after he left the world. He came on earth to bless and not to curse, and blessing he departed.— He came in love and not in anger, and in love he went away.—He came not as a condemning judge, but as a compassionate Friend, and as a Friend he returned to his Father.—He had been a Saviour full of blessings to his little flock while he had been with them. He would be a Saviour full of blessings to them, he would have them know, even after he was taken away.

For ever let our souls lean on the gracious heart of Christ, if we know anything of true religion. We shall never find a heart more tender, more loving, more patient, more compassionate, and more kind. To talk of the Virgin Mary as being more compassionate than Christ is a proof of miserable ignorance. To flee to the saints for comfort, when we may flee to Christ, is an act of mingled stupidity and blasphemy, and a robbery of Christ's crown. Gracious was our Lord Jesus while he lived among his weak disciples,— gracious in the very season of his agony on the cross,—gracious when he rose again and gathered his scattered sheep around him,—gracious in the manner of his departure from this world. It was a departure in the very act of blessing! Gracious, we may be assured, he is at the right hand of God. He is the same yesterday, today, and for ever,—a Saviour ever ready to bless, abounding in blessings.

Let us notice, secondly, in this passage, *the place to which our Lord went when he left the world.* We read that he was 'carried up into heaven.'

The full meaning of these words we cannot of course comprehend. It would be easy to ask questions about the exact residence of Christ's glorified body, which the wisest theologian could never answer. We must not waste our time in unedifying speculations, or 'intrude into things unseen' (*Col.* 2:18). Let it suffice us to know that our Lord Jesus Christ is gone into the presence of God on behalf of all who believe on him, as a Forerunner and a High Priest (*Heb.* 6:20; *John* 14:2).

As a Forerunner, Jesus has gone into heaven to prepare a place for all his members. Our great Head has taken possession of a glorious inheritance in behalf of his mystical body, and holds it as an elder brother and trustee, until the day comes when his body shall be perfected.—As a High Priest, Jesus has gone into heaven to intercede for all who believe on him. There in the holy of holies he presents on their behalf the merit of his own sacrifice, and obtains for them daily supplies of mercy and grace. The grand secret of the perseverance of saints is Christ's appearance for them in heaven. They have an everlasting Advocate with the Father, and therefore they are never cast away (*Heb.* 9:24; *1 John* 2:1).

A day will come when Jesus shall return from heaven, in like manner as he went. He will not always abide within the holy of holies. He will come forth, like the Jewish high priest, to bless the people, to gather his saints together, and to restore all things (*Lev.* 9:23; *Acts* 3:21). For that day let us wait, and long, and pray. Christ dying on the cross for sinners,—Christ living in heaven to intercede,—Christ coming again in glory, are three great objects which ought to stand out prominently before the eyes of every true Christian.

Let us notice, lastly, in this passage, *the feelings of our Lord's disciples when he finally left them and was carried up into heaven.* We read that 'they returned to Jerusalem with great joy, and were continually in the temple, praising and blessing God.'

How shall we account for these joyful feelings? How shall we explain the singular fact, that this little company of weak disciples, left, for the first time, like orphans, in the midst of an angry world, was not cast down, but was full of joy?—The answer to these questions is short and simple. The disciples rejoiced, because now for the first time they saw all things clearly about their Master. The veil was removed from their eyes. The darkness had at length passed away. The meaning of Christ's humiliation and low estate,—the meaning of his mysterious agony, and cross, and passion,—the meaning of his being Messiah and yet a sufferer,—the meaning of his being crucified, and yet being Son of God,—all, all was at length unravelled and made plain. They saw it all. They understood it all. Their doubts were removed. Their stumbling-blocks were taken away. Now at last they possessed clear knowledge, and possessing clear knowledge felt unmingled joy.

Let it be a settled principle with us, that the little degree of joy which many believers feel arises often from want of knowledge. Weak faith and inconsistent practice are doubtless two great reasons why many of God's children enjoy so little peace. But it may well be suspected that dim and indistinct views of the gospel are the true cause of many a believer's discomfort. When the Lord Jesus is not clearly known and understood, it must needs follow that there is little 'joy in the Lord.'

Let us leave the Gospel of St Luke with a settled purpose of heart to seek more spiritual knowledge every year we live. Let us search the Scriptures more deeply, and pray over them more heartily. Too many believers only scratch the surface of Scripture, and know nothing of digging down into its hid treasures. Let the Word dwell in us more richly. Let us read our Bibles more diligently. So doing we shall taste more of joy and peace in believing, and shall know what it is to be 'continually praising and blessing God.'

Notes—Luke 24:50-53

50.—[*Led them out as far as to Bethany.*] There is something very touching in the fact that our Lord's ascension took place close to Bethany. It was a small village bordering on the Mount of Olives, where Mary, and Martha, and Lazarus dwelt. It is probable that they all were present when our Lord left the earth.

[*Lifted up his hands and blessed them.*] This circumstance is full of meaning. The blessing was significant. It showed the spirit in which our Lord parted from his church on earth, and was an earnest of what he would do for them in heaven. It typified his full assumption of his priestly office, and gave assurance of what he will yet do when he comes again.

Gill remarks, 'This lifting up of the hands was not in order to put them on his disciples, nor was it used as a prayer-gesture, nor was the blessing of them prayerwise, or by praying for a blessing on them. As Aaron, his type, lifted up his hands towards the people of Israel, and blessed them when he first offered the offerings for them (*Lev.* 9:22), so Christ as the great High Priest, having offered himself as a sacrifice for the sins of his people, lifted up his hands toward them and blessed them in an authoritative way.'

51.—[*He was parted from them.*] The Greek word so rendered is somewhat remarkable. It signifies literally, 'stood apart.' A German commentator thinks it means 'he went a little distance from them previous to his ascension.' The more common opinion is that the word is only a part of the same incident which is described when it says he was 'carried up into heaven.'

[*Carried up into heaven.*] Where our Lord's body went when so carried up, is an unprofitable speculation. Let it be enough for us to remember that he went into the presence of God for us, and that he will come again exactly in like manner as he went (*Acts* 1:11).

Burgon remarks, 'These beautiful words denote that Jesus was rather *taken away* from the men he loved, than that by an act of his own he left them. For his passion, it is said, that he was impatient (*Luke*

12:50);—for his ascension, not so. He did not *leave* his disciples, but was parted from them.'

52.—[*They worshipped him.*] This is the first formal act of adoration which we ever read of the disciples paying to our Lord. Their knowledge of his Messiahship and divinity was now clear and distinct. Hence came the 'joy' which the verse mentions that they felt. All things were now clear and plain to them concerning their Master. The darkness was past, and the true light shone (*1 John* 2:8).

53.—[*Continually in the temple.*] This expression does not necessarily mean that the disciples were never anywhere else except in the temple. It only means that they made a daily, regular habit of attending the temple services and assembling in the temple courts, and specially at the times of prayer (*Acts* 3:1). It is the same Greek word used about Cornelius, where it says, that 'he prayed to God always' (*Acts* 10:2).

The temple, be it remembered, was a place of resort for all pious Jews in Jerusalem, and in its spacious courts all sorts of worshippers met daily without interruption, or interference with one another. Even of the apostles it is said, that 'daily in the temple, and in every house, they ceased not to teach and preach Jesus Christ' (*Acts* 5:42). It seems to have been such an established custom for all religious-minded persons to assemble in the temple, that the apostles could even preach the gospel there.

Maldonatus remarks, 'that it is a striking fact that St Luke's Gospel begins by describing a scene in the temple, when Zacharias had his vision, and also leaves us in the temple, when it concludes.'

Burgon says, 'They repaired to the temple, and so the temple service became henceforth filled with new meaning. The song of Moses has become to them the song of the Lamb. For them the Psalms speak henceforth another language, for they speak to them only of Christ. Well may they have been henceforth "continually in the temple, praising and blessing God."'

In leaving the Gospel of St Luke, it may prove useful to some readers to give the following list of the principal circumstances which are recorded by Luke alone, and are not mentioned by Matthew, Mark, and John. They are fifty-eight in number.

	Chapter	Verse
1. The vision of Zacharias, and conception of Elizabeth	1	5-25
2. The salutation of the Virgin Mary		26-38
3. Mary's visit to Elizabeth		39-56
4. The birth of John the Baptist, and hymn of Zacharias		57-80
5. The decree of Cæsar Augustus	2	1-3
6. The birth of Christ at Bethlehem		4-7
7. The appearance of angels to the shepherds		8-20
8. The circumcision of Christ		21
9. The presentation of Christ in the temple		22-24
10. The account of Simeon and Anna		25-38
11. Christ found among the doctors		41-52
12. Date of beginning of John's ministry	3	1-2
13. Success of John's ministry		10-15
14. Genealogy of Mary		23-38
15. Christ preaching and rejected at Nazareth	4	15-30
16. Particulars in the call of Simon, James, and John	5	1-10
17. Christ's discourse in the plain	6	17-49
18. Raising of the widow's son at Nain	7	11-17
19. Woman in Simon's house		36-50
20. Women who ministered to Christ	8	1-3
21. James and John desiring fire to come down	9	51-56
22. Mission of seventy disciples	10	1-16
23. Return of seventy disciples		17-24
24. Parable of the good Samaritan		25-37
25. Christ in the house of Martha and Mary		38-42
26. Parable of friend at midnight	11	5-8
27. Christ dining in a Pharisee's house		37-54
28. Discourse to an innumerable multitude	12	1-53
29. Murder of the Galilæans	13	1-5
30. Parable of the barren fig-tree		6-9
31. Case of the woman diseased 18 years		10-20
32. Question on the few that be saved		22-30
33. Reply to the Pharisees' warning about Herod		31-33
34. Case of a dropsical man	14	1-6
35. Parable of the lowest room		7-14
36. Parable of the great supper		15-24
37. Difficulties of Christ's service		25-35
38. Parable of the lost sheep and piece of money	15	1-10
39. Parable of the prodigal son		11-32
40. Parable of the unjust steward	16	1-18
41. Parable of the rich man and Lazarus		19-31
42. Instruction to disciples	17	1-10
43. Healing of ten lepers		12-19
44. Question and answer about coming of God's kingdom.		20-37
45. Parable of the importunate widow	18	1-8
46. Parable of the Pharisee and publican		9-14
47. Calling of Zacchæus	19	2-10